FRONTIER STATIONS

Chief Commissioner's Residence, Gilgit, c. 1993
(Courtesy: Shakil Durrani)

FRONTIER STATIONS

An Account of Public Service in Pakistan

SHAKIL DURRANI

UNIVERSITY PRESS

OXFORD
UNIVERSITY PRESS

Oxford University Press is a department of the University of Oxford.
It furthers the University's objective of excellence in research, scholarship,
and education by publishing worldwide. Oxford is a registered trade mark of
Oxford University Press in the UK and in certain other countries

Published in Pakistan by
Oxford University Press
No. 38, Sector 15, Korangi Industrial Area,
PO Box 8214, Karachi-74900, Pakistan

ISBN 978-0-19-940603-6

Typeset in Adobe Garamond Pro
Printed on 68gsm Offset Paper

Printed by Delta Dot Technologies (Pvt.) Ltd., Karachi

Acknowledgements
The opinions expressed in this book are entirely those of the author
and should not be attributed to OUP

All photographs courtesy of Shakil Durrani
except where indicated otherwise

Cover image courtesy: Abdul Rehman Joyia/Shutterstock

Dedication

To the poor, patient, and neglected people of Pakistan

To the harried mahseer, markhor, chikor, *and* surkhab

To the orphaned mountains and waters awaiting love

To the kind, considerate, and selfless philanthropists

*To the icons, Abdul Sattar Edhi, Abdul Bari,
Adeeb Rizvi, and Ruth Pfau*

To the martyrs, Rachel Corrie and Perween Rehman

And my earnest prayers for a bright future for the Country

Clifton Chapel

To set the Cause above renown,
To love the game beyond the prize,
To honour, while you strike him down,
The foe that comes with fearless eyes:

To count the life of battle good,
And dear the land that gave you birth,
And dearer yet the brotherhood
That binds the brave of all the earth.

My son, the oath is yours: the end
Is His, Who built the world of strife,
Who gave His children Pain for friend,
And Death for surest hope of life.

To-day and here the fight's begun,
Of the great fellowship you're free;
Henceforth the School and you are one,
And what You are, the race shall be.

Sir Henry John Newbolt (1862–1938)
(Inscribed in Hameed Hall, Lawrence College, Murree)

Contents

Preface

During the summer of 1970, I lived in Gulgasht housing colony, opposite Government College, Multan, in central Pakistan. My father worked for the Government Transport Service, having retired from the Army, while I was studying for my Civil Service of Pakistan competitive examinations. In those days, Pakistan was still united and nearly five thousand candidates, almost all post-graduate students, appeared for this examination of whom not more than twenty were finally selected for the prestigious Civil Service of Pakistan. For me, the stakes were very high because there were few alternate job opportunities available with only a Master's degree in Political Science. My dream of serving in the Tribal Areas or becoming a Deputy Commissioner hung by a thread.

One night after completing my studies, I experienced the *Ziarat-e-Mustafa*, a truly amazing experience and one every Muslim dreams of literally. I dreamt of meeting the Holy Prophet, *Hazrat* Muhammad (PBUH), on the marble platform in front of the Taj Mahal in Agra. Even in my dream, I was aware that this was a very special occasion for me. Furthermore, the Holy Prophet (PBUH) addressed me, asking me to give Rs. 14 in Allah's name to the poor. Immediately, I woke up and waited for daybreak to inform my parents about my good luck. My mother, Halima Zaib, named after Bibi Halima who cared for the Holy Prophet (PBUH) during his early days, told me I was very fortunate and that I should say two *rakaat nafil* prayers in gratitude. I did and gave the money to the poor. How fortuitous was it for me to be visited by the Holy Prophet (PBUH) in my dream!

This experience was a life changer and further strengthened my faith in Providence. It resulted in a new confidence which gave me a direction in my life. I tried to walk the correct path with a conviction that Allah would always guide me. In a sense the impact of this event on my life was immediate. Later that year, I sat for the Central Superior Services examinations, and to my great surprise, stood first in the country.

My friend, Nasser Ali Shah from Sargodha, was the one who informed my father of the results, insisting that the my father should get the honour of breaking the news to me. I had, by Allah's grace become an officer in the CSP, the most sought after acronym to add to one's name in the country, the Civil Service of Pakistan. Setting aside modesty for a while, I do wish to record that I had scored a full sixty-nine marks more than the candidate who stood second. Importantly, I was told that I got top marks in all compulsory and optional papers and in the interview as well. To be honest I had only been an above average student for most of my life and my grades during my early school years were never satisfactory. The rest was hard work and I am sure I worked harder than anyone else who sat the competitive exams, and of course, there was Allah's blessing. I always ask if the Rs. 14 I gave as alms have any earthly significance. Somehow I am convinced it did. Rs. 14 is 1,400 paisas which corresponded to the total number of marks in the competitive examinations and viva voce. This may have been sheer coincidence but I have always drawn inspiration from my dream. I also drew a life-long inspiration for sharing money and wealth with those less fortunate as the Holy Prophet (PBUH) had laid great stress on *Zakat* (obligatory charity) and philanthropy.

I have since then had an enjoyable and successful professional career. The Almighty provided me with opportunities and posts that I had never before dreamed or thought of. I served as Chief Secretary at four places and headed two of the country's largest corporations. There have been some personal disappointments, a few mistakes, and a regret or two. There were decisions that could have been different, but then one never knows what the future holds. My deepest regret is the absence of dedicated leadership in Pakistan which has caused much pain to its people. Virtually everyone in authority has underperformed. I can only hope and pray the country survives in a better form. We have seen too many false saviours, most of whom have been exposed, while we await the liberator.

People like me have been amongst the most fortunate ones in the country. It was no more than an accident of birth that was responsible for the joy and comforts of life for me. I have been even more blessed than others in being afforded an opportunity to serve the people in many executive positions where I could help in ways that would make a difference.

I am convinced that my country has honoured me more than save a handful of persons. It is true that the pleasure of giving is much greater than that of receiving. Without being modest I admit to my shortcomings and deficiencies which many a time may have hurt some people. This is the burden I will always carry. An apology would not erase the pain. I have always tried to act humbly with the poor and the defenceless and have been willing to control my ego in the discharge of my duties. Merely being placed in high government posts was a blessing from the Almighty and any display of arrogance would have been the negation of all the honours bestowed on me.

After the declaration of the CSS examination results in 1971, a large number of people came to congratulate me in Peshawar. An elderly friend of my father, however, thought that this was not the right time for felicitations as at present Allah had merely selected me to serve the people. Later, much later and only on the basis of my actual performance would it be time to judge whether I deserved the felicitations or not. The gentleman has since passed away and I would never know whether I had lived up to his expectations. Can those who have occupied the highest posts in the country, truthfully and with a clear conscience, say that they have performed well?

It would have been too presumptuous of me to record my recollections as 'memoirs' but I was advised by the professionals on the subject to write in the first person. I only wished to record my views as these are personal observations, with some post-event reflections, upon a few interesting, profound event that I witnessed, read, or heard about, often first hand. Not that 'I came, I saw, I conquered' in Caesar's style; civil servants generally function under very tight parameters. I did come across important matters that needed to be commented upon, if only because they related closely to the lives of the people in Pakistan. I have tried to follow Jalaludin Rumi who said, 'I want to sing like the birds sing, not worrying about who hears or what they think.'

The thoughts and events are woven around anecdotes, based mostly on memory, and so the absence of references. My word may be taken for the veracity of everything stated and this may not be easy for some. Nearly every anecdote or event mentioned carries an obvious or a subtle lesson.

I tried not to compromise on truth as I knew it, in describing events and have avoided deviation from the accepted rules and conduct. Some notes were available as record for the writing and I did use the internet, of course! I have truthfully and to the best of my memory tried to recall and place in context some of the failings and frustrations in the administration. I have made observations on some individuals and on the people in general in the country. I admit I have avoided mentioning my own shortcomings and failures, and there were many, but that's how it was.

There is much that needs to change for the better in Pakistan and one way of assisting change is by pinpointing the lapses. I have frankly tried to focus on the truth. There may well be factual errors, faulty judgement, and fragments of unkind observations for which I seek prior forgiveness. I wish to thank all whom I have quoted in the book and those who helped me in different ways. I have tried through these pages to suggest better available options.

Over the years, the general outlook in the country has been dark and gloomy. Hope is all I can look forward to. There is however, much to cheer about Pakistan in the years ahead and my earnest prayers are for a bright future for the country.

Shakil Durrani
Islamabad
September 2019

Part 1

A Frontiersman Recalls

1

Fond Memories

There are three parables that I will always remember. These were narrated to me by my mother when I was not quite eight years old. Each one carried a moral and I imagined that there were a number of useful lessoned for me. The first story my mother told me was about two candidates appearing before an army selection board who were asked about the possible motives of a person walking stealthily at night, holding a bag. The first candidate was rejected because he thought it was a thief carrying stolen goods. The one who was selected had suggested that he was a soldier, seeking the enemy. The moral to the first story was that integrity was the most important quality in life! The second story concerned a very wealthy man who sought the advice of a wise man on how best to reduce his wealth. He was told that the easiest way to lose money was to eat corn bread while riding a horse. The rich man did just that but every time he ate the corn bread, the crumbs fell on the ground and he would dismount, collect the crumbs, kiss them, and save them for later use. Soon he became even richer and complained to the wise man that his prescription had been counterproductive. The wise man told the wealthy man that Almighty Allah did not like wastage and extravagance, and if he had continued to drop crumbs Allah would have been displeased, which would have reduced his wealth. On the contrary, since the wealthy man respected every crumb of bread, the Almighty was pleased. Thrift in all matters was of vital importance and thus one saw the constant switching off of unnecessary lights at home! Lastly, my mother mentioned a story about a man who was to be hanged for many serious crimes he had committed. His last wish was to meet his mother and when she met him he told her she was the one who had sentenced him to death because, as a boy, whenever he stole something small, she would laugh it off. Gradually, he had drifted into armed robberies and murders and then the inevitable happened. Honest hard work was the only path to success!

* * *

Like all mothers the world over, my mother, Halima Zaib Durrani was very loving. When I was about ten, I remember being told one morning that my mother had been taken to the hospital in an emergency. As my father, Lieutenant Colonel Shafi Durrani, was away on a military exercise, she left strict instructions that we should only visit her after school hours. Since there were no telephones or cars in those days, my father's batman, Shams Saleh had cycled from our house on 42 Hussar Road in Sialkot cantonment to Regimental bazaar, a mile away, to get a horse-drawn tonga to take her to the hospital in the middle of the night. After an agonizing day at school, I rushed to the hospital and was immensely relieved to learn that her illness was not life threatening. My mother hugged and kissed me. Then she took out, from under her pillow, and gave me a roasted chicken drumstick, wrapped in paper. She had saved it from her hospital meal. Those were modest times and chicken was a once-a-week luxury. But for a sick person to deprive herself of scarce protein for her child was an act only a mother could do. This expression of her love has remained etched in my heart, virtually every day for the past sixty years, I am always reminded of this tender act that for a mother may be a routine matter and most mothers in her place might have done the same. That is why motherhood is so blessed. Her constant prayers for her children were for *umrai khizri aur bakhtai sikandri*, or the wish for the longevity of life such as Hazrat Khizr's and the good fortune of the likes of Alexander the Great.

* * *

My mother would often tell me that my father left for the imminent war in Kashmir just before I was born and had proposed the name 'Shakil' if the newborn was a boy and 'good looking'. A mother's love often clouds her judgement, so the name Shakil was given. She later gave me a pet name 'Shiko', perhaps prompted by the realization that the given name may not have had any relevance to my looks. She always exhibited love and consideration through her austere lifestyle and personal sacrifices for the sake of our education. They say all children are beautiful to their mothers but there was this story, perhaps only alleged, that the mother of a rather well-known person died of shock as soon as she saw the face of her newborn baby boy. Those who later saw him as an adult agreed that his looks were indeed very ordinary. That aside, the power of love is stronger than all the forces in the universe. Love has also been the most talked about subject. Anne Frank was right when she noted that there was more power of love in an open hand than in a closed fist. Many years ago, in a pub on Grosvenor Street in London, a group of young revellers, mostly truants from offices, happily agreed that the real meaning of love was 'caring for someone more than for oneself'. For such a profound definition to emerge, that too after an extended stay in a pub, was a remarkable feat in itself.

* * *

Parental love neither falters nor ceases. Love between siblings cannot be taken for granted. It normally does not last beyond their marriages. With new members and additions to the family come new priorities. Unsurprisingly, love and affection among brothers and sisters generally fades away. My parents worked hard to raise five children. Their thrift saw us through the best schools in the country such as the Convents in Rawalpindi, Sialkot, and Multan, and Grammar School in Quetta. My parents were very strong-willed and rarely compromised on our education and gave us the best. Both remained very proud till the end. They would trace their lineage in support of their contentions. We heard that our paternal grandfather, Khan Bahadur Juma Khan Nurzai Durrani, retired as a Magistrate in the Balochistan civil service in 1919 and settled in Sikander Khan Dheri, close to Sanda Sar in Tehsil Shabqadr. He took great pride in claiming that his library books cost as much as all his other property. His father, Sulaiman, the son of Qutb, the son of Wali, may have been in the Afghan King's guard. He migrated from Afghanistan shortly before the Indian Mutiny of 1857 and joined the British Indian Army perhaps in the Corps of Guides.

My father studied at the Mission School in Kohati Gate and then graduated from Edwardes College, Peshawar, two outstanding educational institutions, which initiated a long family connection with both. He often recounted two of his abiding regrets. When, as a child, he started learning the Holy Quran, his mother Shafaat Begum or 'Adai' of Kagawala, allowed him to carry a gilded copy of the Holy Quran to the mosque. The mullah eyed this exquisite copy. His supposedly benign advice to the boy was to leave the Holy Quran in the mosque in 'his safe custody,' because carrying it to and fro through the bazaar was *gunah* or sinful. My father never saw it again. The only copy of the family genealogical tree, the *shajra-i-nasab*, which was carved on the leather was also lost.

We also heard that our maternal grandfather, Khan Bahadur Abdul Hakim Khan, retired as Superintendent of Police in the 1930s. He would take his children by car to Gulmarg and Pahlgam in Kashmir but no one explained how the driver, the two parents, and their nine children fitted in one car. I realized much later that this was possible because six members of a family routinely ride on one motorbike in Pakistan today! In 1895, Abdul Hakim was part of Colonel Kelly's column sent by the British for the relief of Chitral Fort and was mentioned by Sir George Scott Robertson, the scholar and administrator, in his book on Chitral.

* * *

My mother was adept at embroidery and despite her lack of formal education, she actually wrote an Urdu fictional account based on her life called *Aakhri Station* (The Last Station). In it she had mentioned that, in the mid-sixties of one's life, a train could get derailed. Two decades later, my mother died in her mid-sixties.

My father was an inveterate supporter of Abdul Ghaffar Khan's Indian National Congress party while my mother was inclined towards the Muslim League. My mother recalled that during a heated debate on politics, in the mid-1940s, my father jokingly told her in Pashto: '*taa ba praidum kho Nehru ba prai na dum*' or '*I could leave you but not Nehru*'. However, he voted for the Muslim League during the referendum! This was because Nehru and the Indian leadership had greatly disappointed him. However, he could never tolerate the corrupt and dishonourable conduct of leaders in Pakistan either. In keeping with the ideals of the early days of Pakistan, there was always a picture of the Quaid-i-Azam in our drawing room and

14 August, Independence Day, was celebrated with a private candle-lighting ceremony. This is no longer the case.

Sohail, my elder brother, has been a successful medical doctor and his hobby, surprisingly, is military history. He has lived in America all of his adult life and belongs to the old school belief in parental and sibling love. Few relationships were more sacred to him than those among siblings especially among the brothers, 'Italian style', and he always proved it through his generosity and love. Huma, actually Dure Shawar Tareen, was the eldest and a very affectionate among three sisters; Shehla and Sheree being the younger ones. As time wore on, one realized that sustained affection requires constant effort. Nothing could be taken for granted.

The affections of Hameeda Bano, our maternal aunt, however, were taken for granted by all because she was totally selfless. Every sweater anyone in the family wore was sure to have been knitted by her and paid for, from her modest means. She would also buy a cake of Pears soap every winter when we visited Peshawar and insisted that we only use 'da Pears soap sabun' unaware that *sabun* meant soap. She would often lament the loan of twenty-tola gold bangles she once gave to a relative for the purchase of some property. She never saw the gold or the property again. She gifted my brother, Sohail, a very rare antique green-coloured 'gardanar' tea set made in the porcelain factory established by an Englishman named Gardner, in Czarist Russia. The set survives in America but the factory does not.

* * *

A maternal uncle, Karim Hazeen, alias Khan Bahadur Sahib or Uncle KJ, had no formal education, possibly because of his severe physical disability, but was yet, another remarkable man. Despite his spinal infirmity he remained a keen hunter, an avid card player, and a modest poet. He became pen friends with a Bombay film actress, Manorama, who was so enamoured by his letters and his thinking that she decided to visit him in Peshawar. There the love story ended because he did not want her to see his deformed spine. This was a *zalim samaj*, society at its cruelest! One of his acts of generosity to me was a gift of an old moth eaten copy of the Pears' Cyclopaedia which helped me immensely in understanding science and acquiring general knowledge for my competitive examinations. A few months before he died, he asked me to take away and put to good use his antique carved writing table, which was a gift to my grandfather from the Chief Justice of the Lahore High Court in the 1930s. Perhaps that was the table he wrote his letters to Manorama on! The table remains one of my treasured possessions, containing a letter with a few lines of poetry by David Bates recorded by Uncle KJ. The lines read:

> Speak gently to the aged one,
> Grieve not the careworn heart,
> The sands of life are nearly run,
> Let such in peace depart.

That was his philosophy in life but not many follow this advice in our dear country!

There were other relatives I remember, especially my maternal uncles Rahim and Abid. The former was as generous as he was brave and as Deputy Superintendent of the Rangers was wounded during the 1965 Indo-Pak war. His hunting exploits were legendary, having once shot eleven blackbucks in one hunt. Both shootings left me sad. Brigadier Ghafoor Abid of the 6th and 13th Lancers was a champion Army swimmer and, during the Freedom Movement, while being held as a political prisoner, he climbed the Haripur Jail clock tower and pulled down the Union Jack. He spoke fluent Chinese (having spent a decade in China) and was friends with Zhou Enlai, the then Premier. He would, at times, take evening walks with George Bush Sr. when he was the US representative in Beijing. It was rumoured that there was once a vodka drinking contest in Beijing between him and a Russian Cossack colonel which the latter lost as he could not get up for the fourteenth round.

I will always remember Abid *Mama's* (maternal uncle) affection. My first camera, a Yashica, and my first harmonica, which I never learnt to play, were both gifts from him. I will never forget his generosity in offering us the upper portion of his house to live in until our own house had been constructed after my father's retirement. His love for his wife, the tall and elegant Birgees, was like it was taken from a fairy tale.

* * *

Then there is the fourth generation, that of my sons Arslaan, Danial, and Shamoun, who have had to live in challenging times marked by a near absence of rules and propriety. They are seeing the demise of thrift and humility which is being replaced by vulgar display and influence peddling in society. These young men have worked hard in different ways. I have always admired Arslaan's sincerity and confidence, Danial's intellect and sharp memory, and Shamoun's meticulous care and thoroughness. As a teenager, Arslaan, while driving in Peshawar, once saw a rashly-driven car hit another only to speed off. He chased the escaping car, stopped the driver, and got him to settle matters with the owner of the damaged car. Why did he take the risk? He thought, 'a wrong was committed and it was in everyone's interest to correct a wrong'. This from a teenager! On another occasion, he travelled from Boston to New York and then to Pakistan with only one dollar in his pocket but with the confidence to pull three large bags all the way to the international terminal. He did this because he was too proud to request an uncle for a small loan. I hope they will always understand the core values in life, differentiate substance from form, and understand that the ultimate core values are integrity and hard work. Young people should also learn to seek and respect advice from those they trust because it helps. I was also fortunate in having some very loving cousins in Waheed, Bilal, Sabur, Anis, Bacha, and Ilyas, among others who were considerate and fun to be with.

The story of my Russian cousin, Liliana, is fascinating enough to be shared. In 1920, my mother's step-brother, Qaiyum, left British India for one of the following possible reasons: He either left for Afghanistan and beyond, as he was deeply motivated by the Khilafat Movement that sought to retain the caliphate in Turkey after Mustafa Kemal Ataturk decided to abolish it, or, he left because he did not get along with his wife and his father-in-law (whom he detested). His wife Sanawar, whom I saw in her old age, must have been a most beautiful woman in her time. But then they say most marriages are made in hell! During the next decade, Qaiyum found himself in the newly-created Soviet Union where he fought, either for the Bolsheviks or against them, and then settled down and worked in railways. He married a Russian lady and had two daughters. One became a tail-gunner in a bomber aircraft during the Second World War and would have known the legendary Nadia Popova of the Skirt Regiment of the

Soviet Air Force who led 852 sorties in the war. The other daughter, Liliana, became a soprano for a Russian opera. Imagine a soprano with Peshawar connections! Such was the extent of the Soviet state sponsorship of culture and women's emancipation. Perhaps my fascination with opera, without understanding it much, lay in the family's genes. Many years later, during a visit to Australia, the hosts were kind enough to take us to the iconic Sydney Opera House for a performance. During the interval, the hostess enquired if I went to the opera house in Peshawar regularly. She could not be told that in Pakistan there was a real life opera of constant profanity with politicians as the lead actors.

Soon after the collapse of the Soviet Union, one of the 'Frontier sisters' wrote a letter in the press enquiring about her relatives in Pakistan. My cousin, Waheed, invited her to visit Pakistan to stay with the family. Liliana was in her seventies, her husband had died earlier, and she had a daughter named Sasha. She spoke only Russian, and communication remained, unfortunately, minimal. She only knew three words of Urdu: '*kutay ki bachi*' (the dog's offspring), words she said her father would constantly use when angry. Her face and eyes bore a remarkable similarity to her aunt, my mother. Liliana, despite her personal accomplishments, was concerned about the uncertainties in Russia after communism ended and was quite struck by the cheap availability of cosmetics and consumer goods in Pakistan. Hers was an amazing story, I thought; from Peshawar to Russia for lack of love and then a visit from Russia to Peshawar with love. A small world indeed!

* * *

I wish to recount some details about Major Jaffer Hussain of Chuhan village in Chakwal, a close friend and colleague of my father, who had a profound influence on us. As a *Subedar* in the British Army he was captured in Singapore during the Second World War where he supposedly joined the Indian National Army of Subhas Chandra Bose and was told to train saboteurs who were to be landed by submarine near the Indian coast. As he was seeing off the first batch, he told them in Punjabi to hand themselves to the police as soon as they were ashore. The Japanese found out and decided to make an example of him as only the Japanese could.

He was saved from the firing squad by the timely arrival of Allied troops. Jaffer Hussain, or uncle Jeff as we knew him, spoke delectable English, had a command of the works of Urdu poets Ghalib and Allama Iqbal, and his handwriting was like a fine print. It was he who suggested that my father send us to Lawrence College, to our great gratitude. It was truly amazing that the village schools run by the Government during those days could produce such an accomplished gentleman.

* * *

i. THE SPLENDOUR OF OUR SCHOOLS AND COLLEGES

Childhood memories, albeit on a full stomach, are a delight if providence places you in the top one per cent of the socio-economic bracket. Nevertheless, the rigours of study were daunting. In those days an Army Major's salary could afford five siblings studying in top class schools. Good fortune and my father's postings took me to the Presentation Convent in Rawalpindi, Grammar School in Quetta in 1953, the Convent of Jesus and Mary in Sialkot, and then to Lawrence College in Ghora Gali. At Presentation Convent, Rawalpindi I was weak in studies and always got poor grades in sums, English dictation, Urdu *imla* and drawing, there being only four subjects. Special tuitions was arranged for me in Lal Kurti Bazaar. I will always remember the Sialkot Convent for a non-event on the cricket field. In 1957, while studying in the Second Standard, I sulked when I was not allowed to open the batting, so my generous teammates relented and permitted me to do so. I managed a first ball duck which fittingly ended my cricketing dreams forever. I forget the name of our captain but I do remember our class teachers, Sister Alfreda and Miss Zubeda and class fellows, Adnan, Junaid, Amara and Sherin.

Lawrence College, or Ghora Gali (GG), was the next school and in those days it cost Rs. 150 per month including board and lodging and books and bats. In 1860, Lawrence College was established with the motto 'Never Give In', and was modelled on English Public Schools. It was established in memory of that remarkable humanist and administrator, Sir Henry Lawrence, 'who tried to do his duty', as he wrote in an epitaph for himself a day before he died in Lucknow during the 1857 Mutiny. For some people, public service was the very essence of living. The elite schools of today are beyond the reach of the middle class and appear to be reserved for the most affluent sections of the community only, the Brandeth Road merchants, as someone called them. Other private schools are even costlier. When politicians bring about a uniform system of education in the country, they should note that lowering standards of the better schools is not the way forward of ensuring uniformity.

In 1960, President Ayub Khan was the guest of honour at the centennial celebrations of Lawrence College and the next fifty years passed very quickly. Before one realized it, the 150th anniversary had arrived. Time does indeed fly for those whom life treats kindly. The guest of honour at the 150th celebrations was Prime Minister Yousaf Raza Gillani, who took the salute at the march past with old Gallians parading separately from current students. To keep in step while marching in front of the highest in the land, that also after forty-five years, and without any rehearsal, was a daunting task, and everyone was relieved when the video showed all were marching in relative unison. It was thoughtful of the organizers to invite student representatives from the two Lawrence Colleges in India and also the great-great-grandson of Sir Henry Lawrence from England. Official ceremonies being rather officious, I invited all the old Gallians and guests, about 800 in number, to a raucously informal lunch at the Bhurban Golf Club to reminisce. Never again would they collect in such numbers to relive their stay at Ghora Gali, and the splendor of Lawrence College. Institutions develop excellence and credibility because of their past, as Dr Pont of Edwardes College would say. Lawrence College measured reasonably well on this count.

All the four schools I attended were either missionary institutions or had foreign teachers and the experience was both enjoyable and rewarding. I think I emerged a better Muslim and citizen. Personal hygiene and moral science classes were regularly held to instill humane values. In Lawrence College, there was the redoubtable Miss Glegg, the Head Mistress of Junior School. She would strike terror in the hearts of the youngsters but was also the most admired and missed. On retirement, she returned to England and reportedly refused the pension offered to her because being in the service of the Punjab Education Service, she felt she was not entitled to an English pension. She was a strict disciplinarian in class, dormitory, the sports field, and the dining room, and everyone knew what pranks to desist from. You could never ever, for instance, dip your biscuit in a cup of milk as 'tongawalas do'. Somehow independent Pakistan has not been able to replicate the zeal and devotion of missionary teachers as their numbers continue to dwindle. Mother Andrew of the Convent of Jesus and Mary in Murree was right in suggesting that providing quality education was now the responsibility of the leaders of the independent country. Sadly, after seventy years, they have not been able to achieve a literacy rate above 50 per cent. Education as a lucrative business thrives today and the acquisition of knowledge appears to be a mere by-product. The era of the likes of Margaret Harbottle of the English Department of Peshawar University has long since passed. There will be few like her, to raise and groom at her own expense, a son of a poor peon who later rose to a high rank in the Army. Pakistan was home to her and, therefore, she insisted she be buried in the local Christian cemetery.

The dedication of these teachers was proverbial, perhaps because the system was complete. Such being the quality of teachers many of them left a lasting impression. Mr Munir, Headmaster of Prep School, could be soft as velvet at times and also as hard as nails; Mr Ehsan Elahi was the mathematics teacher and when he said 'now my dear sir', that meant trouble; Mr Naseer of undulating speech 'alu bokhara kishmish chuhara' felt mathematics and logic should be made compulsory subjects; Mr Asghar Ali was friendly and a top-class sportsman and the one who would remind you that a 'snake does not walk but "craals"'; Mrs Sargon would play 'Colonel Bogey' on the piano for the morning assembly and dispense medicines in the evening, and for some reason her tonic mixtures number 'four' and 'five' were in great demand; the physics teacher, Mr Qureshi, and his wife were most uncharitably called 'kheera and kheeri' or 'male and female cucumbers', but both were a pleasant couple; and Mr Zaidi, the history teacher, swore that in his youth he saw bullock carts travel 'at thirty, no forty miles an hour'. When the students expressed disbelief, he would murmur a friendly four-letter word.

Finally, there was Mr T. J. Walters, who taught English but was equally fluent in Latin and Greek. He would throw the book out of the window if students did not appear enthusiastic in his book reading class. Another time he was aghast when he heard a Gallian, yes me, suggest that they should go to see a 'filum'. He explained to my great embarrassment that if I was referring to the cinema then what I wanted to see was a film, pronounced more like 'flmm'. So there were no 'filums' after that. But, old Indian films in Murree remained a craze for Gallians, on twelve anna seats for the late night shows, and without College permission of course. One had to be prepared for the cane if one were caught. There were endless arguments between Mazhar Sher of Wightwick House and Zakaullah Bangoo of Wright House whether Dilip Kumar or Raj Kapoor was the more accomplished actor and who between Rafi and Mukesh was a better singer. Although, everyone concurred that Lata Mangeshkar was incomparable as a singer and it was common to hear the odd Gallian sing and the rest croak her evergreen songs *aye ga aanay wala* from the film *Mahal* and *lo pyar ki ho gai jeet* from *Jadoo*. There was one Gallian, however, who was greatly enamoured with Geeta Dutt. Who else but Geeta Dutt could recommend the most enthralling lines:

Tadbeer say bigri huee taqdeer bana lay
apnay pay bharosa hai to ek dao laga lay.

Or the more inspiring and stirring verse for the young:

Tu duniya main jeenay ka lay lay maza
ya hosh ki bateenh abi bhool ja.

'*Hosh*' (propriety), everyone hoped, would come in good time! Many followed her advice without demurring throughout their lives and at some cost to themselves. Fortunately, there was complete unanimity on the beauty and grace of Madhubala, who had links to our Frontier, the Khyber Pakhtunkhwa province, as the *prima donna* of films and not even the bewitching Rekha in her prime could proffer a challenge to her. Those were the days when Indian heroines were sedate and serious ladies.

The Principals of Lawrence College were gentlemen like Chaudhry Hameed, H. L. O. Flecker, and M. L. Charlesworth, for whom good education and personal conduct were articles of faith. Mr Hameed was the first Muslim Principal of the College and was credited with saving it from the mob which wanted to burn the place during the turbulent days of Independence in 1947. Mr Charlesworth was the last, save one English

Principal, but the only one who thought of constructing a mosque, and that too purely through donations. Another Principal was Mr Moinuddin, who along with his wife, were the most refined but that did not prevent the students from giving them some very uncharitable nicknames. And then there was the genial gentleman Mr Mehboob Ali, a part-time Sports Master, who reportedly got two opposing batsmen out on one ball, a caught and run out. This was long before Imran Khan, the cricketing legend, threatened to get two wickets of his political opponents with one ball during his electioneering. No memory of GG is complete without recalling the head bearer of the dining hall, Chhabu Khan who appeared to be as old as the college itself, or Brutus, the house bearer of Wightwick House who could lift three steel trunks by himself. Then there was Mullah Jaffar, the telephone operator, who would also deputize as the imam and would add to his income by clandestinely selling cigarettes to the boys. Duty and business obviously had separate compartments in his brain. What some of the naughtiest of the boys once did to him, when he had prostrated during prayers, I will not mention. One name every Gallian knew was that of Zakaria Ghaffar from Karachi who was an encyclopaedia on Lawrence College; his friend would jokingly state that he knew the names of every Gallian over the past century. The Lawrence College campus was complete in all respects and it claimed its own resident witch as well called 'Massi Meera'. A few Gallians, not known for truthfulness, insisted on having seen her descend from the wooden ceilings at night. These boys also noticed that her toes were pointed outwards because, after all, no self respecting witch could have straight feet.

Ghora Gali, it was said, was all about the 'GG spirit', connoting camaraderie, courage, sportsmanship, the old school tie, and the national flag. Most Gallians lived up to the expectations but some in politics and in government service did fall short. The most famous Gallian undoubtedly was Zafar Hayat, later a Brigadier, who was a top-class sportsman and was part of the gold medal-winning Olympic hockey team. It was rumoured that during General Zia's rule, the three Gallians who became Federal Ministers in the Cabinet were all expelled from College on disciplinary grounds. They obviously remained very comfortable in Pakistani politics however, which also explains the essence of Pakistani politics! Two Gallians became Prime Ministers of the country. There was Zafarullah Jamali, a class hockey player and a genial soul. In politics he was uninspiring and was always looking over his shoulder to the President, whom he referred to as his 'boss' even though he was the chief executive of the country. He probably regrets having uttered these words! The other Gallian who became Prime Minister was Shahid Khaqan Abbasi. He was elected Prime Minister for an interim period and his performance was impressive.

There were four Houses in GG named after former Principals: Wightwick, Walker, Wright, and Peake. The sports competition to claim the Cock House Shield was intense. In 1960, the centennial year, Wightwick House won the shield, but four years later Wright House claimed it only because of the very poor scores of Wightwick in the Knowledge Cup and the Star and Daggers Cup. This was my House. After the departure of Mr Charlesworth, Lawrence College seemingly went into a tail spin. Some of the later Principals of the College developed tainted reputations, others were too incompetent and one reportedly encouraged cheating in examination to ensure better results. No wonder corruption thrived, indiscipline soared, and a student was actually murdered; this was more in line with the times. Would this be the new Pakistan?

During the early 1960s a number of Muslim students from South Africa joined Lawrence College and some of them became icons for their sporting abilities. Ismail Garda, Cassim Docrat, and the Latib brothers were the main force in the sports tournaments against Aitchison College and other schools like Burn Hall, Cadet College, Hasan Abdal, and Air Force School, Lower Topa. The annual sporting contest with Aitchison College was taken very seriously and it was thrilling to beat them for the 'rubber' in 1964. Lawrence College even won hockey that year to the chants of 'buck up GG' by the on-lookers, the Gallians. The match earned me and another player the College Colours. This friendly rivalry between the two schools continued later in life but in their hearts the Gallians always knew their school was the better one even though I sent two of my boys, Danial and Shamoun to our rival, Aitchison College. Ismail Garda was our top cricketer who later decided to play county cricket in England. However, to his bad luck, each county could accept only one foreign player per side and he had to compete with a cricketer called Sir Garfield Sobers. Cassim Docrat, in due course, became the manager of the South Africa cricket team and toured Pakistan. Abdul Rehman Latib played some professional tennis in America.

Another class fellow of mine from Lawrence College was the unassuming Major Arjumand Malik, who later in life displayed amazing courage worthy of our commandos. He was taken prisoner in East Pakistan in the 1971 War and confined in Ramgarh camp in Bihar from where along with another officer he made a daring escape. They climbed over a barbed wire fence in heavy fog, evaded sentries and scent hounds, spent a night in tiger infested jungles, travelled a thousand miles on foot, train and bus, aroused menacing suspicion half a dozen times but arrived safely after all. Along the way they came across a small village of untouchables growing vegetables. A little girl about ten years old plainly told the commandos on the run that she could not give them water or vegetables because she was forbidden to touch them. (Dr Ambedkar would have turned in his grave hearing the child's innocent words!). They also got Sikh bangles to pass off as locals. What a relief was it to embrace the Desert Rangers when they finally set foot in Pakistan.

The two years at Edwardes College, Peshawar for graduation were a treat. The Principal, an Australian, Dr Phil Edmonds, was fully supported in College affairs by his wife, Belle or *madama*, the Pashto for madam, as she was referred to in her absence. They were always followed by their constant companion, their dog, the spaniel, Titch. For those who had not seen the Raj functioning first hand, Edwardes College showed how one *gora sahib* could transform a native institution into a first class model. Dr Edmonds also proved that it was possible for one well-meaning foreigner, or for the odd local person, to mould hundreds of unmalleable and generally indisciplined Pathan students into useful members of the society. With discipline came excellent examination results, allowing Dr Edmonds to glow with satisfaction. Dr Edmonds took great pains to ensure cleanliness and orderliness. He would inspect all bedrooms of the hostel once a week and would look for dust in the most unlikely places. A student, Zahid ur Rehman, or 'Shorty', could therefore be excused when he was seen walking with a *lota* to the bathroom to clean himself 'because you never know where the Principal might next place his finger looking for dirt'.

Dr Edmonds always had the last word in any oral exchange due to his wit and presence of mind. A student once tried to correct him while he was introducing a new 'green blackboard' in the class. Dr Edmonds quickly admonished him by saying that it was not for him to refine the language. Another time while teaching essay writing, he was at pains to point out that the word 'thing' could only be used for a physical object but when he was reminded that Keats used it differently, Dr Edmonds was stumped. Never one to emerge second best, he quickly retorted: 'but you, Shakil, are not Keats'. Two of his bright students, Gulzar and Ismail, to this day use this ploy when outsmarted in an argument. Dr Edmond's Australian accent however disturbed quite a few students, especially during the weekly College assembly. One student actually tried to confirm the identity of the person who had 'died' as informed by Dr Edmond. He was relieved to be told that no one had died but that the Principal only spoke of *ad majorem die glorium*, to the greater glory of God.

Only once did I see Dr Edmonds pale and shattered, and that was when the college brass bell, originally from the British naval ship, HMS Artifex and gifted to Edwardes College by the Royal Navy, was stolen, reportedly also by an Edwardian. A gloom descended on the College for weeks. It was rumoured that a cavalry regiment of the Army later got possession of it and even half a century later one hopes it will be returned to the College as stolen property is not a war trophy. Dr Edmonds was an icon and the grateful class of 1967, which had produced the highest number of first divisions in Edwardes history, dedicated a stone fountain in his memory. There was something special about the environment in Edwardes College that was captivating and there were teachers like Zia-ul-Qamar, Zakki, and Akhtar, who had Edwardes College in their blood. Long after some of the teachers had left, people could still recall Deliah, Walker, and Thakardur Das. The last individual held mastery over poetry, especially Shakespeare, apart from being an accomplished musician and badminton player. Money never came his way. How could it, when as a lawyer he charged a client only a loaf of bread? It was said of him that, during a radio programme he was hosting, he enquired of the lady he loved: 'darling, are you listening?' Apparently, his was a one-way love.

During those days in Peshawar, no one could forget Professor Hubert Michael Close of both Islamia and Edwardes Colleges whose preferred mode of travel was his bicycle. He spent a lifetime serving the cause of education and even more vigorous were his endeavours to expand blood donation in the Frontier. Sadly, not many turned up at the Church service on his death. That was hardly surprising in Pakistan, where our motto should be 'show me how I may use you'. Then there was David Page, the young English teacher, who after a short stint at Edwardes College developed a life long association with the country and the people. In class one day, he enquired about the purpose behind the use of an 'understatement'. The intense joy on his face was apparent when a Pakhtun Edwardian replied that the purpose was 'to intensify the effect'. Edwardians may not remember much poetry but no one forgot Kabir's lines engraved in marble in the tiny Shalimar Garden which said 'I laugh when I hear that the fish in the water is thirsty; I laugh when I hear that men go on pilgrimage to find God'.

The annual hockey match that Edwardes College played against Islamia College evoked the best spirits in the boys. The game was always keenly contested but the shouting match was infinitely more absorbing. The Islamia crowd chanted '*dal chapatti*' (lentils and bread) and in response the Edwardian battle cry was '*kalay kaway*' (black crows) as Islamia's college uniform was a black achkan. The sporting past of Islamia College, however, was impressive. One of their Principals, Mr Holdsworth, was an Oxford Blue in cricket who had also played for England. He was also known to be a top mountaineer in his time.

The accomplishments of some of my class-fellows in Edwardes College, Peshawar need to be recorded here. There was Colonel Derek Joseph with family roots from Armenia, Senator Brigadier John William, and his younger brother David who joined the Army. All three were decorated for bravery in the 1971 Indo-Pak war. Another brother, Reginald William rose to a high position in the provincial bureaucracy.

* * *

The Punjab University in Lahore was a let-down after studying at Lawrence College and Edwardes College. These were two wasted years except for some friendships I made. It was painful to see lecturers dictating notes at the University level in a Political Science class. No research studies were pursued, no innovative thinking was encouraged, and no thesis development programmes existed and yet a Master's degree was awarded.

Princess Diana being received by Shakil Durrani, Commissioner of Malakand Division on arrival in Chitral in 1991. Also in the photograph is Deputy Commissioner Chitral, Commandant, Chitral Scouts, with Chitrali children presenting flowers.
Photo courtesy: Mian Maqsood

Princess Diana in a *Chugga*, a Chitrali coat and the *Pakol*, the Chitral Scouts
Regimental cap during her visit to Chitral in 1991.
Photo courtesy: Mian Maqsood

Princess Diana, the Peoples' Princess, learns about the Kalash people from the author, Shakil Durrani, Commissioner, Malakand Division during her visit to Chitral in 1991.
Photo courtesy: Mian Maqsood

Subedar Ali Haider of the Frontier Force Regiment who was awarded the Victoria Cross in the Second World War with HRH Prince Charles at a reunion in London.

HRH Princess Anne talking to a tribal Malik as a bemused Colonel Sher Rehman, Commandant of the Khyber Rifles looks on.

Lawrence College, Gora Gali, Murree. Home of the Gallians.

Convent of Jesus and Mary, Murree. The boarding school for girls during twentieth century and
the eternal heartache for the Gallians nearby.
Photo courtesy: Principal, J & M Convent, Murree

The English 'Frontiersman', Feroze Khan with his wife smoking a *chillum*; his request to become a Pakistani citizen was turned down.

Mollie Ellis of Suffolk, UK in 1983. She was kidnapped as a child in Kohat, NWFP in 1923, and returned 60 years later to visit her mother's grave in Kohat.

Mrs Councell visited Kohat in 1986 to see the house where her parents were killed in 1919.

Hollywood super star, Kirk Douglas examining the dagger presented to him;
He wished he had it while filming *Spartacus*.

Muhammad Ali, the greatest boxing champion of all times on a visit to Peshawar in 1988.

CIVIL SERVICE ACADEMY
C. S. P : P. F. S : PROBATIONERS
Session 1971–72, Lahore.

Sitting L to R: Khawaja Zabeer Ahmed CSP, Mohammad Shakil Durrani CSP, Abdul Hameed CSP, Deputy Director, Mahdi Hassan CSP, Director,
Faisal M. Rehan CSP, Asst Director, Shahryar Rashed PFS, Iftikhar-ul-Karim PFS.

Stending 1st Row L to R: Musa Javed Chohan PFS, Tauheed Ahmad PFS, Mirza Shams-uz-Zaman PFS, A.T.M. Nazim Ullah Ch. CSP,
Javad Saddiq Malik CSP, Saleh-ud-Din Ahmad CSP, Ahmad Mahmood-ur-Raza Ch. CSP, Ziaul Islam CSP, Serajul Islam PFS,
Mohammad Ayub CSP, Aziz Ahmad Chowdhury CSP,

Standing 2nd Row L to R: Sher Afgan Khan PFS, Tareque M. Feroze CSP, Syed Masood Alam Rizvi CSP, Iqbal Ahmad Khan PFS, Hassan Sarmad PFS,
Khalid Farid Khan CSP, Alimul Haque PFS, Hussain Hamid CSP, Ashraf Hasan CSP.

ZAIDIS LAHORE

In 1968, the Punjab University arranged a visit to East Pakistan. This was a couple of years before a visa was required to travel to that independent country. The experience was unforgettable. The friendliness and warmth of the Bengalis, soon to become Bangladeshis, was unbelievable for anyone who had not been there. The students of Dacca University were especially hospitable and I still recall the amiability of a student named Tipu. The journey took us to Chittagong, Cox's Bazar, Sylhet, and Shamshernagar tea estates. Friendliness and hospitality followed us everywhere. A picnic was arranged outside Sylhet near a picturesque natural lake. One of the boys from the delegation—there being four boys and six girls—decided to impress the girls with his very ordinary physique and amateur swimming abilities by promptly swimming across the lake. To show off further he swam back thoroughly satisfied with himself. A short time later, the hosts arrived with the food and by way of caution informed everyone not to step into the waters because of the poisonous snakes lurking there. Our Valentino had escaped serious harm by the skin of his teeth but he thought he had made his mark!

What amazed me most about the years in Punjab University were the copious Urdu verses virtually every boy and girl knew by heart. They could recite them by the hundreds and some quite melodiously too. Could that effort not be better employed in scholarship instead? The retort to this view was that good poetry actually balanced learning. They had a point! Nasser Ali Shah, for instance, could recite the Persian poets, Hafiz and Firdusi, for hours. Most others chimed in romantic lines for all occasions. One heard the lament, 'dil nay tarrap kay aah li, puchha kisi nay kya huwa, dil ki khata ka majra ghairon ko kyun sunaun' or something to that effect. I can personally remember only one other verse and that too from my pre-teen days because this was printed under a sketch I would see almost every day: 'saqi teray altaf ka mumnoon hoon lekin, jo kuchh bhi hai is ghum may teri zulf say kam hai' or something to that effect!

* * *

While still in college, on the persuasion of a friend, Major Saeed Akhtar Malik, I applied for the thirty-eighth Long Course in the Pakistan Military Academy. I then decided against taking the tests. My father, Pakistan Army

1376, Lieutenant Colonel Shafi Durrani, who had commanded 11 Field, 12 Medium, 33 Heavy, and 3 SP Artillery regiments, did not want me to join the Army because he thought one had to have a patron in the Army to rise to senior positions. In his case all his patrons were gone for one reason or the other. He was nominated by Brigadier, later General Musa Khan, to a select panel for posting as ADC to the Governor General, the Quaid-i-Azam. He remained a Staff Officer to General Gracey, the Army Chief, who once observed that the young officer had a 'bright career' ahead of him. Then there were stints with Brigadier Sher Khan who was killed in an air crash and General Habibullah who developed differences with General Ayub Khan and left. After retirement, my father served as the Administrator, the mayor, of Peshawar city and was very keen to develop ring-roads to facilitate traffic flow. As for a successful career in the Army, I realized that to succeed in the Pakistan Army one has to work hard at military academics, keep one's mouth shut most of the time, and pray for luck. These three factors lead to success and promotions in the Army even without patrons. Brigadier Yasub Ali Dogar, the Piffer, a distinguished officer and a gentleman was convinced that for senior level promotions in the Army one has to be 'very hardworking and mediocre'. Perhaps the good Brigadier was being too harsh; the Army more than any other career in the country provides one an equal and fair chance to rise to the very top. There are too many examples confirming this. In my time in service, I also tried to speak my mind openly, like my father, but fortunately without serious damage.

The greatest military strategist of the Second World War, Field Marshal Erich von Manstein of Germany, graded Army officers rather differently. He said 'there are only four types of officers. Firstly, there are the lazy, stupid ones. Leave them alone, they do no harm ... secondly, there are the hard-working, intelligent ones. They make excellent staff officers, ensuring that every detail is properly considered. Thirdly, there are the hard-working, stupid ones. These people are a menace and must be fired at once. They create irrelevant work for everybody. Finally, there are the intelligent lazy ones who are suitable for higher office'. I am glad I did not join the Army because I would not have been 'suitable for higher office' and would have retired early. Many of those who planned the puerile Pindi coup against Zulfikar Ali Bhutto in 1972 were known to me.

ii. SOME UNFORGETTABLE PEOPLE

I have been very fortunate to meet some of the most important people of the twentieth century. It was a treat to come across, although fleetingly, Nelson Mandela; 'the people's princess', Princess Diana; the boxing legend Muhammad Ali; the Bollywood screen icon Dilip Kumar; the eminent authority on Sufism, Professor Annemarie Schimmel; the Indian Army Chief Field Marshal Sam Manekshaw; the exceptional cricketers Sachin Tendulkar and Imran Khan; the squash maestro Jehangir Khan; Professor Jeffery Sachs of Harvard University and Columbia University; Ardeshir Cowasjee of the *sala* fame; and philanthropists Abdul Sattar Edhi, Dr Adeeb Rizvi, and Princess Salima Aga Khan. There was also the legendary Abdul Ghaffar Khan, better known as Bacha Khan.

The greatest person I recall meeting and getting to know was a German doctor and a nun, the late Dr Ruth Pfau. This saintly care-giver, through the Marie Adelaide Leprosy Centre, devoted her entire life to eradicating leprosy from Pakistan and later concentrated her efforts on tuberculosis control. She was my hero and it is a small coincidence that we share the same date of birth, 9 September. She was meant to break her journey in Karachi on her way to Bombay in 1960, but thanks to the incompetence of the Indian bureaucracy, her visa was delayed inordinately. She, therefore decided to stay and work in Pakistan. The incompetence of the Indian bureaucracy led to the eradication of leprosy in Pakistan. Dr Pfau lived in Pakistan all her life. I once asked her what one trait she found irksome in the Pakistani people. She was prompt in her reply. Whenever and to whomsoever she made a request for assisting patients, they invariably replied that there was 'no problem madam, no problem'. The problem, she thought, was that 'there was actually a problem' because rarely did people stand by their word. For most Pakistanis a promise or a commitment is vacuous and never really meant to be followed up. There was a lot of lip service but seldom was it followed up. And here I am not speaking of politicians alone. One last word about Dr Pfau is in order. At the golden jubilee celebrations of the successful campaign against leprosy in Swat, the Chief Minister, Mir Afzal Khan was the guest of honour to a lunch, which she insisted, should only be of *'dal, roti, pani'* (lentils, bread, and water), with everyone including the chief guest paying for the food. This was the

only function I have seen where money was actually raised while celebrating
a previous achievement. When will we learn such fine art?

Unarguably, the most interesting person I ever knew well was Maulana
Amir Muhammad Khan or Maulana Bijligar for the laity, who got his
nickname because of being the *pesh imam* (prayer leader) of the Peshawar
thermal power station. *'Pakhtun dai ka langmar'* was how he often, quite
uncharitably, defined people. The Maulana was profanely witty, delightfully
jovial, and an eloquent orator whose lively speeches and sermons were
recorded and sold by the thousands because these were peppered with
sensual innuendoes and outright obscenities. (He once spoke of women's
cricket in rather sexist and derogatory terms, *'pandose ba charta magy'* were
his exact words!).

The Maulana also indulged in politics but quit soon after a new leader
emerged in his party, with whom he did not get along and whom he would
describe quite irreverently. Bijlighar was very public-spirited and helpful to
the District Administration and would often be co-opted during stressful
times to resolve sectarian and other law and order issues. In return, he was
well looked after and there were many occasions at which he was ostensibly
given the resources for the upkeep of his mosque. Once, when he asked
for the replacement of the fans in his mosque in rather quick succession, I
asked him to get better quality fans in future. He understood the joke and
rocked with laughter. He was such a persuasive conversationalist that at
my request, he very hesitantly agreed to record a message in the media in
support of family planning and spacing childbirth. People like him were
rare indeed!

The Maulana had read Rehman Baba, the Sufi poet, and thanked Abdul
Qaiyum Khan, the then Chief Minister, for putting him in Shabqadr Fort
jail where he got the opportunity to devote himself to the most famous
poet of the Pakhtuns. In those days, Air Vice Marshal Bahar was also an
authority on Rehman Baba with each claiming greater scholarship. Bijlighar
joked that he would get the *'bahar'* (spring season) out of the retired Air
Force officer while the latter was convinced that after his renditions there
would be no *'bijli'* or electricity left in the Maulana. Sadly, they never met.

Maulana Bijlighar's death left a void in Bala Mari, Peshawar, and the
Frontier province in more ways than one. Laughter and mirth went out
of fashion. Who would now speak of Prime Minister Nawaz Sharif and

his *maindak* after the elections in the late nineties? Since *maindak* in Urdu means frog, someone resented the Maulana's choice of words but he candidly replied that this word was used by the Prime Minister himself all the time. It transpired that the good Maulana confused the word 'mandate' with *maindak*!

In politics, two of the finest gentlemen I have seen were both from Swat. There was Khaliqdad Khan of Jamaat-i-Islami who was noble, soft spoken, and incapable of deviating from the correct path. The other was Afzal Khan Lala of the Awami National Party with wit and hospitality unmatched. Even as a Member of the National Assembly, Khaliqdad Khan never made a request for himself or another, despite the immense public pressure on him. Hence, the only time he asked for a favour, I was determined to oblige him; in the end all he asked was that I have dinner with him in his village Fiza Ghat! Who could beat that?

Khan Lala was as much a gentleman as he was brave. In politics he would often say there were two types of people. Firstly, there were the truthful, conscientious, and *'wazadar'* sort and the other, and here he paused, were like those one finds in the Pakistan Peoples Party (PPP). Vagaries of politics soon drove him into the cabinet in a coalition government with PPP and then he did not wish to remember his two classifications. Khan Lala's hospitality, like that of his neighbour Dost Muhammad Khan of the PPP, was extraordinary, but there was a small precondition. He would ask one of the guests to lead the prayer, the *'imamat'*, and if there was any reluctance then *'aqamat'* was mandatory, the call before the prayers. Often that was when the chief guest tried not to make eye contact with the host.

Two decades after I was posted out of Swat, I returned to attend the funeral rites for Afzal Khan and by mere chance sat next to an aged man. Neither of us recognized each other. Through discrete enquiry I was told he was the same Khaliqdad Khan, after which I introduced myself. He was ecstatic. He tried, but failed to stand and seldom have I seen a greater spark in human eyes than his, at that moment. In one sitting I bade farewell to one great person and met the other. Is there a pattern in life which creates such coincidences?

There were a few very interesting, and maybe idiosyncratic foreigners I got to know well. The Englishman, Roderick Goldsworthy stood tall amongst them, and he measured six feet four inches. Having served the

British military in the Frontier province before Independence, he remained very partial to the Pakhtuns and also fancied the place. He was clearly unhappy with the Pakistanis and their lack of dedication towards nation-building and spoke his mind openly, causing much embarrassment at times. I once accompanied him in the morning to see the lively General Ghaziuddin Rana, then Inspector General of the Frontier Corps, in Bala Hissar Fort. The good General offered tea or coffee and a visibly irritated Roderick replied 'no thanks, because I just had breakfast and I assume you had too'. He then reminded the General that this was the time to develop the country and not waste it on frivolities. This was one tea invitation too many! Another time in London, Roderick and I decided to visit the India Office library which was about three miles from our rendezvous point. He declined my suggestion that we take a taxi and when I raised the option again, he blew up. 'You Pathans have become weak and look at what is happening to you,' he thundered.

There was another British man with Frontier connections who after converting to Islam called himself Feroze Khan. Past sixty, he wished to live his remaining days as a Pakistani national, teaching either in Kohat or the Khyber Agency and dutifully deposited the fees of Rs. 600,000 required under the nationality law. The intelligence agencies of the State thought otherwise and turned down his request, suspecting that he was a spy. This compelled him to settle in Portugal instead, where he died soon after. Feroze would smoke *chillum*, the Pakhtun smoking pipe, and always carried the local *kasoray* (satchel) to keep the tobacco in. It may be fair to say that thousands of Pakhtuns today cannot speak English correctly because of our Intelligence agencies secret reports.

Equally unforgettable was the American tourist and author, Debra Denker, who at one time wanted to marry a *mujahedeen*. Good that she didn't for the word is a plural for a '*mujahid*' or 'holy warrior' and marrying *mujahedeen* could have caused her all sorts of serious problems! There was also the amiable New York couple Anita and David Christy, well-educated and sedate, who became fond of Chitral and its people. David often had interesting quips to offer but he spoke so softly and so slowly that by the time he ended a sentence, one forgot its beginning.

One cannot forget Anna-Liisa Kaukinen of the Asian Development Bank. She was suave and a great friend and supporter of Pakistan. After

Pakistan tested an atomic bomb, economic sanctions were imposed on the country, therefore the prospects for funding a health project for mothers and children in Swat virtually ceased. She, however, made one final attempt and hastily arranged a lunch meeting for a senior Peshawar-based official with Cinnamon Dornsife, the attractive American Director at the Bank headquarters in Manila. The hope was that he may charm his way in getting approval for the project. There remains no record of whether he ever charmed her but the lunch project was successful as the loan amount was sanctioned. Cinnamon's heart melted when the officer informed her that tens of thousands of mothers and children in Swat would suffer if the project was not approved. The officer deputed, however, did record that he was always prepared to perform such charming duties in the interest of the state, of course! There was another foreigner, the refined Brigitte Sperber, a Scandinavian who was also an accomplished artist having sketched the Kalash people. She was kind enough to do three pencil sketches of my boys and that too within minutes. And then there was Sandra Miller in London, erudite and elegant, who appreciated art and anthropology.

There is also the story of the German couple with the most difficult surname in the world who made Peshawar their home and lived happily ever after. Both Rudolf von Przyborowski and his amazing wife, Ernestine, were hard working and 'hard drinking'! Rudolf owned and operated a quality handmade furniture factory in Peshawar and for a time also made rifle stocks for the Army. For every tree he felled for his trade, he would plant a dozen more and would berate Pakistani timber contractors, most of whom were politicians, for destroying whole forests. In the factory, Ernestine would do what six Pakistani men get paid for; she was the sales person, telephone operator, waitress, record keeper, accountant, and supervisor. The couple also had a rather naughty habit, which one of their close friend found out while visiting the factory one morning with a delegation of senior officials. He soon realized that his glass of coca cola smelt and tasted more like an alcoholic beverage. Could one or both of them have conspired in adding something hard to the soft drink? No liver was safe for long in their company! There were many theories about why Rudolf migrated from Germany after the Second World War but his arrival in Peshawar was a great blessing for friends and a boon for the local furniture and sausage industries. When the couple's livers stopped functioning, they died and left strict instructions that they be buried in the local cemetery.

How could one forget John Briscoe? A great friend of Pakistan, he was originally from South Africa and had settled in America. He had a very distinguished career in the World Bank which lasted twenty-two years. Then, for six years he was at the Kennedy School of Government at Harvard University. He had also won the Stockholm Water Award, the water sector Nobel prize, and was an authority on water issues. Weeks before he died of cancer he emailed his friends: 'it is tricky to know exactly how to communicate one's imminent death. I am now on my last leg and wanted to say goodbye. My life was a lucky one with immense opportunities at every stage.' His last wish was that instead of sending him flowers, people donate to the trust he created for awards in science, technology, and mathematics. The message ended with Conceição Andrade's words: 'imagination is the essence of life.'

I must mention two diplomats, who left an endearing impact on those they knew. Sir Nicholas Barrington, the British High Commissioner, who famously said that whenever he met a Pakistani bureaucrat, even after a few weeks, he asked him what post had he now been transferred to and from politicians he enquired what political party had they joined since they last met. So much for consistency in our dear land! The relaxed and affable Rodolfo Martin-Saravia, the Argentinian Ambassador made Pakistan his home for nearly a decade and the number of his friends increased by geometric progression every year!

Three persons I greatly regret not meeting, were General Vo Nguyen Giap from Vietnam, Fidel Castro of Cuba, and Mother Theresa of Calcutta. They were the towering personalities of the twentieth century. The former two were an anathema to the West and their achievements were played down. General Giap during his times had defeated the major world powers like Japan in the Second World War, the French at Dien Bien Phu in Indo-China, the Americans in Vietnam during the seventies, and contained the Chinese in their brief skirmish later. Even Genghis Khan could not match his war record. Castro was a legend by personally having ousted a corrupt and degenerate leadership and then survived fifty years despite American pressure, aggression, and sanctions. I did not have the resources to meet them when they were younger and by the time I could afford the travel they were too old and ill to meet visitors despite some efforts that were made, by different ambassadors, on my behalf. Truth and sacrifice most certainly were their dominant attributes and it is no small wonder that the Pakistani leadership cannot produce such giants. I also wished I had met Field Marshal Erich von Manstein, the most brilliant strategist of the Second World War after having read his book, *The Lost Victories*, in my teens. He once said 'a war is not lost until you consider it lost,' and these words carry much meaning.

Manstein was on the losing side in the Second World War but among the victors was one Subedar Ali Haider of the Frontier Force Regiment from Hangu, who won the Victoria Cross in Italy. Early in my career as Assistant Commissioner, Hangu, I tried to locate his house. No one knew of Ali Haider which really perplexed me as he was a hero. After some time spent trying to identify him, a young boy enquired if I was looking for *Victoria* and immediately everyone pointed out his house. Now Ali Haider *Victoria* was an interesting chap but was always in dire financial straits and his few admirers tried helping him in small ways. I was told his Regiment had to buy back his war medals which he had sold to pay for his needs. He had no children and in old age the couple's condition was sad and it was left to some officials to keep them alive. In another country, the state would have looked after him better.

The Government, if not the society, also ignored Pakistan's greatest war hero Squadron Leader, later Air Commodore, M. M. Alam, who had shot down a record number of Indian planes during the 1965 Indo-Pak war. He, like another air ace Group Captain Cecil Chaudhry, fell afoul of General Ziaul Haq and the top brass of the Air Force and were largely ignored in life, but thankfully both were given full ceremonial burials by the Pakistan Air Force with the Air Chief present.

There were two Pakistani heroes who in their own ways had major accomplishments to their name in spite of their modest social standing. They would collect, bathe, and bury the unclaimed dead at their own expense. One was a humble office peon, Ghulam Hasan, fondly called *Sadr Sahib* from Muzaffarabad in Azad Kashmir, and the other Taj Muhammad, a watchman at Kalabagh Barrage in Mianwali. For both, making ends meet was a challenge and though they have now passed on, their names and deeds survive them. Once, a Chief Secretary in Azad

Kashmir gladly withdrew from formally opening a bridge over the River Neelum, in favour of Ghulam Hasan in order to honour his memory. Taj, on the other hand was not so lucky as he was allegedly thrown over a bridge by the paramilitary Punjab Rangers for refusing to give them fish, free of cost. A small selfless act is indeed preferable to a life time of empty rituals. Islam teaches us that saving one life is like saving all humanity. A small gesture or a good deed has as much impact as a small act of evil which could cause large scale destruction—as in the case of arson which can also cause devastating forest fires. I am always reminded of a lively friend from Abbottabad who, when most joyous after a few sips of a choice beverage, would produce the tip of a matchstick and announce brazenly that 'this could burn the world!'

The unforgettable few that have been mentioned here were remarkable individuals. Sadly, there were a couple of rather unremarkable persons I came across, whom I regret having met even though my dealings with them were strictly official. I found both of them offensive and insolent in dealing with Pakistanis. One was serving in the United Nations Fund for Population Activities in Pakistan, while the other was serving in the High Commission for Canada in Islamabad. The former considered himself a latter day pro-consul who wanted the national population welfare programme to function according to his whims. The Canadian appeared more as a representative of a hydropower company and its local partners than a representative of his country. He was adamant that the Government of NWFP, now Khyber Pakhtunkhwa, allot the 74 megawatt Malakand Three Hydro Power project to the Canadian company and not develop the very profitable project itself in the public sector. It is said that every person in the world loves two cities; Paris and their own city. What is not known is how these two persons found their way to Pakistan in rapid succession. Could it be that most Pakistanis do not challenge such impolite behaviour as a post-colonial hangover? Or are we so generous to foreigners that some of them take us for granted. Both however, got a taste of their own medicine. The former was reported to the Government for improper conduct, while the French Canadian's haughty behaviour was ground to dust as the Government decided not to allot the hydel project to any foreigner. The newspapers of the period reported that in Canada a scandal involving some politicians and a power company led to the resignation of a provincial premier. It was also noted that there was a connection to a small hydel project in the remote area of NWFP. Today, Malakand Three Power Station earns a net profit of US$20 million annually. In just one year, it provides a hundred times more revenue than the Government spends on one senior officer in his entire career. It may surprise people to know that there were some well-connected Pakistanis in Islamabad who tried their best to gift this project to the Canadians, perhaps for deriving personal benefits. An offer was made to me as well which was turned down contemptuously. Fortunately, President Musharraf, the Governor, NWFP, General Iftikhar Shah, Additional Secretary Ikram Khan, and Dr Zahid Iftikhar were instrumental in ensuring the transfer of Malakand Three Power plant to the provincial government. There was absolutely no reason why Pakistan would gift its best hydel power site to outsiders only to make huge profits.

Ardeshir Cowasjee, was the doyen of the conscience-keepers of the country along with Justices Cornelius, K. M. A. Samdani, Rustam Kayani, Dorab Patel and Rana Bhagwan Das and Jawwad S. Khawaja. The finest ministers I worked with were the suave Salim Saifullah, and surprisingly for some, the streetwise Sheikh Rashid; their official conduct was always correct and professional. Arbab Jehangir, the former Chief Minister of NWFP remains unmatched as a decent and successful politician. When asked whether he was ever jailed for political protest he retorted, 'walay zha darta showda kharaum' or 'place trans do you think I am stupid'. Former Prime Minister Shaukat Aziz, was absolutely brilliant and amazingly quick at decision making. Arbab Zahir and Saalam Khan were gentle, truthful, and sincere unlike most Pakistani politicians.

iii. Recalling Trivia

Looking back, I often recall the innocent feelings of joy, amazement, happy coincidence, and inevitably some passing regrets. Life without such trivia would be rather dull. A totally neat and well-ordered life without anxious moments would be like a military parade, and how long can one parade? So when I was deprived of Rs. 700,000, stolen by a labourer who was doing repair work in my house, I was greatly upset. I did not want to report the matter to the police because that would have meant the arrest of all the labourers when only one was the culprit. And how effective was the police anyway? I was upset, but soon thereafter, a friend, Major Iftikhar Kiyani, asked me to invest in a plot of land when the prices were appreciating daily. I did so and within a month earned a profit of nearly Rs. 700,000. I was fully compensated thanks to the Almighty. At another time during an official visit to Malaysia, we met an amazingly kind and hospitable Tamil-Malaysian gentleman, P. Kenesion, from Accounts Service, whose sense of hospitality would put a Pakhtun or anyone else to shame. He would not let the guests pay for anything, whether it was for a meal or taxi. One day after a particularly leisurely and extended lunch, another guest insisted on paying the bill of US$270, much to this gentleman's annoyance. The meal was followed by a small round of black jack and it was quite a coincidence that the guest won almost exactly the amount paid. As ever, all things considered, a balance was achieved!

Happiness is a strange phenomenon; pure and innocent. Finding a toffee in the school-yard, walking barefoot on grass covered with dew, or sighting a duck on the horizon raises one to a different level. The one happiness I relish, even fifty years later, relates to the red sweater my aunt, Hameeda Bano, knitted and parcelled to me in Sialkot. The Convent of Jesus and Mary School winter uniform was to be worn the next day and I had no red uniform sweater. I begged my mother to let me skip school to save myself from embarrassment. But when it came to school, she would not compromise. Late in the afternoon, as I sat depressed in the veranda of our house on 42 Hussar Road, Sialkot, I could not believe my eyes when I saw the postman walk through the gate and deliver a parcel containing my red sweater. The timing was perfect. I thanked the Almighty and my Aunt Hameeda Bano, with all my heart!

There was another coincidence, which my mother told me about, that in 1953 at the Command and Staff College in Quetta, an officer won a monetary prize during a gymkhana event which he promptly donated to the Red Cross van parked nearby. Thirty-four years later as Commissioner Kohat Division, I was the chief guest at the annual gala dinner event organized by Commodore Khalid in the Inter Services Selection Board. Everyone bought tickets for the raffle to raise money for charity and my wife was asked to pick the winning ticket from a basket. Imagine who was the winner? None other than me! Amidst amiable catcalls of bogey by the audience, I received the prize and I remembered my mother donating the prize to the oldest bearer in the Mess.

One rather bewildering story relates to *nazar lagna*, or the evil eye. While posted as the Chief Secretary, NWFP, my wife hosted a lunch for her lady friends. As the guests were leaving, a very noble and elderly lady advised the hostess not to arrange such gatherings in the future because they attract *nazar* which often has unpleasant consequences. Two days later, I was posted out from my position as the Chief Secretary. The real reason behind my removal was the serious differences I had with the military Governor of the province for his myopic understanding of the Tribal Areas. Others thought that the 'evil eye' had triumphed!

Another time, I experienced much joy. A friend called from London, asking if I needed anything as he was travelling to Pakistan. I requested him for a pair of tan colour Oxford brogues. Imagine the coincidence, for that very same evening my close friend, the Hon'ble Justice Yunus Surakhvi of the Azad Kashmir Supreme Court, came to see me as he would often do. This time he had a packet with him as a gift. I opened it to find a pair of quality English shoes. The colour was tan. This was telepathy!

A kind thought is often worth more than treasure and this was confirmed by a lift operator from the Pakistan Secretariat, long after my retirement. In a chance meeting, all he said was that during my service career he appreciated my carrying my brief case personally at all times! He was most considerate and raised my spirits. Most Ministers and senior bureaucrats in our country would be scandalized if they were seen carrying their brief cases or wheeling their suitcases at airports. I cannot forget a newspaper photograph showing Robert McNamara, the former US Defense Secretary during the Vietnam War, personally carrying two heavy suitcases to his car. Heavens would fall if a senior serving minister or an official stooped to such an act in Pakistan.

I recall that once a small and seemingly trivial decision on my part became a life changer for three young men. In 1983, as Political Agent of Khyber Agency, three students were produced in my court after they were arrested by the local police, the *Khassadars*, while trying to cross into Afghanistan illegally. The boys informed me that after having failed to get admission to professional colleges in Pakistan, they decided to seek admission in the Soviet Union but were caught while crossing through Afghanistan. During those days there were strict orders from President Ziaul Haq to disallow anyone from travelling to the supposedly contaminated and atheist communist country against whom Pakistan was fighting a war in Afghanistan. Here was a dilemma which could have led to disciplinary action against me, for infringing the law. I thought about it for a while and decided to use my discretion humanely. I freed the students with the directive that they be quietly allowed to cross the border. Over a decade later, on an Emirates flight, two young men approached me to confirm my name. After I did so, they informed me that they were two of the students whom I had freed from detention. By then, they had completed their professional studies and were well settled with good jobs. The joy I experienced was indescribable.

The next anecdote was either a coincidence or sheer superstition. Many decades back, the incomparable Indian film playback singers, Lata Mangeshkar and Mukesh travelled to America for a concert. When I arrived at the venue I was saddened to hear that Mukesh had died during the night and the event was cancelled. I had lost the opportunity to hear them sing. Some years later when the singing maestro, Muhammad Rafi, visited England for a similar performance I was most hesitant to buy a ticket for the show fearing a similar fate. I then reminded myself that superstition was forbidden in Islam as 'haraam' and saw the enthralling performance!

I have had many serious regrets in life, some substantive and others trifling. But that is life. I knew a person who said that one of his biggest regrets was the loss of the only peg of an evening drink that he eagerly looked forward to having after a strenuous day. Just as he was getting ready to drink, a cockroach came out of nowhere and flew right into his glass. It must have been a classy cockroach! I too had some regrets in life and not becoming a fighter pilot was one of them. Another regret I had, was the summoning of a particular person to my court, a long time ago. It so happened that someone celebrating the wedding of his son remained oblivious to the common courtesies and peace of mind of the rest of the community. He continued playing loud music until late into the night and refused to desist even after the police had requested him to stop the music. As Assistant Commissioner, I informed the police to summon him to my court the next day. In the court, I learnt to my intense dismay that following a heart attack he had died a few hours earlier. I felt very guilty.

But I assured myself that I was only performing my duties, while he was breaking the law.

There have been compensations as well. This one time, I think I may have saved a life or two in Abbottabad, due to my quick thinking. Driving back from an exhausting tour I saw an angry young Army officer, a rifle in hand, walking briskly while being restrained by another person. I stopped to enquire as to what was happening as I was responsible for life and limb in the area. The officer turned out to be my friend, Major Ejaz Saddozai, who wanted to avenge the insult of a local shopkeeper against his military batman. I managed to take the rifle from him and had the matter resolved without a bullet being fired and without anyone facing the gallows or other legal consequences.

While on the subject of firearms, I often recall the short partridge shoot that the generous Tariq Niazi arranged near Karachi. I was in the city for an official conference after which, still dressed in my formal business suit and Italian shoes, I arrived at the *shikar* site. With a borrowed Russian-made twelve-gauge shotgun, the shoot started till the friendly host, against my preference, insisted that I only use his expensive Holland & Holland shotgun. I did so and a short time later fired at a partridge, dropped it, and realized that the left barrel of the gun had split. Fortunately, there was no injury as vintage English guns do not explode into splinters even when using poor quality local cartridges. I offered to pay for the repairs but the proud Pathan in Tariq would not even hear of it. A lesser firearm could have caused damage as Shamoun my son learnt later. Quality matters and counts in life; the wit had a point when he said that when a Rolls Royce car runs out of fuel, it still travels some miles 'purely on its reputation'.

I recall three incidents that were funny to the point of being farcical. Here, parents with college-going children ought to take note. There was Tassadaq of Edwardes College, who rarely attended classes and got matching results to show for his absence. His past soon caught up with him when he was told to bring his father to see the Principal, Dr Edmonds. Mischief however had taught him to remain one step ahead of the Principal. On the appointed day, he looked around and found a well-dressed middle aged man whom he requested to act as his father in order to 'save his future'. Nothing else, he pleaded! The gentleman, after hearing the Principal's complaints promptly planted a tight slap, as he imagined a father would do, across a bewildered Tassadaq's face. The slap hurt the Principal more than the student but Tassadaq was allowed to stay in College. He emerged from the Principal's office with mixed feelings about his initiative.

Then there was Farooq Ali from Wah, later a Major, who was even more accomplished in pranks. While in his mid-teens at Burn Hall School, Farooq one day decided to bunk classes to window-shop in Abbottabad city. He was caught by his teacher, Father Scardar. He was ordered to sit on Father's motorbike and taken to the Principal for truancy and disciplinary action. Imagine Farooq's presence of mind and guile that he denied going to the city and informed the Principal with a poker-face that he was sitting at the College gate when Father Scardar offered to give him a ride back to the classroom. Now the Principal was at his wit's end as doubt had been created. It was Farooq's word against Father Scardar. The Principal decided to take a lenient approach but once out of the office, Farooq gave a very meaningful smile to a fuming Father Scardar.

Then there were the six Gallians from Lawrence College, Zakaullah Bhangoo, Babar Masood, Mazhar Sher, Hamid Jan, Shaukat Ali, and myself, decided one evening to see an old Indian film in Murree without permission from the College. In those days a cinema ticket cost 12 *annas* or under one rupee. The film was enjoyable until it transpired that two of our teachers were also in the cinema. The boys were duly reported to Mr Naqvi, the stern Headmaster, who interviewed all the offenders separately. The five smart Gallians denied the allegation completely, but I was cornered. The Headmaster had played the oldest trick in the school's discipline book by telling me, the sixth one, that since all the others had confessed and I too should do so. Fuming at the imagined double-cross by my friends, I confessed. The evidence was now complete and the sentence of four cane stripes was given to us all. I was not forgiven by the five smart Gallians till there was another successful foray to the cinema. Happiness in those days was watching an Indian film without permission! Those were simple times as the drugs scene had not arrived in schools and colleges.

There was even greater satisfaction through two small coincidences because the joyful news arrived in the nick of time. General Naseerullah Babar, Sitara-e-Jurat, and Bar, a former Governor of NWFP, had requested a promotion for a relative but as per the rules it was not possible to promote him without qualifying in a routine examination. Meanwhile, the General fell seriously ill and the race was between passing the official examination and the General's health. It was a while before he qualified and a day before General Babar passed away, he was informed of his promotion. We heaved a sigh of relief!

With Malik Habib, a witty and simple person from Peshawar, the timing was even more delicate. He wanted his son employed in a modest post which was notified only hours before he died of a lingering illness. It seemed he was only waiting to see the notification of the appointment before giving up the will to live.

The death in a road accident of Anwar, my Personal Assistant from Bakkar while serving in the Anti-Narcotics Force, was a case of good intentions gone horribly wrong. On a cold and rainy day, as he got ready to ride his motorbike for some errand, I persuaded him to travel in my brand new Peugeot to escape the harsh weather. Minutes later, I was informed of a road accident injuring him and wrecking the car. He was in the premier government hospital in Islamabad for a few days but poor treatment and mismanagement in a government hospital meant that he could not survive. I have felt terribly guilty since and only the appointment of his son, Mubashir, in service mitigated my guilt to an extent. A precious life lost prematurely!

The story of the Peugeot car was interesting and again emerged from the realm of chance. The purchase price was beyond my reach. I was posted as Director Planning in the Anti-Narcotics Force and by sheer coincidence the United Nations Drug Control Programme was looking for a team leader to develop the long-term Master Plan for Drug Abuse Control in Pakistan. Lieutenant General Salahuddin Tirmizi, who headed the Force, insisted that I research and write the plan. I finalized writing the plan, and was pleasantly surprised, that the consultancy fee matched the cost of the car. Shortly, thereafter I lost the car. It seemed that I had worked on the Master Plan more on an honorary basis than on a paid basis! It may be that I had not remembered to share the cash proceeds, by giving *zakaat* for the poor.

Decades later, the death of Kurram Azam, a young man who was a friend of my son Danial, pains me every time I think of him. He brought me a hunting jacket from England which was an act of unforgettable kindness. In a way I am thankful that I never met him. He was the only child of his parents and lived in England but was killed on a visit to Islamabad. The circumstances surrounding his death remain a mystery. Could it have been a gunshot accident or something else? Such is life. The fatal shooting by an outlaw of the very young and handsome Assistant Superintendent Police, Salman Khan, while responding to an emergency outside his jurisdiction in Rawalpindi filled me with much grief even though I had never met him. Then there was Khwaja Ejaz, the Assistant Commissioner in Abbottabad in the second year of his service, who was killed while learning to drive on a hilly road; and he too, I had never met. One recent death, that of Osama Warraich, the budding Deputy Commissioner of Chitral in an air crash brought tears to my eyes. This was criminal negligence by the airline. I did not know him but those who did, spoke highly of his integrity and dynamism. May he rest in peace.

I will forever remember the indignation on the face of this old Jewish man in Amsterdam while I was looking for an antique lamp. His shop was small and cramped and he appeared to be starved for conversation. He was doing two things simultaneously. He was trying to sell the lamp to me while also narrating the agony of life in a Nazi concentration camp. Agreeing with him, I had barely stated I knew how difficult it must have been for him, however he shot back most irritatingly that no one else but him could know how difficult it was in a Nazi camp. He insisted, only he who had suffered knew about the torment that occurred half a century back. I felt sorry for him. He was right as only he had experienced the suffering at the hands of the demonic Nazis. Likewise, when the Israelis later committed major crimes against defenceless men, women, and children in the Palestinian refugee camps of Shabra and Shatilla in Lebanon and killed thousands in Gaza, only those who were there actually knew the suffering they endured.

There was also this regret when, as an Assistant Commissioner (under training) in Peshawar, I was deputed to supervise the burning of narcotics that were seized. As petrol was poured over the contraband goods, a Police Sub-Inspector took away two slabs of *charas* (hashish), stating that he required these to implicate other offenders when there was not enough judicial evidence available. I regret not stopping him for I was on duty and I failed my first test. Maybe I had not learnt to say no as I was still new to service. Regrets never cease. Near the end of my service career as Chief Secretary, Sindh, I toured the Lyari slums which had produced many international medal winners in boxing and football. I was appalled to find the absence of facilities available in their locality. There was no boxing ring and no football stadium worth mentioning. I promised to build for them these facilities to international standards but was transferred from my post a week later because of my differences with the government. My commitment was sadly not honoured and neither the Olympic Association nor the Sindh Government provided such facilities, even though this was the Pakistan Peoples Party's stronghold.

My greatest regret was the aborted chance to make big money in England. I missed becoming a millionaire by not betting enough on a race horse called Henbit, that went on to win the Derby. I only had five pounds to bet on Henbit but the takings did not even last me an evening. For Henbit this was probably his only major win as he broke a leg and then started siring future thoroughbred horses. Happily, there is much to look forward to in life even with a broken leg! Then there was the regret, when not heeding advice, I declined to invest in a hill resort property in Pakistan where prices later increased two hundred times. And there was also an acute embarrassment experienced in Japan, which I wish had never occurred. The Japanese host was walking me by a stream, lined with cherry blossom trees and it being late in the season, most of the blossoms had withered and fallen. I, however, plucked one cherry blossom and placed it in the lapel of my jacket. Judging from my host's demeanour, I am sure he did not approve. Moral of the story was to never pluck blossoms of any kind without permission! There are other regrets and one of them was that a servant from the Water and Power Authority, perhaps Kamran or Riaz, stole the Rolex watch my father had given me a few days before he died and its loss still rankles me.

There was another occasion when on an official visit to India in 1995, I requested the young lady at the guests' relation desk at the Maurya Sheraton Hotel to confirm my return airline ticket. Later that day, she did so but looked very pale and sick I could not resist asking her if she was ill. In her condition, I think, all she wanted was to pour out her heart to anyone willing to listen. She was very upset because of some issues with her in-laws, being stopped from seeing her infant daughter, and was not getting access to her academic degrees. How could I help in a foreign land? As a District officer by training, resolving problems as soon as they are identified was my forte. Humanity transcends borders. I suggested that since I was from an identical service background, I could call the Commissioner or the Deputy Commissioner of her area to help her. Moments later, I withdrew the offer as I felt this could cause her further trouble and this time from the government and intelligence agencies, since only spies deal with the enemy and here she was an Indian, and I Pakistani considered the number one enemy. State regulations in the subcontinent transcend humanity! I hope her travails have since ended!

Another close call was while still in my teens, in Kakul, where my father was posted to the military academy; in those days, there were no electric or gas water-heating geysers. The preferred mode was to heat the water in the bathroom in a metallic vessel, the *hamam*, which used rock coal for heating. The bathroom door was locked and because of the cold winter, the window was also shut, hence allowing the lethal gas to spread. I faintly remember a sweetish feeling overpowering me but somehow I managed to unlatch the door and stumble out. Not having clothes on was not the highest priority at such a time. I had just survived! There was another bathroom incident in Turbat in Balochistan, this time involving a huge scorpion. Just as my son, Danial, then twelve-years-old, stepped in barefooted, a foot away from the waiting scorpion; I woke up miraculously and switched the lights on. Only then did we see the scorpion with the sting ready in attack mode and averted a very serious accident.

iv. THE CIVIL SERVICE OF PAKISTAN

I am among those fortunate ones who spent their entire lives in one career. In my case, I worked only in the Civil Service of Pakistan, later called the District Management Group, and more recently, the Pakistan Administrative Service. I had previously been selected as a lecturer of Political Science in the provincial government and had been posted to the Government College in Mardan, but never delivered a single lecture as the summer vacations had commenced. The three months' pay that I received was given to the poor on my father's specific instructions, although I had a different plan for using that money.

A year earlier, I had applied for the Army's first Graduate Course merely to experience going through the entire process. After passing the test, including the obstacles course, I was selected by the Inter-Service Selection Board in Kohat. However, I had no intention of joining the Army. After being informed about my selection, I was brash enough to ask for an interview with the President of the Board and somehow managed to speak with him. I spoke to him about one of the tests consisting of writing eighty sentences in English after words were flashed for only a few seconds. I said I must have written all eighty sentences correctly but felt that if I had to do the same exercise in Urdu, I would barely have completed one-fourth of the answers. To me, this test merely demonstrated proficiency in the English language and nothing more. Some years later, I learnt that an Urdu option was introduced! Two decades later, when I was Commissioner Kohat Division, I requested to see my grading by the Army Selection Board. It was 'Alpha Alpha Delta', whatever that means! The Institute of International Development at the Kennedy School of Harvard University was more considerate in grading me three decades later. The fifty-odd senior executives attending the Environmental Economics course voted that both a Mexican economist and I, give an after dinner speech at the Golden Night's dinner. This was totally unexpected as I had voted for the Mexican economist. Some Egyptian course-mates later mentioned that they had voted for me. I must admit I was thrilled and honoured to address the final dinner gathering at the Harvard Club in a most jovial atmosphere.

I am glad I chose the Civil Service of Pakistan as a career. Had I joined the Army, I would have retired early because I have inherited my father's habit of speaking my mind openly. I, however, miss being a part of Queen Victoria's Own Corps of Guides, the Army unit I would have joined. In the Civil Service, I had the opportunity to serve with and get to know ordinary Pakistanis better and to appreciate their issues and problems. More than that, I saw our rulers upclose, and therefore, I am not surprised at how poorly the country has fared under them. The Civil Service was more compassionate in those days. Now, all that the politicians demand is a master-servant relationship with the bureaucracy.

I now know well why the country failed to come to grips with its problems: it was because of the greed and crass selfishness of most of the rulers. A career in the Civil Service provided executive authority to 'do good', to resist the infringement of law by the powerful, and of course to savour the excitement of seeing new places and meeting new people. Generally, officers confined themselves to routine work only, even though many did not deny themselves some undue benefits that came their way. However, what one most missed in government service was the independence of mind and the frankness of spirit to objectively influence important decisions. These days, politicians in power, do not consider impartiality a virtue; they demand blind obedience. I have had as many and varied experiences of dealing with ordinary people as with the high and mighty. Once, in 1996, while serving in the Planning Wing of the Anti-Narcotics Force, I was summoned by the late Prime Minister Benazir Bhutto. She wished to post me as Commissioner of Rawalpindi Division because she felt that this position should not be occupied by anyone from the Punjab for reasons unknown to me. I was told that General Naseerullah Babar and Aftab Sherpao thought I would be an appropriate choice in Rawalpindi, which was adjacent to the capital, Islamabad. I would, in a sense, be their nominee. When I arrived, the Prime Minister was unavailable, so I met her husband, Asif Zardari instead. I declined the offer politely since I felt they must have some unfair expectations from me which I may not be able to fulfill. We then started discussing environmental issues and I found many of Mr Zardari's suggestions quite agreeable. He then asked me to become Additional Secretary in the Environment Division, which I again declined and repeated that I was not senior enough for the position. He said that he would fix that. Somehow, nothing came of it but I liked Mr Zardari's relaxed approach to issues and his trusting nature. I was glad I escaped both offers!

There was another escape some years later, when I was holding another top position. A very attractive young lady came to see me in my office, through the intercession of someone at the apex of power. She demanded that a particular media contract, running into the tens of millions of rupees, be awarded to her favoured company. When I quoted the rules to her she was visibly annoyed and could not understand how I was not complying with the directions received from 'above'. Her annoyance soon turned into anger and that was when I encountered a fierce amalgam of good looks and an abusively sharp tongue. Thankfully, no harm came my way from 'above'!

The years in the Civil Service were a delight, apart from the fact that the batch of 1971 was the last one in which East Pakistan was represented.

We were also fortunate that Qasim Rizvi was the Director at the time. He was a consummate orator and a brilliant administrator. Very early on in the Academy, he advised the probationers not to waste 'a lovely year in the Academy by poring over academics and class work', because 'you do not have to prove anything more'. Instead, he thought it was important to learn conventions and etiquette and to enjoy Lahore, especially in the winter, because there was no place in the country like Lahore and, as they say in Punjabi, 'Lahore Lahore ay'! Some of us, including Javed Sadiq Malik and Hussain Hamid, took his words to heart and said an early goodbye to our course books—at the cost of the final rankings in the service seniority.

For the next forty years, I had the privilege of serving the country as a civil servant and was very fortunate as far as my postings were concerned. It was a blessing that I spent nearly a decade in the Tribal Areas of Orakzai, Mohmand, and Khyber as a Political Agent and then as a Commissioner in the Kohat and Malakand Divisions. Later, as Chief Secretary North West Frontier Province; I was responsible for all tribal agencies. Perhaps the most memorable time was spent as Deputy Commissioner of Chitral; Swat was a lovely experience. To add to this was the Gilgit-Baltistan stint, and words are not enough to describe the people or the place. I have always thanked the Almighty that I had the opportunity to serve as the Chief Secretary at four places: Gilgit-Baltistan, Azad Kashmir, North West Frontier Province, and Sindh. It was a privilege never provided to anyone before me or since. To have later become chairman of the two largest public sector organizations, Pakistan Railways and the Water and Power Development Authority (WAPDA), was also a huge honour. Whether I made any significant contributions wielding these powers, I cannot judge for myself. However, there are three contributions I recall with great satisfaction. Firstly, I was able to retrieve from private individuals the ownership of the 1,450 megawatt Tarbela Four hydropower plant and transfer it back to the government. Similar was the case with the 840 megawatt Munda-Mohmand and the smaller Malakand Three hydel power projects, which were going to be gifted to the private sector. The annual profits from these three huge units run into hundreds of millions of dollars. I managed the transfer of these three exceptionally profitable projects to the public sector, which may not have been possible had I not resorted to an unconventional stratagem. I approached three chief justices and explained how private individuals were being favoured, by those who mattered, at the cost of the people of Pakistan. Unsurprisingly, they agreed with my public interest sentiments.

It is the rulers who take all major decisions, and very often enrich themselves in the process, but when it comes down to accountability, the officials mostly suffer alone. The erstwhile rulers cut convenient and mutually beneficial deals with those who replace them. The accountability system in place, largely ignores the billions syphoned off by the rulers through their approvals of non-transparent contracts and speed money deals, but remains focused on petty thievery by officials. The accountability laws, the organizational structure, and the senior-level appointments do not permit meaningful accountability. Ultimately, corruption can only be mitigated by ensuring transparency at the department's apex decision-making level when approving projects, contracts, and appropriations. There is a need to associate the representatives of the Auditor General of Pakistan and the National Accountability Bureau, at the approval stage so that years and decades later the officials are not hounded for the decisions taken by them. Moreover, while approving proposals the Prime Minister, the Chief Minister, and Ministers must, by law, place their signatures on file to acknowledge their ownership.

In Pakistan, accountability turns to witch-hunting as happened during General Musharraf's tenure; he was convinced that he had the answers to all of the country's problem. One of the problems he wanted to tackle was the high-level corruption amongst the politicians and government officials. The judiciary and the military were of course exempt from these proceedings. The National Accountability Bureau (NAB) was created under the strict General Syed Amjad to punish those deemed corrupt with a battalion of Army officials in support. There were a number of Gallians, Lawrence College alumni, serving under him. The performance of the Bureau was modest as General Musharraf used the setup for political purposes. This agency had sweeping powers to consign an accused to be imprisoned for ninety days where he would be deprived of company, sunlight, and more so human dignity. General Musharraf was told that if he were to allow the investigators, ten by ten treatment, about US$26 billion allegedly siphoned off through corruption, equal to the country's debt, would be recovered. Musharraf agreed to the suggestion and so all of the accused were confined to small ten by ten feet cells carved out of basement rooms, to incarcerate them. Photographs of the accused would be displayed in the media after their arrests to cause maximum shame to them and their families. The recovery of illegitimate gains were to be ensured through humiliation, harassment, and sleep deprivation. In such an environment, General Musharraf called a meeting of the Federal Ministers, Permanent Secretaries, and the Chief Secretaries in February 2001 to highlight his vision for the future of Pakistan.

I was at that time the Chief Secretary, Azad Kashmir and thought I would raise the issue of the humiliating treatment of the citizens of Pakistan by NAB. I remained very worried about the General's likely reaction, harsh as it would certainly be. I decided to seek the advice of my father, Colonel Shafi Durrani, who was living in retirement in Peshawar. He told me that if I believed strongly in the principle involved, I should raise the matter before the President and that in such cases the consequences do not matter.

I felt strengthened and accordingly raised the matter publicly before the President calling the NAB treatment a *ziyadati*, an unfair practice which unlike *sakhti*, or harshness, is morally repugnant. Severity was acceptable but injustice was not, as our tribesmen say. It was brought to the notice of the President that the families of the officers whose photographs were flashed in the media would avoid leaving their homes and their children would skip school even before their fathers had been convicted by courts. The interaction with the President lasted about ten minutes, following which I think he ran out of arguments and in the end told me bluntly that what he was doing was correct. This was the limit of my *jihad* and of course, I felt most relieved for at least having sensitized him. After the refreshments, as the President was leaving I noticed that he was looking for someone in the gathering and I prayed it may not be me. When our eyes met, he came straight towards me, shook my hand, and said that he really enjoyed the discussions on the subject. Yet, another close shave but I was grateful to him for his magnanimity. Once again, thank you Mr President!

The NAB could have been an effective organization but soon lost its direction because of political interference. There were excesses committed by NAB in Pakistan which as Chief Secretary, I was determined to avoid in Azad Kashmir. With the support of General Ashfaq Parvez Kayani, the respected General Officer Commanding 12 Division and Barrister

Sultan Mehmood Chaudhry , Prime Minister of Azad Kashmir, most of
the harsh practices were mitigated. Human dignity needs to be protected
at all times. Unnecessary handcuffs and underground cells without beds
and lights were done away with, and police remands were reduced from
ninety to thirty days.

The NAB, despite convicting a large number of corrupt senior officials
and politicians, lost much credibility over the years with at least one of
the Generals that followed General Amjad, being accused of corruption.
In addition, General Musharraf employed blackmail and strong-arm
intimidation tactics against politicians to compel them into supporting
his political dispensation. With the passage of time, General Musharraf's
passion for good governance waned and having decided to extend his rule,
politicians were cunningly wooed. His policy of seeking a rapprochement
with the same corrupt politicians he had denounced earlier, was objected to
by the few public-spirited politicians who withdrew their support for him.
Some chose deliberate exile while others informally decided to politically lie
low for a time, but many joined the Musharraf bandwagon. If you cannot
beat them, join them! Some of the biggest scoundrels in the political history
of Pakistan had a field day during and after General Musharraf's rule, while
bureaucrats who did not have social connections were targeted. If there still
were some politicians whose sins remained unwashed, General Musharraf
provided them one more opportunity to clear their names. He enacted the
infamous and dubiously named National Reconciliation Ordinance (NRO)
forgiving them their past misdemeanors if they would team up with him
in future. Many took the bait and joined him—prominent among them
being Benazir Bhutto.

In a few cases, NAB erred hugely in arresting and humiliating officials
whose character, reputation, and integrity was unsurpassed. There were
arrests in cases where the exercise of routine administrative discretion,
decades earlier, was challenged and held against the officers. In one instance,
an entire committee that had taken a decision ten years back on a routine
matter and was part of a chain of command, was arrested. These included
a senior Secretariat Group officer, who was among the most honest and
competent officers in the country but was incarcerated for a long period
due to being a member of this committee. For someone like him, who
could not even afford an air conditioner at home, finding a lawyer was an

arduous test! The courts acquitted him but who would answer for the years lost in jail and moreover, for his dignity stolen by the state? This happened at a time when thousands of crooks walked free. A consensus appears to have been developed that because of the manner in which accountability laws are being enforced, bold decision-making and exercising discretion, the bedrock of effective administration, have been sacrificed.

The above narrative, in a sense, was my contribution to the people of Pakistan and it would not have been possible had I not been in the Civil Service. However, having spent nearly half a century in public service, I left with the impression that these days it is rarely possible for an officer to positively influence policies, where personal agendas of the rulers are involved.

v. ALPHA TO OMEGA

From the start of my service in Abbottabad to my final posting in Karachi, life in the Civil Service of Pakistan was a great joy. My first regular posting was as Assistant Commissioner, Abbottabad where I was born twenty-five years earlier. It was here, that as a young Assistant Commissioner I learnt what it means to 'take the initiative' in government service. The year was 1973, the venue the Governor's House in the hill resort town of Nathiagali. Prime Minister, Zulfikar Ali Bhutto, along with his wife Begum Nusrat Bhutto, was visiting to inspect the place for a meeting with Indira Gandhi, Prime Minister of India, following the Simla Conference. After walking around what arguably is the most beautiful building in Pakistan, the dignitaries were served tea in the rear veranda overlooking the rolling lawns. A while later, Begum Bhutto looked up at the swallows which had built a dozen nests on the ceiling. Moments later, the Prime Minister also looked up and when the Prime Minister looks up, everyone looks up. The swallows were gracefully floating in and out of the nests, like Olympic gymnasts. Now where there are swallows there are swallow droppings as well, but no harm befell anyone that day. The agitated engineer of the public works department responsible for the maintenance of the building looked at the swallows encroaching on the ceiling of a government building and became very nervous—imagining that the nests were causing a concern to the Prime Minister. He took the initiative by boldly announcing that he would remove the nests by that evening.

Begum Bhutto was livid, stared at the engineer and before the Prime Minister could react said that this was the silliest thing she had ever heard. The poor engineer sank into his chair, having been insulted so publicly. As a young Assistant Commissioner, Abbottabad, I had learnt my first lesson in taking initiatives; speak only when you are spoken to!

Around this time, a ceremony was held in Abbottabad to distribute land titles to tenants who had benefited from the land reforms. The Governor of NWFP (now KPK) attended as chief guest. As the Governor started speaking, the public address system broke down and even though the function had been organized by the Board of Revenue, the District Administration was always involved in these matters. The cause was traced to a television cameraman having plugged into the weak electricity connection powering the microphone. The Governor raged and fumed with anger, and the consummate orator that he was, what he most missed was listening to his own voice. As a public speaker, Aslam Khattak had no peer with the exception of Attaullah Shah Bokhari, especially when speaking in his soft Pashto dialect. The Chairman of the Board of Revenue was not amused at the lapse and looked at the Commissioner with concern, who relayed a more serious look of scorn towards the Deputy Commissioner Hazara. He in turn gave a dirty look to me while I was meekly looking down at the floor, praying to the Almighty for a miracle to happen so that I do not lose my new job.

The miracle happened slowly. At this point, the Director Information, Iqtidar Ali Mazhar, a very genial person, decided to take the initiative, which would have consequences for him. He was not responsible for the problem, but went to inspect the burnt-out socket all the same. Walking up and down quite unnecessarily, he caught the eye of the Governor who promptly gave him a tongue lashing of his life. Words were heard to the effect that the director would soon lose his trousers. Meanwhile, the miracle, the befuddled Assistant Commissioner was praying for, actually happened and the microphone came back to life two minutes later. Luckily, the age of miracles was not over! The function ended peacefully but, if the Director's trousers were actually removed later, no one knew. I had learnt a second lesson in damage control to behave normally if you are not responsible.

Fast forward thirty-four years and I had risen from the post of an Assistant Commissioner to Chief Secretary of Sindh. The venue was Karachi and the date was the infamous 12 May 2007. The President and the Sindh Government had decided that the Chief Justice of Pakistan, Iftikhar Muhammad Chaudhry, would not be allowed to enter Karachi. I tried to instill sense and reason into the political leadership repeatedly, but failed. In accordance with the insidious plan of the provincial government, the main roads were blocked and normal life completely disrupted. Masked gunmen, ostensibly with the support of the government, killed forty-eight innocent persons all of whom were poor street vendors, watchmen, and daily wage earners. For days before the arrival of the Chief Justice, regular meetings were held by the Governor, Chief Minister, intelligence agencies, police, and senior administration officers to ensure that the absurd orders of those in authority were strictly complied with, and that no laxity was shown to the Chief Justice and his supporters. As Chief Secretary, armed with the sole support of the Home Secretary, I tried to caution restraint but in vain. I then decided to take some initiatives to contest the government's orders in all meetings. I later called the Prime Minister's office to inform them of the gravity of the situation. When every effort failed, I expressed open dissent to the Chief Minister and sent copies of my note to the Prime Minister and the Governor. Politicians in power do not brook opposition from bureaucrats no matter how valid their views. Soon after the gory events that I had predicted occurred, I was removed from my position as Chief Secretary. This was a small price to pay for speaking truth.

The point to note is that the three initiative takers in Nathiagali, Abbottabad, and Karachi suffered a little momentary inconvenience but they actually did not fare badly in the long run. The engineer, who had merely been politically incorrect as far as swallows and wildlife were concerned, retired peacefully but after a promotion; the Director of Information rose honourably in rank and was much respected; and the Chief Secretary's opinions were not only later appreciated by the Prime Minister but after retirement he was given what was perhaps the best corporate job in the country for a full five years. Being correct is more important than being successful. One of Pakistan's greatest and most honourable citizens, the late Justice Cornelius, had been the President of the Cricket Board. Once, in Lahore, inadvertently he was not sent a ticket to a Test match. Never the one to complain or admonish, he simply and quietly queued up and bought himself a ticket. With this single action he set an example that people still remember, a half-century later. Winston Churchill would say that he judged his generals not by the results of the battle but by the quality of their efforts. In service, from the beginning to the end, or from Alpha to Omega, there is milk and honey for those who wish to work with dedication and have a positive approach. I feel that character and courage, which in essence are the same, are the most important values in public service. Such values alone ensure, that threats and inducements are resisted.

(I had originally written the above segment for a speech to be given at the annual dinner of the Pakistan Administrative Service but the speech was not delivered).

2

The Transient Tenures of a Chief Secretary

i. GILGIT-BALTISTAN

It is at the Chief Secretary's level that the administrative stream meets the apex political leadership of the province; this is where the buck stops. This is where the best Chief Secretaries either fall or those with less conviction are retained. All rulers need them. Generally, disagreements at the lower tiers of administration are often resolved by accommodating the politicians' unfair demands by relaxing rules and procedures. At the highest level, an agreement is difficult to achieve if the views of a correct and impartial Chief Secretary clashes with the politicians who are bent upon achieving political mileage, at the cost of the law. The nature of politics being what it is in our country, one should have one's spine removed surgically before stepping into the Chief Secretary's chair! For the most part, the weaker the Chief Secretary, the better it is for the politicians! For those with any dignity, it is advisable to serve with just enough clothes to fill a single suitcase so that the position is quickly vacated. Most Chief Secretaries are not destined to complete their full tenures because of the unfair expectations of the rulers while others simply serve as doormats. Chief Secretaries have been known to win over wavering opposition members in the service of their masters. In Azad Kashmir, during the 1970s, a Chief Secretary enthusiastically lent his shoulder to remove his president and prime minister on the directions of the rulers in Islamabad. He also boasted that he was authorized to kill two hundred people, if required, to accomplish the task.

One honourable Chief Secretary was removed summarily, merely because he conveyed to the Prime Minister an uncorroborated report from the Political Agent, North Waziristan Agency. In 1998, an inaccurate sitrep was received by him regarding the American Cruise missiles, launched against

Osama bin Laden, having landed in Pakistan. In fact the missiles had landed inside Afghanistan. The Prime Minister, without confirming the report, promptly complained to President Bill Clinton about the infringement of our sovereignty. Later, when it transpired that the missiles had not landed inside Pakistan, the Prime Minister was obviously embarrassed. These missiles were fired much before the American drones regularly began targeting militants in Waziristan without any regard for our sovereignty. Sovereignty appears to be a loose term in more ways than one!

While in service, I was honoured for serving as Chief Secretary at four different places but I also hold the record for not completing my tenure at any of these posts! The competent authority always removed me prematurely because of my differences with them. In truth, I always found the 'competent authority' pretty incompetent! My first appointment as Chief Secretary, then called Chief Commissioner, was in the Northern Areas (now, Gilgit-Baltistan). This was the area where the three empires met in the nineteenth century: the Czarist Russian Empire, the Chinese Empire, and the British Empire. It was here that the Great Game commenced. During the British rule, the Governor of a smaller or newly formed province was often called Chief Commissioner, with limited powers than those of the Governor.

My posting to Gilgit-Baltistan will always be a pleasant memory, more so, after I was transferred. Here was a place where the mythical Shangri-La was said to exist, a name that evokes a picture of snow-covered mountains, low-hanging clouds, fast-flowing cold streams with rainbow trout, ibex aplenty, snow leopards stalking prey in the snow covered mountains, and delicious fruit that is appropriate for intoxicating brews. Imagine an area where even the names of the wildlife are alluring. Here, one finds the Astore markhor, the Himalayan ibex, the Marco Polo sheep, the Shimshal blue sheep, the Deosai brown bear, the *Shapu* Urial, the Golden marmot, the Western Tragopan pheasant, the Monal pheasant, and of course the *Ram chakor* or Himalayan snowcock. It was said that the 'the wildest dreams of Kew are the facts of Kathmandu' but more so of Gilgit-Baltistan. The people are no less remarkable; stout, good-looking, and peaceful with not a care in the world until bigotry arrived from the plains of Pakistan. I will always be proud of establishing the Deosai National Wilderness Park in Skardu in 1993, which is a vast plateau at an altitude of nearly

13,000 feet and must rank as one of the natural wonders of the world. The goal was to retain the area as the Almighty had created it so that no human construction such as paved roads, electric power lines, or buildings would be permitted. During late summer, the area is covered in wild colourful flowers stretching across about forty square kilometers. This plateau is home to the brown bear, the Kashmir stag, and the golden marmot all of whom are threatened species.

For the traveller's information, Gilgit-Baltistan is where the Himalayas, the Karakoram, and the Hindu Kush mountain ranges merge. My fascination with the area was triggered because of three reasons. There was a 'hundred-year reason' since my maternal grandfather, Abdul Hakim Khan of the Frontier Border Military Police, had been part of Colonel Kelly's column that marched through this area in 1895, for the relief of Chitral. Then there was a 'fifty-year reason' as my father, Major Shafi Durrani, would often travel to Gilgit and Skardu during and after the Kashmir War of 1948 and he would have much to tell about it. My 'own reason' was more prosaic. This was the place where a lot of outdoor activity was possible. I requested a posting which was easily granted because the security conditions at that time were so bad that no career officer wanted to dampen his future prospects, by serving here. I was, however, unhappy with the advice given by the then Governor of the Frontier province, a retired Army man, who from the goodness of his heart tried to dissuade me from taking up the tough assignment; he thought it would damage my future career because there would be too many problems. A British Governor similarly placed, might have encouraged a young officer to serve Queen and country in the wilds and the wilderness; for Pakistanis, ideals are more for 'self and pelf'.

Not having considered the Governor's advice, I started the journey to Gilgit and on arrival at the Chief Commissioner's House, late in the evening, was greeted by a huge blast from very close. For a moment, it appeared that the Governor's concerns may have been apt. I was worried for about two minutes. Mercifully, the explosion was traced to an electric transformer malfunction. From then on, Gilgit and Skardu were a joy and a challenge even though this was truly the most stressful posting of my career. Sectarian violence had become the norm and there was an absence of law and order. The weak and pusillanimous policies of our leadership had allowed the area to become lawless; instead sabotage and sectarian murders, became the rule. Service was no doubt stressful, but more painful was the neglect of the government towards problems. No one in the Federal Government had the time to listen. After the withdrawal of the Frontier Crimes Regulations (FCR) and the promulgation of the new judicial procedural laws by the Zulfikar Ali Bhutto government, very few criminals, let alone those responsible for sectarian violence, were penalized. This was an incentive to murder and to kidnap in the name of faith, knowing that the state would only watch benignly. It was the norm for the police, the prosecutor, the judge, and other officials to first cater to the demands of those that belonged to their sect before applying higher impartial standards.

Every request to the Federal Government for posting good officers cadre, went unanswered. In 1993, the interim Prime Minister, Moeen Qureishi, was among the very few who cared but had little time to redress the situation. He visited Gilgit with General Waheed Kakar, the Army Chief, to assess the situation. A presentation was to be made by the Chief Commissioner and General Fazle Ghafoor, the Force Commander, Northern Areas. Since the venue was the military headquarters, General Fazle Ghafoor was to speak first and he was prepared thoroughly with all kinds of charts and slides, as military men always do. The night before the visit, he asked for a copy of my presentation so that it could be 'placed' ahead of time, in the slide projector. I forwarded my presentation which had four points on a sheet of paper, against the better judgment of my colleagues. The next day, the General spoke for fifty of the allotted sixty minutes for both of us! What was amusing was that he spoke on my four points as well. I, therefore, requested that I not speak since the issues had already been alluded to but the Prime Minister insisted that I speak. I then elaborated on the points, without mincing words and was very critical of the Federal Government, for ignoring the Northern Areas. It was clear, I said, that foreign countries were supporting different sectarian groups in the area with arms and resources which needed to be dealt with, without being 'apologetic'. As I finished speaking, I remained apprehensive of the likely reaction of the two most powerful persons in the country to my strong opinions. I was in for a surprise. As soon as the presentation ended both the Prime Minister and the Army Chief moved straight towards me, hugged me warmly, and greatly appreciated my four 'bold' observations. I heaved a sigh of relief.

The Prime Minister's tenure was less than three months which was not enough to change the status quo. How one wished all our presidents and prime ministers had learnt from dedicated and honourable people like Moeen Qureshi. That was not the case and before long, and purely out of frustration, I requested a different posting. The Establishment Division, however, declined saying that my tenure was too short and in any case they could not find any volunteer to replace me. Then with a sleight-of-hand, I managed to get my name included for the Administrative Staff College course in Lahore which could not be denied to me, as I was in the 'promotion zone'. I was allowed to leave. I realized that the greatest joy in serving in Gilgit-Baltistan would be experienced after one was posted out of there; only then one could reminisce and relish the time spent there.

Sadly, I experienced great helplessness in Gilgit-Baltistan during my short stint and wondered when would the Federal Government provide support positively? So much could have been achieved but was left unfulfilled. All that I received was lip service by the politicians. As for the bureaucrats, the better ones kept clear of the place, reserving their talents for Lahore, Islamabad, and Karachi. One reason why people have little faith and trust in the administration of Gilgit-Baltistan was because of inexperienced officers being posted to the top positions. There was this provincial service 'officer' from Punjab, whose sole qualification for being posted as Chief Commissioner was his subservience to the rulers of the day whose tired legs he reportedly massaged while posted as the Deputy Commissioner in Sheikhupura. In any case, his stay lasted only two months. The local people need to trust the officials if the latter are to succeed. The following example is worth noting. The construction of the District hospital in Chilas was delayed for a few months because the architectural design was not suitable for the hot summers but local notables thought that the Chief Commissioner wanted to transfer the funds to another place in Skardu. They would just not believe me till the new hospital was actually built in Chilas. As for Skardu, a Cadet College was promised by the Chief Commissioner, but people became apprehensive when it too was delayed for a year.

In Gilgit, I was fortunate to have served with the two Federal Ministers, Sardar Mehtab Ahmad and Afzal Khan who were exceptionally decent human beings. Once a minor incident took place with the former Federal

Minister, Sardar Mehtab Ahmad; just before he was to plant a ceremonial sapling in the garden, he had a lit cigarette in his hand and asked me to hold it while he planted the sapling. I thought that a Chief Commissioner could not be seen holding a Minister's cigarette and asked another person to hold it for him. I think he was a bit miffed at this but our relationship was not strained.

There are many and varied anecdotes from public service; one of these related to my stay in Gilgit. The local people face myriad problems, some serious others apparently trivial, but it is for the administration to resolve these expeditiously. The quality of any administration depends upon how effectively it resolves these problems. At times the approach adopted to redress a grievance is, to say the least, rather unconventional as the following story would show. Once a young woman badly bruised and battered with black eyes came to see me in the office. She complained that her husband would beat her every day and that she could not cope with the situation any longer. I ordered some tea for her and telephoned the concerned official, the *Tehsildar*, to summon the husband and give him a tight slap in the privacy of his office. This was done perhaps not effectively enough, as the young woman returned a week later with the same complaint. The *Tehsildar* was then reprimanded for inefficiency and told to get more vigorous. He assured me that he would take action and this time dealt with the offending husband more effectively. For the next one month, I did not hear from the woman and was understandably worried. Had she been murdered or divorced? Such thoughts crossed my mind. Fortunately, she was soon located in excellent health and spirits and she had a message for the Chief Commissioner. Her husband had become very loving and supportive. Little did she know the reason why! The moral of the story is that prompt and inexpensive justice is required in a vast majority of cases. In certain cases, a loving slap correctly executed is more effective and can in certain situations keep the police and the courts away.

I'll end by recalling some of the outstanding officers such as Hafiz Sanaullah, Sohail Rashid, Khwaja Shamail, Brigadier Rahim, Rehmani, and Asad Zaidi, the politician who served the people with utmost dedication. Here I would like to mention the Biddulph Library in Gilgit which was lovingly maintained and preserved over the years by a Sherbaz Bercha, the lone librarian. He would rue the loss of the habit of reading books amongst people; the simple soul should have known that instant gratification was the new game in town. This was my Gilgit-Baltistan tenure and the time I spent there were one-and-a-half years.

ii. Azad Jammu and Kashmir

The territory of Azad Jammu and Kashmir, in terms of the sheer beauty of its mountains, meadows, lakes, and rivers—all the way from Taobat in the north to Bhimber in the east—stands out from the rest of the region. Few areas in the world can surpass its natural beauty. Kashmir, unfortunately, has suffered for a long time from every conceivable natural and human disaster. Earthquakes, snow storms, floods, famine, and pestilence have ravaged this area. To this, one can add invasions, murders, cruelty, and plunder for hundreds of years. Hindu Dogras, Sikh Maharajas, Muslim Afghans, Timurid Mughals, and now 'democratic' Indians have all inflicted extreme pain and cruelty on the Kashmiris. Today, the Indians have over half a million security personnel entirely controlling the territory against the will of the people. Most Kashmiris are familiar with the legend of Chiragh Beg, who was selected from Kabul by a group of Kashmiris to become their Governor on account of his saintly looks. As he was travelling in a royal procession back to Kashmir, he saw a corpse being taken for burial. He stopped and ordered that the ears of the dead man be chopped off so that the latter could inform those in the 'hereafter' of the new Governor's arrival. As for the living Kashmiris, they would soon get to know him, he said. And they did.

Shortly after General Musharraf's coup, I was sacked from the position of Additional Chief Secretary in the Frontier province and became an officer on special duty (OSD). An OSD has no work or duty to perform and is told to stay at home until the authorities decide to absolve him of his alleged 'crimes'. I was lucky to find a great posting, thanks to the efforts of another military man, the suave General Ehsan ul Haq, who helped me get 'considered' for the post of Chief Secretary Azad Kashmir. This was a great experience both in terms of defining good governance and in developing some lifelong friendships. I realized that so much could be done effortlessly and all that was required was dedication and integrity. Rarely during my forty years of service, have I come across these two attributes in the rulers of the land; Azad Kashmir was an exception. Every day there was some innovation or improvement in administration. Small proposals such as developing a quick disbursement mechanism for the grant of monetary relief for those subjected to firing by Indian troops from across the Line of Control, were quite gratifying. Establishing an endowment fund for the free treatment of people suffering from serious diseases was seen as continuous relief, a *sadqa jaria* more so, because this money had been misused previously. And then, the completion of the Jagran hydropower plant in the Neelum Valley, despite the machinations of some selfish officials and politicians, proved to be a boon. In this case, for years, the French and Swedish contractors were up against a wall of official indifference fuelled by corruption. The contractors had rightly refused to test the hydel power project till they were paid their legitimate dues, already authorized by the consultants. The amount in question was less than the contractor's security deposits available with the government, yet for two years the project was not allowed to be tested because some officials wanted to blackmail the foreign contractors. All this while, the project's benefits were being denied to the people. Barrister Sultan Mehmood who was Prime Minister of Azad Kashmir from July 1996 to July 2001, was the one who agreed to a proposal for making the payment due to the foreign contractors and in just a year the revenue from the project was five times the value of the dues paid. Barrister Sultan Mehmood never unnecessarily interfered in administrative matters and would insist on taking decisions on merit. Close to the general elections, I provided him with the unsolicited opinion to the effect that he would lose the elections by a wide margin. He vehemently disagreed but lost as I had predicted.

Government service in Pakistan is a path strewn with pitfalls. The worst of these is a premature transfer of an official for no fault of his. One afternoon—a moment that every bureaucrat dreads—happened while I was on tour of Bhimber. I received abrupt transfer orders in an emergency and on enquiring was told by the Establishment Secretary that I was fortunate for not being suspended from service as that was what General Musharraf had ordered. This worried me, as I was not aware of any charges against me. I prayed that I not be charged with any anti-state activities but then who can stop the authorities from raising claims like espionage or sedition against someone. I soon found out the reason. The Federal Minister for

Kashmir Affairs, was the one responsible for complaining about me to General Musharraf, for not 'following the Federal Government's policy'. This revelation was quite a relief, although it was a preposterous allegation. Our tribal friends often say that '*marg ta eh neesa tbay ta ba razaa she*'; or 'when you threaten someone with death he is likely to bargain for a fever'. It was a great comfort to know that at least I was not a traitor! I left charge in deference to official posting orders. That is when matters got rough for the Minister. Half a dozen generals came to my rescue and they were a handful without their battalions! Generals Mahmud Ahmad of the Inter-Services Intelligence; Aziz Khan, Corps Commander; Yusaf Khan, Vice Chief of the Army; Parvez Kayani, Director General, Military Operations; Rao Zulfiqar, Army Engineers; and Javed Alam from Inter-Services Intelligence all bombarded fellow General Musharraf in my support and the orders were soon cancelled. When it comes to friendship, the military man remains more steadfast in his support than civilians and as for the politicians, the less said the better. The reason lies embedded in the military's basic duties which are not possible to perform without trust, loyalty, and camaraderie. Most bureaucrats, and all but a few among politicians, thrive on the absence of these values. I may mention that the Minister's grouse may have been caused by my opposition to his plan of inaugurating a new bridge during Muharram, this is when the police were deployed on security duties to maintain law and order. All's well that ends well and this tenure ended well.

Two trite incidents relating to my stay in Azad Kashmir remain etched in my mind. Both were rather amusing. An Army Engineering battalion working on a road construction project was not being allowed access by a private landowner on one pretext or the other. The *subedar* in charge, was understandingly rankled when one day the owner of the land presented him with an injunction from a court prohibiting him from any construction. Steadfast in the course of duty, the *subedar* placed the injunction notice on the engine of the bulldozer, loudly informing it that a stay order had been issued by the court. The engine did not take notice the first time, nor the second time, and that is when the *subedar* told the petitioner he was helpless as the bulldozer would not listen to him! The grant of unnecessary stay orders from courts is the bane of any administration. These injunctions resulted in the escalation of the project's cost and delays in the accrual of benefits.

On another occasion, as Chief Secretary, I ordered that a house precariously perched on the edge of a precipice be vacated as it was endangering not only the occupants but the traffic on the road below. The owner approached the Chief Justice of the High Court of Azad Jammu and Kashmir (AJK). I was summoned by the Court but for some reason the summon was not served and the next thing I knew, the Chief Justice in a pique had fined me—the head of the State administration—Rs. 2,000 for not attending the court. Till then I was oblivious to this petty drama. Fortunately, the good Justice Yunus Surakhvi of the AJK Supreme Court quashed the order an hour after it was issued. Some people in high positions can really stoop low! The people of Azad Kashmir, especially from Mirpur and those from the Suddan tribe, are trustworthy friends and generous to a fault. They never forget a favour or a good deed. Many have migrated to England and other foreign lands never forgetting their origins or their homeland and are in the forefront as far as philanthropy and generosity is concerned. It was most pleasant to find so many honourable people like Sardar Ibrahim Khan, General Aziz Khan, K. H. Khurshid, Barrister Sultan Mehmood, General Anwar, Sardar Sikander Hayat, Raja Farooq Haider, Raja Zulqarnain, Justice Yunus Surakhvi, Chaudhry Hameed Poti, Sheikh Hafeez, Iqbal Ratyal, Khalid Farook Ibrahim, and a host of others in a place as small as Azad Jammu and Kashmir. These people retain the friendships which was best exemplified by the example of one Colonel Sher Khan of Rawlakot. A close friend of his from Swabi in the Khyber Pakhtunkhwa province was so devoted to him that he decided to name his grandson *Karnal* (as in 'colonel') Sher Khan after him. The boy later joined the army and on promotion, *Karnal* Sher Khan became Captain *Karnal* Sher Khan who during the Kargil war of 1999 won Pakistan's highest medal for bravery, the Nishan-e-Haider. I left Azad Kashmir with a heavy heart, after serving for about two years.

iii. NORTH WEST FRONTIER (KHYBER PAKHTUNKHWA) PROVINCE

I experienced another jolt while leaving Azad Kashmir, as originally the government had posted me as Chief Secretary of Balochistan, but the orders were cancelled three days later (reportedly on the instructions of the Corps Commander). What the reasons for the cancellations were, I do not know, but immediately afterwards I received the orders of being posted as the Chief Secretary of the once-fabled and lately-troubled North West Frontier Province. Soon thereafter, even the romance of the name was no more and the province is now indistinctively called Khyber Pakhtunkhwa.

The events surrounding my posting were unfavourable as the events of 9/11 had unfolded a few weeks prior to my arrival. The US invasion of Afghanistan had started with the bombing of the imagined hiding place of Osama bin Laden in Tora Bora. Worse still, the Devolution Plan dealing with the cataclysmic restructuring of the civil administration in the provinces had been initiated. It would be many years before the damages unleashed by this 'reform' would be undone.

This was the period when General Musharraf had conducted the farcical referendum to gain five additional years in office and he went about addressing rallies in cities in his military uniform and tribal headgear, along with his Corps Commanders. Voting was free for all, including under-aged children, it was open in the literal sense, and unfair in the extreme. Even unregistered persons could vote and many voted for the General dozens of times. The precedent for a referendum had been established by another General, Ziaul Haq, two decades earlier. It was painful to see bureaucrats outdoing each other in stuffing the ballot boxes with a 'yes' vote, ostensibly to support 'the General's cause of enforcing Islamic injunctions'. I remember voting no in both referendums and that was the limit of my resistance to the farce.

With his own position secure for five years, Musharraf allowed holding of the General Elections in 2002. The collection of right-wing political parties, the Muttahida Majlis-e-Amal or the MMA won a landslide victory in NWFP and Balochistan. How the MMA was created, I do not know for certain. It appeared that there was some official support provided, although there was none on polling day. There was no rigging of the ballot box and the alliance won because of their religious manifesto and the reaction to the American invasion in Afghanistan. Before the elections, Khalid Masood, the competent head of the Provincial Special Branch of the Police, and I, would constantly analyse the likely election trends and two weeks ahead of the polls I informed the Governor that the MMA would win about 28 seats of a total 35. The Governor was furious and nearly hit the roof because 'his intelligence service experience' told him that their seats would only be half as many. As it turned out, the MMA won twenty-eight seats.

The military government was most surprised with the election results and became noticeably edgy, even though the MMA had developed a basic political understanding with the military. Under these circumstances, a major general of the Intelligence Services contacted me in Peshawar and demanded that my father-in-law, Saranjam Khan, then the Secretary General of Muslim League (Nawaz), be asked to join the governing Pakistan Muslim League Quaid-i-Azam (PML-Q) and support General Musharraf. I was aghast but kept my wits about me; telling the general that this directive was beyond my charter of duties; that I would convey no such request and that I was prepared for a transfer out of the province. I was retained but only till the 'forces' got a more plausible reason to remove me. Despite all efforts, General Musharraf's nominee for the Prime Minister's position, Zafarullah Jamali, could not muster the bare majority required in the National Assembly. I had learnt that at least two of the National Assembly members of the MMA from the Tribal Areas had secretly switched sides in return for substantial personal gains and informed the Chief Minister, Akram Durrani accordingly. Both, him and Maulana Fazlur-Rahman refused to believe this but as a precautionary measure they confined all their members in the Chief Minister's House as the Maulana had his own ambitions for the top slot. General Musharraf's game plan was noticed and began to crumble. The Governor was then told to conjure up some tricks and he cunningly came up with the antidote. He spoke to the Chief Minister on the telephone but only after placing a company of Frontier Corps troops close by. The Governor requested that all tribal area members only be allowed to meet him formally since he was the Agent to the President for FATA. I learnt through my own sources that the troops were to be employed to forcibly seize the two members if there was resistance from the Police. I advised the Chief Minister about the sly move of the Governor knowing full well what the Governor's intentions were. The Chief Minister was quite naïve but then like all politicians was convinced he was a political *Aflatoon*, or Plato, and allowed the members to meet the Governor. A couple of hours later, when two tribal members failed to return from the Governor's House, the Chief Minister was thoroughly shaken and admitted that he had made a mistake by not heeding my advice. By then, the two members were whisked away, with their consent, to Islamabad to cast their votes for Mr Jamali who was to become the Prime Minister. It was rumoured that both members were richer by Rs. 50 million in the process.

It was difficult to say whether the Chief Minister was more angry or embarrassed. He ordered the Inspector General of Police to get the East Cantonment Police Station, *Sharqi Thana*, to register a First Information Report (FIR) against the Governor by name for the kidnapping of the two MNAs. The police, as is their norm, complied readily and a short time later the Police Inspector arrived with Register Number One at the Chief Minister's House to register the case. As soon as I got to know of this, I advised the Chief Minister against such a juvenile move, warning him that it would blowback against him as the members had already been won over by the Generals in power. An affidavit by these two would have led to charges being filed against the Chief Minister and he would have lost his position, only a week after being sworn in. Better sense prevailed and the next day the Chief Minister decided against the move and called to thank me for my timely advice. In other matters of administration where personal, party, or financial interests were involved, he unfortunately, never followed my advice.

The Federal Government soon got tired of the MMA but the provincial Governor got tired of the Chief Secretary sooner. As Chief Secretary, I seriously objected, in writing, the Governor's attempt to sequester the FATA administration into a separate secretariat which I knew would lead to the creation of a separate province, in due course. My letter said that this was a serious infringement of the Constitution and the Rules of Business and the Governor was advised against such a move. The Governor did not like the advice and ten days later, he ensured that I was removed unceremoniously as Chief Secretary.

The provincial Governor contrived a cunning scheme to have me removed as Chief Secretary because of my policy differences with him. It so happened that the Jamaat-i-Islami, a party which was part of the provincial government, decided to stage a protest rally in Peshawar for gaining some obscure political advantage. The Chief Secretary directed the Inspector General Police and the Capital City Police Officer by word and through letter that such a rally should not be permitted, as there was likely mischief behind it. The warning was reiterated a day before the protest to the Police Chief but again no preventive measures were taken. The CCPO actually feigned illness on the appointed day and was not available even on police wireless. The police allowed the rally of some two hundred people, who marched down a road damaging the hoardings of an international soft drink company. I do not know if I could claim damages from the company! The President and the provincial Governor were besides themselves with fake anger, and showed their deep concern by posting the Inspector General Police and me out of the province. Apparently, they wanted to score points against the right-wing government of the MMA, just ahead of the President's visit to the United States. As for the Governor, he wanted to square up with me for writing a 'harsh' letter to him critical of his handling of the Tribal Areas. So, two birds were taken down with one stone! At about the same time, around forty police recruits in Quetta were killed in an ambush by militants and the only reaction of the military government was to transfer the Station House Officer (SHO) of the concerned Police Station. To this day, I do not know why the Inspector General of Police did not follow clear orders in preempting the rally although he did inform me that his subordinate was the culprit. The latter confessed to me that the fault lay with him. I somehow felt that an IGP should have asserted himself more strongly.

On the subject of the police, I wish to recount an unusual incident that occurred near the Pishtakhara Police Station outside Peshawar. Early one morning a crowd had blocked the road in protest against load-shedding of electricity. Since there were no executive magistrates in the country after General Musharraf's Devolution programme, the police alone confronted the crowd. Soon a fracas developed which led to police firing and killing one person. In retaliation, the large crowd held a dozen policemen hostage in the Police Station and started firing at it. For the next eight hours there was no communication between the police and the villagers and as such there was growing concern for the safety of the police hostages. The protestors refused to talk to the police; the elected Nazim had hidden himself in a nearby hospital because most of the local villagers were from a different political party; and there was no Magistrate, Assistant Commissioner, or Deputy Commissioner on the ground. The Home Secretary, Brigadier Mahmood Shah, was a noble person but had only recently been inducted from the Army and did not have field-duty experience. As such, there was no other option for me, as Chief Secretary of the province, to visit the site and manage the situation. The police were told to remain well clear of the area to avoid further provocation. I first went with my driver to the village guest house (*hujra*) to offer condolence prayers for the deceased person, which helped reduce tensions. I then promised an enquiry into the incident, took some refreshments with the local people, and finally requested them to hand over all policemen to me. They agreed. Such fine people. This was one more price that the people paid, for abolishing executive magistrates!

Over time, the frustration of working with an incompetent and self-centred leadership in the Frontier was difficult to sustain. I thought both the governor and the chief minister were unequal to their tasks. The General was bent upon hoisting the disjointed and impracticable devolution plan at all costs while the chief minister deviated from the rules on merit and objectivity. The Government of MMA was determined on bypassing all rules and regulations and came up with the idea of enacting the *Hisba* Act. Under this proposed law, the chief minister was to be made the absolute and final authority on executive, judicial, and financial matters with flimsy legislation in place for form's sake only. Fortunately, it took the Supreme Court only an hour to undo the intentions of the chief minister and his cohorts.

Despite such adversity, there were a few memorable moments to savour. Three public welfare institutions were constructed to support the much needed development for the well-being of the people. The SOS village for orphans was being planned in Peshawar with the support of the devoted humanitarian, Begum Salima Aga Khan but the land was neither available nor was there money to acquire it. Secondly, there was a need to establish a proper hospital for the mentally challenged patients complete with visitors' rooms for parents and families of the patients. Lastly, Edwardes College School required space for its junior school, a hundred years after the college was built. I ensured that money was sanctioned for all three projects, but not before the finance minister raised all sorts of obscure objections to all three proposals. Some years later, the SOS building was finally completed.

I spent a total of twenty months in NWFP.

iv. SINDH

After serving in the NWFP, I spent a delectable year as Secretary, Ministry Population Welfare, a department deliberately miscalled to cushion any resentment against the family planning programme. This dealt with the most important issue facing the country but sadly operated with very limited commitment from the government. In the years ahead, our population growth rate would be our undoing! After President Ayub Khan, no leader had the vision to actively patronize the family planning effort.

Later, for the next three years, I was appointed Permanent Secretary, Ministry of Railways which meant I was also the Chairman of Pakistan Railways, an organization which had suffered decades of neglect. Then, with only six months left before my superannuation, I was posted for the fourth and the last time as the Chief Secretary, this time to the Sindh province. It transpired that President Musharraf and Prime Minister Shaukat Aziz were not satisfied with the state of the administration in the Sindh province and decided to replace Fazalur Rehman, a kind and genial officer from the Accounts Service. The fault perhaps did not lie with the Chief Secretary but in the Sindh administrative system which thrived on corruption, threats, and blackmail. After assuming of charge in Karachi, I straightaway informed the Governor and the Chief Minister that I would not accept any extension or re-employment in service as Chief Secretary after superannuation because the law and more so conventions did not permit this. In any case, this was not necessary as I was removed earlier due to my serious differences with the government.

Amongst the four provinces in the country, the worst governance was in the Sindh province, perhaps because it was rich in resources, but more so because of its corrupt and highly partisan political leadership. Many officials took the cue from the politicians. In Sindh, there was little or no regard for law and rules and what the books said could be conveniently ignored or relaxed by the governor, chief minister, and the ministers. The provincial Rules of Business gave more powers and discretion to the ministers than was the case in any other province. Prior consent of the chief minister was often required even before a summary could be initiated for his orders. Junior officials from one department were promoted out of turn and posted to lucrative and corrupt departments like Food and Excise and Taxation against higher posts. Police Inspectors were known to get shoulder promotions to the ranks of Senior Superintendents of Police and even higher positions on whims of those who mattered, and they in return obliged their benefactors in every way. Well-connected police officials from the provincial cadre were often promoted for displaying courage in fake encounters against imaginary criminals because no firm parameters for promotion existed. In one case, a particularly influential provincial police officer had forwarded his case for a second out-of-turn promotion, which despite my objections as the Chief Secretary, was approved by the Chief Minister. I was of the view that bravery in operations, even when corroborated by independent sources, should lead to award of medals and cash rewards so that the promotion rights of others were not compromised. This was not the case in Sindh.

There is a particularly perverse administrative culture in Sindh in which the chief minister and the ministers are not bothered with legal requirements, rules, and propriety. For them the law is hardly something to be respected. Highly-rated officers who do not blend into this culture are hounded out early. The Sindhi and later the Muttahida Qaumi Movement (MQM) comprising Urdu-speaking politicians, controlled every matter in their Ministries, no matter how trifling. In power, but only when in power, they were convinced that by threatening and bullying officers their objectives were easily achieved. Bullying and blackmail remained the ultimate administrative norm and no wonder the province stands stuck in its muck today. Accountability does not exist. Once out of power, these same politicians become totally docile and obsequious. The shamefully corrupt and incompetent administration in Sindh has caused immense damage to the people of Sindh.

One of the biggest disservices done to the state, which is a crime, relates to the allotment of state-land at throwaway prices to friends and associates. Almost all chief ministers in Sindh, including some in other provinces as well, were responsible for this crime of allotment of state-lands and bungalows free of cost as Mughal princes would do. One additional reason for my removal as Chief Secretary was because of my refusal to become party to a foul deed; quite literally, a land deed. My goose was cooked by the events of 12 May 2007, which led to the deaths of 48 innocent people, and despite the support of the Prime Minister and the Governor Sindh, it was clear that others were waiting for an opportunity to axe me. The opportunity came sooner than expected. The Chief Minister had planned allotment of scores of acres of prized state-land to a close friend who was a prominent businessman of Karachi, at less than one-fourth its market value. The Land Utilization Department in the Provincial Government was headed by a capable officer with integrity, Siddique Memon. He was compelled to initiate a summary on the subject for chief minister's approval. The officer discussed the case with me and it was agreed that he would initiate the summary without making any recommendation. I, as Chief Secretary, would then oppose in writing the grant of land without calling for open bids as stipulated in the law. The chief minister was not amused even when he was informed that the Government of Sindh would lose up to Rs. 2 billion if the land award was not advertised. I did not comply with this order. It appeared that the businessman was being rewarded by Providence for his generosity to the poor. Following an election meeting of President Musharraf in Nawakot in Mirpurkhas, the four of us were returning to Karachi in an official Toyota Land Cruiser; as we were leaving the Nawakot Fort, an old beggar woman stretched her hand for alms. A minute elapsed as I struggled to get my wallet from my pocket, intending to give her Rs. 10. The businessman who was in the driver's seat, quickly produced two bank notes to give to the beggar, and I realized that each was a Rs. 5,000 note. I quickly withdrew the notes intending to hand these back, thinking he had made a mistake but he insisted that the money be paid to the beggar. He was a generous person, but then generosity like charity should begin at home.

After about four months as Chief Secretary, the Chief Minister decided that I had to leave the province and leave soon. He proceeded to Islamabad to see the President and threatened that he would not return to Karachi without my transfer orders. While the powers that be, pondered over his ultimatum, the Chief Minister played his master card by predicting that General Musharraf could not be re-elected in the presence of such a 'non-cooperative' Chief Secretary. The decision to transfer me did not take long after that. The Governor Sindh, Ishrat-ul-Abad, who remained very considerate towards me, did make an effort to retain me but fortunately it was to no avail. Prime Minister Shaukat Aziz, wisely thought that any further retention would only add to my differences with the Chief Minister.

I was posted back again as Secretary Railways and soon afterwards was appointed as Chairman of the Water and Power Development Authority (WAPDA) by the Prime Minister on a five-year contract. What happened to the generous award of state-land to the businessman? I was told that the Chief Minister did approve the concessional grant, in violation of the rules, but only after I had left. Since the Chief Minister's tenure ended soon thereafter, I doubt if the land was actually transferred but I think the chief minister should have been confronted and stopped from this illegal act by those who succeeded me.

In another case, a group of Arabs and Europeans enjoying full support from the President's House wanted a transfer of a few thousand acres of state-land near Hawkes Bay, virtually free of cost, for the 'joint development' of real estate. This scam was stopped with great difficulty. Anything can happen in Sindh; there was this Sindhi minister who reportedly placed a gun to the head of a provincial secretary to get approval for a case while another would routinely kidnap businessmen, especially from religious minorities, to extort money. Some officials were murdered for not complying with illegal orders. This was democracy Sindhi style! During my short stay in Sindh, a large delegation from Qatar, which included a well-known Pakistani entrepreneur, visited the province to seek projects for investment. The fact of the matter was that their interest was confined to obtaining the transfer of a hundred acres of prime land on Drigh Road, housing the Karachi Water and Sewerage Board, at throwaway terms. The 'investors' proposed that they would construct hotels, commercial businesses, and luxury housing at the site but without paying for the land cost. Instead, they offered to provide a small share of the income accrued, to the province, and wished to raise the money from local public offering. This scheme was unacceptable to me and the Arab brothers were told that both parties must first equally contribute US$40 million to the provincial treasury to cover the cost of the land. That was when the delegation beat a hasty retreat! All the while, receptions and dinners were heavy on the itinerary of the guests; expensive rugs, carpets, and other items were presented to them. The Arabs apparently felt embarrassed as they did not reciprocate the gifts. The Pakistani entrepreneur, however, informed me that their gifts were in their aircraft parked at the airport and that someone had been sent to bring these. This was worrisome and I requested him that to avoid embarrassment no gift be provided to the Chief Secretary as I was the chief host. Fortunately, no embarrassment was caused to the Chief Secretary or others because gifts from the aircraft never arrived; and how could they when the deal was not struck?

I have known Pakistani politicians and officials hinting and expecting lavish gifts including luxury cars, watches, and diamonds from the Arab sheikhs, almost as a right. There was this one chief minister from the Punjab who reportedly requested his Arab host to replace the gifted Toyota car with a Mercedes. They obliged. I also knew that most Arab dignitaries had a low opinion of Pakistanis whether he was a leader or a manual labourer. They were derisively called *maskeen* (humble souls). I had, therefore, decided a long time back that I would never accept a personal gift from them.

Some years later, I visited Qatar with a delegation led by Prime Minister Yousaf Raza Gillani and hoped that no gift be presented to me on this visit. Thankfully, no gift was given. On our return to Pakistan, I received a packet from the Foreign Office. It was an expensive wristwatch reportedly valued at US$2,000. I had two options: the first, which was to send it back to the Foreign Office but was dissuaded from doing so as someone else would have appropriated it. I, however, paid the value determined by the Cabinet Division's *tosha-khanna* and never having used the watch sold it for charity. Nevertheless, I am grateful to the Amir of Qatar for the present.

The following anecdote explains Pakistan's social structure which does not brook discussion, dialogue, or debate. In the administration, even a short delay in executing a command, any command, is frowned upon. In the Sindh province, the situation is infinitely worse because government affairs are seen as a continuation of the iniquitous social system based on a master-client relationship. As Chief Secretary Sindh, I received directions from the Principal Secretary to the Chief Minister to issue suspension orders for Ms Faryal Talpur, the District Nazim of Nawabshah district. I was accustomed to the ways of the Frontier province and was disturbed by such arbitrary orders. My queries on the matter were not appreciated; I was told to comply with the 'sahib's orders'. However, I refused to take any action until I had enquired into the matter first. I thereafter, called Ms Faryal Talpur and Ahmed Bux Khokhar, the District Coordination Officer (DCO) of Nawabshah, to personally enquire into the matter. It transpired that Ms Talpur, the sister of Asif Zardari of the Pakistan Peoples

Party, was the only opposition Nazim in the province who incidentally was selected by a toss of a coin after a tie in the votes, among some thirty district nazims in the province. I learnt from the Nazim that because of her being from the opposition all development and operational funds under six heads of accounts had been denied to her, in order to teach her and her supporters a lesson. DCO Khokhar, after some initial obfuscation, was honest enough to admit that it was under directions from the Chief Minister that he had withheld the grants. This was an open and shut case and a choice had to be made either in favour of the law or in compliance with an unjust command. Both options were difficult but the latter choice was most distasteful. To ease the burden on the DCO, I asked him to apply for a long leave, which was granted immediately. As for suspending Ms Talpur from office, I refused to do so, and gave my reasons in the Enquiry Report to the Chief Minister. He was not pleased at my refusal and decided to refer the case to the Local Government Commission, to probe the charges against her. The Local Government Commission was a farcical handpicked body ingeniously crafted by the National Reconstruction Bureau (NRB) which had a pathological hatred for the Civil Service. Meanwhile, other events overtook the enquiry and Ms Talpur retained her position. I was soon removed as Chief Secretary for other whimsical reasons by the Chief Minister.

Again a similar incident occurred, a short time later. This time the Chief Minister ordered an enquiry and the arrest of a senior police officer. The police officer in question, was at that time a Deputy Inspector General, a 'very controversial officer'. There were rumours that he had a brush with the law a few times both in the Punjab and the Frontier provinces over some embarrassing incidents. Between him and the chief minister, there was no love lost and the cause this time was the alleged kidnapping of a family in the Tharparkar area, which was a case he was investigating. The Supreme Court had also taken notice of the matter, which annoyed the Sindh Government. It, therefore, registered its own case against the DIG and the focus was on having him arrested to embarrass the Court. The sharp 'policia' that he was, he managed to be bailed out in this case. This was too much for the chief minister and he ordered Asad Ashraf Malik, the competent Director General of the Anti-Corruption Establishment of Sindh, to file a corruption charge against the officer. To initiate such an enquiry, the permission of the Chief Secretary was a prerequisite and this permission was granted. Much to my amazement, the Director General came back a day later recommending his arrest since according to him the charges in the enquiry had been proved. I was not pleased and from an earlier meeting, knew that there were hundreds of cases where enquiries had been pending for months and years. I admonished him and he was frank enough to admit that the Chief Minister was hounding him to arrest the officer immediately. The permission for arrest was not allowed. The Chief Minister was livid, accustomed as he was to Sindhi officers who do not resist any orders and told his Principal Secretary to order the Chief Secretary to ensure that the police officer was arrested. Despite the Chief Minister's order, he was not arrested. Such are the deeds of chief ministers and principal secretaries in failing states. Banana republics, as someone said, are better because at least you get free bananas! The same chief minister, most surprisingly, would dutifully follow the rituals of faith, quite diligently. Once when he saw me leave a meeting to offer the afternoon prayers he said that he was most impressed as senior officers in Sindh seldom said their prayers.

They say that existing realities are never permanent realities. How true! The Chief Minister, was soon out of power and spent five years in exile but not before he got a taste of his own medicine. A person from Sindh hit him with a shoe and the surname of the attacker happened to be Durrani, as reported by the newspapers. This was poetic justice but I actually felt sorry at the act. On the other hand, Ms Faryal Talpur was later elected to the National Assembly and wielded extreme authority as by then her once-exiled brother, Asif Zardari, had become President of Pakistan. Serving under the Peoples Party was a trying experience; most (if not all) ministers and parliamentarians were rude, corrupt, and uncouth. I was, however, grateful to Ms Talpur for the respect and consideration she showed me even though I could not comply with the requests she would forward. I was also told that President Zardari once mentioned to someone, that I stood by my conscience in their support when they had to face serious challenges.

Meanwhile, my differences with the Chief Minister were coming to a head. The summary for the grant of land at a throwaway price was among the many other cases sent by various departments where the chief minister overruled the chief secretary even though the former was in blatant violation of the Rules. As all summaries on return from the Chief Minister were routed through the Chief Secretary for implementation, I held those back where the rules were infringed. The Chief Minister was incensed when he came to know that I was not implementing his decisions and he then tried to teach me the 'Rules of Business'. He telephoned me at home when a few people were visiting, and so I decided to dramatize the conversation. As he called me 'Chief Secretary *Sahib*' I replied that I was not the actual Chief Secretary but was only living in the Chief Secretary's Residence. The chief secretary was one whose advice and recommendations were sought and seriously considered but such a practice had not occurred during my four month stay in Sindh. I, however, reiterated that the files which were not being acted upon would continue to lie unattended till the rules were followed.

It was sad to observe that the politicians in Sindh seldom took a principled stand on law. Most chief executives of the province were more adept at exercising their discretion for personal or party benefits. No one challenged them. I feel there was little benefit in retaining seemingly elite service groups where officials cannot display courage and integrity, especially at the level of chief secretary and the inspector general of the police. There were honourable exceptions to this rule but their numbers were small.

It is observed that a politics of gain governs all decisions in the country. Who is to blame for the famine in Thar which is a disgrace for the provincial government. In the district government departments like irrigation, public health, works, education, health, and livestock seldom provide any worthwhile facilities to the people. Amazingly, the common people continue to vote for the same political parties and individuals and this remains a concern. The district administration and the police are barely able to carry out their duties. Crime and insecurity is the rule while ordinary people remain at the mercy of the landlords, criminals, and the police with each outdoing the other in collecting their share. One can only pray to the Almighty for divine assistance.

The total time I spent in Sindh was four months.

* * *

There was one additional opportunity of becoming a 'Chief', this time as a caretaker Chief Minister of Khyber Pakhtunkhwa before the elections of 2013. After my tenure ended as Chairman of WAPDA, I remained as an Advisor with the Diamer Basha Dam project, as the Prime Minister supported the project. Although I had neither desired nor lobbied for a three-month stint as caretaker Chief Minister of NWFP, the press repeatedly mentioned my name along with the two candidates shortlisted for the position. Under the law, the outgoing chief minister and the leader of the opposition were to select the caretaker chief minister through a consensus between them. A suggestion by some well-meaning persons to approach and request the two Parliamentarians—whom I knew very well—for their support was of course, impossible. I telephoned the Chief Minister, Amir Haider Hoti to convey to him that I was not interested in the position but was unable to speak to him as he was in a conference. The Chief Secretary and the Additional Chief Secretary were then told emphatically that I would not accept the offer as reported in the press. They informed the Chief Minister immediately. The media soon reported my refusal, much to my relief. Three months is not enough to achieve anything worthwhile, even though being Chief Minister is an honour. I could, however, not tolerate the thought of any politician sitting in judgment on me, on an issue like this.

3

Tales from the Frontier

I n 1849, the British annexed the trans-Indus River Pakhtun territories following the Second Sikh war but, this area officially became the North West Frontier Province (NWFP), in 1901. It would be fair to say that the British were fascinated by the territory because of its strategic importance, the physical risks prevalent, and the rough, tough, and egalitarian spirit of its people. Although economic and social changes have considerably tamed the rebellious nature of the Pakhtuns during the past seventy years, their excessive pride and haughty temper continues to exhibit itself in violence and vengeance every now and then. I am sharing some tales and anecdotes observed from close quarters as I not only belong to the 'frontier' province but have spent most of my career as a field officer in the Tribal Areas and the adjoining districts.

i. A Tale of Two Gallantry Awards

One of the more fascinating stories to emerge from the First World War relates to two Afridi brothers from the Khyber Agency who won the highest military awards for gallantry—but from opposing countries. In March 1915, the Germans pinned the Iron Cross on *Jamadar* Mir Mast Qambarkhel Afridi while on 26 April in the same year, *Jamadar* Mir Dast Afridi became the proud recipient of the Victoria Cross. Both brothers had displayed extreme valour in the battles around Ypres, fighting for different armies. How and why the two brothers ended up in opposite camps is intriguing. Mir Mast joined the 58 Frontier Force (FF), the Vaughan's Rifles, which was ordered to go to Europe at the beginning of the war. Operations started almost immediately and these were no ordinary operations. The world had never seen such gore and brutality before. This was the infamous trench warfare which was viciously augmented by poison gas where tens of thousands perished for a yard, gained or lost. *Jamadar* Mir Mast was known to be politically aware and was a strident supporter of the Turkish caliphate. He thought that the best way he could resist the British Empire was by fighting it. One night, he, along with fourteen fellow Pakhtuns, crossed over to the German lines and in the following days he fought against his erstwhile companions in Ypres. After a particularly belligerent engagement against the British troops resulting in savage losses, he was awarded the Iron Cross, the supreme German medal for gallantry, by the *Kaiser*. His brother, *Jamadar* Mir Dast, had enlisted in the 55 Frontier Force better known as Coke's Rifles. Both units were sent to Europe but soon Mir Dast was attached to the 57 FF, Wilde's Rifles. He participated in many engagements, but on 26 April 1915, enemy fire and poison gas took a severe toll on the unit. Mir Dast was the man of the moment. Even though he was wounded and affected by gas, he was still active in recovering eight seriously wounded English and Indian officers, from the battlefield. For his bravery, he was awarded the Victoria Cross. The King personally pinned the Victoria Cross on him. After the war, both brothers returned home to Tirah in the Khyber Agency. The Iron Cross-holder never crossed paths with the government but Sir George Roos-Keppel, the Chief Commissioner, tried hard to corner him. Mir Mast was determined to raise a force with Turkish and German assistance to resist the British. He even established contact with Haji Sahib of Turangzai who was fighting in the nearby Mohmand areas. On the other hand, the Victoria Cross veteran, Mir Dast, was the toast of the country, regaling troops with his amazing war-time experiences. As Political Agent in the Khyber Agency, I met the grandchildren of the veterans long afterwards but even a century later two issues remain central to the tale, one physical and one moral. Physically, without doubt both award holders were exceptionally daring men. The moral issue was more subjective. Mir Mast violated his oath by crossing over to the enemy but for a higher moral calling. Mir Dast was honour-bound to his oath and always felt he had 'merely performed his duty'.

* * *

ii. MOLLIE ELLIS OF SUFFOLK AND KOHAT

Between the First and Second World Wars two people, a woman and the other a man, one English and the other a local tribesman, became part of the folklore of the Frontier. The girl was sixteen-year-old Mollie Ellis, the daughter of Major Ellis who had been kidnapped from Kohat Cantonment by the Afridi tribal gang. The man was Mirza Ali Khan, known to history as the Fakir of Ipi, who came to prominence because of the return of one Ram Kori, a Hindu girl to her parents. She became Islam Bibi after reportedly converting to Islam. Mollie Ellis was rescued and the episode was resolved within a few weeks; the Fakir of Ipi's freedom struggle lasted a quarter of a century.

A gang of Adamkhel Afridis of Darra, led by Ajab Khan and his brother Shahzada. were suspected of conducting thefts and raids in nearby Kohat town. A contingent of Frontier Constabulary took preventive measures through a *barampta* to arrest those responsible. It was reported that the main accused would flee the house wearing women's clothes. The Constabulary therefore started checking all inmates, which included few women who were leaving. Ajab Khan saw this act of checking the women insulting and an affront to local conventions. He promised revenge, and shortly thereafter led a gang at night and entered the house of Major Ellis in Kohat Cantonment. The Major was away on military exercises but his wife, on hearing footsteps, blew the whistle provided for such an emergency. To prevent the alarm being raised, Shahzada stabbed and killed Mrs Ellis and forcibly took away the girl, Mollie. They spent the next day in the hills, deliberately moving away from where the police would be looking for them. Mollie recognized the surroundings as she spotted the peak called the 'old woman's nose' while she was being led away. During the night, they crossed the Darra-Kohat road and travelled westwards towards the Orakzai tribes finally taking refuge with the Mamuzai tribe. The Akhunzada of the Mamuzai was a spiritual leader of great significance and enjoyed wide esteem. This was a lucky break for Mollie.

The kidnapping of an English girl from the well-protected cantonment was deeply humiliating for the government. Two Army Divisions were immediately mobilized. Tribal Maliks and elders from amongst the Afridi tribes in Darra Adamkhel, Khyber Agency, and from the other

Agencies were despatched to first locate the kidnapper and then to use all political means or non-violent recourse to secure her release. Three prominent Pakhtun government officials, Sheikh Mahboob Ali, Mughal Baz Khan Afridi, and Quli Khan Khattak assisted the tribal *jirga*. The Chief Commissioner NWFP, Sir Harold Dean personally supervised the recovery effort from Kohat, Hangu, and Shinawari Fort which was the gateway to the Orakzai tribe. Simultaneously, troops started assembling to march into Orakzai and Afridi territories should Mollie come to any harm or was not returned.

Once the *jirga* had established contact with Mahmud Akhundzada and other tribal elders, it was decided that a volunteer nurse, Lillian Starr from the Mission Hospital, Peshawar, be sent deep into the Tribal Areas with some supplies for Mollie. The devoted efforts of the tribal *jirga* coupled with the threat of the army divisions that were deployed had the desired result. Lillian Starr was soon able to bring back Mollie through the Yakho Kandao Pass to the Shinawari Fort and was received in great style by the Chief Commissioner and the military officers. 'My father was waiting. I don't think we said a word, we just fell into each other's arms,' she recalled. She was unharmed and unmolested to the great relief of everyone as mentioned by Lillian Starr in her book *Tales from Tirah and Lesser Tibet*, published in 1923. 'I knew the Pathans didn't molest women. They'd kill you, but they wouldn't molest you,' she further added. The Pakhtun kidnappers behaved 'honourably' on one count, at least.

Mollie and her father returned to England, after Mrs Ellis's burial in Kohat cemetery where her tombstone reminds one that life ''tis but a little while' and no more. After sixty years, 'a little while' later, Mollie Wade née Ellis visited Pakistan, where a relative was posted in the British High Commission but the main purpose of her visit was to see her mother's grave in Kohat cemetery. A new tombstone was created from a photograph provided by Mollie.

The kidnapping issue, however, did not end with the return of Mollie as the British administration made sure that they punished the gang by exiling them all to northern Afghanistan and then razing their village in Darra Adamkhel, to the ground. One from the gang, perhaps a Malikdin Khel Afridi, was arrested, tried, and executed. Ajab Khan and Shahzada died natural deaths in Afghanistan. Some of their sons and grandsons were killed during the Soviet occupation of Afghanistan; the rest arrived in Pakistan as war refugees.

In 1979, while I was in England for an advanced degree course in Economics. I tried to contact Mollie Wade, as she was then called, through newspapers and the BBC but they were unable to oblige for privacy reasons. Political Officers, however, know how to get things done the 'Frontier' way. A letter was sent to the grand old man of the Frontier, Sir Olaf Caroe, the last British Governor of NWFP, then living in retirement in Steyning on the English Channel. His reply was deeply moving when he spoke of his pleasure in writing to a 'Durrani', the 'rulers of Afghanistan from Ahmad Shah to Zahir Shah and Sardar Daud'. The Soviet occupation of Afghanistan was another move in the Great Game that began early in the nineteenth century, involving the then superpowers, the British Empire and Czarist Russia. There would be much blood and brutality by the time the Great Game ended. It also led to a large shift in the world of geopolitics as communism crumbled in the old Soviet Union, after a hold of seventy years.

After having established contact with Mollie in England, she needed to be convinced that I was not a journalist and with her permission I drove to Suffolk, on the east coast of England, to meet her. She was quite frail by then but in one breath spoke of the sad events of the early part of the century and then in the next breath, switched the subject to the apples growing in her small garden. Perhaps her mother's memory continued to hurt her. She did wonder how ordinary people through sheer chance could shape history and how many thousands could have been killed as a result. I carried some gifts for her including cognac and she provided me with a penned-down version of her accounts. She still felt the pain of her mother's murder after all those years and was angry with some of the film producers for falsifying her role in the tragedy. Her husband had by then died and her son was a brigadier in the British Army who was subsequently posted to Pakistan. Mollie was keen for her mother's grave to be repaired and when this was done, she was 'most grateful for the effort'.

A few years later, when I was Political Agent in the Khyber Agency, Mollie visited Pakistan. The obvious first stop was Kohat and though the bungalow she was kidnapped from was no longer there, she placed a marble tablet in the Inter-Service Selection Board House commemorating her visit. The President of the Board, Brigadier Zafar Hayat, a former hockey Olympian, had her name engraved as Mollie Alice and insisted on the spelling but after some discussion, the good Brigadier was persuaded to alter it. She also visited the *Khassadar* Piquet, named 'Ellis Piquet' after her father, as that was the site from where the kidnappers crossed the road into Tirah. During the visit, the Khyber Rifles in Landikotal invited her to an elaborate tribal lunch in their mess complete with a pipe band and its accompanying protocol. There will hardly be a military mess in the world which will see more dignitaries than the Khyber Rifles Mess. While at lunch, I learnt of a dinner invitation later that evening from the Governor of NWFP, General Fazle Haq, at the Governor's House. Someone not very familiar with her, had planned to act as the great re-conciliator and suggested to the Governor to invite both Mollie and the sons of Ajab Khan who were living as Afghan refugees in Pakistan to the dinner. The Governor was thrilled and looked forward to a historic handshake which would end sixty year's of rancour. I was not so sure about her response to the proposed meeting with the children of the men who had murdered her mother. I told the Governor that I would give him a definitive answer on her likely response within the hour. I then put the scenario to her as a hypothetical question, as a political officer would often do, soliciting her reaction. She plainly said that let alone shaking hands, she would not even look at the people who had killed her mother. I conveyed the outcome to the Governor and requested him to disinvite one party. Mollie was the one who attended the dinner.

iii. MAMA'S ROOM

Early in 1920, Colonel T. H. Foulkes of the Indian Medical Service and his wife were killed by tribesmen in a bungalow in the Kohat Cantonment. Their only daughter, who later became Mrs Councell, was at that time ten years old. In the mid-1980s, nostalgia brought her back to Kohat with her son, a British Airways pilot. She herself had escaped death or capture that horrible night because she had hidden under the bed. She did not have an address or a picture of the house and her only recollection was its close proximity to the Resident Commissioner's bungalow. I was then Commissioner of the Kohat Division, living close by in the Cavagnari

House—one of the most splendid buildings in the country. Incidentally, Sir Louis Cavagnari, who had built the house, was a senior political officer with the British Army in Kabul during the Second Afghan War and it was he who had sent the famous telegram to Delhi intimating that the situation in Kabul was peaceful and that 'the natives were most friendly'. Two hours later, the Kabulis stormed the Residency, killing Cavagnari and his escort. After some scouting, Mrs Councell managed to locate Colonel Faulke's bungalow and the moment she entered the house she was transported some sixty-five years back in time. 'This was mama's room, this is the drawing room, the *ayah's* room', she said as she excitedly went about remembering an era now long gone. She was a brave lady indeed, looking for the house that had brought her much pain. Was there a departure from *Pakhtunwali*, the Pakhtun code of conduct concerning women? Probably yes.

iv. *Pakhtunwali*

Many decades later, an event took place in war-torn Afghanistan, which was deemed the veritable epitome of *Pakhtunwali*. It is interesting enough to be shared as it revealed the different mindsets of an average Pakhtun and a typical American. There are four main canons of the Pakhtun code of conduct called *Pakhtunwali*. The code is unwritten and any violation is held, or should be held, in perpetual contempt. It comprises of *melmastia*, meaning hospitality; *nanawatai*, the giving of refuge to those seeking it; *badal*, or revenge, best served cold; and finally, *nang* which means honour. There are also a few unsavoury customs among Pakhtuns like *swara*, a forced marriage to settle a wrong; *ghag*, which refers to compelling a family to give their daughter in marriage against her wishes; and *mirata*, the elimination of all family members of an enemy, including infants. I hope these customs are done away with so that the Pakhtuns emerge as better human beings.

In June 2005, a military engagement was initiated by the American forces against the Taliban through a four-man US Navy Seal team in the Korengal Valley of the Kunar province in Afghanistan. It was called Operation Red Wings and resulted in the deaths of three Americans. A rescue attempt led to the shooting down of a Chinook helicopter with the loss of a further sixteen troops. The one remaining Seal Petty Officer,

Marcus Luttrell, was wounded but could not be evacuated. He staggered
into the forests and hid himself for some days near the village of Sabri
Minah inhabited by the Pakhtuns till he came across some local people
from the Sabri tribe. Luttrell gave himself over to the tribesman once the
latter assured him that they meant no harm. Gulab, a Pakhtun tribesman
brought him home, cared for him, and made attempts to contact the
American forces at Camp Blessing to hand him back. The Taliban in turn
offered Gulab a bounty for handing the Seal Petty Officer over to them
but were prepared to use force against him in case of a refusal. His family
and tribe, on learning of the threat, assured him of their support and they
gathered with arms to defend him and their guest. They were defending
the guest even though he was an enemy soldier because of the *Pakhtunwali*
code of *'nanawatai'* which made it obligatory to provide asylum and refuge
to anyone. A short time later, the Seal Petty Officer was safely returned to
the Americans who reportedly offered Gulab a reward of US$200,000 for
his brave efforts. He refused to accept the money for fear of defiling the
Pakhtun code. Meanwhile, life became unbearable for him in his village
and he was compelled to migrate with his wife and six children to a safer
place. He got a job at an American facility for US$280 per month but
continued to lead a traumatized life. Once during a security check, he was
taken into custody but released soon afterwards. Here was a lesson that he
learnt in reverse-hospitality!

Once the American Seal was safe and back at home he never contacted
Gulab again, even though he owed his life to him, and neither did anyone
from the US armed forces attempt to interact with him. The incident
showed the wide chasm between the thinking of the occidental and the
oriental people. For the Westerner, everything in life is a transaction and
they try to place a monetary value on friendship, honour, and sacrifice,
which are payable through financial compensation and soon forgotten.
For the Pakhtun, a traditional or a religious obligation cannot be translated
into lucre. This act was beyond a financial gain and was actually the very
lifeblood that strengthens the Pakhtun code of conduct. The inter-state
relations of the West and particularly that of the Americans are not much
different either. Long-term friendships barely exist because the focus is
only on self-interest. The former US Secretary of State, Hillary Clinton

was correct when she said that much of this region's travails were due to the American policy of abandoning the people as soon as the Soviet Union was ousted from the area. Nature, however, moves slowly and takes a long-term view of events and this is why there is greater sustainability and balance in nature. This trait is absent in human relationships in the West and the East is catching up fast.

A similar incident of actualizing the Pakhtun code of conduct in practice was seen among the Afghan refugees in the Kurram Agency during the mid-1980s. An Afghan refugee from Logar had a monetary dispute with some people from the Afghan Mangal tribe, and the latter kidnapped and incarcerated the refugee for a while. One day, the kidnapped person managed to flee from captivity and took refuge in the temporary settlement of another family of Mangal tribe. Soon the settlement was surrounded demanding the return of their captive. At that time, the male elders were away and it fell upon a brave grandmother to assume command of the situation. She made it clear to all those present that returning the captive was contrary to *Pakhtunwali* and would never be countenanced even if that meant the deaths of all of them. As the standoff continued, the local administration under Abdullah Khan Masud, the redoubtable Assistant Political Agent arrived at the scene, recovered the kidnapped person and arrested a large number of the attackers. The matter was referred to a *jirga* of elders of the area who soon resolved the dispute as *Pakhtunwali* blossomed. I was also informed of a village near Waziristan where a serious security situation compelled the women and the children to seek refuge amongst the adjoining Marwat tribe who were their traditional enemies. For the duration of their sojourn the male members of the Marwat tribe did not even visit their own village to avoid any suggestion of impropriety.

Similarly, Khushal Khan Khattak, the warrior poet, while a prisoner of the Mughal Emperor Aurangzeb in Ranthambore, is reported to have directed his clan to send their women and children to his sworn enemies, the Yusafzai Pakhtuns, to escape the Mughal army. He said that the Yusafzais were his enemies no doubt, but that 'they were also Pakhtuns'.

v. LOWIS AND HIS WRISTWATCH

There was an Englishman, R. H. D. Lowis, Assistant Political Agent, who was originally from the Indian Political Department was sent to serve in the Tribal Areas and the Indian States. Officers from this service would mainly serve in NWFP, Balochistan, the Tribal Areas, and also in China, Iran, and the Gulf States. Lowis had served with distinction in Chitral, Kohat, Waziristan and other places during the decades before Partition. In 1937, he was serving in South Waziristan Agency when the Shahur Tangi ambush occurred, resulting in heavy British Army casualties. During the 1980s, his daughter, Joanna was posted to the British High Commission in Pakistan and was obviously very keen to see and experience the areas she had heard of and learned so much about from her father. Interestingly, she carried a photograph of herself at the age of two posing with her tricycle in front of the Cavagnari House in Kohat where her father had lived as Deputy Commissioner. Half a century later she was requested to pose again at exactly the same spot, this time in front of the bicycle that belonged to my youngest son, Shamoun, then aged two.

She was well informed about the conditions of the Frontier in the past and recalled many anecdotes. During British Raj, while Lowis was posted as the Assistant Political Agent in South Waziristan, one of his duties was to drop leaflets to warn tribesmen to vacate their houses, before the Royal Air Force bombed their homes to punish them for serious offences. This was a civilized way of dealing with offences, considering that nowadays no such warning is given even when children are being targetted. Once while dropping the leaflets, Lowis lost his wristwatch which fell on the ground. A few days later he could not believe his luck when a *malik*, a tribal elder, brought his wristwatch back which was still working, stating that a shepherd had found it. Decades later our Lowis of the Frontier, long after his return to England, went to the Caribbean for a vacation. While angling in a boat he lost his watch, or was it a ring, this time to the sea, and he hoped that some angler would recover and bring it back to him. Sadly, there was no Frontier man who could inform him that '*Sahib*, I caught a fish with your watch inside'. The Caribbean was not the Frontier!

Such was life on the Frontier that virtually every Frontiersman, military or civilian, had experienced great personal threats and dangers. Lowis, safe in England and as an old man, would at times wake up in a delirious state, ordering everyone to take positions behind makeshift trenches made from sofas because he imagined that the tribesmen were attacking. Being sniped at was considered a 'christening' in the Tribal Areas and one was not 'political' in the real sense, without experiencing it in the field.

vi. FIELD MARSHAL SAM MANEKSHAW AND GENERAL YAHYA KHAN

In 1995, on an official visit to India, by chance I saw Field Marshal Sam Manekshaw at the Sheraton Hotel in New Delhi. I know New Delhi is hardly the Frontier, but since the Field Marshal spoke extensively of NWFP province, to which General Yahya also belonged, I feel I must mention it in this chapter. When I called his room from the hotel reception he answered 'Field Marshal', and later personally made me a cup of coffee. He was not condescending and tried to avoid the subject of the 1971 Indo-Pakistan war. He was brave enough to admit that Indian troops greatly outnumbered those from Pakistan by three to one in some sectors, while the disparity was much greater in most others. In a few sectors, the ratio favouring the Indians was as high as ten to one and at one place twenty-three Indians to one Pakistani soldier. The Field Marshal was a lively and interesting person. On hearing about my Frontier province background, he reminisced about his early days fondly, remembering the 5 Lockhart Lane house of 'Ganga', later General Mian Hayauddin, in the Peshawar Cantonment. He recalled Kohat, Bannu, and Zhob of the days gone by and was particularly keen to hear about the Late Justice Dorab Patel of Quetta.

Manekshaw spoke about his friendship with General Yahya Khan with considerable affection and narrated an amusing anecdote relating to the days immediately preceding the 1971 war. The Field Marshal mentioned that he told the returning Indian Military Attaché in Islamabad to convey his best wishes to General Yahya and his wife and to remind him that he was still waiting for 'his thousand rupees'. Just after Partition, when Yahya Khan was leaving for Pakistan, he requested Manekshaw to sell him his motorbike for a thousand rupees as he urgently needed conveyance. Manekshaw initially showed some reluctance at parting with the bike but relented on Yahya's insistence. He asked the latter to pay him immediately. Yahya took the bike, thought for a while and said 'actually Sam I do not

have a thousand rupees' but that he would send him the money as soon
as he reached Pakistan. Twenty-four years later, the Field Marshal recalled
laughingly, that he was still waiting for the money. It must be said to
Manekshaw's credit that he felt uncomfortable talking about the war and
showed extreme humility about the events, constantly reminding me a
number of times that it was an unequal contest.

The contest was also unequal in terms of competence and character of
the commanders. An Army officer once told me that Lieutenant General
Amir Abdullah Khan Niazi, the Commander Eastern Command, who
surrendered to the Indians in Dakka in 1971 was not considered fit to be
promoted from a major's rank, early in his career. He reportedly sought
the help of Lieutenant Colonel, later Lieutenant General Akhtar Hussain
Malik to intercede with Niazi's battalion commander to promote him to a
Lieutenant Colonel's rank and he was ultimately promoted. Akhtar jokingly
also mentioned in Punjabi *'is nay khitay gernail bana ay'* or who would make
him a general. The rest they say is history.

Decades later, General Sahibzada Yaqub, formerly the Corps Commander, told me there were no easy solutions to the difficulties in East
Pakistan but that these were made worse by the absence of clarity and
objective analysis of top commanders. On the lighter side, he said all
meetings with General Yahya Khan and others would almost always be
scheduled for the evening, for conducting business while sitting on casual
drawing room sofas. Before you knew it, whisky would be served, clouding
out any chance of clear straight thinking or objective planning. Straight-
backed chairs and a conference table may not have altered the course of
the war, but the commanders' mind-set and deliberations may have been
different. The whisky-induced 'Dutch courage' was mock audacity, an art
perfected by the Dutch themselves at Srebrenica in Bosnia decades later,
when they failed to prevent the massacre of 8,000 unarmed Muslims by
the Serbs.

Life is full of ironies and more so in General Yahya's case. After
Bangladesh was created and Zulfikar Ali Bhutto assumed power in Pakistan,
the former President General Yahya Khan was placed under house arrest in
a rest house in Abbottabad. There he would spend time gardening, much
like Napoleon in St. Helena. The rest house shared a boundary with the
Baloch Regimental mess, where in better days General Yahya, himself from

the Baloch Regiment, would be feted and regaled, as Pakistan Army Chief. During formal dinners for dignitaries at the Military Mess, the guests dined to the accompaniment of music and there was always a choice between the pipe and brass bands. How painful was it for the incarcerated General to hear the real music of life from such close quarters? It was during those days that the author, as a young Assistant Commissioner in Abbottabad received a petition from General Yahya's son requesting a permit to buy, on payment from the authorized shop, a tin of *ghee* (clarified butter), because there was an acute shortage in the market. Until a few months earlier the words of this General would have moved heaven and earth and here he was requesting something as small as a tin of *ghee*! Perhaps Shelley was right when he wrote philosophically:

> My name is Ozymandias, King of Kings;
> Look on my Works, ye Mighty, and despair!
> Nothing beside remains. Round the decay
> Of that colossal Wreck, boundless and bare
> The lone and level sands stretch far away.

Human glory was short lived as one was taught in school.

vii. An Earth Shaking Experience

In order to survive a variety of dangers in a third-world country like Pakistan, one needs to have lots of luck. A friend's mother, deep in conversation, leaned forward to listen to others in the group when a stray bullet hit her in the head. Had she been sitting upright on the *charpoy* (a traditional woven bed) she would have been alive today. Officers who served in the Tribal Areas were more likely to be a target of a sniper which would have ended many careers, if they are unlucky. Travelling by road in any mode in Pakistan is riskier than stray bullets. A long time back, General Naseerullah Babar, while appreciating the performance of a political agent in Orakzai Agency, cautioned him all the same 'because you are riding a tiger'. In government service, most officials, most of the time are either riding a tiger or are facing one! There are many risks to life and limb!

During the 1980s, the mountainous Chitral District may have held the world record in sheer number of dangerous mule tracks used for mechanized vehicles and yet, these were called roads. A loaded mule would have found the going tough particularly in Mastuj and Turko subdivisions in Chitral. In one stretch on the 'road' at Tao, you were no more than six inches away from the mountain side while on the other you could see the stream a few thousand feet below. There was no need to crane one's neck. To tackle the bends one had to apply forward and reverse gears repeatedly. It was therefore, close to madness that in 1981, as Deputy Commissioner Chitral, I decided to take a risky two hundred mile trip by jeep to Gilgit over the Shandur Top. Sensible people travelled by horse. The luxury of staying in Hunza Hut within the Chief Commissioner's residency, however, originally built for Prime Minister Zulfikar Ali Bhutto, was compensation enough for the arduous journey.

The next day while travelling to Hunza, our jeep had a puncture. As it was being replaced, we heard repeated mortar-like firing sounds from both sides of the valley. Everyone looked around in total confusion for the possible cause of the sound and then saw with horror heavy dust rising all over the mountain slopes. We were in the midst of a severe earthquake! A few minutes later, one could not see beyond a few feet while the pounding of the rocks, some bigger than the jeep, continued unabated. How one evades rocks in zero visibility was not a lesson taught in survival schools! Somehow we managed to climb the boundary wall of a small Army Engineers post and prayed that no falling rock had our names written on it. It was half an hour before the dust settled enough to see hundreds of rocks spread all over the place. Only then did we notice a couple of Army soldiers who were also perched on the boundary wall with us. One of them asked me what I did for a living and on being told that I was the Deputy Commissioner Chitral, had the presence of mind to spontaneously ask for a license for a rifle. Remarkable man with great initiative indeed! This led to others making similar requests, which were honoured later. It is sad to realize that there is total discretion of officials and politicians in Pakistan; that very few people can claim a gun license as a right? After the earthquake, the gun license requests were taken care of, and then there was the issue of climbing down from a wall that we had scaled within seconds, when danger stared us in the face. Someone had to place a chair next to the wall for the frightened souls to clamber down!

Discretion being the better part of valour, we decided to return to Chitral because the rough road and earthquake had sapped all our enthusiasm. Midway, there was some spirit left in us and we decided to fish for trout in the clear waters; every journey must have a high point! By evening as we crossed the Shandur plateau and reached the new wooden bridge in Mastuj, where there was another big blast awaiting us. As we prepared to cross the bridge, a loaded jeep from the opposite direction reached the bridge first. Surprisingly this jeep instead of driving across the sixty-foot bridge stopped in the middle while the driver got down to inspect the engine. This was very annoying for we were tired and weary having just braved an earthquake till we realized that the jeep had stalled and moments later, it caught fire. The deputy commissioner by law and convention is responsible for virtually everything happening in his district. Instinctively, I ran to the stranded jeep, now engulfed in a raging fire accompanied by officers, Major Zamir and Nasir the engineer, and we managed to push the burning jeep away from the bridge and doused the fire with our jackets and blankets. It was then that the jeep driver lifted the tarpaulin to reveal four barrels full of petrol he was transporting with the sides of the barrels already hot. This was a close call. The jeep and its cargo had been saved. Also saved, was the new bridge that had cost the government Rs. 3 million. More than anything else, all of us had escaped by the skin of our teeth. No medals were pinned on any chest because in Pakistan ribbons are often granted for 'personal' and 'political' reasons. However, the reward for a good deed, is having done it!

viii. *Laas Dai Azad* (GO TO HELL AND DO WHATEVER!)

The literal meaning of this title is *go to hell and do whatever*. I had just been posted as the Political Agent, Orakzai Agency, somewhat early in my career, since the total period of my service was less than three years. The elected member of the National Assembly from the area was a retired army officer who was then elevated to the position of Minister for Establishment, responsible for all federal government officials, including myself. He was a quiet gentleman and civil but the nature of a Political Agent's job was such that you could not please everyone all the time. Once, some elders from his Mullakhel tribe criticized the Political Agent in his presence for ignoring them deliberately and he reportedly told them that he 'would take care of me'. He might or might not have said these words and I doubt that he would have acted against me, but as a very young officer I remained worried. I did not want to be known as a 'loser', at least so early in my career. I called Mr Nasruminallah, the tough and dynamic Chief Secretary, to report the alleged meeting. He was busy and was only able to return my call at 1 a.m. When I informed him of what the Minister had said about me, his response was that I need not worry and then ordered me to see the Minister, right then, in the middle of the night to convey the Chief Secretary message *laas dai azad* in Pashto. This would have been one communication too many!

Relieved as I was, I must have laughed involuntarily which annoyed the Chief Secretary and he emphatically ordered that after I had conveyed the words to the Minister I was supposed to call him back that night. The matter ended there but I did not travel to communicate with the Minister. The situation however, became normal soon.

ix. HIGH RISK HONEYMOON

Not for anything has the phrase 'honeymoon period' been coined. In this instance, it happened literally. I had a miraculous escape from serious injury or worse, both physically and socially, only a month into my marriage while posted as the Political Agent, Mohmand Agency. Never in contemporary times, to rephrase Churchill's lines, has a newly wedded couple spent a honeymoon in a place more desolate, in an environment more barren, and surroundings more dangerous than in Agency headquarters at Ghallanai! The offices and residences of the officials were newly built in an amphitheatre-like compound surrounded by bare stony mountains. Water had to be transported from a distance of 5 miles. There were no trees, shrubs, or grass, instead there were plenty of snakes, scorpions, and spiders of the poisonous variety *ghandalay*. The newly built house of the Political Agent was on a knoll and the unimaginative architect who had designed it, put full length French windows all around the house. The Mohmand tribes are generally friendly people and all made the effort to make the place livable so that the administration of the Agency could be run smoothly, scorpions or no scorpions.

There was one eventuality we had not envisioned. Very late one night, when we were asleep, there was a deafening sound in our room as the heavy, wall to wall wooden ventilator frame, weighing a quarter ton, came crashing down missing the heads of the newly wedded couple by no more than a foot. Were the bed a foot closer to the wall, there would have been some explaining to do, but in a marriage so new a lot of questions would have been asked of the occupant of the house if there was a serious injury!

A week earlier, actually a day before the wedding, I faced a logistical problem which could not easily be resolved while living in an urban area. Over a hundred tribesmen I knew, decided to gift me a sheep each in accordance with their wedding customs. I was at my wits end not knowing where to keep the animals and how to maintain hygiene. There was only one way out; most of the gifts accordingly were gifted to friends while Saida Jan Shinwari made delectable *tikkas* and *laralay* of the remaining, for all and sundry.

x. The Chief Secretary Summons

Some people worry unnecessarily or take official business more seriously than is required. There are others who are committed to the dictum 'never do today what could be postponed till tomorrow'. I think I fall in the first category and have a real life situation as proof. Once, late in the day, while serving as Political Agent, Mohmand Agency, I was conveyed a message from the office of the Chief Secretary, Munir Hussain, to meet with him after the weekend. Munir Hussain was a kind and considerate officer but until I was ushered into his office, I remained deeply worried and anxious. I envisaged all the possible reasons why he wished to see and question me. Sleep eluded me for two days. Where did I go wrong? I practiced responses to all possible scenarios again and again. The fateful day arrived and I was shown into the presence of the provincial government's senior most officer. The few seconds before the conversation began, seemed like hours and then the Chief Secretary finally spoke. 'Well Shakil, I wanted to speak to you,' he started and then paused for a moment, making me even more miserable. 'I wanted to talk to you about arranging a duck shoot in the Warsak Lake as the area has had plenty of ducks in the past.' That is when I heaved a sigh of relief, sat back in the chair, put the teacup to my lips, and my confidence having been restored said, 'It will be a delight, Sir.' Moral to the story: Happiness is when the Chief Secretary speaks to you only about *shikar*!

Munir Hussain was one of the most gentle Chief Secretaries I have served, yet there was an occasion when I was severely shaken, by those sitting next to him. In 1976, following the civil disturbances in Upper Dir district regarding the forest royalty issue when the Army and Air Force undertook a military operation in the area. I had just returned from a holiday in the US and was urgently summoned to the Chief Secretary's office. There with him, were two close confidantes of the late Prime Minister Zulfikar Ali Bhutto, a politician, and a former police officer. After a brief discussion on the military action in the area, there were some laudatory words for me from the courteous Chief Secretary. This was like fattening the turkey before Thanksgiving. I was informed that the people of Dir district were very 'poor and deprived' who needed great care and support from the administration. It was then that I was told about being selected as the new Deputy Commissioner and that I was to ensure greater efficiency in performance of duties. Now the Dir district was always known as a troublesome and difficult place to administer but I concurred with the posting, as was expected of an officer. Just as I was leaving the office, one of the two persons volunteered the very loaded statement that the poor must be supported at all times and that workers of the Pakistan Peoples Party in Dir were 'poor and deprived'. At the time, I had no idea that Zulfikar Ali Bhutto was planning on holding General Elections in early 1977 but the statement made it clear that the powers that be, had some expectations from me to assist the ruling party in some ways. I was confused because the law differentiates only right from wrong and does not speak of any special assistance to be provided to the poor. I had five seconds to respond. The Almighty came to my rescue and provided me the strength to mumble the sentence, 'Sir I would do my best and there would never be any complaint against me of being partial towards any one'. Impartiality perhaps was not the uppermost concern in the minds of the two persons. In the aforementioned event I was never notified as the

Deputy Commissioner, as they were not looking for impartial officials. They were looking for pets!

xi. A Midnight Call from the President

The telephone call that really frightened me was the one I received when I was Deputy Commissioner, Chitral. This was from General Ziaul Haq, the military President of Pakistan, at midnight, during the dead of winter. The year was 1981, when the Soviet Union was firmly installed in Afghanistan, and I thought the President would inform me that the Soviet Union had invaded Chitral during the night. Short of that eventuality, the President of Pakistan would never call the Deputy Commissioner that late in the night. Would the President ask me why I was not aware of the invasion and if so, what would I say? Literally shivering because of the cold and the possible Soviet invasion with the telephone receiver held tight to my ear, I dreaded the questioning. In those days, Chitral town had ten telephone sets, with the Deputy Commissioner holding the telephone numbers one and two. Number one was under great stress at that moment. The telephone operator continued enquiring if his voice was audible and the technology was such that the voice would fade and appear, at intervals. He then connected me to the Military Secretary to the President who also asked if I could hear him clearly. I said yes and then the voice disappeared but by then it was too late and the President was on line. I heard him say in Urdu that he was Ziaul Haq speaking but then nothing was audible thereafter, for nearly half a minute. At that moment, I thought it was important to learn what the President was saying since the stakes were high for the country. I managed to mutter to the President that I was having difficulty hearing him. The President apparently annoyed said 'so rahay ho ya jag rahay ho' enquiring if I was awake or asleep. He should have known that no one sleeps when speaking to the highest in the land even though at that time only owls are awake. Anyway, I did hear the President mention the words *rawaiti mehmanawazi* or the traditional hospitality of the Frontier and was relieved that there was no Soviet invasion after all. One was not expected to be hospitable to invaders but then why did he call?

As I prepared to investigate the reason for the President's midnight call, Colonel Murad Nayyar of the Chitral Scouts and Brigadier Salauddin of the Frontier Works Organization telephoned and informed me that they too were called by the President. It then transpired that an important guest of the President was to visit Chitral the next morning and we wondered who it was that made him call three officials, in the middle of the night.

Early the next day, we were at the airport and as the Deputy Commissioner represented the state I thought I would present the guest a local *chuga* or gown made of hand-spun wool. The Commandant of the Scouts and the Brigadier would have none of it and insisted they offer similar presents to the valued guest. So there were three sets of gifts because these officers jokingly said '*hum nay be nokri banani hay*' or 'we need to be on the right side of the boss'. As the white Presidential Puma helicopter came in to land, we queued up to receive the important guest in quest of our *nokri* or the retention in service. A cameraman alighted with some equipment and a haversack on his back and one does not give much importance to a cameraman when a presidential guest is on board. After a minute, the pilot emerged and we eagerly enquired about 'the guest', and were informed that the man in jeans with the camera was actually the President's guest. We accordingly sprinted towards him, shook his hands with mock enthusiasm and forced three sets of gifts on him. The perplexed guest turned out to be a Mr O'Neill, Editor of the *Asia Week*, a soft spoken and courteous gentleman. In those days General Zia desperately cultivated foreign journalists because of his pariah status due to imposing Martial Law and hanging Mr Bhutto. So every foreign journalist was a valued guest.

Mr O'Neill was taken around to different places and served lunch at the Chitral Scouts Mess at Darosh, complete with a pipe band in attendance and the local Chitrali *stukk* dancing. One has to be really blessed to be served in style at the Darosh Mess. Mr O'Neill spoke to me at length on the proposed Lowari Tunnel and the war in Afghanistan. I think he gave me more time than he had given to the President himself. Next week when the *Asia Week* article appeared, there was a picture of me with supporting write-up but no mention of the President, which must have been very disturbing to him. The President's rights ostensibly were usurped by me but thankfully he did not mind. Often, retention in service or *nokri* is suspended by a thin thread in our country as the next anecdote explains.

xii. HANG THE DEPUTY COMMISSIONER!

In another episode in Chitral, the President from whom I had received a midnight call, threatened not just my job but my neck as well. A certain *Subedar* Dilawar of the Chitral Border Police did not wish to retire from service and every year before his date of retirement he would tamper with his service record, for a price, by lowering his age. Now Dilawar was an interesting and likable person but after a while this habit of his was becoming tiresome. He was finally retired, his papers completed and he started receiving his pension. But he still wanted to be back at his job and conceived an ingenious ploy to achieve it. During Ramadan, the month of fasting, *Subedar* Dilawar made his way to the small mosque inside the President House in Rawalpindi and shed a steady flow of crocodile tears as soon as he saw the President and began to criticize the Deputy Commissioner profusely. What apparently impressed the President most, was his claim of liberating Kargil as part of Brigadier Aslam's force during the 1948 War. The President immediately called me in Chitral but I was in America for my mother's treatment and this enraged the President further. Next he called the Commissioner Malakand Division, Islam Bahadur and severely castigated the 'cruel Deputy Commissioner' who was treating a *mujahid* improperly. The worst was still to come when he fumed that unless the issue was quickly rectified, he would 'hang' the Deputy Commissioner. When the Commissioner a few days later, informed me laughingly about the matter, I told him this was no laughing matter because the President means every word he says, having hanged Mr Bhutto a short time earlier. An enquiry later established that *Subedar* Dilawar was validly retired and General Fazle Haq had been very helpful in this regard. I was in a sense quite impressed by Dilawar for having thought of such a clever stratagem.

xiii. AN UNFLATTERING REPORT ON THE MILITARY

In 1982, the Defence Attachés of several embassies were visiting the Khyber Rifles in Landikotal for a routine round of presentations and festivities. At the eleventh hour, the British Military Attaché decided to travel by helicopter and directed his driver to bring the car from Peshawar. After the function ended and all guests had returned to Peshawar, it became apparent that the driver along with the official vehicle was missing and presumed to have been seized by offenders. The offence was serious, we all knew, but why was the Defence Attaché so deeply worried? Over the next forty-eight hours, the vehicle was traced and soon recovered along with the driver by the officials and the *Khassadars,* the tribal police.

As the vehicle was brought into the Roos-Keppel House—the official residence of the Political Agent, the Defence Attaché quickly lifted the boot of the car, opened a small briefcase and checked some papers inside. Finding these papers intact left him much relieved; he thanked those responsible for the car's recovery and left.

It was then that Zarif Khan Mohmand, the sharp and clever Political *Tehsildar* of Jamrud, handed me a sheaf of photocopied papers. He explained that before handing over the car, he had thoroughly checked it to ensure that there were no explosives placed. He also had the papers in the brief case photocopied for being 'case property'. One look at the 'case property' caused quite a flutter. It was a secret report on the capabilities and preparedness of Pakistan Defence Forces where the competence of some Generals was derided. The Pakistan Air Force was described as not quite a 'Sunday afternoon flying club' but not too professional either. I sent copies to all concerned but I assume the military was not too amused by what it stated about the Generals. This was the period when the Army was in power and General Ziaul Haq was lord and master. About the same time, the Siachen Heights were occupied forcibly by the Indians and General Ziaul Haq and his Generals got considerable flak for it. The British Military Attaché may well have been right about the quality of some of the Army Generals! The Pakistan Air Force, however, I think was unfairly commented upon in the report. This was the period when PAF started flying the F-16s, the Fighting Falcon jets, which had vanquished over a dozen Soviet Union planes in aerial combat, without a single loss.

xiv. The Commissioner's Jurisdiction

The people of Pakistan are easily governable if executive officers are fair and firm. In the past 150 years, the people have learnt to respect the law, while the law is expected to be impartial. Prior to this period, like a Mughal *mansabdar,* (a military unit within the administrative system of the Mughal

Empire introduced by Emperor Akbar), the Commisioner was suspect in the eyes of the people but once he proved his genuineness, the people's hospitality was overwhelming as I experienced.

As Commissioner, Kohat Division I once had to travel to Islamabad from Kohat over the Khushal Garh Bridge, an engineering marvel, while carrying a large amount of cash to make the down-payment for my brother's house in Islamabad. This was unwise on my part, as I forgot that banks existed in Kohat and Islamabad and I could have transferred the money. When I reached the outskirts of Jund village, I found the road blocked by thousands of irate people protesting against the local *Tehsildar*, a class-two magistrate, who had locked up a few shopkeepers on the charge of profiteering. Dozens of buses and cars were stranded on a hot summer day and the sufferings of the villagers were pretty apparent. In the intense heat the standoff had lasted some hours. On reaching, I introduced myself and tried to find out reasons for the road blockade. I volunteered to assist outside my jurisdiction on the condition that the crowd allow the traffic to move freely. It was then time, to establish contact with the other party, the Government officials, who had ensconced themselves in the nearby Union Council office. I approached them and introduced myself as the Commissioner, Kohat Division but I could gather that the *Tehsildar* was not too impressed. This was ominous because if the situation deteriorated, the angry crowd could have caused harm to the officials and the two policemen guarding them. Much as I tried, the *Tehsildar* was not amenable to reason even as I explained that he had no force with him and the immediate priority was to disperse the protestors peacefully and later to attend to the merits of the charge. The *Tehsildar* remained obstinate and was abusing people continuously as often happens in Punjab. I had to formally warn him against his conduct and threatened to inform his superior officers of the happenings. Still, there was no positive response. With no option remaining, I left the office to address the crowd telling them that I would report the entire episode to the Commissioner, Rawalpindi Division, Saeed Mehdi but with the request that they disperse peacefully. They agreed but I was a bit embarrassed when they raised full-throated slogans 'Commissioner Kohat *zinda baad*' or long live the Commissioner.

The road was cleared and as soon as I reached Rawalpindi, I contacted the Commissioner, Rawalpindi from some shop as this was before the advent of cell phones and provided him all the details. He was most grateful for my resolving the issue which was outside my jurisdiction, and according to law I could exercise authority only 'within my sphere of competence'. I learnt later, that the matter was subsequently resolved and a penalty imposed on the *Tehsildar*. Three lessons were gleaned from the experience. Firstly, that the particular *Tehsildar* was an idiot, secondly there is great importance in retaining All Pakistan Services, and thirdly that the Commissioner, Kohat was quite foolish in carrying heavy cash in an age of banks.

xv. A Public Park on Church Ground, Kohat

Most Pakistani generals wish to be remembered even if for non-military achievements. Welfare projects are closest to their hearts. This in effect, may be their alibi for not being remembered on a victory honour board. One General Officer Commanding, 9 (Fort) Division was no different. To be remembered as a builder, he wished to convert the large Church Grounds adjacent to the Inter-Service Selection Board in Kohat into a public park on 'self-help' basis. The good General conveyed his proposals to the Chief Minister, NWFP in a semi-official letter in the early 1990s but quite brazenly also asked for Rs. 10 million for the venture. 'Self-help' complemented by Rs. 10 million! The letter was marked to me as the Secretary, Tourism and Sports Department and I was at a loss to understand why the money was required when the land and the labour did not have a cost. I opposed the request, mentioning that the land and labour being free, the equipment could be installed by the private sector very conveniently at no cost. Deep foresight however, was one of Chief Minister's traits and he favoured the proposal 'because it was best to remain on the right side of Generals'. A decade later, I had to pay dearly for this slight. Fast forward to the coup led by General Musharraf, and the events of October 1999, the GOC was promoted as Corps Commander in Peshawar and I was the Additional Chief Secretary of Planning and Development in Khyber Pakhtunkhwa province and subsequently had to suffer for not supporting the 'self-help' proposal.

One of the first orders of the Corps Commander, now the *satrap* in the province, was to remove me from this post and to transfer me to the sublime post of officer on special duty (OSD), pending removal from the province. Fortunately, a week into the military rule, a Civil Service Officer named Abdullah was appointed Chief Secretary. Abdullah was a bold officer of impeccable integrity and character, who during his student days was a top English debater in the country, inspite of having studied in the local government schools. Courageous as always, the new Chief Secretary told the General that posting the Additional Chief Secretary out was a mistake and needed to be rectified. Since another officer had already been appointed to the post, they decided to create a new post of Additional Chief Secretary (Health) for me. Although, I was quite relieved to be offered another position, I did not accept it as it was junior to my former post.

Senior officers in the Secretariat urged me not to offend the military and to accept the position. Junior officers, as well as my children, were unanimous in their belief that it would be shameful to accept a lower post and that they would lose all respect were I to accept it. So, the new post, no matter how grand it sounded, was refused. The General was furious by the refusal as no 'bloody civilian' was expected to refuse the General's orders. The General waited for an opportunity to square up such a brash civil officer and soon found one. In a meeting with General Musharraf a few days later, he narrated the incident, saying that the officer had refused to obey orders and needed to be disciplined. General Musharraf, who styled himself the Chief Executive of the country (his was a modern day coup), did not support the logic of his Corps Commander. Candid as always, he reportedly told the Corps Commander that the officer's refusal was legitimate because, 'can you post a Major General to a Brigadier's post?' The crestfallen expressions of the Corps Commander were unfortunately not recorded by any photographer. I was grateful to General Musharraf!

xvi. HIGHJACK ALARM IN KABUL

The visit to Kabul was official although the delegation and Prime Minister Shaukat Aziz travelled by separate aircrafts. What struck me most about Afghanistan on my first visit to the country, was how dry it was compared to the greenery of Pakistan. Our country is clearly blessed by nature with abundant water, forested mountains, and fertile plains. One day I hope the two countries will cooperate to develop hydropower and water storages for the benefit of the people of both countries.

On arrival in Kabul, a caring individual had arranged a private dinner for the delegation with a choice menu meant to relax and revive the tired travellers. The meetings the next day kept every one so busy that the hotel staff was requested to pack our bags and send them directly to the airport. One bag somehow contained the remains of the beverage from the dinner. For the flight back home, the team was to travel by the Prime Minister's aircraft, everyone was asked to report early. One by one, the officials started boarding the aircraft but each refused the offer of the Embassy's well-meaning bearded Pakhtun Office Assistant of carrying their hand baggage up the stairs. Having seen half a dozen delegates turn down his request, I thought I would save him further embarrassment and allowed him to take my hand luggage inside the aircraft. He did that but then decided to take a leisurely stroll up and down the aisle till he reached the Prime Minister's seat. That was when the alarm bells rang and the security people woke up. The Assistant was immediately seized and frisked and so shaken was the poor soul he just could not remember whose bag he had brought in. Meanwhile, I was oblivious to the commotion and was catching up on newspapers of the past couple of days. The moment I saw him, I informed the security officials that he had carried my bag and that he was from the Embassy. Everyone started breathing more easily as the possibility of hijacking receded. Just then orders were announced on the public address system that all the luggage of the Federal Secretaries was to be removed from the plane and rechecked. Those junior to the Federal Secretaries were not covered by the order. The baggage was promptly removed and the plane started taxiing out when it was realized that the simple assistant was still on board. The pilot was told to stop the plane but by then the stairs had been removed by the ground staff. To save time, some clever bloke decided to land him on the tarmac the unconventional way and without the assistance of stairs. Accordingly, the aircraft door was opened and two security persons held him by his arms, while another two on ground carefully grabbed him by his feet all in full view of international camera crews. Anything can be expected from our national airline, even when the Prime Minister is on board!

The plane then took off and the Pakistani television started reporting the 'breaking news' of the presence of a 'terrorist' on board the Prime Minister's aircraft. The plane however reached Islamabad without any further drama save one. The senior-most officer in the country responsible for checking contraband articles, who was present at the dinner the night before, found to his disbelief that the remnants of the contraband was neatly packed by the hotel staff in his bag and placed in the Prime Minister's aircraft. That was indeed a narrow escape for him. The story had two morals. If you are allowed entry into a VIP plane, don't go about exploring, and more importantly pack your bag yourself.

xvii. You Scratch My Back and I'll Scratch Yours

There is a General Headquarters letter available in the Government Secretariat in Peshawar; I have the other copy which asks the provincial government to provide 10,000 acres of state-land free of cost in Dera Ismail Khan for distribution among senior military officers. The letter was as short as that. The military Governor of the province marked the letter to me as Chief Secretary for 'necessary action'. I thought this transfer was improper, that the land be used for the benefit of the province, and the matter kept pending. The Governor was keen that the land be transferred quickly. On the other hand, I wanted the matter delayed so that the new civilian government could reverse the decision, convinced that they would never countenance this transfer of state-land.

Soon the Log Area Commander visited my office and enquired under whose name my agricultural land totaling 1000 *kanals* or 125 acres in Dera Ismail Khan should be transferred to. I was taken by surprise, and plainly told him I had no land in Dera Ismail Khan and that is when the cat was out of the bag. He informed me smilingly that a certain senior officer, who was responsible for such matters in the GHQ, had offered this land to the Chief Secretary, in return for transferring the remaining 10,000 acres to the military. I was livid and told the brigadier that it was a shame he was trying to bribe the custodian of the properties of the provincial government. After the elections, the new Chief Minister was advised that this land should not be transferred free of cost for distribution among senior military officers. It was recommended that part of the land be allotted to the families of those killed in action, the *shaheeds* (martrys), of the three defense forces, the police, paramilitary, and civil government employees who died while performing their duty. The remaining land should be auctioned with the right of first refusal given to the local tenants and the money utilized to pay off provincial debt, which was around Rs. 60 billion. A short time later when the new civilian government assumed office, I thought as a religious-oriented entity it would not handover the state-land, in keeping with Islamic principles of equality and equity. I accordingly placed this issue at the top of the agenda for the first meeting of the provincial cabinet, convinced that the cabinet would reject it. It transpired that the cabinet supported the grant and appointed a committee under a senior minister to examine various options. The senior minister was not in any mood of denying the land to the military either. Bearing in mind the opposition of the Chief Secretary and the Senior Member Board of Revenue, he forwarded three options to the cabinet, i) the land may be transferred to the army, ii) the land not be transferred to the army, or iii) the land be put to any other use. So much for precision! Most politicians in Pakistan have little courage and here was another example. On my transfer from NWFP, I briefed the new Chief Secretary about the unjust and unfair proposal. Sometime later, the newspapers reported that the land was approved for distribution after all. Some of the dominant political and administration officials in the government at that time had also benefited from the *bandarbaant* (monkey business) award. It seems that my loss was someone else's gain; you scratch my back, I scratch yours, and between the two grab our land as well!

xviii. MAYDAY! MAYDAY!

One lesson that I would wish everyone learn and practice is to seek sound advice. However, there is an intrinsic problem with that, as one can only find out after the event what is and what is not sound. I have realized that in life the winners always and actively consult the wise. The losers think they know what is best for them and lose out in the process. Taking a decision purely on impulse and not seeking sound advice is often a recipe for failure. I was involved in a most harrowing and risky event which need not have occurred, had I accepted expert advice.

There were three of us who were to return from Gilgit in a small four-seater chartered plane to Islamabad after an official visit. The flight back could have ended in tragedy. Heavy clouds had started gathering as we got ready to takeoff in the afternoon and the senior pilot suggested we cancel the flight. As the senior-most officer in the group that had chartered the plane, I prevailed on the junior pilot to takeoff against the better advice of the senior pilot who too acquiesced to my decision against his better judgement. After takeoff the clouds continued to gather and soon visibility was near zero. The light plane could climb no higher than 18,000 feet while the surrounding peaks in the Chilas and Kaghan area were over 22,000 feet. For nearly forty-five minutes we were flying on autopilot without any visibility. A strong gust of wind could have pushed the plane into the mountain side but we were extremely lucky that day. My advice to all is that risks that can be avoided must be avoided and that never overrule the advice of those professionally and better qualified, in all walks of life. During the tense hour in the air, the two senior engineers from WAPDA, Dr Izhar and Abdul Khaliq, and myself decided to focus not on the surrounding dangers but we didn't know how to. We then found a way; we ate the last lunch if not the last supper! What better way to keep the unpleasant thoughts away than by eating from the lunch boxes that were provided?

Forty years earlier, when I was Assistant Commissioner in Abbottabad we were warned against crossing a flooded stream near Haripur but experienced advice was spurned with the driver Zardad insisting that the Toyota jeep HA 74 would ford through. Midway, the jeep got stuck and just then a huge wall of water turned the jeep over. I managed to get out quickly along with those in the back but it was quite an effort to pull old Zardad out. Was I more at fault than him?

There was another close call while travelling by a twin engine helicopter to the Diamer Basha dam site. This time, none on board was at fault, but all came perilously close to a crash. The Minister of Water and Power, Pervez Ashraf and the permanent secretary, Ismail Qureishi were on board with me in the helicopter loaned by the Prime Minister. After flying over the towns of Abbottabad and Battagram, as we neared the Indus River, I noticed a slight change in the whirring sound of the engine and saw the pilot turn left towards Tarbela rather than right towards Basha. I knew the area well

from my previous posting in Gilgit and immediately enquired from the
pilots, Majors Asad and Ahsan, if the going was good. Their thumb down
signal indicated that one of the engines had packed up and the pilots had
decided to return to base in Rawalpindi. I was concerned but not unduly
worried, knowing that the chances of a second engine failing were remote
and decided against informing the two important passengers who were
asleep. For them, ignorance was bliss but as I looked down I saw to my
horror a small graveyard right below us. Was there a message? I quickly
said a prayer and sought the blessings of the Almighty. After a while, the
minister and the secretary were informed of the engine failure and all of
us suggested to the pilots to land either on the cropped terraces or at the
runway close by in Tarbela. They did not approve of the idea, later telling
us that a helicopter uses maximum power both while rising and landing
and with only one engine left, they did not have the power to put the
helicopter down safely.

The hour before the helicopter arrived back at the Dhamial Base was the
longest I have known. Every minute was as long as an hour. Finally, we were
right over the base, but unknown to us there was another serious problem
to override. The helicopter had steel landing skids but no wheels, and which
meant that there was no guarantee the helicopter would stay upright and
more so that the landing friction could cause a fire. In the event, the senior
pilot very deftly and with our prayers landed smoothly even though the
helicopter skidded nearly fifty feet on the tarmac. It was only after we had
alighted from the helicopter that we became aware of the seriousness of the
event. When the pilots were asked if they had experienced a similar event,
their answer shook all of us as this was their first such experience! Small
wonder that shortly thereafter the Prime Minister got two new replacement
helicopters and never used the old one again. A prayer however, comes
readily for the dedicated Army Aviation pilots who daringly operate in the
skies in war time and in peace.

xix. A Chief Minister is Appointed

Just before the General Elections in 2013, Imran Khan, the famous
cricketer and chairman of Pakistan Tehreek-e-Insaf (PTI), a political party,
had a nasty fall while climbing up to a platform for a political rally. He

was rushed to the hospital. Having known him for twenty-five years or so I decided to visit and sympathize with him. I also wished to advise him to maintain very friendly relations with the federal government. During the conversation Imran sought my opinion on who should be the next Chief Minister of the Khyber province. He had a particular person in mind but I suggested the name of Pervez Khattak, a late entrant to Imran's party, yet one senior enough to be appointed the party's Secretary General. I told him that he had a fair reputation and that I was not aware of any scandal associated with his name either. I garnered another reason as well in support of my suggestion. I thought that were Pervez Khattak not appointed Chief Minister he would create, within twenty-four hours, a 'forward bloc' in the party with his supporters, join forces with other like-minded opposition members in the Khyber provincial assembly, and get himself nominated as Chief Minister. His extensive experience in political wheeling-dealing would ensure that he remained in power because no one minds at what cost one ascends to power, which is usually paid by the common people. No one is bothered by the absence of good governance. Pervez Khattak got the office but his administration remained marginal and unimpressive. Mounds of garbage and vast lakes of sewage were seen everywhere in the province while road traffic became a nightmare, especially due to the construction of the unsightly and costly elevated metro system. The sewerage rats got lucky and made a public comeback! There was said to be reduced higher-level corruption but in the main, no worthwhile improvement in governance was evident.

It was sad to see the continuation of the traditional political mind-set of the rulers with focus on nepotism, favouritism, and subjective decision-making to the detriment of good governance. During this period, I was appointed Chairman of the Board of the provincial Energy Development Organization, but with no salary or any other benefits, because of my experience in heading the huge Water and Power Authority earlier. I hastily resigned within a few months because of the Government's unwillingness to stem out incompetence and deviation from the rules in the organization. For instance, the PTI government awarded the Koto and Lawi hydro-power projects against the rules to a non-compliant Chinese company. Why, it may be asked? The biggest failure of Pervez Khattak's government lay in not developing the immense potential of the hydropower sector and in particular the Munda-Mohmand Dam. This was tragic, as the absence of the dam cost the state billions of rupees in lost revenue while cheap electricity could have been generated, forming the basis for industrial development. Foreign funding was available for the project which would have neutralized the dangers of floods in Peshawar valley, besides generating much needed financial profits for the country. Once a group of Chinese investors, wishing to invest one billion dollars in the province could not meet the Chief Minister after waiting for a week; the same team instead met Shahbaz Sharif, the Punjab Chief Minister, within twenty-four hours. So much for the *tabdili* or change that PTI had been loudly claiming. The lacklustre performance in the KPK province should be blamed on the sycophancy and ineptitude of Ministers, the relaxed approach of the Chief Minister, and the rank incompetence of the private-sector mercenaries appointed, especially in the power sector. The electorate in KPK normally does not give a second chance to an incumbent government but such was Imran Khan's charisma and commitment that his party was re-elected with a larger majority.

xx. Hajj: The Ultimate Experience

A friend of mine from the Punjab once told me that Pathans observe their daily prayers and fasting in Ramzan too seriously. He could have also added the performance of the obligatory Hajj pilgrimage to Makkah for those who could afford it. I wanted to send three or four persons, who did not have the financial means, in my place to perform Hajj. I thought this would bring great blessings to all. However, during the last year of his life, my father had suggested many times that I perform Hajj. After the decision was made for me, all the necessary preparations were finalized for my wife, Sabrina, and myself to travel to Madina Munawara, while experiencing the usual hassles of the local authorities retaining passports so that pilgrims do not stay back. The three days of prayers and *ibadat* right next to the Prophet's mosque were an enthralling experience. Then it was time to move to Makkah Mukarramah by coach. At the appointed time neither the travel agent, of a fickle and dishonest Pakistani company, nor the coach could be found. It arrived five hours late with the usual excuses our countrymen are capable of concocting. The vehicle must have been one of the most obsolete, still on road, but for intending *hajis,* there was no choice. The thermostat did not work either. One moment it became freezing cold and then it became searing hot. The temperature variations continued all the way to Makkah Mukarramah. Morning saw us arrive at our destination, a triple-storied rented building without lifts and with sewage flowing into the rooms. Our group simply refused to move in and for good reason too. I was horrified to learn that the additional payments I made for a room in the five-star hotel, extremely close to the Khana Kaaba, was not even booked for me. After much debate, we were all taken to the office of our *muallim,* a Saudi man of great influence, but with little concern. As tea was being served, we learnt that an older woman from Mardan who had travelled in our bus had died probably due to exhaustion and exertion of travel by road. It was sad that someone who had come with hopes of performing Hajj would depart forever, so suddenly. As we were discussing burial arrangements with their family, my wife collapsed and fell to the ground. An ambulance quickly arrived to take us, clad in our *ahrams* to the nearby Al Nur Hospital. I was at my wits end, deeply shaken at the prospects of returning home without performing the pilgrimage. The thought was not a happy one for me as many people would enjoy my discomfiture. The inevitable comment would have been that Providence had made sure that I did not fulfill the Hajj obligations. So near and yet so far!

Deeply worried and confused, I prayed to the Almighty and to the Holy Prophet Muhammad (PBUH), from my heart, to save me the stigma of returning without doing Hajj. I then called Major Tariq, my Staff Officer in Pakistan, who picked up the telephone at the first ring and he immediately contacted my cousin Bilal who had a friend in Makkah Mukarramah. Now Bilal, a gentleman at large, normally wakes up around noon and turns off his telephones at night. Thankfully that morning, he answered the phone promptly and in turn contacted the caring brothers Tariq and Tanvir, sons of the very hospitable Chaudhry Nazir. They immediately contacted Khalid, an engineer working with their company in Makkah. All this must have taken less than fifteen minutes and soon Khalid, a real saint for me, arrived at the hospital. By then the doctors had revived my wife who was tired and dehydrated but on her feet. Khalid took us to their guest house and ushered us into a very large room containing all manners of food and beverages, notably *laban* the yogurt drink. The domestic help, originally

from Maralla near Sialkot, served us a princely breakfast of *parathas* with
omelette which was most appropriate for dehydrated pilgrims who had
the misfortune of trusting Pakistani travel agents. Recovered and rested,
we undertook the obligatory practices so much so that the *Tawaaf* around
Khana Kaaba and *Sai* between Safa and Marwa was done comfortably. The
stay in Mina was equally a blessing and so was the sojourn at Arafat and
Muzdalifah. We were amongst the first few to leave Muzdalifah for *rajam*
or the ritual stoning of Satan. The initial travails notwithstanding, few
people in life would have performed Hajj in such seven-star comfort and
I could never thank the Almighty enough for making it all possible for us.

Life is all about struggles and there remained two such tests before
the Hajj could be completed. The *Tawaaf-e-Ziarat*, the final ritual of
seven circumambulations of the Khana Kaaba, is mandatory and the large
numbers of Hajjis in the compound, means that only the physically fit are
in a position to complete the rounds and at least once get to touch the
blessed House. Near the end of the sixth circumambulation, I felt that my
wife's grip had slackened and then I realized that she had almost fainted.
I wrapped my arm around her and somehow managed to keep her on her
feet, while dragging her along in the multitude Hajjis. I am convinced
that I had Divine help. Moving a near unconscious person fifty yards out
of a milling crowd to safety, was one of the most arduous experiences of
my life. The moving multitude could not stop to provide us space even if
they wanted to be helpful and a fall meant instant trampling by thousands.
I had the Almighty on my side and I said another prayer from my heart.
The prayers were answered and slowly and gradually, I managed to reach
the safety of the steps where Saudi medics provided relief.

I remain convinced that Providence alone made Hajj possible in such
great comfort. I recalled that two decades earlier I had travelled to Makkah
with a delegation of journalists for Umrah. The leader of our delegation,
Hajji Javed, the Provincial Minister for Information, had informed Saudi
Protocol about our visit moments before our departure. For reasons no one
knew, Saudi Protocol decided to treat the delegation as royal guests. One
moment, we were carrying our luggage to the coaches to take us to the
hotel and the next we experienced big limousines at the tarmac, staying at
the royal *Qasr-e-Ziyafa* adjacent to the Khana Kaaba, and all else that goes
with being guests of the king. Providence was indeed helpful.

The Hajj was over, and it was time to leave for the airport. If I thought that our troubles were over, I was mistaken because the Saudi Airways was determined to provide us one parting 'gift'. For reasons that no one could fathom, then or now, the airline decided that there would be 'free seating' for all passengers in the aircraft and that economy class passengers could sit in business class seats if they got there first. The certified Pakistani Hajjis accordingly made a lunge for the business class seats which was a sickening sight. I was prepared to accept this inequity only if it would hasten my return home but the fellow business class passengers steadfastly refused to countenance the injustice of free seating. It was another two hours before the higher management of the airline took the considered decision that all passengers would sit in their respective seats and all complied reluctantly. Delay and frustration apart, I have often pondered over those bizarre orders which no thoughtful person would have ever taken in the first place. Arriving home was the greatest relief.

Part 2

Romance of the Frontier

4

The Former Princely States: Chitral, Swat, and Dir

i. CHITRAL

There is a mystique and romance about the three former princely states of Chitral, Swat, and Dir which have engaged outsiders for centuries. Their history is extraordinary, their geography inviting, the climate mild, and the inhabitants distinct from other people in the country. The three states are also quite different from each other. In 1970, the former states of Chitral, Swat, and Dir became the Provincially Administered Tribal Areas (PATA), and also a part of Khyber Pakhtunkhwa Province as regular districts with representation in the Provincial Assembly. This new name, given without a consensus, is devoid of the romance that the frontier conjures. These districts are subject to the High Court and almost all regular laws apply except those relating to taxation. The Criminal and Civil Procedure Codes have been extended, and also the *Nizam-i-Adal*, which is the Islamic Sharia law. Before the merger of the princely states there was little crime but over the past half a century serious crime has soared and the social stability that once existed is gradually disappearing.

Chitral District is situated on the Chitral River in northern Khyber Pakhtunkhwa. Its climate is alpine, the rivers are stocked with trout, while the hills and ponds abound with exotic winged wildlife. This is also the place, where the rarest of the big cats, the snow leopard, was first filmed in the wilds by George Schaller, world's preeminent field biologist studying wildlife throughout Africa, Asia, and South America. The snow leopard, or *purdam* as the locals call it, would often wander into the Deputy Commissioner's bungalow during the winter. On one occasion, the guard on duty apologized to me, regretting not shooting the animal during the night, and pledged that next time no lapse would occur. He was warned that were he to shoot a leopard, there would also be one guard less the next

110

day! This is also the District with the fabled Tirich Mir, the 26,000 feet peak, which was my morning's first inspiration from the bedroom window of the deputy commissioner's house. A foreign visitor thought the view was worth a million dollars, which was just as well, as the monthly salary of the occupant at that time, was not more than US$200. I always found Chitral, a dreamy place straight out of fairy tales. What more could one want than to spend two years there and reminisce about it, for the rest of one's life, and that too at the cost of the state?

There are over a hundred districts in Pakistan, but Chitral is special as the land, people, and culture are in a class by themselves. Most of the inhabitants are *Khawars* of Central Asia with their own language and a very distinct lifestyle and culture. In the South, there are some Pakhtuns and along the western border with Afghanistan, survive four thousand Kalash people. On return from England after a post-graduate degree in Development Economics and Project Planning, the Governor of the Frontier province, General Fazle Haq, offered me a choice of posting between Bajaur, Mansehra, and Chitral. Chitral obviously, was my first choice and thus began a very close and memorable association with the people and the area.

The Chitralis are trustworthy and friendly and absolutely adore the outdoors. Thousands of businesses in Peshawar and Karachi are left to Chitrali accountants and salesmen, without any complaints of theft or misappropriation of goods. Although, there must have been at least one crooked person in Chitral—the one who stole the copy of a hand-written Quran that I presented to the Shahi Mosque.

The Mehtar of Chitral was the state's hereditary ruler, until Chitral was merged with Pakistan in 1970. Included among his many duties (of sorts), was one of contracting multiple marriages and therefore, it is not surprising to see a disproportionate number of princes and royals from the Katoor Dynasty. It is alleged that they were masters in cunning, treachery and intrigue, with poison being one of the favoured means of conducting affairs of the state while settling inheritances and other differences. This was very convenient too, as the brother or the cousin was eliminated with no shots fired and there was no trace of blood either. Plausible deniability, was first perfected by these rulers.

The history of Chitral from the final years of the nineteenth century onwards has been absorbing. In 1892, following the death of the Mehtar Aman ul-Mulk, there was extensive civil strife and various pretenders sought to gain the throne. This was too good an opportunity for Umra Khan, the Nawab of Jandul, which was near the state of Dir, and for the Afghans to miss. Umra Khan besieged Naghore, the fort in Chitral in 1895. The skirmishes continued for days in which Surgeon Captain Harry Frederick Whitchurch was awarded the Victoria Cross, close to where the Deputy Commissioner House is now situated. The small detachment of British troops under Captain Townsend had no option but to seek shelter in the fort and await the arrival of reinforcements from British India. Two columns were assembled for providing relief. The lighter one under Colonel Kelly moved from Kashmir to Gilgit, braved the Shandur Top snows in the winters and arrived in the nick of time, to save the besieged garrison compelling Umra Khan to retreat to Jandul. My maternal grandfather Abdul Hakim, of the Samana Rifles and Border Police, was part of this column. The defense and then the relief of Chitral was a story of heroism with few parallels in modern times. The British remembered the courage and sacrifices of the officers and troops who remained steadfast during the siege. A Russel terrier, Buddy, belonging to one of the British officers, had its name recorded in the history books by being awarded an Indian Service Medal with the medal clasp 'Relief of Chitral'. Over a century later in Afghanistan, Sasha, a Labrador, was awarded the Dickin Medal, the animals' Victoria Cross, for detecting explosives in many places and saving lives. The 'Brits' are really an eccentric lot!

A month later, a larger force under General Sir Robert Low, after fighting a number of battles in Malakand and Dir, entered Chitral through the Lowari Pass. The force was to prove the resolve of the British Government to defend every single British Indian Army soldier, regardless of the cost. They lost Colonel Battye commanding officer of Queen Victoria's Corps of the Guides near Jandul but the advance continued. The memory of the siege of Chitral remained etched in the mind of Captain Townsend and two decades later during the First World War, he rose to the rank of Major General, only to surrender at the siege of Kut in Mesopotamia to the Ottoman Turks. His command of the garrison was severely criticized, but in his defence, it was pointed out, that the psychological influence of the siege of Chitral in 1895, persisted.

In the years following the retreat of Umra Khan, one of his sons, also known as Jandul Khan, settled permanently in Chitral. During his advancing years, we would often meet while I was the Deputy Commissioner. A few years later, on my promotion as Commissioner Malakand Division, and during a tour of Chitral, Jandul Khan came to call on me. He was most excited, effusive, and at the same time short of breath as he had so much to say. In the middle of the conversation, he tried to get up, closed his eyes, collapsed in my arms, and died in the same Deputy Commissioner's office where in happier times he had recounted tales from the past. Such is life! Latif Khan, the son of Jandul Khan, was a police officer who kept in touch for old times' sake. With some people, friendship ranked just below faith among the ultimate values. The elderly Chiragh Hussain of Sweer was another such friend.

The Chitralis are law-abiding and peaceful people but are excitable as well. Once in a while they do get worked up but never more than when the daily flight is cancelled, due to inclement weather, in winters. In those days, it meant no newspapers, no fresh vegetables, and the feeling of being completely isolated from the rest of the country, as the only land link through the Lowari Pass is usually closed because of snow. This was when the Chitralis would protest loudly and raise slogans, bordering on sedition. One way they would vent their frustration was, by sticking anonymous notes on the dangerously tilted wooden bridge, conveying light hearted criticism and threats, against the administration. Only rarely would matters boil over when a crowd would organize a protest demonstration. They once surrounded the helicopter of the Inspector General of Frontier Corps, Naseerullah Babar with the intention to burn it. Many years later, a group threatened to march to the Deputy Commissioner's bungalow to protest. The march was stopped, after strategically placing a machine gun manned by a professional local soldier, Major Sardar of the Chitral Scouts, who refused to be taken in by pleas of the common cause against outsiders. On another occasion, the students of the local college locked up their principal for failing to resolve some real or imagined grievances. The Assistant Commissioner was sent to free him and settle the issue. He, too, was locked up but he refused to use force to free the principal. As Deputy

Commissioner, I had no option but to sort things out myself. I went in alone, keeping the police away from the students in order not to provoke them further. Muhammad Khan, the driver, insisted that I take my Luger pistol, which he offered to carry to the college—'corral' at high noon! The negotiations soon turned friendly, and thankfully there was no gunfight at sunset!

Most Chitralis appear to be quite different from the rest of the people in the country. Virtually, everyone can dance, sing, or play a musical instrument. Many still brew their own wine. One Chitrali fooled the French Ambassador to India. He mistook Shahzada Burhanuddin's 'shagore' water for an Italian brew. Italian, he insisted, but not a French wine to be sure! The French and the Japanese, more than other foreigners, adored Chitral, especially the Kalash people. Occassionaly, the tourists got more than they expected. There were these two petite Japanese girls, Keiko Murase and Keiko Shinamura, who fell in love with Chitral but got the shock of their lives when they were woken up in the middle of the night by the Senior Civil Judge. The judge, perhaps, had other ideas and was not known to be very stable. He insisted on verifying the girls' visas, even though he had no authority to do so. With the greatest of difficulty, they managed to ward off danger and informed the authorities. The matter was then reported to the High Court and the judge was disciplined and removed.

The Chitralis absolutely love outdoor activity. The polo season starts officially on Nowruz, the 21st of March, the first day in the Persian calendar with the Deputy Commissioner, astride his charger, leading the horsemen to the polo ground. Half the town turns up for the polo matches. In Booni and the northern villages, even the womenfolk come out to watch the matches.

Everyone looks forward to springtime when the 'leaf of the Chinar tree is as big as a child's hand'. The two top teams, Jang Bazaar, sponsored by the Deputy Commissioner, and Chitral Scouts attract large crowds. All teams along with players, sports enthusiasts and dignitaries first assemble at the Town Hall in the afternoon. After refreshments, the assembled teams move on horseback, to the beat of the drum. Most Deputy Commissioners endear themselves to the people, if they can ride a horse and play polo. Top polo players like old Muzaffar, his son Maqbool, Sikander-ul-Mulk, Ayyaz and Saeed were held in great public esteem. Many polo players were of modest means but would save every rupee to maintain a horse. There were others like *Subedar* Sarwar Lal of Reshun who loved horses and pedigree dogs. The good *Subedar*, who could only speak Chitrali, once offered to gift his springer spaniel to me as it was rare for a Deputy Commissioner to visit a far-off village. I declined the offer, and reminded him that giving away a pet dog is like giving away a child. A few days later, the same dog was found with an officer of the Chitral Scouts who had earlier accompanied me to the village! The Scouts officer was admonished for accepting the pet as a gift which he unconvincingly said, had been forced upon him by the *Subedar*. The officer may not have been very truthful, but he was now the official owner of a lovely dog! Those in Chitral who do not appreciate polo, switch to football or the blood sports of fishing and hunting for ibex, water fowl, and *chukar* partridge or the chakor.

Paradise Lost

Kalash: The Paradise Lost (1992) is a book about the plight of the Kalash people of Chitral, written by Mohammad Alaudin of the Civil Service of Pakistan. The book laments the fact that the state has largely ignored the institutional efforts in ensuring the Kalash peoples survival. The main reason why Chitral is such an enchanting place for tourists is because of the presence of the Kalash people, but sadly their numbers continue to decline. Some historians trace their lineage to the Greeks, descendants of Alexander the Great, as many of them are fair-complexioned, blue-eyed, and blonde. Rudyard Kipling may have been inspired by them for his novella *The Man Who Would Be King*. Whatever their origins, they remain one of the most fascinating people in the country. Song and dance is in their blood and there is much rejoicing at festivals marking the four reasons.

There is little or no crime among the Kalash people, unless one considers a wife voluntarily leaving her husband for another man, a crime. In such cases, which are common, the new husband pays twice the bride's price to the former husband and everyone goes home happy. However, there have been many cases where after their conversion to Islam, the erstwhile Kalash take to serious crime. Many years ago, a Swiss couple trekking in the Kalash Valleys, who had an expensive camera and other valuable items, were murdered by their guides who were recent converts. They then fled across the border to Afghanistan. The administration sent a team led by *Havaldar* Shahab of the Chitral Border Police, the Deputy Commissioner's force, to arrest the culprits and bring them to trial. While the two culprits were being brought back, one of them attempted suicide by trying to crush his manhood with a rock. He survived the attempt and was sent to the gallows, after being sentenced by the court. He could have jumped down a ravine to kill himself but then perhaps he had his brains in the wrong place!

The population of Kalash people appears to have plateaued and they number approximately 4000 men, women, and children. Their cousins, the 'Red Kalash', who lived in Afghanistan, were all forcibly converted, killed, or exiled by Amir Abdul Rehman Khan at the end of the nineteenth century. The Kalash people, survived because of the tolerance of the Mehtar of Chitral, Sir Shuja ul-Mulk, and the benign presence of the British Administration. They survived, but just barely, as there still is considerable discrimination against them. This is clearly apparent from their socio-economic indicators: lower life span, poor health and education levels, limited employment opportunities and low income earnings.

The Kalash Environmental Protection Society was established by the late Maureen Lines, formerly from Hampshire in England and later a Pakistani citizen, with the support of Raza Kuli Khan, MP Bhandara, and the author, to assist the Kalash people in coping with the pressures and challenges of life. Those who know the Kalash well, realize that they are their own worst enemies. The few among them who are educated or are economically well off, remain self-centred and have little time or care for ordinary Kalash people. Foreign researchers and academicians are also to blame. They undertake research, write their books and research papers, but this scholarship has not benefited the Kalash. Pakistani tourists are a double-edged sword, as they behave in the most uncivilized manner, having heard of titillating, but untrue tales, about Kalash women. They visit in droves and are very noisy but inspite of the tourist trade, the economic conditions of the Kalash do not seem to improve. Money spent by tourists, benefits the non-Kalash, as the tourist trade, the taxi-jeeps, and restaurants mostly do not belong to Kalash people. The main fault lies with the provincial government and a succession of deputy commissioners of Chitral who have been guilty of dereliction of duty towards the minorities. Little has been done for the welfare and survival of these indigenous and vibrant people living in their idyllic surroundings and valleys. Their school teachers were non-Kalash, who were inconsiderate of their traditional beliefs. At times they have been known to use insulting language with small Kalash boys and girls. In the late 1990s, a development project was started to train Kalash teachers for their schools. But such was the apathy of the average Deputy Commissioner that it would be a miracle if the scheme is still working. Chitral also receives another type of tourists, the perverse type, who wish to buy beautiful brides often for men three times the girl's age. Once, a famous film comedian from Lahore arrived in Chitral, in a very non-comic role. He was accompanied by an Arab who was looking for his 'nth' wife. Such people, on occasions, would buy Chitrali girls ostensibly for marriage, misuse them and then sold them for other purposes. The comedian and his partner were detained and put on the next flight back. Why would a Pakistani pander to the desires of a foreigner at the cost of someone's life? Earlier, an American had cunningly married a Chitrali girl, and after a while, left her in dire circumstances in New York. Were it not for the assistance of some fellow countrymen, her nightmare would have lasted a long time.

Perhaps the best stroke of luck the Kalash ever experienced was the grant of Rs. 5 million by President Ziaul Haq for saving their walnut trees which were mortgaged to the Muslims of Ayun and other places. This was a worthy act of a General known to be a fundamentalist. In 1981, the proposal of the Deputy Commissioner was followed up by the energetic and well-meaning Governor of the Frontier, General Fazle Haq. The Kalash people, unfortunately, know no thrift and spent much more than they earn. They would mortgage the fruits of their walnut trees for petty amounts, running into a few hundred rupees to outsiders. One Kalash man reportedly mortgaged his walnut tree for the cost of a *pakol*, a Chitrali cap. Under the Walnut Tree Redemption Policy, the government redeemed all these trees by providing a one-time grant. It was felt that now the Kalash would be free to invest the profits earned from the sale of walnuts into productive income-generating venture. This was not to be. Most of them promptly re-mortgaged their trees to the same people. This was frustrating as people who do not want to rid themselves of poverty, cannot be helped. Moreover, the money allocated for the Kalash is, more often than not, misused on fancy projects or those unrelated to core issues. Most visitors to Kalash valley, both locals and foreigners, are uncaring, and offer some sympathy but nothing material to these people. The wife of a top British executive of the Imperial Chemical Industry, for instance, once donated a sum of Rs. 10 for the Kalash Fund. This, in those days, amounted to one-fifth of a pound sterling. This was very generous of her indeed and as they say in Pushto, *'piyaz ee pa niyaz ee'*, or even an offering of an onion is a gift from the heart.

In 1981, a museum with Kalash artefacts was constructed near the polo ground on land that was donated by Shahzada Asad ul-Mulk, to encourage tourism and a better understanding of the Kalash and the Chitrali people. In a bizarre move a few years later, the Deputy Commissioner decided to convert the museum into a thermal power station to ingratiate himself with the rulers of the day. Some years later, the Commissioner of Malakand Division restored the museum to the relief of all.

Polo Tournament at 12,000 Feet above Sea Level

Chitral is also famous for the Shandur Top 'rough and tough' polo. This sport of the kings originated perhaps not too far from this area. Lieutenant Colonel Cobb, an Assistant Political Agent in Chitral, who later became the Political Agent of Malakand Agency and was the pioneer of polo festivities during the 1930s. Friendly polo matches were played in the summer on the Shandur Top at an altitude of 12,500 feet. The Top formed the border and the watershed between Chitral and Gilgit. This amazing plateau, a few miles long, has the world's highest polo ground. These polo matches were discontinued after Independence but were resumed as an annual event in 1981 while I was the Deputy Commissioner. There are thousands of people from Chitral, Gilgit, and overseas who visit Shandur during the second week of July to attend the Shandur Polo Tournament. The whole area takes on the look of an army encampment with food, drinks, and other items sold in a makeshift bazaar, which lasts for a week. Minor league matches are followed by the main Chitral versus Gilgit final which is always very keenly contested. The Deputy Commissioner of Chitral is expected to support his side. But if the same officer is transferred as Chief Commissioner of Gilgit-Baltistan, the Chitralis are upset when he roots for his new team. This is the local people's sense of ownership over some officers.

Thirty years after the highly contested polo matches resumed at Shandur, it was noted by the enthusiasts of the game that competitive fast-paced polo was not meant to be played at such a high altitude. Many horses collapsed and died due to the lack of oxygen. There should only be friendly polo matches in Shandur and the horses need to be changed at short intervals. It is however, most gratifying, to see so many people from Chitral and Gilgit and from different parts of the country, congregate at Shandur in a picnic-like atmosphere to regale themselves. Interestingly, Shandur Top, since the mid-eighties has its own five-hole golf course that was created beside the lake.

The golf course was especially made for General Ziaul Haq, who was the guest of honour that year. The Pakistani underlings, military or civil, do not waste any opportunity in ingratiating themselves with the high and the mighty! Despite the golf, polo, and a lunch fit for royalty, General Ziaul Haq lost his temper during this visit. In the welcome address, a local politician bemoaning the non-fulfillment of some promises made by the President a year earlier, innocently mentioned that his critics were right when they said 'that you, Mr President, do not honour your promises'. Now this really incensed 'Mr President' who was also the Chief Martial Law Administrator or CMLA, which people translated as 'Cancel My Last Announcement'. The local politician got the tongue-lashing of his life.

Sadly for Shandur Top, the Chitral Scouts and later a Deputy Commissioner during the 1980s, added a grotesque concrete structure with some latrines which were prominently visible from afar, the most pristine area of the country. A latrine or two could be built but it should have been concealed and tucked under some rocky outcrop so that the undulating landscape retained its purity.

The Commandant of Chitral Scouts

No story about Chitral is complete without mentioning the late Lieutenant Colonel Murad Nayyar, Commandant of the Chitral Scouts for nearly ten years. After his initial three-year tenure ended, President Ziaul Haq granted him an extension, and then further extensions continued. The

1980s were a difficult period for Pakistan following the Soviet Union's invasion of Afghanistan and the subsequent flow of five million refugees to Pakistan. The first refugees arrived in Chitral and the local administration and the Scouts remained busy for the next decade, providing them logistics. Colonel Murad was also responsible for increasing the size of Chitral Scouts from three to six wings that not only provided local employment but also strengthened the border posts. The credit belongs to the Colonel for building defense bunkers on the borders and for the living accommodations he developed for his troops. The Chitral Scout Messes at Chitral and Drosh owe their smart look to him where civil and Scout officers, along with Shahzadas Shams and Siraj, spent many an evening regaling in song and *stukk*, the local dance.

Colonel Murad belonged to Piffers—the Punjab Irregular Frontier Force—a Frontier Force Regiment very proud of its history. He was from Gujrat in Punjab but spoke fluent Pashto. He brought back memories of the British Army officers of the distant past like Lumsden and Warburton, of Battye and Nicholson, who had spent a lifetime with their troops administering the tribes. The people of Chitral, despite their generosity had one failing and I hope over the years this would be made good. They would seldom donate blood. Once the Chitral Scouts personnel refused to provide blood, following an emergency, when a group of people were trapped and injured trying to cross the Lowari Top in winter. A final warning was issued to the Scouts to donate blood but on their refusal, they were cashiered from service. An outsider was intrigued as to the reason behind it. He was told that the people believed that ten drops of *ghee* or animal fat produces one drop of blood and ten drops of blood produces one drop of the seed of life in a male. Such was the priority placed on human life compared to the human seed!

In 1989, following General Ziaul Haq's death, Colonel Murad's tenure finally came to an end. For a few months before he retired, he was a changed man, abstaining from the many blessings of life. Once in the presence of many people, he boldly enquired from a doctor what part of the body should be aimed at for ensuring instant death. He felt that life after a long command in Chitral Scouts would not be worth much as he did not want to be involved in finding rented accommodation, a cook, a *dhobi*, a barber, a doctor, and so forth. The night before he was to retire, he left his will in his briefcase and shot himself in the head. He had willed his limited property to his sisters, his belongings and his books to those who had served him. He lies buried on the banks of the Chitral River in Drosh, where he spent his best years.

The Legendary Major Langlands

Easily the most famous person in Chitral was Major Geoffrey Langlands, the Principal of the Langland School and College. He served as a commando in the British Army during the Second World War and after early retirement and on the suggestion of General Ayub Khan, joined Aitchison College in Lahore as a teacher. During summer vacations, he would trek in the mountains of Swat, Chitral, and Gilgit, and train urban Aitchisonians in the outdoors. Later, he became Principal of Razmak Cadet College in Waziristan, a tough assignment even for a commando. How tough life was in Waziristan, he soon found out when he was kidnapped by local tribesman, but was released shortly thereafter. He was then offered the position of Principal at the Public School in Chitral established by a deputy commissioner. Major Langlands was principal for nearly a quarter of a century and during this period, he developed this school into a first-class institution with emphasis on academic achievements. Grooming young people as conscientious and confident members of society was a priority for him. Students from this school have done well in life and shine as examples of the rewards that quality education bestows. In its initial years, British university students taking time off would often spend a year or two as volunteer teachers in this school.

Owing to his decades of devoted service, Geoffrey Langlands always had a big advantage over others in collecting grants and donations for the college. In 2013, he was succeeded by another educationist from Britain, Carey Schofield, who had served in the school earlier. In 2019, Major Langlands passed away at the grand age of one hundred and one and was greatly mourned by all Pakistanis who knew him or had heard of him.

A Princess visits Chitral

The former princely state of Chitral waited a long time for a visit by a Princess, and Lady Diana was no ordinary Princess. In the summer of

1991, the most famous and adored person on the planet finally came to visit Chitral. Ten minutes before her plane was to land, the administration was informed that the visit was cancelled because of low clouds. There was disappointment all around but suddenly the Princess's aircraft appeared. The British plan their events well in advance and I remember Sir Nicholas Barrington, the British High Commissioner, enquiring a year earlier if it was possible for the Princess to visit Chitral.

A dispute arose straightaway between the civil administration and the military on the visit. The Chitral Scouts, a paramilitary unit, proposed that in view of the security, protocol and other facilities available with them, the royal programme should be conducted in the Chitral Scouts Mess. The Tudor-style Officers Mess of the Chitral Scouts was undoubtedly impressive, more so because as legend has it, its foundations were 'well and truly laid' over bottles of champagne. But after considerable lobbying, it was decided that her programme would be confined to the imposing lawns of the Deputy Commissioner's House. The House was nearly a century old and though renovated in 1981, it retained its imposing style. There were seven terraces in the compound including one each for a tennis court and a swimming pool. There were three majestic towering *Chinar* trees, much like the Sycamore tree, hundreds of years old, under which the royal party was seated. A troupe of Kalash girls had been invited to perform their traditional dance but the main purpose was to introduce them to the Princess. The Princess was presented with a hand-woven ladies *chuga*, a Chitrali gown, and the Chitral Scout's iconic cap with the regimental insignia and plume by the Commandant of Chitral Scouts. She liked the gifts and looked resplendent in the *chuga* and the Chitral Scouts cap, as if she had worn them all her life. I also presented Chitrali gowns for two young boys about the ages of Princes William and Harry without mentioning them. As soon as she realized that the ages matched those of her sons, she appeared most pleased.

It was clear immediately that the *people's princess* was not very comfortable with formal protocol arrangements. More than once, she asked to let her move around and meet the large crowds which had gathered to see her, which included British and local people. This of course was done. The District administration had ensured that the presence of uniformed personnel was kept at a minimum apart from the security detail at the fringes. Only one speech was permitted by a Federal Minister from Chitral, who took a lifetime to read from a prepared text. What he spoke, or tried to speak, was mostly unintelligible but the Princess was much amused by the comical rendition. She was however, keen to hear from Shoaib Sultan, the Chief Executive of the Aga Khan Rural Support Programme for the innovative projects in community development.

The Princess's interest lay in the minority Kalash people and their dwindling numbers They survive but just barely. When the Princess was informed about the plight of the Kalash people, she was moved and agreed to my suggestion to lend her name as a patron for the Kalash Welfare project. This was thrilling news and Sir Nicholas Barrington, the British High Commissioner was also very pleased. But then nothing came of it. The Kalash may have been unlucky as I did not follow up with the Princess about a proposal for the next six years and then she was no more with us. This has been my abiding regret. Someday, I hope to take up the proposal with her sons, Princes William and Harry, if for no other reason than for the Princess's visit to Chitral and her photograph wearing the Chitrali cap!

The Princess's visit was short and as she sat in the jeep that was to take her back to the airport for the return flight, Ishtiak Ahmad, the Deputy Commissioner of Chitral was pushed into the driver's seat in place of the professional driver. Before her security team could react, the convoy for the airport started to move. Ishtiak had been the actual host while the Commissioner was only pulling rank by monopolizing the occasion. And there was Princess Diana with two Chitrali children sitting in her lap, waving and touching thousands of hands all the way to the airport. The Royal advance-party security team, which had surveyed the area a couple of months earlier, had been absolutely adamant that no local officer would drive the Princess's vehicle and only a professional driver would do so, and there is no denying that the standard operating procedures must be followed at all times. This was a lucky break!

There was a drama staged by the Special Branch of Police the evening before the Princess's visit to save their skin in case something went wrong. The Deputy Inspector General of the Special Branch informed me that a 'source report' had intimated that the Princess's aircraft would be attacked with a missile on way to Chitral and in case the attempt failed she would be subjected to small arms fire in Chitral. Having known the concerned officer well and the Special Branch even better, I took full responsibility for the security and told them this was a bogus and concocted report with no basis at all and that I was disregarding it completely. The Special Branch's real purpose was only to place it on record, 'just in case', something serious did occur which is another police face-saving mechanism. I acknowledged the receipt of the report in the presence of the Deputy Inspector General of Malakand Range. I, however, insisted that no fourth person should know about this so that the visit was not jeopardized. Nothing untoward happened and the visit went smoothly. The staff with the Princess told us later that she enjoyed the Chitral visit the most because the presence of uniformed security forces was kept to the minimum and there was a relaxed ambiance.

At the end of the visit, Mir Afzal Khan, the Chief Minister, asked me about the Princess's expressions and her frame of mind. I thought she had incredibly sad eyes, as if she was missing something in life. Only later did her unhappiness and separation make the news. And then, a few years later, very tragically, the Princess was dead.

After the Princess left Chitral, there was a near tragedy involving the senior officers, including myself while returning to our duty stations. As the convoy of vehicles reached Ziarat Post of the Chitral Scouts, a few pebbles started falling on to the road from the mountain. The experienced driver braked immediately, reversed the lead jeep and moments later an avalanche of rocks hit the road. We experienced a lucky break.

ii. Swat

Fittingly, the most scenically beautiful part of Pakistan was once upon a time, also its best governed region. Sir Winston Churchill, when he was a Lieutenant, was 'struck with the beauty of the scenery' and had the memory of 'a beautiful valley, where the green of the rice fields was separated from the blue of the sky by the glittering snow peaks of the Himalayas.'

Some areas in Swat appear as an extension of Switzerland but only as far as geography is concerned. In governance, after its merger with Pakistan, the comparison would be more apt with the Congo, the Sudan, or Chad. The newly built-up areas in Swat would rank with the worst planned in the world and in the absence of land use regulations, Swat's rivers and mountains are being degraded every day. The principal reason for the colossal damages caused by the 2010 floods was that influential people, mostly outsiders, had built homes and hotels well below maximum flood levels which is absolutely taboo everywhere in the world except in our country. Hundreds of powerful people had encroached into the Swat River for fun and play thereby creating dam-like hindrances to any increased flow. Thousands paid with their lives and properties for defying and defiling Mother Nature.

The Swat of the last Wali, Miangul Jehanzeb, was near idyllic. Public buildings, schools, hospitals, and offices remained in pristine conditions fifty years after the merger. After the earthquake in 1991, only a few of the buildings constructed during the Wali's reign had developed cracks. In contrast, virtually every structure built after Swat's merger into Pakistan was damaged if not destroyed. Many of the roads in Swat were unpaved but remained smooth due to excellent maintenance. The paved roads of course were top class. A decade after the merger, someone asked the witty provincial civil service officer Sahibzada Yunas if the merger of the State was complete. 'No,' came the reply 'because the premerger roads still remain in a much better shape than those built later'. The Swat Hotel, now the Swat Serena, was lovingly built by the Wali and was a reflection of the times past; it was what hotels should be like. Large rooms with spacious bathrooms and high ceilings compared to pigeon-hole rooms of other conventional hotels. The Commissioner's office was grand with trophies of a Kashmir stag and Markhor heads and a large fireplace that was put to regular use in winters. The Commissioner House, actually built for President Ayub Khan, whose two daughters were married to the Wali's two sons, was again pure luxury. Everything in Swat at that time appeared well planned and laws were implemented strictly. If a vehicle hit a goat or a chicken on the road, the owners of the goat or chicken were penalized. There were a large number of professionals like lawyers, doctors, educationist engineers, and businessmen from outside Swat who were encouraged to live and work permanently in Swat and many incentives were provided to them.

An insight on how the Wali of Swat responded to circumstances was provided by Saranjam Khan of Baghdada, Mardan. Every time he visited Swat he would call on the Wali and was allowed an audience immediately.

Often the Wali, out of sheer kindness, would offer him a timber permit which was always declined politely. Once however, he accepted the permit so as not to annoy the Wali. It so happened that the very next day Saranjam Khan had some important issue to discuss with the Wali but this time the latter kept him waiting for hours before seeing him. With a timber permit in hand the visitor was compromised to a certain extent. When the Wali did see him he enquired about the purpose of the visit. Saranjam Khan, having understood the reason for the delayed audience, merely told him that he had come to return the permit. He did not mention the actual reason but the sharp witted Wali understood! His respect for the 'Mardan Khan' increased and he insisted he have lunch with him. On another level we see this happen every day in Pakistan!

The Wali's state was undoubtedly an autocracy and he, like his father, could be very harsh when it came to challenging his personal interests. Exiling his enemies from the state was his preferred form of disposing any threat. The ordinary people however, remembered him most fondly for the prompt disposal of all cases, whether administrative or judicial.

The care and responsibility that marked the rule of the Wali of Swat remains unsurpassed except for the State of Bahawalpur. The earthquake referred to earlier was also like an inspection visit to check good governance. Interestingly, only a few hours after the earthquake struck, Abdul Sattar Edhi called to inform that his relief helicopter was on its way and that the local administration may buy whatever it required from the markets to provide relief to the people. As the Commissioner, since my training was in government manuals only, I daftly inquired if there was a ceiling to the purchases and whether any formalities were to be observed. The reply was reassuring. He stated that the ceiling was as high as the requirements of the people were. And as for observance of codal formalities he said, 'If I do not trust the Commissioner who do I trust?' No wonder Edhi was revered! Since the earthquake had struck in winter, when snow blocks many of the distant roads in Swat, a request was made to the Federal Cabinet Division to deploy two of its Emergency Relief helicopters. But none was available. A similar request to the Army also went unanswered. A few months earlier, six military helicopters had descended at the Kabal golf course to bring the top brass for the military chiefs' golf tournament.

After Swat's integration into Pakistan, a new judicial procedural code called the Provincially Administered Tribal Areas (PATA) Regulations was formulated by the remarkable administrator, Rashid Khan of Matta Mughal Khel to dispense quick justice. The new dispensation was not without its problems, but inexplicably the Peshawar High Court, two decades later, declared it unconstitutional because the law was different from the laws elsewhere in the country. PATA Regulations experienced problems but the correct option was to make it effective through the required amendments. The people were greatly annoyed by the High Court order. Here was one issue on which there was near unanimity among the people of Swat except for the lawyers. Someone once asked Sufi Muhammad of the Tehrik-i-Nifaz-i-Shariat what constituted 'Sharia', or Islamic jurisprudence, and without wasting any time, he said that fairly resolving all civil and criminal cases within a week was a sufficient definition. The people of Malakand Division, he added, observed all basic tenets of Islam such as *tauheed, namaz, roza, zakat,* and *hajj* but what was missing was an effective system of adjudication of disputes.

The Wali of Swat actually provided all essential ingredients of a modern state while other rulers in the country only made promises. Swat was a functional state, unlike the weak and wobbly structure in the rest of the country. There was an efficient hierarchy of executive officials and the *Qazis'* duties lay in ensuring that the problems of the people were resolved quickly and fairly. The socio-economic infrastructure was adequate, with good schools, colleges, dispensaries, and hospitals. There was no question of seeing schools without teachers and hospitals and medical dispensaries without qualified staff, contrary to what is the norm today in Pakistan. The state even had its own museum, rest-houses, and hotels. An airport at Kanjo was built and there was also an eighteen-hole golf course at Kabal. A convent school for girls was established at Sangota with nuns and missionaries invited from outside the state. Next to the convent, was the Swat Public School for boys with boarding facilities, resembling the Senior School of Lawrence College, Ghora Gali, which was established by the author in 1990. Later the school was renamed the Excelsior School.

The Kabal golf course became an object of contention between the Army and the Commissioner, during the nineties. The Army Chief, was determined to take it over. He wanted it for 'better maintenance' and nothing else, of course! When reminded that there was no Army unit located in Swat, he countered it by stating that the Dir Scouts would be responsible for it. The Kabal golf course was one of the very few facilities still in the hands of 'the bloody civilians' and I wanted to keep it that way. Further discourse not being possible with the Army Chief, I protested to Chief Minister, asking him to post me out, as the transfer of the golf course amounted to a show of no confidence in me. I also questioned on how the Dir Scouts would manage to spare a platoon when they routinely regretted providing troops citing manpower shortages, whenever a request was made for operations. Fortunately, the Chief Minister sided with me but he was perplexed at my emotional attachment to the golf course. 'Da faujiano sra talakaat sata', or 'always maintain good relationships with the Army', was his sane advice. That reminded me of what General Fazle Haq had said to me in the late 1960s: 'Forget the Civil Service of Pakistan, join the Army, as it will always be in power in Pakistan'. Time would tell how far General Fazle Haq was right because the great sage, Zhou Enlai, reportedly said two hundred years after the French Revolution was too early to assess the impact of the Revolution!

Despite the generally benign rule of the Wali of Swat, honourable people like Afzal Khan Lala of DurushKhela protested that there was no alternative to representative government and adult franchise in the twentieth century. Swat, remains a special place for the locals and the visitors. It was home to some exceptionally refined and hospitable persons like Dost Muhammad from Matta, Senator Kamran and his sons Shuja and Nasir, Dr Najeeb, the brothers Taj and Khurshid, Salimullah, the Sports Officer, Bakht Roshan, Khanzada from Kalaam and from Shangla, Sher Muhammad, Fawad Khan, Kamal Khan of Matka, and Mehmood Khan not forgetting Rashid from the Commissioner's office. Two of the finest persons I met in life, Afzal Khan Lala of Awami National Party and Khaliqdad Khan from Jamaat-i-Islami were both from Swat.

During the first decade of the new century, Swat, like many other places, suffered much civil strife and dislocation. The causes behind the short lived insurgency of the 1990s and the more widespread one over the last decade, could have been the failure of the State to provide justice and redress grievances promptly. Unlike the people of the rest of the country, those in Swat, had actually experienced a more efficient administrative and judicial system. Serious crime was rare and only an odd case of murder or kidnapping would occur. Punishments were swift and retribution effective, that deterred others. The essence of Sharia is the quick and cheap disposal of criminal and civil cases. Today the courts or the *katcheries* are non-performing, the police corrupt and oppressive, and the revenue administration most inefficient and bloodsucking. These have become the much despised and distrusted symbols of the state.

The state's organs and institutions are established to address the problems and remove the frustrations of the people; these frustrations can only be resolved through appropriate enabling laws. Why not amend or adjust criminal and civil codes to bring them more in line with the local conditions and traditions of the people for providing quick justice? Why adhere to foreign codes incorporated a long time back, when they cannot fully deliver now? The 'fault ... lies not in the stars but in ourselves...'

iii. DIR

The third former princely state, Dir, has always been difficult to administer both because of its terrain and the temperament of its people. Except for a few plains, the area is marked by mountains with narrow valleys making access difficult. In other places like Brawal and Jandul, on the border with Afghanistan, the government's control was weak. Here, Deputy Commissioners were advised to tread cautiously to avoid any serious backlash. The Nawab of Dir, Shah Jahan, was not known to be as benign as the Wali of Swat. After the Dir-Bajaur operations of 1960–61, Shah Jahan was unseated and exiled to Lahore with one of his sons. The standard of road communications, schools, and hospitals compared very poorly to those of Swat. His detractors would often criticize him for developing a better veterinary dispensary for his dogs than health facilities for his people. The importance of Dir remained paramount following the disturbance of the 1960s, because rebels from across the border in Jandul, Shahi, and Brawal would often stir trouble. Since the road to Chitral passed through Dir, the Government always remained attentive. Once in a while, there would be a complete breakdown of security as in 1976. A dispute on the sharing of the forest royalty payments between the stakeholders and the Government was poorly managed by the local administration and the political leadership in

Peshawar. To regain control and restore order, the 7th Army Division from Peshawar, commanded by General Fazle Haq and supported by Air Force bombardment, was sent to restore calm. The Headquarters of the Force were in the Chakdara Fishing Hut and it was well that this place existed. To a friend's query, the General replied that he was there merely 'sorting out the clan' and would return soon. Return soon he did, but not before the government conceded a much larger share of the royalty payments than those demanded by the people and which halted the military operations. This was a case of becoming wise after the event.

For some reason, a religious political party, the Jamaat-i-Islami, always had an effective presence in Dir District even though it barely existed elsewhere in the Province. Dr Yaqub, Sardar Alam Badshah, and Siraj ul Haq, among others, would normally win a few provincial assembly seats for the Jamaat-i-Islami and were quite demanding. The rules of business of the government demand that all verbal orders be reduced to writing in the shortest time possible before action is initiated. In such cases officials are issued orders verbally and told to comply or else directed to forward such proposals in writing, giving the impression that these emanated from the officials.

A member of the provincial assembly unhappy with the administration for not doing his bidding, waited for an opportunity to turn the tables on the officials. He imagined he would settle scores with the senior officers on the distribution of the relief items collected after an earthquake that struck the area in 1991. A committee was formed by the Government to evaluate the fairness or otherwise in the distribution of relief goods with him as one of the members. He tried his best to find out any shortcomings but he was disappointed as the able and conscientious Secretary to the Commissioner, Waqar Ayub, had each item, down to soap cakes and slippers, fully documented. The member then approached a few persons on the side and enquired if they had paid any bribes to the officials to get relief items. On getting a negative response, he suggested that in that case they must have paid some 'sherini' or sweets to officials. The reply again disappointed him as all rules of transparency and equity were followed by the administration.

Another member of the provincial assembly from Jandul was distinct in his own ways. He often employed bluffs and threats to get past obstacles.

Abdul Sattar Edhi, one of the greatest humanitarian
and social worker at the Karachi Literature Festival 2013.
Photo courtesy: Oxford University Press

Dr Ruth Pfau (1929–2017),
who devoted her life to eradicating leprosy in Pakistan.
Photo courtesy: Shahid Hussain

Iconic Ardeshir Cowasjee (1926–2012), a fearless businessman, columnist, and philanthropist.

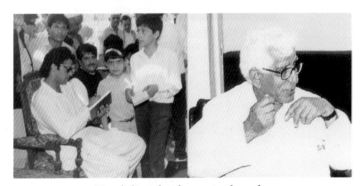

Two dedicated and committed people.
Imran Khan   Dr Adeeb Rizvi,

The Former Interim Prime Minister (July–Oct. 1993), Moeen Qureishi (left).
One of the best that served our country.

Athar Tahir, sporting a beard, with Lieutenant General (retd) Ali Muhammad Jan Orakzai,
Governor NWFP at the launch of his book Frontier Facets.

Lord Linlithgow, the Viceroy of India with Sir George Cunningham, Governor of NWFP,
at the inauguration of the Jabban Hydroelectric Project in 1938.
Photo courtesy: WAPDA archives

Chairman, WAPDA and Commissioner, Malakand Division inspecting project's expansion while
riding on the mechanical trolley that was used in 1938, and still in use 2010!
These trolleys were built to last!

The Inauguration of Cadet College Skardu, 1994.

A Watermelon presented to the author by Bacha Khan, 1977.
It turned out to be rotten!

Once in 1990, in Samarbagh, a violent crowd from Jandul, which was dissatisfied with the local administration on some minor matter, set fire to a small government building. When the suspects were not handed over to the government within the appointed time there was no option left for me as Commissioner, but to 'show the flag'. A Wing of Dir Scouts was deployed just in case some hotheads tried to bluster. The MPA arrived with a few hundred people and promptly threatened the Commissioner stating, that if force was used against his people, he would not be responsible for the consequences. I reminded him that as the Commissioner of Malakand Division, I knew the law and that nowhere in the statutes was there any mention of the responsibility for 'law and order', resting with any provincial assembly member'. Everyone understood the context well and the persons responsible for arson were handed over to the administration. However, the house of the main accused was spared at the intercession of the *jirga*.

The *Dirugees*, or the people of Dir, often became great favourites of the officers serving in the region for their straight talk and hospitality. The most memorable of them of course was Zahir Shah Khan of Och, an Awami National Party activist and a close friend of hundreds of officials who served in the area. The depth of his knowledge of the area, the people, and the issues was amazing and he was always a friend of the Government. Zahir Shah Khan's hospitality was proverbial and almost anyone known to him passing through the area, including Bacha Khan, would stop by at his *baitak* and be regaled by the experience. Then there were Haji Sarfaraz, Sher Azam, and Anwar Khan from Panakot, all fine people and always helpful to the Government. Not to be forgotten was one Saeed-ul-Haq, who claimed telepathic powers through numerology to reach back to one's past and tell the future. There were many embarrassed faces, while he divulged a particular person's past. But then most saints, they say, have had a past! It may surprise many to learn that Saeed was in great demand by politicians and senior military officers in Islamabad, who by relying on the occult, were desperate to know their future prospects in careers. There is no shortage of politicians and officials with blind faith in magic and sorcery.

Here, I must mention Chakdara, which is the heart if not the epicenter of Malakand Division. The rest-house, called the Fishing Hut, lies on the confluence of the Chakdara stream with the Swat River. The building of the Fishing Hut has been claimed by many Political Agents because it is as picturesque as it is functional. It is a rest-house, a dining place, a conference center, a musical evening hotspot, and, of course, a fishing hut. There is no comparable facility in the country. Serious anglers from all over the country would cast for a prize *Mahseer*, a carp-family game fish found here. The doyen of anglers, Aziz *shikari* from Peshawar, must have baited hundreds of *Mahseers* here and he has photographs as evidence. Colonel Cobb, a British Political Agent, is said to have caught an eighty-six pounder *Mahseer*. It was difficult to question the claims of the Political Agent then but it is generally acknowledged to be the biggest *Mahseer* caught in the Swat River. My own record was a modest six-pounder but was released soon after. However, a Political *Tehsildar* from the area and later a Magistrate, Ghulam Habib—an avid hunter and an even more avid a bragger—whose tales were mostly uncorroborated, insisted that the one he caught was bigger than Cobb's. He would hold audiences spell bound for hours recounting his interesting exploits and it was a sheer delight to be in his company. A *Mahseer* breeding fish farm, developed with Nepalese assistance near Chakdara, was constructed to generate an increase in the falling numbers of *Mahseer* population, but the results were unknown.

Standing sentinel to the Chakdara fort, was the famous Churchill Piquet, which the young Winston Churchill supposedly visited as a war correspondent during the 1897 campaign in the area. Queen Elizabeth II's visited Swat in 1961, which included a visit to Malakand Pass where once Winston Churchill had been sending war reports from his pickets now known as Churchill's pickets. The British were great ones for history and romance! The picket was close to Jalala, near Thana, where, during the 1897 operations, as Churchill described first-hand, Colonel Adams and Lord Fincastle won the Victoria Cross.

iv. MALAKAND AGENCY

The constitutional status of the former princely states of Chitral, Dir, and Swat were determined in 1970 when these states were absorbed in the Frontier Province and administratively placed under the Commissioner of the new Malakand Division. Prior to 1970, they were the responsibility of the Political Agent of Malakand Agency, who in addition was also the executive head of the territory of Malakand. After the merger of the states with Pakistan, the new Malakand Division was called the Provincially Administered Tribal Areas or PATA. Before Partition, the Political Agent of Malakand Agency also functioned as the Resident for the three States. For district level officers, a posting to the Malakand Agency was a crowning achievement, just as the Assistant Commissioner, the 'Chota Sahib' of Hangu Sub Division in Kohat was top-ranked for entry-level position for the Indian Civil Service and later for Civil Service of Pakistan. Such was the prestige of the post of the Political Agent, Malakand Agency that Aslam Khattak, the late Governor, once narrated that as a young man, the then Governor of NWFP told him he could not appoint him the King who was in England but he could appoint him as Emperor by posting him as Political Agent of Malakand Agency.

The present day Malakand Division was part of the Gandhara Empire nearly 2,000 years ago. Stamps, statues, and artifacts from the period are spread all over. One small statue, called the terracotta Buddha, was so unique that a foreign archaeologist half-jokingly said 'it was worth a small kingdom'. It was once stolen from the Museum and sold by intermediaries to Mir Afzal Khan of Mardan who graciously returned it to the Chakdara Museum. Years later, during student disturbances in the area, the Museum was attacked fortunately without any damage being caused to the 'small kingdom'. The terracotta Buddha was then ordered to be shifted to the Peshawar Museum, as no one can afford to lose even a small kingdom. There were small Gandhara statues and friezes in the bungalow of the Political Agent of Malakand Agency painstakingly gathered over the years by the British. An officer posted there, after Partition found the idols sacrilegious and reportedly chopped some heads off and destroyed the rest. Tolerance is a virtue greater than all other virtues and no society has been known to progress without it.

The Malakand Agency had the rightful claim of initiating economic development in the Frontier Province because the diversionary works of the Swat River were located at Amandara Headworks and the two hydel power stations of Jaban and Dargai generated hydropower in the 1930s. Lord Linlithgow, the Viceroy, inaugurated the facility. Some of the equipment, such as the mechanical trolley, is still in operation 80 years after its installation! The people of Malakand would often complain that the Agency did not have a quality school. In the 1990s, with the assistance of Humayun Khan, the locally elected representative, I spearheaded the building of a public school at Rangmalla much to the gratitude of the inhabitants. The facility was later used as a rehabilitation center and it was everybody's hope that a school would be established in the vicinity.

The Agency also housed an infantry battalion in the fort shared with the Political Agent, which often led to minor skirmishes. The military is most adept at safeguarding their land and properties, much like their regimental silver. So adept are they that very often they take 'temporary' custody of properties that are not their own. It is almost impossible to retrieve such civil properties 'temporarily' in occupation of the Army. One such piece of land was in Malakand Agency which the Army refused to return because according to their military records they got possession of it by rights of 'military conquest'. One had heard of the 'doctrine of necessity', which was endorsed by the law courts of the land, but employing the doctrine of the 'right of military conquest' was something else! Game, set and match! This dispute arose because of some century-old and costly *shisham* trees on the land under their 'temporary custody'. Mercifully, the minor issue was resolved.

Malakand has a famous love story in its folklore that could surpass all love stories. Once upon a time, there lived the handsome Adam Khan, who was equally adept at playing the 'Rabab' (Rubab) as wielding the sword and there was Durkhanai, unarguably the prettiest girl of them all. They suffered many trials and tribulations but their union remained elusive. On their death, they were buried in separate graves but villagers swore that over time, their skeletons were found locked in embrace. Pushto ballads and poetry soon followed and there was one from faraway Ireland, by Tomas Ó Cárthaigh, appropriately titled 'Lovers of Bazdara'. (Incidentally in Mardan the district adjoining Malakand, home to the forbears of the famed Bollywood heroine Madhubala, remember an equally compelling romantic folklore. In the village of Turlandi there was the debonair Yusaf Khan who pined for the enchantingly beautiful Sher Bano but what followed was tragic; serene love could not withstand intrigue and fate).

Lovers of Bazdara
Tomas Ó Cárthaigh

Silent now her tambourine
She played while yearning for Adam Khan
For whom she fell at fleeting glance
As only true lovers can

Durkhanai won his heart too
As he caught her peeping over the wall
On the urging of her friends who said he was beautiful
Modest she hid, and hard did fall.

Adam Khan to his friend declared
She was the one for his life
But he was too late, in the Pashtun way
She was to be another's wife.

Friends being friends did what they could
Found a way to get the lovers to meet
Delighted, they exchanged gifts
Their time together it was, too short, too strong, too sweet.

The madness of the heart seizes Adam again
He wanders and cries until he is struck blind with tears
Asks kind strangers to her home to be brought
He drops dead as her home he nears.

She on hearing this to her bed she takes
Till death in its kindness takes her from her pain
The lovers who in life could not be together
In death would lie in one grave for all time to remain.

Some time on, the grave by the villagers was opened
Shocked they were there to find
Not two skeletons side by side as buried they were
But in an embrace, entwined!

Kindness and sense this time prevailed
It was decided so that they could stay
So they lie, awaiting the Day of Judgment
The Lovers of Bazdara, to this very day!

5

The Erstwhile Tribal Areas:
A Forbidding Past and an Uncertain Future

i. The Early Visitors

For reasons of pure historical romance, if not for their strategic importance, there are few areas in the world as fascinating as the Federally Administered Tribal Areas of Pakistan, earlier known by its rather nondescript acronym, FATA. Its past has been most eventful but its future remains a matter of concern despite its merger with the Khyber Pakhtunkhwa province. In fact, it may not even be possible to predict the future accurately as that 'very special person', Lord Nathaniel Curzon, former Viceroy of India, shrewdly observed. He prophetically stated that anyone who makes a prediction about this Frontier area has not read a page of its history. Even today as violence and uncertainty envelop it, opinions and diagnoses of experts are varied and often contradictory. How would treatment be prescribed when neither the ailment nor its prognosis is clear? Let alone predicting the future, contemporary assessments about present events are equally contentious. It is hardly surprising that even among experts there is no consensus about the causes of the recent wave of militancy following the events 9/11, its depth, or the motivation behind it. Two respected commentators on the situation, both from the Civil Service, having served as Political Agents in Waziristan, Commissioners, and Chief Secretaries of the North West Frontier Province, often hold different opinions about the causes of the present troubles and the means of resolving it. If Khalid Aziz and Rustam Shah Mohmand do not agree on even the basics, the situation is probably very complicated and will take a long time to normalize. The situation on ground remains complex and appears to be far removed from the pious hopes and simplistic solutions offered by those with a superficial understanding of the situation. Perhaps the views of the local people, who have a vital stake for the future, is not being heard. The government, the parliament, the judiciary, the military, and the media need to keep their ears to the ground to determine the real aspirations of the tribesmen.

It must be remembered that for the immediate future the society would remain tribal, as their response to external or local stimuli remains collective or tribal, whether or not these areas are called merged districts.

History records that Colonel H. D. Hutchinson, author of the book, *The Campaign in Tirah 1897–1898*, was equally unclear a century ago when he wrote about the reasons which led to the British forces invading Khyber Tirah in 1897–98:

> But I am quite sure that, even now that it is all over if you button-hole ten intelligent men, and ask them "all about the war, and what they killed each other for?", you will get a different answer from each, and no two will agree in essential particulars!

This is an amazing assertion to make but not far from the truth.

Well into the 1970s, in UK, many Frontier veterans would saunter into their local pub, often with the war medals on their aging chests, enquiring from other 'old chaps' how 'the situation was that day on the North West Frontier'. You could get the British out of the Frontier but you could not get the Frontier out of them! Romance reminded them of the Crown Jewels and the Frontier was the centrepiece. It was here that they found their match.

For the Raj enthusiast and the military historian, the Khyber Pass ranks as a must-see battleground alongside Panipat, Thermopylae, Flanders, Ypres, Kharkov, and El Alamein. All these battles shaped history. Many well-known military captains and warriors, known to history, played their role in these theatres of war. The most famous of them all, Alexander the Great, entered India through the northern Nawa Pass, although the bulk of his forces swept down the Khyber Pass which was just as well for him. Had he not travelled the way he did, he would not have come across, and taken fancy to, a beautiful local girl from Kalkot, near Chakdarra, whom he married. Alexander and his Greek troops apparently had much time for fun and frolics judging by the number of Grecian-looking descendants they left behind. The Kalash people of Chitral are said to be of Greek origin, and then how do you explain the aquiline-nosed Pathans in the area? There is an amazing similarity between the sketch of Alexander on the cover of Sir Olaf Caroe's book, *The Pathans*, and some living today. The nose of one civil servant is embarrassingly similar too! There was this British Army officer on his first posting to India who was convinced that he had seen his Indian batman earlier, even though the latter had never set foot abroad. It transpired that the batman's features were identical to those of Alexander, whose painting he had seen in his Mess back home. A case study revealed that the batman's village was precisely on this invader's route. And genes never lie!

There were many other mercenary soldiers who etched their bloody deeds and made their fortunes from the Khyber region. Amongst those better known were Mahmud Ghaznavi, remembered for the plundering of the Somanath temple; Genghis Khan, the military genius who was known as the scourge of the earth; Amir Taimur, the great warrior Tamerlane; Babur, founder of the magnificent Mughal Empire; Nadir Shah Afshar, infamously associated with the word *nadirshahi* which means the mass murder in Delhi in 1739 and Ahmad Shah Durrani, the Afghan King and poet of Panipat in 1761, was the last of the successful invaders from the north. Later, came Maharaja Ranjit Singh, the remarkable Sikh potentate, and his bold general Hari Singh Nalwa from Punjab. Besides these famous names, there were dozens of lesser-known marauders from different tribes and bands. There were high-cheek-boned and slit-eyed Scythians, Bactrians, Huns, and big-eyed but equally desperate Turks, Afghans, and Persians, all mesmerized by the fabled wealth and alluring womenfolk of India. Every invader wished to return home with the *Koh-i-Noor*, the most desirable diamond in the world and the *Noors* of pleasure! Modern day warriors of business and finance remain as motivated by such prizes as the invaders of the past. The entry gate to the subcontinent in most cases was marked 'Khyber' and there were no complimentary invitations. Everyone had to earn their way through force, guile, or bribe and all who experienced the place were impressed. Actually there may be one person in the world who remained unimpressed by the Khyber and he was the Indian cricket spinner, Chandrasekhar. After visiting the Pass, he found the place rather ordinary and too dusty, *dhool bohat hai*. Who said Indian spinners preferred dusty wickets?

After Alexander's brief sojourn, it was 2,000 years before the next European invader stepped into the region. The area was too important to ignore and so against the general tide of the invaders, the British decided to show the flag from the south. Only once before in history has there been a mass movement from India, and a very successful one at that, but that was a religious and cultural invasion. The great Mauryan Emperor, Asoka, was so distraught with blood and gore after the Kalinga War that he adopted Buddhism and devoted the rest of his life to *Ahimsa* or non-violence. He was responsible for the spread of Buddhism to Central Asia and beyond. Khyber, with its remaining Buddhist stupas, was also the springboard for this invasion from the south. This invasion however, had a more lasting impact than purely military conquests.

In 1839, during the First Afghan War the British first entered the Tribal Areas on their way to Kabul, although only a few of those who survived returned to tell their horrific tales of war. The immortal sketch showing Dr William Brydon on his horse near Jalalabad as 'the sole survivor' in this theatre of war was a telling commentary on the misadventure. Misfortune dogged this same survivor Dr Brydon, even during the Mutiny in 1857, when he was incapacitated, by a gunshot, in the loins in the Lucknow Residency. He survived again. 'Forward Policy' advocates, like Lord Auckland and subsequent 'Great Gamers', put up every argument in an effort to thwart Czarist Russia from moving towards the warm waters of the Arabian Sea and the Crown Jewel. Generals Robert of Peiwar, Sam Browne, Robert Low, William Lockhart, and Bindon Blood were all present in the Tribal Areas fighting for Queen and country, in the nineteenth century. They were followed in the twentieth century, when still young, by Field Marshals Montgomery, Alexander, and Auchinleck. Not to miss out on the opportunity for fame and future, was a young war correspondent known to history as Sir Winston Churchill, who visited Malakand, Dir, and Bajaur during the Great Pathan Revolt in the closing years of the nineteenth century. He must have honed his writing skills during those early years, compiling *The Story of the Malakand Field Force*. This may have set the stage for the Nobel Prize for Literature, he won half a century later for his epic volumes on the Second World War, in which he was also a star performer.

It appears that some lucky people do get another chance in life to redeem themself, if the first attempt fails. Churchill was one of them. The author of the disastrous attack on Gallipoli, the 'soft underbelly' of Turkey during the First World War, survived to lead his country to distinction in the Second World War. His account of the battles in Malakand is riveting and his ability to analyze the area and the people he barely knew, is remarkable. Throughout history, the people of Khyber and its surrounding areas never stopped hurling projectiles of all kinds at invaders; it was rocks and arrows at one time; Jezails and blunderbusses at another; and automatic rifles and rocket propelled grenades more recently. Their primary business was intimidating opponents, much like fast bowlers do with the cricket ball at Lord's.

Over the last five hundred years, for which records are available, document that peace was an exception to the rule in the Tribal Areas. The invader and the trader could traverse the area but only with the consent of local tribes. Money, in fact, opened gates quicker than the sword. The fact that tribesmen lived in an economically unsustainable area, left them with few options but to raid the fertile plains for sheer survival. Forays into settled areas became an economic necessity, which led to countermeasures by whoever administered the plains. For the Mughals, the tribes were a constant thorn, and quite obviously the victors of any skirmish exacted a terrible vengeance on the vanquished. The Emperor Humayun had prominent Wazir and Mehsud tribesmen strung by the neck all the way from Gomal to Bannu after his rear-guard troops were massacred in Gomal. The egalitarian *Roshaniya*, literally 'light' movement, but contemptuously dubbed *Taariqi*, or 'darkness', by the Mughals, operated out of Waziristan and resisted the imperial troops for decades. The Mughals remained sworn enemies of the Pakhtuns for the primary reason that they seized power from Ibrahim Lodhi and Sher Shah Suri, both Pakhtuns, and saw them as their mortal enemy. Some of the biggest names in the Mughal armies died fighting these tribesmen. In 1586, the Karakar Pass outside Swat saw the Mughals, under their commander Zain Khan, defeated with heavy losses. The body of Raja Birbal, one of Emperor Akbar's favourite courtiers, was never found. In 1672, almost a century later, one of the bloodiest battles ever fought was around Ali Masjid in the Khyber Pass. The Mughals under Amir Khan were vanquished with the loss of 40,000 soldiers. Also killed in Jamrud was the redoubtable Rana Jaswant Singh, sent in support by Emperor Aurangzeb. He left nine wives to mourn him, and reportedly, some 1,600 concubines. Seven of his widows committed suttee. The Pakhtun confederacy, consisting of Afridi, Mohmand, Safi, and Khattak tribes, was victorious, but the dead included both their commanders Aimal Khan Mohmand and Darya Khan Afridi. Soon after, Khushal Khan Khattak, the warrior-poet instrumental in forging a Pakhtun alliance, suffered a grievous loss. One of his fifty-six sons, Bahram, betrayed him to the Mughals, prompting him to lament that 'my one demerit devours all my merits that I am Bahram's father and Bahram is my son'. The Pakhtun has many qualities but intrigue and treachery remain embedded in him. Khushal Khan Khattak, along with Sher Shah Suri and Ahmad Shah Durrani, were the greatest Pakhtuns of the last five hundred years. If he could be betrayed by a son, so could all Pakhtuns by other Pakhtuns!

The Sikhs were scarcely more welcome. Although, they controlled much of the Peshawar valley, they never had much respite. Their dealings with the tribes were generally conducted through *arbabs*, who were prominent local landlords. Maharaja Ranjit Singh was more successful as his interest lay in collecting the annual tribute without bothering to occupy the Tribal Areas. It has been suggested that tyrannical rulers like Ranjit Singh were more suitable to governing unruly subjects by effectively providing security for the people. This may have been one of his strengths as he is known as the greatest Punjabi leader in a thousand years. The other attributes of Ranjit Singh are well summed up by P. E. Roberts: 'Ranjit Singh is one of the great personalities of Indian history. A born leader of men, gifted with an iron will, selfish, brave, and avaricious, he possessed just that combination of virtues and vices which is best adapted for building an oriental Empire.'

He may, in course of time, be forgotten, but his governor, the Neapolitan adventurer Paolo Avitabile would be remembered for reasons of his own in Peshawar. Memories of 'his moral delinquencies and fiendish cruelties' would survive the millennium. He maintained his 'wise and vigorous management' of this turbulent area by routinely hurling mere suspects to their deaths from the Gorgatri towers in Peshawar city and insisting on hanging 'Khyberres' and the troublesome locals on gibbets outside Peshawar on the smallest pretext. Avitabile's sense of retribution was always unambiguous. He once had an ear cut off of each of two mischievous youths

for the capital crime of stealing oranges from a garden near Wazirabad. The
'fruits of their errand' were more than what they had bargained for! Ranjit
Singh's most famous General, Hari Singh Nalwa spent a considerable time
fighting in the area and was killed in Jamrud, resisting Afghan troops
supported by local tribesmen. The battle was not decisive and the invaders
soon withdrew, it is said, because the dead body of the general was displayed
in such a way that he seemed alive to the enemy and to his own troops,
who thought he was still in command.

The withdrawal of the Afghans after the Battle of Jamrud against the
Sikhs in 1837 marked the last time any invader entered India, from the
North. Thereafter, the disciplined presence of the British in the Peshawar
valley, discouraged any future adventures. This was a momentous change
much as if the sea waves had decided to cease lashing at the shores. War
and invasion, which had been regular features for thousands of years finally
ended. Henceforth, only the foolhardy would pit themselves against the
Raj. For historians, the last recorded successful invasion of India from
the north was led by Ahmad Shah Durrani, who after constant battles
with the Sikhs, finally decimated the Maratha Confederacy in the Third
Battle of Panipat in 1761. Interestingly, Muslims fought on both sides,
this being quite a common phenomenon in almost all battles fought in
India. Historians record that more Muslims were killed fighting their co-
religionists than in wars with non-Muslims. Conviction was not always
valued high; what mattered most was the collection of the war booty for
these inhabitants of deserts and the dry hills.

ii. MODERN VISITORS AND DIGNITARIES

It was not only the military rank and file that remained fascinated with
the Tribal Areas; the ordinary folks were equally interested in enjoying
the Tribal Areas. The founder of Pakistan, Quaid-i-Azam Mohammad Ali
Jinnah, visited soon after the creation of the country and shook hands with
Afghan border sentries. In 1961, a high point of Queen Elizabeth II's tour,
was her visit to the Khyber Pass.

The mystery, danger, intrigue, and uncertainty actually add to the
fascination and mystique. In 1983, Princess Anne was justifiably incensed
when she was informed that because of possible physical dangers due to the

punitive action taken against heroin dealers in the Khyber Pass, she would have to travel by helicopter rather than by road to the Landikotal Scouts Camp. She was adamant that she would only travel by car and, if that was not possible, her visit to Khyber Rifles Mess should be cancelled. She felt that there was little purpose in visiting the Khyber Pass if she could not feel the ground the British regiments had once marched upon, or immerse herself in the mountains full of crags, deep defiles, watchtowers, and of course ambush sites. She wanted to absorb and experience the spirit of the emblems and badges of British regiments which had served here, from up close. Ultimately, she had her way although, I, as the Political Agent in the Khyber Pass, and the security team remained nervous wrecks that day. Her courage more than made up for her lofty behaviour.

In 1979, after the Soviet invasion of Afghanistan, there was a constant stream of visitors to the Khyber Pass, as dignitaries of all shape, shade, and size wanted to be seen furthering the war effort against the invading Communists. Ministers and permanent secretaries to the Government, parliamentarians, and journalists came in droves. Some were bright; others were politicians. One politician, Stephen Solarz, the Congressman from New York, and a perpetual Pakistan-basher, was however very sharp. The British visitors were always better briefed and asked intelligent questions, unlike the Americans, who often made elementary-school level queries. These trite questions betrayed mediocrity, and there was never a place for mediocrity in the Khyber. One had to be brave and a visionary to survive in this theatre. I was amazed to think that such persons managed the policies of the Great Powers and the results were before us. Quite naturally, there were few successes and many blunders. Some would become wise after the event and this was very true in the dealings with the Afghans! The Soviets and the Americans may never have invaded Afghanistan had they read the incisive British House of Commons debates, following the failures of the Anglo-Afghan wars of the nineteenth century. In hindsight, it was clear that in Afghanistan, as in Vietnam, the battles might be won by the invader but the ultimate winner in this theatre was always the victim, backed by their terrain. The barren plains and scorched rocks of Afghanistan would always be hostile to any invader, just like the thick jungles and waterways of Vietnam. The Afghans got it right; the invader had the watch but they had the time. No one can fight the terrain which ultimately exhausts everyone. This was in essence Paul Kennedy's 'imperial overstretch'.

There were however, some brilliant American visitors, the exception to the daft rule, and one of them as Zbigniew Kazimierz Brzezinski. He was a clear-headed man and the only thing complicated about him was the name his mother gave him! He appeared familiar with the history of the region and was cognizant of the grand strategy to deal with the issues in Afghanistan. Vietnam had taught him that there would be no need to expend American blood because all it takes is to pay one to fight one. His observations and questions were of a high standard and appropriate to the situation. The thinking strategist, however, almost lost his life because of the stupidity of a non-thinking American accompanying him. The latter insisted on sitting in the anti-aircraft gunner's seat apparently for a photograph for folks, back home. What followed was a nightmare for the hosts, as the amateur guest tried to monkey with the gun placed at Michni Post very close to the border. The gun swiveled around violently and a few rounds were accidentally fired in the air but fortunately with no loss. The master strategist came close to becoming the highest ranking western casualty of the Afghan war!

Then there was the visit of the famous actor Kirk Douglas from Hollywood. He was a very genial person, pleasant in conversation, but a showman down to his boots. Each time the camera was on him, one could see him strike a pose. While accepting a tribal dagger, I presented to him, he agreed with the suggestion that had this been presented earlier, it could have been usefully employed in the film Spartacus!

For junior officers in the Khyber Agency, escorting foreign dignitaries to the Khyber Pass by limousines was fun, barring one small olfactory issue, associated with some Western visitors. They often did not mind the voluntary egress of intestinal gases, while travelling! This for the Pakhtuns, was the ultimate dishonour and for the host the embarrassment was rather pungent. Belching, on the other hand, was anathema for the Westerners but not viewed with disdain by Oriental people. Habits and values as such are very different; the forced passage of air from one end or the other are interpreted differently, proving Kipling right that the east and west were poles apart. And the 'twain shall never meet'!

The former British Prime Minister Margaret Thatcher, the veritable Iron Lady, also marked her presence in Khyber to show solidarity with the Afghan Mujahideen, resisting Soviet occupation. Her visit was meant to acknowledge the support the Americans had provided her during the Falklands War. In accordance with the standard format for visitors she first met the Afghan refugees in the camp outside Peshawar, where an Afghan elder made a short speech highlighting their struggle against the Soviet Union's occupation of their country. The interpreter that day was a highup Pakistani official, responsible for Afghan refugees and when the elder spoke of their resolve to rid the foreign invaders from their land, the officer deliberately mistranslated his words to say that they were resisting the Soviets for the sake of their faith. The Afghan elder who understood some English, was not amused and he got up to emphasize that their struggle was primarily to cleanse their land of foreigners. Future invaders must take note! From the refugee camp, Mrs Thatcher travelled to Michni piquet, where she was shown the rocky Pakistan-Afghan border by the Political Agent of Khyber Agency. Now, the Political Agent was a very fine gentleman. Pointing to the grey rocks at the centre which had turned white due to rainwater, he ingenuously told the British Prime Minister that the 'white white *chuna*' was the border line. *'Chuna* in Urdu is powdered limestone, used to whitewash walls. The translation being rather inept, Governor General Fazle Haq became angry and showered some choice expletives at a bemused Political Agent, fortunately, in Pashto. After that, no one ever likened the border to *chuna!*

iii. *'A Riddle wrapped in Mystery inside an Enigma'*
Winston Churchill

How well the Frontier tribes have been absorbed into mainstream Pakistani society, is often debated. Most analysts see it as a very successful example of a merger of an insulated people with a mainstream group in modern times. There are others who point out that certain Tribal Areas still remain isolated, with the writ of the State not covering all the area. In fact, even before the present insurgency spread in the Tribal Areas, a majority of the inhabitants had started living in the Settled Areas. This was both to escape the risk and uncertainty of the area, and more so to pursue rewarding economic activity. Some of the most capable officers in the 'Political' administration working for the State actually hailed from the Tribal Areas. These *pultikals*, served the State loyally at great personal risk.

The uncertainty and unpredictability of the Tribal Areas, however, is all that remains certain and predictable. Old Curzon was indeed prophetic. During peace, no one could make any predictions about the future. It does not take long for a real or imagined hurt to convert a minor eddy into a turbulent storm. As Robert Warburton was leaving the Khyber after eighteen successful years (1879–1898) as Political Agent, he revelled over the peace and tranquility he had brought about among the frontier tribes. In 1897, within a year, the Great Pathan revolt was in full swing, all the way from Malakand to Waziristan, with severe hostilities that consumed tens of thousands of troops in Bajaur, Mohmand, Khyber, and Orakzai territories.

It happened again, during the 1930s, when there was large-scale unrest that engulfed the entire Tribal Areas, and at its center was the Faqir of Ipi, also known as Ghazi Mirzali Khan, a Pakhtun tribal leader. Decades later, after the unrest subsided, it re-erupted after 9/11 at the turn of the century. On 9 September 2001, two passenger planes struck the World Trade Center in New York and a two decade-long war started half way round the world, in Afghanistan and the Tribal Areas of Pakistan. No one could have imagined that the area would turn into an inferno for an incident that occurred in the West, thousands of miles away. Just a year earlier, political officers could travel across the Tribal Areas even at night, with only a gunman. General Fazle Haq famously said that there was little fight left in the tribesmen except when a religious issue cropped up. He was probably correct as any sustained hostility would need to be covered in religious garb. After the US invasion of Afghanistan, and to the amazement of experts, a widespread insurgency lasting for more than a decade started within no time in Pakistan, all the way from Swat to Waziristan. The main impetus, of course, was the US invasion of Afghanistan to dislodge the Taliban. This led to the relocation of tens of thousands of fighters and refugees from across the border into the Tribal Areas, where they consolidated themselves under the banner of religion. As the Pakistani state had little or no writ over large expanses of this territory, it was easy for militants to occupy these areas.

This was dissimilar to the situation that occurred thirty years earlier when the Soviet Union invaded Afghanistan, as that tumult was confined to Afghanistan only. There was no hostile reaction in the Tribal Areas despite all the mischievous attempts of the Soviet and Afghan Intelligence. What could be the main reason Pakistan experienced widespread insurgency later? Could it be that Pakistan was seen as complicit with Americans in the war? Or was it because this time around, there was a power vacuum in the Tribal Areas, and Pakistan was seen as a weak and failing state? If it is the former, then the insurgency should vanish soon after the Americans leave the area. If not, these troubles will continue to persist until the power vacuum exists. It is for this reason that the Pakistan army is building a formidable border fence, roads, and establishing its writ over the entire area. Whatever the scenario and true to form, the unfolding events in the Tribal Areas once again, could not be predicted.

iv. THE TRIBESMEN AND THEIR MOTIVATION

The tribesmen loathe any control by outsiders. The British ruled in what is now Pakistan for a hundred years, having wrested power from the Sikhs following the latter's defeat in the Second Anglo-Sikh War of 1849. Over the next half-century, they gained control over the Tribal Areas gradually through force of arms, and occasionally through peaceful persuasion. They were more successful than others and therefore in time, acquired greater control. This meant that the military skirmishes and the annual punitive expeditions never ceased. Nor was there any shortage of reasons for the British or 'tribal divines' inciting believers to action against anyone deemed an infidel. Almost overnight ordinary individuals became fearsome adversaries with the likes of Mast Mulla in Malakand, Hadda Mulla in Mohmand, Powinda Mullah in South Waziristan, and Mullah Said Akbar Akhund amongst the Afridis, leading large *lashkars* to jihad. During the last few years of the nineteenth century, the tribesmen had realized that the British had come to occupy their homeland. They were uneasy with the demarcation of the Durand Line and the construction of numerous forts and camps in Khyber, Malakand, Samana, Shabqadr, and Waziristan. The war clouds were looming on the horizon but the ground antennae had not picked up the signals. When war did erupt, the strategic policies and tactical maps were redrawn, and subsequently led to increased military obligations, on a permanent basis. A quarter-century after this, a minor fracas over a Hindu girl developed into the Waziristan version of the Thirty Years' War. The tribesmen were enraged by the reported return to her parents of a Hindu girl who had allegedly embraced Islam. This eruption led to the emergence on the scene of one Mirzali Khan, more popularly known as the Fakir of Ipi, who stoked unrest all over Waziristan in the south of the Frontier. Religion remains the dominant factor in the tribesman's motivation towards life, coupled with his fierce sense of independence. These traits are there to stay.

The northern tribes were not far behind in resisting the British and there arose a social reformer by the name of Badshah Gul (BG) of Turangzai village in Charsadda. To distinguish him from his successors, he was classified BG 1 in official reports followed by BG 2 and BG 3, all raised armed calls for freedom. Long afterwards, he shifted to the Mohmand tribal region and continued his struggle. The Guides Hill, in Upper Mohmand Agency where Captain Godfrey Meynell won the Victoria Cross in 1935, bears testimony to the ferocity of action. M. M. Kaye, author of *The Far Pavilions*, who had relatives in Queen Victoria's Own Corps of Guides, as well as her husband General Hamilton, who had served in the Tribal Areas, seemed to remember almost everything about the regiment. This was also the action where legend has it, that the head of a young British soldier was washed down the Subhan Khwar stream during floods, and was picked up by a local Pakhtun *malik* who ruefully remarked 'Da gulab da wajallo wo', 'Was it fair to kill this rose?'

In war, the tribesmen always entrust military leadership, at the beginning of hostilities, to a spiritual divine, a prominent *mullah* or an imam of the main mosque. Pakhtuns distrust each other and do not tolerate anyone from amongst themselves gaining pre-eminence, however fleetingly. Once the hostilities were over, the spiritual leader headed back to his traditional mosque duties while the tribal elders returned to their own ways. As such, no permanent tribal leader is created! The Pakhtuns are totally unlike the Baloch sardars, who are the acknowledged leaders of their tribes with powers of life and death, over their people. Administration under the 'Sandeman System' was thus easier as the residing political officer dealt with only one sardar. This was not possible amongst Pakhtun tribesmen, each of whom was convinced that he was as good as anyone else. In the Mohmand area an educated young man, once greatly impressed visiting senior officers from Peshawar. Not only was he eloquent in word and verse, but made useful suggestions for the area's development as well. Every official thought, he was destined to make an impact in the future. A wise old man, however, predicted a sad and quick end to his life as jealous family members could never countenance a '*tarbur*', a Pushto word used both for a first cousin and an enemy rising to prominence. The young man was found dead a short time later.

Fascination with the Tribal Areas apart, there is the seamier side which visitors do not get to see. With few economic resources available, eking a living is tough and the absence of effective social structures denies ordinary tribesmen human and social rights taken for granted by people elsewhere. Compassion and philanthropy are not common. Life for the weak borders on the unbearable, both economically and socially. For the very rich it is even more risky. That is why a majority of the tribesmen over the past half-century chose to live and work in more secure settled districts in different provinces. One of the country's largest industrial empires has been developed by an Afridi family near Lahore, because business and industry demands security and rule of law. In the Tribal Areas, one has to be strong, especially in terms of money and number of armed supporters. Countering enemies to the extent of their total elimination is worth aspiring for, and even small children are not spared. The lives of the women, though having improved with the spread of education, still leave much to be desired. There is the tale of the accidental killing of a young man from another family, with the killer's mother advising her son to immediately shoot his own wife and claim it as honour killing. With the wife killed, the son would escape being killed in revenge. In another case, after a tribesman was murdered, his family shot dead a woman from the killer's family who was married years earlier as a *sowra* into their family to settle a previous enmity. Even though a tribal *jirga* enjoys some sanctity and authority, very often tribal *jirga(s)* that are not governed by the state are known to favour the powerful and the affluent.

After the creation of Pakistan, when relative calm prevailed in the Tribal Areas, there arose another group of trouble makers called the *Pakhtunistanis* or hostiles. Their modus operandi was less of conviction and more for blackmail. They were a handful of men, unhappy with the status quo or who were involved in personal feuds and who went across the Durand Line and were generously funded by the Afghan government. Though the Afghan government was generally not overtly hostile towards Pakistan, but they did provide support to the external hostiles just to be on the safe side. The tribesmen being masters of anecdote and narrating of moral stories, the case of one Zar Akhmad was interesting. Zar, the genial Mullagori from Khyber Agency, had opted to become a *Pakhtunistani* and was granted some benefits by Afghanistan. He was invited by the Political Agent to switch sides but during the conversation the officer used abusive language towards him which upset Zar Akhmad. Zar then went on to recount a short story of two brothers, Abdullah the wicked and Lala the simpleton. Whenever there was an occasion for rejoicing and getting extra food, Abdullah would tell his brother that as the elder he was bound to join in the festivities. But when there was danger, war or need for sacrifice, Lala was told to step forward to do his duty. 'Political Agent Sahib if you want to rally all tribesmen towards Pakistan, stop behaving like Abdullah,' advised Zar Akhmad. Some years later, his home was provided with piped water. This was while I was the Political Agent, but the primary school promised to him was never established, since he did not bribe the officials of the Political and Education Departments. These officers too, were more Abdullah than Lala!

Despite minor disturbances, during the first thirty years after Partition, the Tribal Areas remained fairly peaceful, except in 1961 when a Pakistani hostile from Jandul in Dir raised a *lashkar*, an armed body of men, to support his claim for the Nawabship of Dir State. A large number of tribesmen from Afghanistan provided him support and to counter him the Army's 15th Infantry Division, a Roman five each for Victory, Valour, and Valhalla, was moved to Munda Qila, Lower Dir. The Dir-Bajaur operation ended quickly after the 12 Medium Artillery, commanded by Lieutenant Colonel Shafi Durrani chastised the rebellious spirit of the pretender to the Nawabship of Dir State. The Bajaur Scouts were then raised under the redoubtable Colonel Karim which led to peace for the next fifty years.

During this period, the *Paktunistani* hostiles were supported by the Afghan authorities as the latter opposed the Durand Line, the international border between Afghanistan and Pakistan. They were encouraged to place small explosives under bridges in the Tribal Areas without causing too much damage, and were told to toe the Afghan line generally. They were publicly seen on *Pakhtunistan* day and other ceremonial occasions in Kabul and Jalalabad. It mattered little to the Afghan authorities that apart from these few hostiles, no one else from the Tribal Areas was concerned about the Durand Line issue, engrossed as they were in making their livelihood within the Pakistan's economy. During the time that I served in the region, I hardly came across a tribesman who did not wish to remain part of Pakistan. Some acts of espionage, intrigue, arson and bomb blasts continued for a time but it was on a small scale. The later days political officers, denied a role in the more famous 'Great Game', played this minor one to the hilt. The blackmail value of the *Pakhtunistanis* lasted till the Soviet tanks rolled into Afghanistan late in the 1970s, after which the erstwhile hostiles made a quick dash back to their homeland in Pakistan. The new Afghan issue had very serious international geopolitical implications and there was no place in it for the handful of *Pakhtunistanis*. They were actually small pawns with an exaggerated opinion of themselves. With a change in the international environment, they scurried back home and lived happily ever after! Even commanding figures like Bacha Khan and Ajmal Khattak, who found shelter in Afghanistan, the latter after being hounded out by Zulfikar Ali Bhutto, returned home. Important and honourable tribal chiefs such as Malik Wali Khan Kuki Khel, Malik Nadir Khan Zakakhel, Mira Jan Sial, Amin Khoda Khel Mohmand, and others, who had lived for long in Afghanistan, were ultimately compelled to return and live among their Pakistani brothers. They had convictions but now the times had changed.

One of the more interesting players in this small game was Gran Mohmand, originally from Kunar province in Afghanistan, who was persuaded to work for the Political Agents in return for some favours. Gran lived permanently in Pakistan but either patriotism or some other incentive motivated him to fight the Soviets, following the invasion of Afghanistan. Having no rifle, he borrowed an old .303 rifle from the author without disclosing the reasons for the request. Soon he and his group were in Afghanistan where they laid an ambush for a detachment of state troops. Having killed one soldier, Gran, against better advice, rushed to claim the dead trooper's AK-47 automatic rifle which was quite a novelty then. He was instantly shot dead by the remaining soldiers and his body was taken away. Among the papers recovered from him, there was a letter from a former Political Agent which the Soviets cited as proof that Pakistan was supporting the locals. To an extent they were right because Gran's rifle had indeed been provided by a government officer.

The above digression aside, it may be rightly said that with the arrival of the British in the trans-Indus region, it soon became clear to the tribesmen that the presence of the *pehrangai*—the foreigner, soldier, and the political sahib, did not augur well for their freedom. Earlier, they saw armies only on the move up or down their terrain which were not to be garrisoned locally. For the British, a longer stay was manifest destiny. Interestingly, for once both the British and the tribesmen had met their match in each other. A love-hate bond developed between them. They remained in close contact assiduously looking for chinks in the opponents' armour. If there were no chinks, they would resolve matters through sweet argument, well supplemented by ready cash it may be emphasized. When the tribesmen found a major weakness on the ground, they would opt for a clash of arms but when defeated they would conveniently blame it on some hot-heads who had gone astray.

This uneasy relationship continued for a century, during which period there were nearly a hundred military expeditions launched against the tribesmen. The British tried to sustain the new status quo which the tribesmen were loath to accept. It would be another century before the tribesmen understood that prosperity depended on peace and that there could be freedom even with roads, schools, and hospitals providing modern comforts. A level of respect had developed between the tribesmen and the ingenious British who were not much interested in gaining territorial control of the barren tribal lands and wished to avoid the heavy cost in blood and money. Their main interest lay in denying control of the area to Russia before the First Great War and between the wars to Germany. The Germans took considerable interest in the Tribal Areas, especially during the unrest caused by the Fakir of Ipi and in the princely states of Swat and Dir, judging from the weapons they provided to some of the local people. Even today, there are a large number of Lugers and Mausers pistols available that had been sent from Germany a hundred years ago.

It was said of the British Foreign Office of the nineteenth century that they used small scale maps in assessing the dangers of a Russian attack on

India. They feared an attack through Khyber and Kurram Passes and also through the almost impassable Broghil Pass in Chitral. This amused the Russians, one of whom is said to have told a British traveller to Central Asia that they would be out of their minds to attack India through such narrow defiles when the best invasion routes were available lower down in the Kharan and Keitu gaps. The British however, took no chances and continued to strengthen their hold. Elaborate underground bunkers, dragon teeth defences, pillboxes, and picquets were built. Such was the sturdy quality of these concrete picquets that when the Pakistan Army tried to widen machine gun emplacements, after the Soviet invasion of Afghanistan, no crowbar could chip the concrete. There is no doubt that the presence of the Government had a lasting impact in the region, as the area was gradually pacified and a development process started which absorbed the tribesmen into the mainstream of the society. The extreme poverty in the Tribal Areas started being addressed only after the government initiated its development programme during Zulfikar Ali Bhutto's tenure and then again more recently. However, much more needs to be done.

'Where insecurity ends civilization begins,' as Ijlal Haider Zaidi, a former Chief Secretary, would constantly remind younger officers. How the British maintained security is a story in statecraft and benign administration which few colonial powers except the British understood. They did not resort to the repression, extortion, and savage killings committed by Spain and Portugal in South America, by Belgium and Italy in Africa, by France in the Maghreb and Indo-China, and by Japan in China and Southeast Asia. The British wisely did not introduce foreign ideas or build European models, but worked on existing concepts by adapting local tribal institutions to suit their immediate needs. Tribal structures and customs were not disturbed. They were allowed maximum local autonomy in their affairs. Today, over three score and ten years later and despite the merger of the tribal areas in the legal statutes the merged areas administration is barely functional because the tribal institutions have not been adapted to serve the present needs. This adds to the frustration of the people.

v. THE VICEROY'S AGENT IS A BOXWALLAH

The miracle of British administration lay in its retaining control over the rough badlands of the Tribal Areas through just one British officer, the Political Agent. He was the Political and Administrative agent of the Government of India through the Governor, and in the case of Indian states through the Agent to the Governor General or the AGG. He was the Viceroy's Agent to the concerned tribe. He was supported by a few Indian political subordinates, actually native civil administrators who managed the difficult tribal wards through personal courage, wit, and determination. The officers were taught to be 'firm, fair, and friendly', pretty empty words when the chips were down, but cardinal principles of sound administration nevertheless. During the British Raj, the Political Agent for the Frontier tribes needed to be 'lean and keen' while 'the fat and the good natured' were useful for the Indian states. Tribesmen have always been most astute observers and quickly evaluate a new Political Agent on arrival and then decide how to deal with him. Threats, blandishments, or sycophancy work with some officers but the tribesman knows who to respect, and these are the ones who normally succeed. Tribesmen expect higher moral standards of their Political Agents and have been known to advise political officers not to lie or cheat even if they themselves indulge in these traits. Sir George Cunningham, the Governor of NWFP, would post his brightest officers and bold risk-takers to the Tribal Areas, and would often ignore their minor improprieties. For postings in the Secretariat and Accounts offices, he would look for the sedentary *lakeer ka fakeer*, one who follows rules stringently and never deviates from prescribed texts. The more modest ones were not suitable for the rough and tumble of the Tribal Areas, where every Political Agent defined his own administration style.

The position of the Political Agent is central to the affairs of the Agency. Administration is highly individualized and prescribed texts do not always work. He needs to carry the Maliks and the tribes with him, to ensure that there is relative peace in the Agency. This means that the roads must remain open, small business encouraged, and development activity pursued. He is deemed to be successful if he achieves these aims without the constant use of the Scouts. Often he is so keen to avoid the use of force that he is seen as standing 'between the soldier and his war medal'. The position was considered very important. A former British High Commissioner to Pakistan, Sir Oliver Foster, once told me while I was the Political Agent Khyber, that by the time he finished his university studies, the Raj had ended, otherwise the one position he would have loved to hold was that of a political agent.

For the political agent, patience, tact, and wit are important, but nothing is more crucial than character, courage, and integrity. Tribesmen often test new officers with threats and inducements, more so in Waziristan and Khyber. The Political Agent however, cannot submit to threats, empty as these may be. Once he commits to a course of action he must follow through or face ridicule for the remainder of his tenure. A mature political officer would win tribesmen through adherence to the law and regular *mullaqat* or meetings, approachability towards the administration's supporters, the odd favour to show recognition, and a refusal to be intimidated by fear, buys their respect. Courage, like cowardice, is contagious and works wonders. But total reliance on force and the militia does not always succeed. Officers with *boxwallah* reputations or those looking for financial gains, failed to leave any impact. Some good officers like Abdul Hameed Kusuria in North Waziristan, Taj Muhammad Khan in Kurram, and Javed Khanzada in Khyber Agencies came to grief by acting impulsively and being unable to balance the different options available. Kusuria was killed during a Tochi Scouts action to recover a stolen rifle even though there were a dozen non-violent ways of recovering stolen rifles. It was rumoured that his assistant political agent used abusive words for a tribesman, who was preparing to get them refreshments, which resulted in fatal shots being fired at them. Taj Muhammad Safi was known to be a tough officer but was shot and wounded by a mob in Parachinar that demanded the restoration of water lines that were disconnected for non-payment of bills during Ramzan, the month of fasting. Javed Khanzada, formerly of the 13 Lancers, an aviator and hunter, was of a special breed of men. Posted to the Khyber Agency without any prior experience in the Tribal Areas, he was immediately thrown into the deep end. With little understanding of tribal administration, he relied on force alone and saw no peace during his tenure. The cardinal rule was to employ the carrot-and-stick principle, which he did not comprehend.

The physical risks and strenuous duties of office were partially compensated by the small perks in the past, although these days the financial incentives are of a different kind. A number of political officers were killed or injured in line of duty in the Tribal Areas, both during the British era and later. Three Political Agents died a violent death in South Waziristan prior to Independence, with their names starting with the alphabet 'D', namely Dodd, Donald, and Duncan. Durbar Ali Shah, a post-Independence Political Agent, was therefore perpetually worried and would go to great lengths to avoid risks!

The role and position of the political agent is unlike any other devised by management practitioners. Nowhere in the world, is someone so young entrusted with so many powers and responsibilities. The political agent is vested with immense authority in executive, judicial, financial, and developmental areas. He commands the levies and *khassadars*, who number between two to three thousand in each Agency, and has overall supervisory control over all Government departments in the Agency. He is also in law, if no longer in practice, the immediate superior of the Commandant of the Frontier Corps unit, the Scouts, and can order the deployment of the troops to control any situation. The job of the political agent, however, is very demanding and inherently risky. His main reward is the boost to his ego that the post gives him, and he is compensated through discretionary funds and allowances for secret service and entertainment. The political agent is also authorized to issue permits for the import into the Agency of timber and goods from Afghanistan and the export of food items to that country. The permits are meant as payments to tribesmen for various services rendered for the administration, though there is considerable misappropriation in the system. Some officers, even in the past, and most today, were infamously associated with the misuse of permits. It is one thing to be able to live comfortably during a tenure in the Tribal Area, but quite another to amass a fortune to purchase properties.

For governors and chief secretaries, the test always lies in selecting the most effective and honourable officers as political agents. The rest follows in routine. An all-round merit, which can only be based on reputation, is the sole criterion and the results normally vindicate the choice. Over the years, aberrations have set in and corrupt practices have developed. What was worse was to follow over the last twenty years. It was rumoured that many a governor and some serving generals would appoint the highest bidder to the political agent's post. A few years back, reportedly, one contender paid Rs. 200 million to the governor for a prized position in the Tribal Areas. This was hardly surprising, since some governors themselves have been known to pay hefty amounts to their political sponsors in Islamabad to buy their gubernatorial positions. There appears to be no limit to greed and there is no hitting rock bottom either, as the administration continued to become morally bankrupt. A new breed of investors has now emerged who invest in political agents and other office holders including, the governor's office for financial gains. There always was, an element of corruption, in the Tribal Areas with political agents and their subordinates syphoning money through the issue of food or timber permits. In the Khyber Agency as in all others, the Politicals, the Khyber Rifles, the *Khassadars*, and all Intelligence agencies were 'on the take' and the amounts collected were huge. British Political Officers, someone remembered, would only accept cake and drinks as gifts on Christmas. A week into my posting as Political Agent Khyber Agency, a subordinate, with embarrassment written all over him, mumbled and asked where my share from the permits should be deposited. He told me that all officials of the political administration, the Khyber Rifles, the *Khassadars*, and the four intelligence agencies received their daily share. I declined to be part of such thievery and I imagine they would have distributed my share among themselves. In Balochistan, the enrichment from such illegal trade in the Frontier Corps, the Customs, and the others is said to be much higher. One tenure of 'duty' suffices for a couple of generations.

It is therefore, not difficult to understand why the writ and authority of the state had collapsed and the state faced serious difficulties in restoring it. The reason is due to general incompetence and some shamefully corrupt officers and politicians placed in positions of power, over the last few decades. 'Thank God for the creation of Pakistan or I would be a *subedar* and you an overseer,' said Colonel Qadir Khan of the Frontier Corps, pointing towards a Superintending Engineer. Three former Governors, Sir Olaf Caroe, Sir George Cunningham, and Sir George Roos-Keppel would have turned in their graves were they to learn about the new ways and methods of their successors. Other Englishmen, including the Governor-General of Bengal, Lord Clive and Warren Hastings, during the eighteenth century, would have been more at peace with this Pakistani arrangement. Clive is reported to have stated at his trial for corruption that he was surprised at his own 'moderation' in amassing wealth in India, while in the service of the Honourable East India Company. He was acquitted after a long trial.

The Government must not only post honest and competent officers to the Tribal Areas but also support them in their pursuit of state policy. Soon after the creation of Pakistan, the tribal hostiles, who with the covert support of the Afghans, sponsored a *lashkar* in Tirah which started moving towards the Bara plains near Peshawar. The Political Agent of Khyber, Sardar Muhamad Alam from Kot Najibullah in Haripur, on the advice of the Governor, publicly warned the *lashkar* not to cross a certain line, failing which, he would order action by the Pakistan Air Force. The *lashkar* however, crossed the line, meanwhile the Government decided to act discretely and wished to start negotiations instead. Sardar Muhammad Alam had a huge moustache and having heard that the Governor had revised his position, requested that a barber be summoned immediately so that he could shave his moustache before facing the tribal *jirga* again to convey to them the change in policy. 'Saving face' was important. It was only then that the air bombardment was ordered and normalcy restored. The massive moustache of Sardar Sahib was also the subject of comment earlier when he was Political Agent in Gilgit-Baltistan. One morning at the airport, he was seen walking briskly near the runway and was frantically cautioned by a visiting American official to slow down lest he take off!

By and large, the tribe always understood the government's resolve in cases when there was a real threat to the state's sovereignty. For any threat short of that, the political agent had different means to deal with the developing situation and these means normally 'delivered' the objective sought. This of course was always complemented by the silent persuasion of the paramilitary Scouts, camped nearby or the battalion stationed close by. The Political Agent however, has to take stock of the 'political' and tactical ground situation before he decides to use force and then only when he is certain of success. For example, it is just not possible to employ the Frontier Corps against the whole tribe or even a large segment of it or when sensitive issues are involved. It is essential to isolate and reduce to a small minority those tribesmen against whom action is contemplated. As Chief Secretary, Frontier Province in 2002, I was quite baffled when the Political Agent of Khyber, Fida Wazir, informed me in a chance meeting that Governor Iftikhar Hussain had ordered him to use the Khyber Rifles to recover electricity bills from the dominant Zaka Khel Afridi tribe. This could have led to large scale casualties for limited or no gain. Only a novice could have issued such orders and I dissuaded the Governor from such a foolish course of action. Serious matters such as these are best resolved through tribal *jirga(s)* and consensus building.

The British, unlike the French and the Spanish, were very wise in not burdening the tribes with foreign administrative instruments and legal codes. They chose to manage the Agency's affairs through the tribes' own customs and usages with a few adaptations where these were essentially required. The dos and don'ts of the treaties between the various tribes and the Government were laid out in the *Collection of Treaties, Engagements and Sanads Relating to India and Neighbouring Countries* by Charles U Aitchison, published in 1909. The treaties were also known as the Aitchison Treaties. One of the central features of these treaties called for the return of any tribal woman who flees her home and seeks refuge in the Settled Areas. This provision was a tricky one, since the return of the woman to the tribe meant instant death while not returning her, contravened the treaty's clauses. The condition of women, as far as human rights were concerned, were non-existent and generally elaborate excuses were put up by the Government to either delay or deny the return of the women.

As late as the mid-seventies, the Rabia Khel Orakzais attacked the town of Hangu because a young woman from their tribe had decided to marry against the wishes of her parents. The police was outgunned and the Frontier Constabulary was hesitant to fire the first shot unless specifically ordered by the Assistant Commissioner or the Deputy Superintendent of Police, both of whom got cold feet. As the firing intensified, the Political Agent of Orakzai Agency, whose headquarters were in Hangu town, tried to get the two Settled Officers to resolve the issue but to no avail. He then asked the courageous District Officer of the Constabulary, if he would obey his orders to repel the tribesmen by force of arms, even though the area was outside the Political Agent's jurisdiction. Masta Mir was a most remarkable man who had risen from the ranks and spoke only Masud Pashto and no English or Urdu. He replied that he was prepared to take action on the condition that I issue written orders and take full responsibility for the consequences, whenever an enquiry was held. This being the proper course, I gladly agreed to do so. The Constabulary thereafter, fired a few bursts of machine gun fire over the heads of the invading tribesmen and next thing one saw was hundreds of Rabia Khel Orakzais fleeing as fast as their feet could carry them. The situation was retrieved, peace restored, and the fugitive pair were taken into protective custody. People remained appreciative of the brave woman who continued to fire back when under intense attack. Love indeed is blind, as the Hangu man was said to be pockmarked and of pedestrian looks.

Often during the course of duty, the political agent had to come to the aid of destitute men and women. After the Soviet invasion of Afghanistan, millions of refugees poured into Pakistan and there were times that a steady stream of homeless orphans and displaced children would make their way to the refugee camps, on this side of the border. Once such a young girl, without any parental support, arrived at Torkham, a major border crossing between Pakistan and Afghanistan. Suddenly there appeared dozens of good Samaritan tribesmen volunteering to house and support her. This was a tricky situation and the little dove had to be kept out of the hawk's reach. The family of an official driver was told to look after her till a blood relative was traced, much to the annoyance of the not so good Samaritans!

vi. The Tribal Institutions

For the British, the matter of immediate concern after gaining control of a tribal area, was establishing government offices, camps, cantonments, residential buildings, bazaars, and the roads which were deemed 'administered' or 'settled' areas. In such pockets, magistrates and session judges could exercise judicial powers under the Indian Penal Code, although it was rarely used. This was a small grey area and bordered the 'Protected Areas' where the tribes lived and where the Government occasionally intervened through the Frontier Crimes Regulation when the law and order and security conditions, so demanded. In cases of serious intra-tribal violence, kidnapping, thefts, and smuggling, the *Khassadars* and the Scouts were employed to restore order. There was another subdivision as well, the 'Non-Protected Area' or Tribal Territory, the 'TT' of the political officers, which was physically inaccessible. In every Agency, there were such pockets with no roads and the tribes were left to their own device. The state generally remained indifferent to them except when there were reports of

Russian, German, Afghan, or Indian anti-state elements present. This was when there was no shortage of loyal *maliks*, offering to neutralize them indirectly, provided the political agent armed them with sacks full of money.

The British tried not to disturb the traditional life and customs of the tribesmen as they were their main stabilizing force in the area. Tribal institutions, as stated, were employed and where required local customs were codified and gradually adapted and modernized. It was recognized that economically, the area was non-sustainable. Apart from provision of employment in the government services, some financial rewards were dispensed through the bi-annual tribal allowance, the *muwajib*. This meant the grant of money to the tribe for maintaining good behaviour. Social stability was achieved through the recognition of the traditional tribal elders and grey beards, the *maliks* and *spingeeray*, who wielded power and influence in their tribe. They in turn interacted with the tribesmen in all matters and were held responsible to the State in return. Finally, holding the entire tribe or a sub-tribe responsible, for *nafa* and *nuqsan* or profit and loss, through the concept of collective tribal responsibility meant that every adult male from that sub-tribe, the *tappa* or *kundi*, was accountable for the conduct of any one of its member. This inculcated restraint among the tribes, as each member was deemed a fair game and could be arrested by the government for a crime committed by any other member of that sub-section of the tribe. This system was also derived from the prevalent custom among the tribes. For the Government, this practice helped to control crime and ensured social stability during that period. Over the years as the Tribal Areas were opened through the construction of roads, bringing in socio-economic development, while the tribesmen started availing opportunities for trade, business, and professional activities. Under the current scenario, the system of tribal collective responsibility has lost much of its effectiveness and needs to be modified. In any case, in the twenty-first century, it would not be correct for any number of reasons, to imprison routinely fellow tribesmen and distant family members for the conduct of one accused. It would not be possible today to take into custody a government officer, a doctor or a banker, for instance, for the real or alleged sins of a close blood relative! However, in cases of serious crimes like kidnapping for ransom, terrorism, and extortion, despite the protests of the human rights organizations, pressurizing close family members until the accused is arrested is a practice widely exercised by the Punjab and Sindh Police with effective results. After the merger of the Tribal Areas the Deputy Commissioners of the Districts as successors to the Political Agents would need to ensure that the system was not abused and the rights of the people were respected.

The administration in the Tribal Agencies nevertheless was based on the cooperation of the tribal elders, the *maliks*, and it is always important that the Political Agent keep them in good humour. Their success or failure depends on this vital relationship. A *malik*, as a representative of his tribe or sub-section of a tribe, is no more than the first among equals. He cannot ride roughshod over the collective views of the tribe which he is bound to consult. The *jirga*, or the tribal council, thus carries much importance as it is a body that is thousands of years old. Everyone in the tribe wants to be heard, or at least be seen to be heard, in the consultative *jirga*. The *jirga* arrives at its decisions through a consensus of the assembled and it is difficult for the tribal *malik* or the political officer to impose his decision over their verdict. The village organizations, currently being advocated by international community and development specialists are a poor version of the village *jirga*. There was this occasion when the International Fund for Agricultural Development declined to fund a development project in the Tribal Areas because their charter stated that they could only work through Village Organizations. They were advised by the Additional Chief Secretary of NWFP to select Waziristan for their programme, rather than choosing the settled areas and to see matters at first hand by observing the functioning of the tribal *jirga*. After they saw the actual working of the consensual *jirga* during the visit, they enthusiastically agreed to undertake their project in the Tribal Areas. It was, however made very clear to them that the lady consultants should be appropriately dressed and covered. Moreover, only women would be allowed to work with and speak to tribal women. They were also told to concentrate on their immediate duties and to avoid lecturing anyone on women's emancipation as emancipation is easier brought about by education and poverty alleviation. The ground rules were adhered to and the project proceeded comfortably until the events of 9/11. Some NGOs are reviled locally; years earlier an elderly man from Dir told the Commissioner that he had seen an 'NGO and she was half-naked'!

There are times when a *malik* does not want to assist the political agent for reasons of his own and checkmates him through subterfuge, intrigue, or hostility. There are other times when to attract the attention of the political agent, a tribesman may get someone to snipe at the political agent's office or the Scouts Camp at night. This causes no material damage but the nuisance value of the individual is established. The *maliks* have to be dealt with, in a friendly manner which is another way of saying that they have to be supplied with favours. The grant of tradable permits, award of development projects, where the *malik* is also the nominated contractor, employing a *khassadar* or two, and the official recognition in functions are what the *maliks* crave most. In return they help keep peace, assist the development process, and ignore the government's retaliatory measures against criminals and offenders. Generally, they have their bread buttered on both sides! Protocol is important for the leading *maliks* and they must be seen to be in the forefront by others, such as when offering the traditional sheep to visiting dignitaries. The presented sheep is in fact paid for, by the State but is returned to the *maliks* after the dignitary pats it on the head to acknowledge the gift. The poor sheep is then put to the more conventional use by the *maliks*; it is slaughtered and consumed in the form of *tikka* and *laralay* by them, as soon as the visitor departs. Giving this gift and then consuming is the convention! Only once was this convention not observed. That was when the then Governor Frontier Province, Khwaja Shahabud Din of Dakka and Kashmir, decided to take the presented sheep back to the Governor House for future use. The tribesmen never forgave him for the deviation from convention and remembered it forty years later. Another time when Malik Gulla Khan invited two officers to his home for lunch and presented a wristwatch to each, Gulzar Khan of the Civil Service, mischievously enquired if the wristwatches were also to be returned like the gifted sheep!

Every *malik* demands *mullaqat*, a one-on-one meeting, with the political agent. The duration and frequency of this is determined by the importance of the *malik*. He may or may not provide confidential information to the political agent, but this is the investment that has to be made for any support that may be required by the political agent in future. Often the *maliks* freely criticize and backbite their peers, if only to draw greater attention to themselves. The *Mullaqat*, to be of any value, must be strictly confidential. It is amazing what a tribesman can reveal in the secrecy of an office. One simple political agent, having read the handing-over confidential report of his predecessor, confronted an intelligence source in public, demanding why the latter had not provided any secret information on kidnappers and car thieves to him as he would to his predecessor. This was like a death sentence for the informer. The bonds of friendship and mutual self-interest of the tribesman and the political officers was proverbial. Malik Darya Khan, the sagacious elder from North Waziristan, would always caution fellow *maliks* against constant animosity towards the political agent, saying that the latter was the biggest malik in the tribal Agency and the Government the biggest tribe. Fighting this powerful 'tribe' would in time definitely cause their ruin.

The tribal institution of levies and *khassadars* consists of tribesmen provided by the concerned tribe as a mark of allegiance but they are also paid by the government. Increasingly, they perform security, watch and ward duties in the northern Agencies. In Waziristan, however they have a less defined role. In places where the grip of the administration was firmer, they became the Political Agent's police force. From marauders, they became a force to check marauding. The *khassadars* were as much a local security unit as they were 'hostages' provided by the tribe to the state for ensuring good behaviour. They had the advantage, as local tribesmen, in being able to deal effectively with their fellow tribesmen. Levies were recruited in those parts of the Tribal Areas, where the state had greater control such as in Upper Kurram, home to the Turi tribe, and in the old Malakand Agency. The Levies did not need to bring their own rifles, unlike the *khassadars*, as rifles were provided by the state. Their position was not hereditary and anyone from a sub-section of the tribe could be recruited when someone retired. Except in Waziristan, the levies and *khassadars* would wear a dark grey militia uniform with shoulder badges often inaccurately announcing them as a 'force' even though they were more of a tribal institution. In Waziristan, the *khassadars* rarely wore uniforms, but that did not mean they did not claim the allowance for it. Now that the tribal areas have been merged into the settled districts of Khyber Pukhtunkhwa Province, the khassadars and levies would need to be quickly reorganized as a Levy Police force, armed and trained for security duties and crime investigation. The establishment of Levy Police Stations, in different parts of the Agency, after the merger with the settled areas, is now an urgent requirement. The writ of the state has to be established and governance improved. The *khassadars*, being a more informal tribal institution, should be converted into the Levy Police force under an organized command system with proper recruitment, training, investigation, and prosecution regimes so that crimes could be reported, criminals apprehended, and cases investigated and prosecuted in courts.

One tribal custom which the more influential tribesman shares with other Pakhtuns is the *hujra* or guest house for visitors and a meeting place for the villagers. In the Tribal Areas, a guest on entry into the *hujra*, traditionally hands over his weapons to the host, as security is the latter's responsibility. What is always even more endearing is watching one of the hosts rearrange the shoes, which the guest removes on entering the *hujra*. Touching the shoes, merely conveys the message that the guest is held in high esteem. This is a very moving experience!

Judging by the events of the last thirty years, it is clear that many of the tribal customs have been superseded by time and events as these are no longer very effective in maintaining, let alone extending the writ of the state. Although the tribesmen have been well-integrated into Pakistan's economy and the mainstream of society, the Tribal Areas still have a lot of catching up to do in terms of development. Almost all governments with the exception of Zulfikar Ali Bhutto's, were guilty of this 'masterly neglect' which was an invitation to trouble. The majority of the rulers neither cared about the area nor found the time to visit the people to address the problems. Had Bhutto stayed longer in power, the Tribal Areas would have been much more developed economically and politically. It is therefore, not surprising that decades of neglect have been responsible for the turmoil and civil strife the Tribal Areas are now experiencing.

Following the US invasion of Afghanistan, the indigenous and foreign powers became stronger in the Tribal Areas because of the vacuum that existed. Traditional organizations like the *maliks*, *khassadars*, and 'collective tribal responsibility' were all brushed aside like a house of cards. Hundreds of *maliks* were killed, schools blown up, and the authority of the state pulverized. The blame for this neglect rests squarely with the past 'rulers', presidents, prime ministers, governors, chief secretaries, and the senior Frontier officers, who either did not have long-term vision, or else were content to bide their time in office by shying away from difficult and risky actions. The Army and the Frontier Corps for their part were equally oblivious to the dangerous vacuum that had been created over the years in the Tribal Areas. There were very few officers with a vision, both in the Frontier Secretariat and the Frontier Corps. The majority could not comprehend the issues that could erupt in the future. Those who understood the need for opening up the Tribal Areas included Chief Secretaries NWFP like Nasruminallah, Ijlal Haider Zaidi, and Omar Afridi; and among the Inspector Generals of Frontier Corps there were Generals Naseerullah Babar and Tariq Khan who were willing to show the flag. For the rest, a tenure of service in the Tribal Areas merely beefed up their resumes. The Pakistani leadership should have taken a leaf from both the Czarist and Communist Russians who opened up all parts of the Central Asian Republics very early on and thus extended socio-economic benefits to the people. Sadly, we let time slip by and time does not forgive!

vii. THE FRONTIER CRIMES REGULATIONS (FCR)

Over the past 2,000 years, the British alone were successful in establishing a measure of control in the Tribal Areas. This was no small achievement and was largely the result of adopting a policy of least possible interference in the daily affairs of the tribesmen. One of the policies adopted was the Frontier Crimes Regulation (FCR), an amalgam of limited criminal and civil procedural codes which were adapted from the tribal customs in practice. Normally their application was restricted to the *Administered* or *Protected* areas that were accessible in the Agency such as government offices, roads, bazaars, and camps but rarely in the *Non-Protected* areas which were outside. The purpose was to establish law and order and legitimized British authority, while providing prompt and cheap justice in keeping with the tribal traditions.

Tribal folklore has it that when the British first interacted with the tribesmen, their views were sought on the type of laws to be applied to them. *Sharia*, the Islamic law, was first suggested but the tribe balked at the thought of losing their hands for the crime of stealing. The Indian Penal Code was then proposed but the tribesmen felt that this placed a premium on providing truthful evidence which they would find most difficult to ensure. Exasperated the British official asked in Pushto *bya ba so kau* and pat came the reply *bya ba guzara kau*. *Guzara* was accepted by the tribe but it defies definition. It could be described as showing flexibility and lenience; a pardon today and a penalty tomorrow. And tomorrow is another day anyway.

The FCR is in some respects like *guzara*, was an instrument in the hands of the administrator, to be employed carefully in the larger interest of stability of the tribal society. A term of imprisonment could be scrapped if the tribe shows up collectively as a *jirga* requesting a pardon. The award of punishment displayed the sovereign status of the state, but the grant of pardon was a concession from authority in accordance with the traditions of the tribe. The spirit of *guzara* was to *live and let live*. Any request from a *jirga* suggests the tacit acceptance of responsibility by them for the future and that is why it was rarely spurned. The *jirga* resolves the problem and provides some guarantees for future good behaviour of the individual or a section of the tribe. The tribal agency is a hostile and dangerous place where brute force is not always the best solution. The Political Agent may be required to take one step forward and two steps backwards, depending upon the surrounding conditions. Many years ago, a Federal Minister of Water and Power having heard that a request from a *jirga* is normally accepted in Pakhtun culture came to see the Chairman, Water and Power Development Authority (WAPDA) in a *jirga*, requesting that a Rs. 7 billion contract for a small dam be awarded to a close friend. The Pakhtun chairman was at a loss trying to explain to the Minister that government rules did not permit him to grant the contract, and in any case only a personal request from a *jirga* could be accepted. The Punjabi Minister was not impressed!

The FCR is a time-honoured and fair customary code but unfortunately much maligned by people who do not understand its spirit. Laws in a special area must reflect the objective conditions and requirements of that area. The local people would not be stable or develop economically if the laws in practice were unable to address the local conditions effectively. The FCR is effective because its spirit is diametrically opposed to the philosophy of retribution in criminal court system, in the settled areas. The *jirga* basically tries to ease the vengeance, honour, and anger of the victim rather than to punish the guilty. The underlying assumption is that the victim party must be fully satisfied with the award of the *jirga*. That alone would drain out the vengeful spirit while no amount of punishment to the guilty may end his grievance. In the settled districts, very often when the accused is convicted by the court and after serving the jail term, the victim's party strikes to exact personal revenge. Thus, people suffer the consequences of insecurity and recurrent crime. This causes entrepreneurs and capital to migrate to safer areas. This cycle continues till one party throws in the towel and leaves the area or when both parties become bankrupt. Where redress of disputes is not possible and delays and heavy expenses are the rule, people find it difficult to utilize the investable economic surplus for generating economic activity. There were some deficiencies in the penal and security provisions of the FCR but as a procedural code, both in criminal and civil disputes, the *jirga* system functioned effectively. The State needs to choose a judicial system that delivers effectively rather than pander to the personal interests of any influential sections of society.

The great advantage of the FCR was the simplicity in processing of criminal and civil cases. The key issue lay in the selection of the *jirga* members, as tribesmen become partial to their kin or to the lure of money. Assuming that the political officer responsible for processing the *jirga* acts honestly and competently in accordance with the law, the trial takes just a few days and the conviction rate is very high. This is because the facts of a crime or the truth behind civil disputes are generally known to the local people so the manipulation of the Evidence Act and the intricacies of the Civil and Criminal Codes are avoided. Officers who have been part of the *jirga* trials in the Tribal Areas for decades and have disposed hundreds of cases insist that there are few occasions where there is miscarriage of justice on grounds of corruption or partiality shown to a party. The performance of some judges of the superior courts has not been beyond reproach either. During my long stints in the Tribal Areas, I can vouch for the fact that after hearing and pronouncing verdicts in hundreds of cases, I never missed a good night's sleep. All that the FCR courts require, is a honourable trial officer and honest *jirga* members. The complexities of law and corrupt practices are a bane in the justice system in the courts of the settled districts as well. These drawbacks are well-known to the tribesmen but after the merger, the application of procedural laws needs to be evaluated objectively. Integrity is both a financial and intellectual property and is not the preserve of a class. The fault then does not lie in the particular codes, but in those who are responsible for executing the codes. The greatest vindication of the FCR as a procedural code in the Tribal Areas is that the majority of tribesmen, (with the exception of the tribal lawyers), remain supportive of the *jirga* trials and have not shown any partiality to the court system in the settled areas. In the past, the preventive and security sections were deemed offensive by the tribesmen but now with the abolition of the Frontier Crimes Regulation (FCR) those sections dealing with 'preventive security' would be replaced with the preventive security laws in practice in the rest of the country which are very stringent as well. Additionally, the jurisdiction of the Peshawar High Court and the Supreme Court of Pakistan has been extended to the Tribal Areas and will lead to prompt and inexpensive justice which sadly has not been seen in the settled districts since Partition.

It may be remembered that traditional *jirga(s)*, as opposed to vigilante *jirga(s)*, remain in practice all across Pakistan but they function informally. Where the parties trust the elders of the area, these are a prompt and cost effective means of resolving dangerous and protracted disputes in a manner that neither of the parties 'loses face'. Not losing face is always crucial for the tribal community and the tribesmen accept a harsh decision or order by the Government but would never allow a minor concession to the adversary. Such a process was adopted some decades back to resolve the serious dispute between Katiakhel Kukikhel Afridi and Shalober Qamber Khel Afridis in the Khyber Agency which had defied resolution for decades and consumed many lives. Every few months, a *tiga* or ceasefire, when a stone is symbolically placed between the warring parties, would temporarily bring about a cessation of hostilities, but could not settle the dispute permanently. Ultimately, both the adversaries asked the political agent to act as the arbitrator to resolve the issue. Ordinarily, the political agent should not take over this role as he is bound to annoy one of the parties. In the event, he announced that the central part of the disputed land was to be awarded free of cost to the government to construct a quality public school and distributed the rest of the land between the parties which was gladly accepted by both parties. For the Pakhtun, a personal loss is gladly acceptable as long as the enemy does not gain. Sadly, even after 30 years, the quality school was never built. The decision of the Government in 2020 to permit select Elders in the merged areas to resolve civil disputes through an Alternate Dispute Resolution mode is a welcome step towards satisfying the peoples' needs. The criminal cases should similarly be adjudicated like the jury system around the world.

viii. THE FRONTIER CORPS

The Frontier Corps, the federal para-military force in the former Tribal Areas, is popularly called the Scouts or the Militia. The Scouts in the Khyber Pukhtunkhwa province (KPK) is a separate force from the Frontier Corps in Balochistan province. Some years ago the Frontier Corps (KPK) was subdivided into separate Northern and Southern commands each under a Major General from the Pakistan Army. The tribes that are allowed to enlist in the Frontier Corps include the Masuds, Wazirs, Turis, Orakzais, Afridis, Mullaghoris, Bhittanis, Shilmanis, and Mohmands while the balance came from the settled districts tribes of Khattaks, Bangash, Yusafzais, Chitralis, and others. Chitralis are the only non-Pakhtun tribes that are notified for enrolment in the Scouts. The dark grey cloth used for making their uniform is also called *militia*, although lately the army-khaki uniform has been introduced for the Frontier Corps.

The forerunner of the Frontier Corps 15 units was the Khyber Rifles (1878) following which the Kurram Militia (1892), the Tochi Scouts (1894), the South Waziristan Scouts (1900) and the Chitral Scouts (1903) were raised. The Masud Scouts were established just before Partition and the Thall Scouts shortly thereafter. The Bajaur Scouts was created after the Dir-Bajaur operations in 1960–61 while the Dir Scouts came into existence after the State was merged in 1970. The Mohmand Rifles in Yusuf Khel-Ghallanai and the Shawal Rifles in Razmak were created as part of the opening up of the Tribal Areas in the early 1970s. More recently, following the post-9/11 operations in the tribal belt and Malakand division, the Swat Scouts, the Orakzai Scouts, the Khattak Scouts and the Bhittani Rifles were raised.

The Scouts are a fleet-footed and lightly armed force of naturally trained climbers. During *baramtas* (security operations), road protection duties and especially Road Opening Days (ROD) in the past they would occupy the adjoining hills and vantage positions to ensure security and to ensure safe passage. The Scouts were able to scale mountains, easily not only because they were hill people but due to their regulation uniform of the loose *shalwar kameez*, made for effortless climbing. Their food, especially the dry rations were modest, actually very modest. In 1983, the Columbia Broadcasting System (CBS) team while filming the heroin trail for the TV programme *Sixty Minutes*, wanted to see the Khyber Rifles in action and taste the food a rifleman carried in his haversack. The request was turned down by the Political Agent politely because the dry rations which consisted of nothing more than the humble *gur* or jiggery, and the poorest quality grams could not be shown to the world. Modest food notwithstanding, the Scouts have a proud history of courage and sacrifice, stretching well over a century.

Sadly, over time the Scouts have lost their distinct identity and have increasingly morphed into army-type battalions in structure and operations. For Political officers, merely requisitioning them for action, is a demanding exercise that takes many days. The Scouts officers, like the Army, now tend to adopt stricter hierarchical approach and have lost the flexibility that was the operational norm of Scouts in the past. During the British Raj, before an officer was accepted for service in the Scouts, he would be subjected to gruelling scrutiny and was then posted, initially, only on probation. For a while, the experiment of recruiting officers specifically for Frontier Corps service was also tried but quickly phased out for good measure. Such Scouts officers, generally, were not properly trained and over time acted more like 'Political' officers, than military ones. They were forever pleading against the use of force and would recommend the use of peaceful means to bring a tribe to heel. The best officers in the Frontier Corps were those who spent only one tenure and then returned to the Army. There were, however, some interesting and genial Scouts Commission officers in the Frontier Corps, like Colonels Abdul Qadir of Thana, Mohsam Khan of Bannu, and Major Jalil Afridi. They were relaxed and never tired of storytelling.

Service in the Tribal Areas has always been a risk for life and limb, and those posted in such difficult places are generally not averse to feathering their nests. This was relatively easy because of smuggling or trading of goods to and from Afghanistan. This however was the Pakistani way of life and few in society were above it.

One fact that was indisputable was the friendly, yet suspicious and an innocent distrust of the 'Politicals' by the Scouts and vice versa. There was a time when the political agent was the acknowledged head of the Agency's administration, so much so that in the annual parade the Political Agent would take the salute. When General Afzal, Inspector General Frontier Corps, wanted to reintroduce the annual parade in Waziristan, one Commandant actually thought this was a retrogressive step. The Commandant was never comfortable with a subordinate role to the political agent and was fond of quoting from the *Warrant of Precedence* that identifies the seniority positions of government officials. This *Warrant* was a flexible document that was regularly revised for the military's benefit every time there was martial law in the country, which, of course, was a regular occurrence. The 'Political' on his part, would quote the *Frontier Corps Act* which from the British days gave pre-eminence to the position of the political agent, in ordering troop deployment and conducting operations. However, getting the Commandant to actually deploy and employ troops for action on orders of the political agent, was an arduous task. The Commandant would raise every excuse in the book to delay if not avoid compliance. He would always consult the Frontier Corps Headquarters in Bala Hisar before even routine deployment could take place, and once approval was granted, he would demand civil transport to move the troops. This delayed matters and gave the wrong message to the tribe.

The Scouts were never meant to be independent of the 'Politicals' but have become so now. Some of the Commandants behaved so independently that the Khyber Rifles would openly entertain tribal *maliks* blacklisted by the political agent. Of late, one of the prime reasons for the withering away of the authority of the state in the Tribal Areas has been the downgrading of the role and status of the political agent by the Government of General Musharraf and the military. The political agent's role has been substituted by the military intelligence agencies whose diktat is now deemed final, in most matters. The Scouts and the intelligence officers are concerned only with immediate security matters, while the political agent was the actual *more plar*, or the father, the care giver for the tribesmen. He was the one responsible for all aspects of the tribesmen lives and over a century the two had developed conventions they generally abided by. Things have reached such a pass during the past few years that a Brigade Commander in South Waziristan Agency deliberately made the political agent wait outside his office for an hour along with the other tribesmen, before seeing him. He said later that he did this on purpose to show the political agent his *right place*. What the ignorant Brigadier did not realize was that great damage was being caused to the writ of the state and not to an individual.

By and large, the Scout Commandants were mature officers and some of them, like Colonel Sher Rehman Sheru from the Khyber Rifles and Colonel Fazle Mahbud from Masud Scouts, both winners of Sitara-i-Jurat which is the equivalent of the Military Cross, were exceptionally competent. Colonel Shera would keep himself occupied in the mess bar all night before a *baramta* raid alongside Laiq Hussain, the Assistant Political Agent and Major Mahmood of Sargodha *to discuss strategy*. Nothing else they joked! They would proceed straight from the bar to the operations area before first light. Then very alert, he would approach the political agent whose presence was required in operations, salute and inform him most candidly that he would be responsible for the operation only till he was alive. After that you would be on your own! Fortunately, for the political agent, he survived dozens of such operations and was always successful. Rarely did the need arise to even fire a shot. Other Commandants were not so forthright. One Commandant would constantly remind the Politicals that this was not the militia of the British Raj and they could not be relied on. The fact remained that, as is said about the Army, the Scouts are also as good as their officers were.

A level of maturity also needs to be shown by the 'Politicals' in dealing with the Scout officers. Some political agents were particularly friendly with the Scouts Commandants. One of them was Sahibzada Yunis, then serving in Kurram Agency. He like other political agents would pay a routine allowance to the Scouts, outside the books, with a promise of a, monthly increment if matters remained satisfactory.

When security conditions permitted, senior Scout officers savoured their stay in the tribal areas. Often the Mess with its Bar was the focal point. The most remembered senior officer was the Inspector General Agha Zulfiqar, who was tough in office, but relaxed later. He was known to loath consuming contraband beverages in tea cups during President Ziaul Haq's rule. On one occasion during a dance performance in the Mess, a suitably inebriated Major bodily lifted the lady dancer and placed her onto a bewildered General's lap breaking the chair in the process. The Inspector General promptly ordered a court martial of the Major and announced

the sentence forthwith; two bottles of Scotch for the Mess! This was a stiff
sentence quite literally, recalled Ismail Niazi, because Charles, the Prince of
Wales, had merely fined a naval mate a bar of 'Mars' chocolate for taking
a bite from his cucumber sandwich without permission.

ix. THE NEW FORWARD POLICY OF ZULFIKAR ALI BHUTTO

Ever since Pakistan came into being in 1947, there has been little debate
and much ambiguity regarding how best to manage the Tribal Areas. The
Quaid-i-Azam's vision was clear and he wanted the Army to be moved out
of the Tribal Areas to show goodwill, cut costs, and concentrate the troops
on the eastern border. Accordingly, under Operation Curzon, the Army
was evacuated from Waziristan. The Quaid stood vindicated as there was
peace and stability for the next half-century in the area. Even during the
two wars with India, there was no hostile military pressure from the tribes
or indeed from Afghanistan.

As noted earlier, during this long period there was only one leader who
exhibited a deep interest in the development of the Tribal Areas. He was
Zulfikar Ali Bhutto. A politician from Sindh with foreign affairs experience,
Bhutto knew intuitively that the Tribal Areas needed to be developed
economically for ensuring both social and strategic stability. The area had
to be integrated politically and structurally with the rest of the country, so
that it could be led into the twentieth century.

In 1973, a new Forward Policy was planned and executed by two
brave and knowledgeable officers under Zulfikar Ali Bhutto's orders.
Nasruminallah was appointed Chief Secretary and Brigadier (later
Major General) Naseerullah Babar, was posted as Inspector General
Frontier Corps. Together, they initiated the move towards opening up
the inaccessible Tribal Areas. The opening was to be made through the
'Politicals', which meant peaceful initiatives while the efforts of the tribal
maliks would lead the strategy. The use of force was to be avoided. This
policy proved to be very successful.

It must be remembered that this area was called *tribal* not only because
tribal people lived here, but because the people responded collectively to
external stimuli. The concept of *collective* tribal responsibility, stipulated
that for all acts of omissions of the tribesmen, the sub-section of his

tribe would be collectively responsible to the administration and held accountable, had, over the years become anachronistic. This was the central principle on which the Tribal Areas functioned in the past because the concept was ingrained within the tribal structure as well. Now with most of the tribesmen living and working outside the Tribal Areas, and with the traditional power structure no longer relevant because of the impact and influence of education, employment, money, trade, and industry, and lately because of politics, it had lost its effectiveness. The merger of the former Tribal Areas into the Khyber Pukhtunkhwa province was therefore only a matter of time and in 2016, the committee headed by Sartaj Aziz made the correct recommendation of merging it with the province during the tenure of Prime Minister Nawaz Sharif. After the merger, the role and function of the state would expand to ensure effective management of security, control of crime and development of the area.

Unfortunately, the role and responsibilities of the state in the Tribal Areas had lagged far behind the requirements of the time. Little effort was made to open up the inaccessible areas to economic development, based on sound administration. This default, in due course, posed very serious problems for the state. Without effective state control over the area, the lives of the people could not be improved. The czars and the communists in Russia were able to provide universal literacy and full health coverage to the Central Asian Republics, because they opened up all inaccessible areas through a network of roads and railways. A hands off attitude towards the Tribal Areas, would not work. Presidents Ziaul Haq, Ghulam Ishaq, Farooq Leghari, Rafiq Tarar, Pervez Musharraf, Aisf Zardari, and Mamnoon Hussain barely found time to visit the Tribal Areas. Zulfikar Ali Bhutto was the only Prime Minister who traveled widely in the Tribal Areas.

Bhutto's new Forward Policy showed the way ahead. It basically extended the writ of the state in the Tribal Areas by re-occupying forts and areas abandoned after the creation of Pakistan. New roads were constructed and the territory opened up to the Durand Line, the border with Afghanistan. On the demarcation of the Durand Line in 1893, Afghanistan was allowed limited informal influence and consultation with some sections of tribes, who lived on both sides of the border. This was accepted as a temporary measure for preserving security and stability in an otherwise volatile area, but it was made clear that the Tribal Areas formed part of the British Indian

Empire. At times Afghanistan did try and provoke disaffection among the tribes but without much impact. It happened in early 1950s, when Malik Wali Khan, Malik Kukikhel, and Malik Nadir Khan Zakkakhel were provided shelter and support by Afghanistan. This led to the bombardment of strongholds of *Pakhtunistani* hostiles in Tirah and peace was soon restored. In 1975, the hostiles also opposed the construction of roads to Tirah in the Khyber and Orakzai Agencies which also led to a light skirmish with a hostile *lashkar* in Sheen Qamar near Khujauri plains. The *lashkar* after pushing back the ineffective *khassadars* decamped with their wireless equipment. In contrast, there were also times when the government and people of Afghanistan provided much needed support to Pakistan in its hour of need, as was the case when the country was at war with India.

There is no denying the great need for restoration of good neighbourly relationship between Pakistan and Afghanistan. Although, any claims on Pakistan's sovereignty cannot be countenanced, there are issues like sharing the water flow from the Kabul and Kaitu Rivers and other smaller streams that originate in Afghanistan, which need to be resolved, perhaps with the intervention of the World Bank. Pakistan should also assist Afghanistan in the development of water and power resources and it would be appropriate to finance and construct a dam for the Afghan people on the Kabul-Kunar River.

In 1973, King Zahir Shah of Afghanistan, was overthrown by his cousin, Sardar Daud Khan, who was a staunch *Pakhtunistani*. He was expected to stoke up much trouble in the Tribal Areas. There are minutes available of a meeting, quoting Prime Minister Zulfikar Ali Bhutto, that all inaccessible areas in the tribal belt be opened through the construction of roads before the new Afghan leadership could oppose the effort. This was also the period when sections of the Pakistan establishment clandestinely supported, with arms and finances, groups opposed to Daud Khan. This ill-conceived policy would haunt Pakistan for decades. In the event, Daud Khan turned out to be a very reasonable and wise leader who genuinely wanted to establish permanent peace with Pakistan. His meeting with Zulfikar Ali Bhutto in Murree and Rawalpindi in 1976, developed the basic groundwork of future relations with Pakistan. It was said that Bhutto felt that in the Foreign Office there were some senior policy makers from the Punjab who did not favour the restoration of normalcy with Afghanistan.

THE ERSTWHILE TRIBAL AREAS

This observation may or may not have been accurate, but there is little doubt that Pakistan's failure in extending its effective writ to the Tribal Areas was the primary cause of strained relations with Afghanistan. The lack of the state's presence also provided the opportunity to anti-state elements, who with the assistance of hostile powers, created serious law and order problems for Pakistan. However, through Zulfikar Ali Bhutto and Sardar Daud Khan, efforts for peaceful resolution of the issues were initiated. But time was not on their side. Bhutto was embroiled in elections and electoral misconduct during the period 1976–77. Sardar Daud Khan was assassinated in 1978 by extremist ideological forces in Afghanistan. Since those days, Afghanistan, and to a large extent Pakistan as well, have been caught in a vortex of turbulence and no one knows when thise will abate. Durable peace in the region, remains the precondition for resolving political, social, and water issues between both, Pakistan and Afghanistan. The former King Zahir Shah could have made the difference after his return to Afghanistan following the departure of Soviet Union by rallying the diverse people together as one nation. This was not to be, even though his name had a two hundred year old royal lineage and political legitimacy. Sadly, neither he nor anyone close to him had the resolve or was given the opportunity to better the circumstances of people of Afghanistan. There was a view prevalent that Zahir Shah did not have the capacity for the task of uniting the country since he had lived comfortably in Rome for decades while his country burned. Louis Dupree, a senior research associate, Islamic and Arabian Development Studies, would say that Zahir Shah was 'not a leader of men; he was a follower of women'.

The new Forward Policy was implemented by a breed of young and energetic officers who were appointed as Political Agents. Many were just thrown into the deep end to perform as they learned on the job. Conventional wisdom on the Tribal Areas also held that senior and experienced officers alone should be sent to these areas, but the Chief Secretary, Nasruminallah thought otherwise. Inayatullah and then Abdullah were sent to South Waziristan while Sulaiman Salim was posted to Miramshah in North Waziristan. Khalid Aziz administered Khyber Agency, while I was posted as Political Agent to the Orakzai Agency. At that time, the number of years I had served was less than three years, half of which was spent under training in the Civil Service Academy at

Lahore and Peshawar. A few senior provincial service officers like Afzal Khan Baruch, Sahibzada Yunis, Mohib Kiyani, Iqbal Swati, and Abdul Rahim were posted to some of the tribal Agencies, for a period. These five were experienced Political Agents, well-versed in administration and were expected to win over the tribal *maliks* through *jirga(s)* and negotiations to establish road communications in their areas. Bhutto allowed the Chief Secretary complete freedom of choice in the selection of officers, and more so, in implementing the policy. The foremost responsibility of this corps of officers was the opening up of the Tirah, Shawal, Khwazai-Baizai, Safi, Orakzai, Mamund, and Salarzai areas through a network of roads and development which was partially successful.

Apart from opening up the inaccessible areas, the summer resort town of Razmak—*Chota* or Little England—in the heart of Waziristan, with its alpine climate, extensive infrastructure and many forts were quickly taken over by the Frontier Corps. A Cadet College was also established for the tribesmen's children. Road communications to Ghulam Khan, Datta Khel, Gariom, Kankarwaam, Makin, Ladda, Birmal, Angor Adda, and Kaniguram were improved or extended. Bridges, long damaged by nature or man were rebuilt. Schools, especially for girls, hospitals and dispensaries were established. Irrigation and drinking water projects were set up and two factories were established in the public sector for making *chaplis* (footwear) and *machus* (match-boxes), units in Waziristan. The Shawal Scouts was established to show the Government's presence in the region. In the Khyber, Orakzai, and Kurram Agencies, the main focus was on building three roads into Tirah leading from Peshawar, Hangu, and Sadda. In Kurram, the road from Sadda to Badama and Dogar came close to the Afridi border. Early in 1975, in Orakzai, the roads from Hangu to Ghiljo and then across Sampagha Pass to Daburi were completed in heavy snow and rain. Maidan in the Khyber Agency was about twenty kilometres away.

In Khyber, efforts at road building from Khaujuri plains along the Bara River to Tirah were not successful. One of the main reasons was the complete prohibition on use of force for the purpose. If in early 1975, a Company or two of the Mehsud Scouts had been deployed at Shin Qamar in the Khyber Agency, the results would have been different, as was proved in the Mohmand Agency earlier. Besides this hundreds of schools, health units and drinking-water supply projects were undertaken. The Bara Dam

in Khyber and the Shalozan irrigation project in Kurrram were completed
and small industrial units for cigarette manufacture and fruit preservation
were established. In Mohmand and Bajaur Agencies, major roads were
carved out. The one from Yakka Ghund leading to Yusafkel and the
Nahakki Pass onto Khar in Bajaur Agency, was a singular success. Local
tribesmen by and large supported road building and there were always
tribesmen like Malik Yar Badshah of Kamali Halimzai whose efforts were
most laudable. A side road from Lakaro in Mohmand Agency was extended
toward Charmarkand and Nawa Pass, the pass from where Alexander
the Great entered India. Lakaro was also the place where a bomb blast
occurred during Prime Minister Bhutto's visit that killed the local Assistant
Political Agent in 1975. The opening of the Mamund and Salarzai valleys in
Bajaur Agency was a notable achievement as it was undertaken peacefully.
Churchill knew both these areas well, and he wrote extolling the fighting
qualities of these tribes. With the roads extended, the responsibilities of the
State increased as well, necessitating the creation of the Mohmand Rifles
and establishing new sub-divisions and tehsils. Again schools and hospitals
were granted top priority and, as in other Agencies, two small factories were
established. The one in Mohmand used locally available silica sand to make
crude bottles. In Khar, a vegetable oil extraction plant was set up, based
on the abundant mustard grown there. The winds of change it seemed
had finally started blowing across the Tribal Areas. These soon stopped
when the Chief Secretary Mr Nasruminallah was transferred following the
assassination of the Senior Minister, Hayat Sherpao in 1975 and two years
later, Mr Bhutto was removed from power.

Visionary leadership is now required to take bold decisions. The
introduction of adult franchise in 1997, spearheaded by the Minister
Mr Omar Afridi, was one such bold decision taken by the interim
government. Earlier even senior Army officers and ranking bureaucrats
from the Tribal Areas were denied the right to vote if they were not notified
as *maliks* officially. The first lady in the Pakistan Administrative Service, Ali
Begum of Kurram Agency, would not have been allowed to vote because
women did not have voting rights. Luckily, the heavens did not fall when
adult franchise was finally introduced. In 2002, sadly some unconstitutional
changes in the established system were undertaken by an ill-informed
and inexperienced Governor. He created a separate Secretariat under him

for the Tribal Areas which caused needless duplication and wastage of resources. This change proved damaging to orderly administration in the short period it has existed as it split apart the laws and conventions of people living side by side for millennia. It may be noted that the geography, history, economics, and the socio-cultural traditions of the people of Tribal Areas have always been extensively interwoven with the Frontier province. The Sartaj Aziz Reforms would save the area from further damage but only if a generous development package is provided for the next couple of decades. Change and innovation are important in any society and need to be thoroughly debated and then introduced for the benefit of the people. Rustam Shah Mohmand, ruing the fall in administrative and ethical standards, would often say that whenever in doubt, first check what the British did, in similar circumstances. The British kept innovating objectively and they generally got it right because they would carefully identify the problem in accordance with the needs of the times before finding an effective solution. Dr Abdul Hakim of Mardan, the Agency Surgeon in South Waziristan Agency at the time of Independence, had an interesting anecdote to recount. The night before the British left India, the officers of the South Waziristan Scouts in Wana, having savoured the delights that the Mess Bar offered, then turned upside down all the furniture and pictures in the Mess. This 'would be the state of your new country', they said. Seventy years later, many would agree!

x. Post 9/11 Events and the Merger of Tribal Areas

The impact upon the Tribal Areas of the events in Afghanistan, starting from the Saur Revolution in 1978 leading to the decade long Soviet invasion, the ten years of Taliban domination, the 9/11 events culminating in the US led invasion, and Pakistan's military operations to establish its writ, have been huge. These events have had major repercussions in the Tribal Areas as the traditional institutions are barely recognizable now. The Americans, either due to hubris or faulty reading of Afghan history, made the same mistakes made by imperial powers in the past. In Afghanistan the biggest adversary has always been the rugged and barren mountainous terrain, much as the vast snowy plains of Russia were for Napoleon and Hitler. The geographic obstacles were complemented by the fighting prowess of the people. I had suggested to General Sahibzada Yaqub, the former Foreign Minister, in a chance meeting shortly after 9/11 to tell the Americans, that they would be well advised not to invade and occupy Afghanistan. That was not to be. The General had read Afghanistan's history; the Americans had not. The rest, as they say, is history.

The impact of the post 9/11 events in Pakistan and especially in the Tribal Areas were devastating. The Khyber Pakhtunkhwa province, including former Tribal Areas had still not recovered from the effects of the Soviet invasion of Afghanistan in 1979 which had led to the influx of nearly five million Afghan refugees in Pakistan with almost all of them sent to Khyber Pakhtunkhwa, and Balochistan Provinces. War and violence in Afghanistan following the US invasion in 2001 led to severe insecurity in the Khyber Pakhtunkhwa province and the Tribal Areas. Economic activity almost ceased, there was a flight of local industry to other provinces, wholesale and retail businesses were monopolized by Afghan traders, who were already dominant in the road transport sector. Unemployment and loss of business was acutely felt by the local people. The economic losses since the US led war in Afghanistan have been estimated at US$100 billion over the last two decades almost all of which was suffered by the people of the two western provinces and the Tribal Areas.

After 9/11, the Tribal areas have once again gained importance. The hasty American decision of ignoring this region after the defeat and retreat of Soviet Union from Afghanistan in 1989 would continue to haunt them for long. Sadly, either on account of insecure local conditions or lack of interest, the expected level of economic and social development has not been seen in the area. During the 1990s, the Government of Pakistan had plenty of development funds for constructing motorways, highways and elevated expressways, development of new cities and pet projects for parliamentarians but not enough for the infrastructure or social services in the Tribal Areas. In any other country, the bulk of the funds would have been earmarked for the strife-affected areas. No compensation was given to the affected people although Prime Minister Imran Khan is committed to following the recommendations made by Sartaj Aziz to provide a sizable development package for the Khyber Pakhtunkhwa province and the newly merged areas. Fortunately, the Gomal Zam Dam in South Waziristan was completed in 2012, while the Kurram Tangi Dam in North Waziristan and Munda-Mohmand Dam in Mohmand Agency are presently under construction; the latter two dams became possible only because of the fortuitous presence of a sympathetic Pakhtun officer in the Federal water sector's administrative loop.

Ensuring economic development and peaceful communal living demands that there is universal application of equitable and objective laws and legislation dealing with land settlement, land use and town planning, road construction, and provision of electricity and irrigation infrastructure. Custom-based laws, for quick and cheap resolution of disputes among the tribesmen, need to be strengthened and codified. All laws have to be sanctioned and enforced by the State, for where there is default of writ, extra-constitutional forces move in. Such unconstitutional forces are oblivious to matters of formal sovereignty. The development and the functioning of the modern state is an all-encompassing exercise which cuts across individual and tribal holdings. It is just not possible to construct electric transmission lines, roads, and water channels unless the entire area is treated as one unit in every Agency and District. Further, taxes and user charges have to be recovered from the people for services provided and for maintenance of developmental assets. Without the supremacy of law overseen by an effective judicial system, material progress is not possible. No State can tolerate its citizens, tribesmen, or others settling their disputes with heavy machine guns and rocket launchers. If enabling enactments are non-existent or if laws cannot be enforced because of limited state sovereignty, the newly merged Tribal Areas may remain deprived as they were before.

The merger of the Tribal Areas with Khyber Pakhtunkhwa province was constitutionally completed in 2018 but there is a need to redress the problems mentioned. The issues of the twenty-first century are different from those of the earlier period and require a long-term Master Plan of fifty years to be rigorously followed and funded. There is no option except providing three per cent of the resources from the Federal Divisble Pool specifically for the former Tribal Areas, for ten years. The foot dragging by three provinces must not be allowed to delay the mainstreaming of these areas into Pakistan so that there is no repetition of the devastation experienced over the past few decades.

The strategic decisions which Pakistan had avoided taking for over half a century were ultimately forced on it by the situation in Afghanistan and its impact on the Tribal Areas. The presence of militancy in large pockets, compelled the country to neutralize these elements by forcibly occupying all areas where the state's writ was absent. Starting from Swat in 2009, the rest of Malakand division was cleared and the writ of the state was established in Bajaur and Mohmand Agencies. This was followed by reinforcing the State's writ in Kurram, Orakzai, and Khyber Agencies before North and South Waziristan, notably Shawal and the Maddakhel areas, were also cleared. In the end, Khyber Tirah was occupied to pre-empt any further disruption. The border fence that Pakistan has been constructing since 2016 along the Durand Line will provide security and monitor all movement to and from Afghanistan. It will, in time, be recognized as the international border. Another positive decision taken by Pakistan after establishing its hold in the Tribal Areas was to merge it into the Khyber Pakhtunkhwa province with the support of the local tribesmen who had suffered immensely over the past few decades.

Two decades after the US invasion of Afghanistan with the loss of thousands of foreign soldiers and billions of dollars spent, the adage that it is easy to invade Afghanistan but difficult to exit, has been confirmed. The area is indeed the 'graveyard of empires'!

The resistance to foreign troops in Afghanistan would continue to impact the erstwhile Tribal Areas and indeed the provinces of Khyber Pakhtunkhwa and Balochistan, for some time to come. Without a cessation of hostilities and a return to peace in Afghanistan, there would remain much instability inspite of using modern armaments and the mother of all bombs. There would be a need to negotiate with the Taliban and other local ethnic groups. Russia, China, Iran, and of course, Pakistan must be involved so that no one takes advantage to the others' detriment. Encouraging local autonomy for diverse ethnic groups in a loose federation of Afghanistan would be required to be built into the agreement. This should be sealed with generous foreign assistance and the presence of neutral United Nation peacekeepers.

Just as important as extending the writ of the state and the merger of the Tribal Areas is the need to stamp out any subversive activities that hostile countries stir up in these territories. The long-term Indian aim of weakening

Pakistan through proxy interference would need to be countered. There has been enough evidence to support the contention that outside forces have and would always aid, abet, and arm inimical elements in the Tribal Areas and Balochistan to destabilize Pakistan. India and its allies were complicit in assisting the anti-state elements in East Pakistan in 1971 and it would not desist to weaken Pakistan so that it exists as a weak satellite state. Even a low budget subversion plan by India could create serious problems for Pakistan as the recent past has shown. All the Indian rulers from Nehru to Narendra Modi, despite variations in their posturing, had little love for Pakistan and as seen in the past, they would go to any extent in destablizing its neighbour. Pakistan will have to remain doubly watchful and more importantly it must remain strong on the ground, while ensuring a healthy economic growth.

6

The Seven Tribal Agencies, now the Merged Districts

The present day Khyber Pukhtunkhwa (KPK) province was largely wrested from the Sikhs by the British after their victory in the Second Sikh war in 1849. Thereafter, for nearly one hundred and fifty years the Tribal Areas adjoining the North Western Frontier Province were administered by officers working as political agents of the Viceroy of India and after Partition, the President of Pakistan, to different tribes residing there. The seven Agencies were Bajaur, Mohmand, Khyber, Kurram, Orakzai, North Waziristan, and South Waziristan and in addition there were some Frontier Regions (FR) like Adamkhel Afridis, Ahmedzai Wazirs, Bhittanis, Sheranis, and other smaller tribes which were attached to the nearest district.

In 2018, the special status of the Tribal Areas under the constitution ended and the seven administrative Tribal Agencies were merged into the KPK province as separate districts. The old nomenclature of Agencies is however used in the text to describe the conditions obtaining there since Partition. It must be understood that the new districts are still technically not settled through land settlements while the independent functioning of the police and the courts does not appear to have taken hold so far. The seven Tribal Agencies have few affiliations with each other but on the contrary, there are enmities and border disputes among most of the adjoining Agencies. All Tribal Agencies over the course of a century have developed economic and social affiliations horizontally with the adjoining settled districts. It would, therefore, never be practical or economically feasible to consider the Tribal Areas as a separate provincial or political entity as the tribes never owed allegiance to a single leader among them and never comprised one organic entity. The fact that a majority of the tribesmen now live and work in the settled areas and only occasionally visit the Tribal Agencies underlines this point further. These tribes were gradually absorbed economically and then administratively into the North West Frontier Province. Here are some personal glimpses, of each of the seven administrative Tribal Agencies.

i. KHYBER AGENCY

The Khyber Agency is often considered the doyen of the tribal Agencies and is inhabited by eight sub-sections of Afridi and the smaller Shinwari, Mullogori, and Shilmani tribes. The area, for one reason or another, has remained central to the subcontinent right from the times of Alexander the Great, Genghis Khan, Tamerlane, the Mughals, Nadir Shah Afshar, the Sikhs, and the British. Much later, the Russians and Americans decided to explore and invade the adjoining Afghan territory, at, considerable cost to themselves. The Agency has experienced relentless invasion, plunder, blood feud, and treachery, most of which was facilitated because of its location on the main caravan and trade route from Central Asia to India and its proximity to the commercial hub of Peshawar.

The Khyber Pass, has gathered fame, notoriety, and surprisingly much romance too. The Agency also has more than its share of crime such as car thefts, kidnapping, smuggling, and narcotic trafficking, which has given the area a blemished reputation. Due to serious security and crime issues in the Frontier and the Tribal Areas in particular, the civil administration, the police, and the Frontier Constabulary always remain over stretched in tackling never-ending offences. The colloquially known *Sab Accha* Register, literally translated as 'All Okay Register', which records serious crimes, always remained full in the Khyber Agency. The first report to the District or Agency officer by the senior subordinate always concerned the *Sab Accha* report. So when on return to my office one day, *Subedar* Ghazi Marjan Qambarkhel Afridi informed me, as Political Agent in the Khyber Agency, that everything was *sab accha* (all was okay), I felt relaxed. As we stepped forward, Ghazi casually informed that early that day, eight desperadoes had been shot dead by the family they had snatched a rifle from some days ago. The fact that the boy's mother was accompanying him at the time of the snatching was considered particularly repulsive. As we moved on, he provided additional information about a bus that had fallen into a ravine, killing three persons. Ghazi followed this news by revealing that there were casualties in two other firing cases as well. So much for *sub accha* report! However, controlling serious crime remained the foremost duty of Political Officers in the Khyber Agency.

In the Khyber Pakhtunkhwa province, serious crime remains the top priority for the government. There is little doubt that this situation owes much to its location adjoining the Tribal Areas. The state's writ in the Tribal Areas has declined while crime has become more complex. There is a need to make the administration much more effective to ensure security in the Agencies and the Districts. There are of course other factors responsible for crime as well besides the proximity to the Tribal Areas, as there is much crime in Karachi, Lahore, and in rural Sindh and Punjab. The lax control of the state in the Tribal Areas and the inability to expand the writ of the state has contributed to the insecurity. Some of the most dreaded names in the world of crime, during the past century, have had a Khyber connection. Many were neutralized or exiled, while others turned over a new leaf in life by focusing on religion or in assisting the administration to fight crimes. One such individual was Muhammad Jan Kukikhel, popularly known as Majaan, who was initially a desperado but later reformed himself and became a friend of the administration. Long after his conversion to good citizenship he knew precisely which culprits were responsible for most of the serious crimes that were committed. The recovery of stolen vehicles or tracing kidnapped persons, became relatively easy because of his source of information. Later in life, he, along with his son Zaver, spent much time concentrating on children's education and on *tabligh* (reaching out and spreading Islam). His story had a happy ending.

The importance of Khyber, for different reasons, was so great that some of the most famous personages in British India served in this Agency. Better known among these individuals included Sir Robert Warburton, the son of an Afghan princess and an English father; Sir George Roos-Keppel, who later became the Chief Commissioner NWFP; Major General Iskander Mirza, who became the President of Pakistan; and Sir Sahibzada Qaiyum, who rose to be the Chief Minister. They had all earned their spurs as Political Agents. Later day officers, with only a few exceptions, were also high achievers in the administrative hierarchy. No wonder, there was so much romance associated with the Khyber, described aptly by John Masters. An English officer while taking an evening stroll in Peshawar sees an Afridi tribesman walk past him without uttering a word or conveying any greetings. His young daughter, accompanying him enquires of her father why this 'Indian' did not greet them. The father, who was well-schooled in Frontier affairs replied truthfully and frankly 'because, my dear this is not India'. In the Tribal Areas, there was little obsequiousness or flattery. The tribesman demanded acceptance as an equal and could alter the environment and the administration. There was, thus, a constant 'give and take' between the Political Agent and the tribal *Malik* with an agreeable compromise always emerging in the end; a decisive victory for any side could mean future disequilibrium. Differences were patched up, later if not sooner, but it was important not to break the dialogue. This process was colloquially called *pulticali* or the skills of the Political Officer. Once trust was developed between the Political Officer and the tribesman, one could be assured of their support even if it was grudgingly provided.

Until recently, only a third of the Khyber Agency had been within reach of the government. The accessible portion was called the Protected Areas and it was here that the government was able to exercise a measure of control. The construction of roads and the extension of socio-economic facilities were only undertaken in relation to strategic necessity and that to, in spurts by the British. The entire Afridi Tirah and the Bazaar Valley, remained largely inaccessible to the state until 9/11 when the army moved in. It took the government over 140 years from the time the Agency was established before these two areas were finally opened. One fact that was not openly acknowledged, for understandable reasons, was that the British had greater writ and control in the Khyber Agency more than a half a century ago than was the case long after Independence. British officers would visit Qadam, Shin Qamar, Tatara, and even the Bazaar valley on the outskirts, routinely and often with their families. This was not possible after they left, because the Pakistani administration adopted a hands-off approach.

The happenings in the Khyber Agency have always had a great bearing on the security of the districts of the Frontier Province, much like the conditions in Waziristan today that affect the Province. The boundary between the Peshawar district and Khyber Agency, the Maffey-Griffith Line, was always marked by insecurity and its implementation remained a nightmare for the administration. The line itself was contentious and there was seldom much peace on either side of it. Territorial disputes existed between the Mullaghori tribe and the village of Kafur Dheri, and between the Kukikhel Afridi tribe and the inhabitants of Regi Lalma. Virtually every village in Jamrud, Shah Kas plains, and the Khajuri area in Khyber Agency had disputed land ownership with the settled villages of Sheikhan, Badabher, and Mattani. Slowly and gradually as insecurity increased, tribesmen started buying or encroaching upon land across the Maffey-Griffith Line. This belt of land became a *de facto* Tribal Area. The Frontier Constabulary, which was responsible for holding the line, was no longer effective in protecting it and failed to deal with the new informal extensions. This was an incentive for new incursions as the districts continued to shrink.

The Frontier Constabulary was initially established by merging the Samana Rifles with the Border Military Police and it was given the responsibility of checking tribal raids. Over the past few decades, sadly, this role has been performed, more by default. Serious crime has continued to rise. For example, one hot summer evening in 1981, a day before the Eid festival, a section of Kukikhel tribe invaded and occupied a disputed area in the general direction of Islamia College Peshawar. The out-gunned Frontier Constabulary platoons did not offer resistance and promptly surrendered their weapons and fled. They were preceded in the race by the police, many of whom also shed their uniforms. As the Political Agent Khyber, I was called frantically by the Commissioner Jehanzeb Khan and the Deputy Inspector General Police Masud Shah and asked to employ political expertise in evicting the invaders. Before sending a *jirga* or the conciliators to the offending tribe, I considered it necessary to deploy a battery of artillery guns in the area. The sight of the guns is normally very persuasive. The *jirga* was directed to give an ultimatum to the invaders to vacate the occupied area within half an hour or be prepared for the consequences. In the event, the time allotted proved much longer than required. The Kukikhels showed surprising speed! The rifles were returned later, with no remorse felt by the Frontier Constabulary, as no one in the force was disciplined for dereliction of duty. It later transpired that the Deputy Commandant of the Frontier Constabulary had allowed most of the force deployed in the disputed area to go on leave for Eid holidays without informing the Political Agent or even the local police. He may have been kind to his troops but was oblivious to the security requirements of the area. This attitude was not surprising since very few errant officials in government are penalized for dereliction of duty. Decades later, seventy Constabulary recruits were killed in a suicide attack outside the Shabqadr Fort but no questions were asked of anyone.

The Frontier Constabulary was an immensely proud and effective force during its heyday when officers of the calibre of Eric Charles Handyside, the District Officer, were in command. It was said that never was a weapon stolen from the Frontier Constabulary because of its class and tribal composition. Later, with mediocre persons in command and without the requisite and focused training, the high standards maintained by the force were bound to decline. And they did. These days an ill-trained, badly-led, and poorly-motivated FC is not much better than a Frontier Chowkidar force as they are mostly deployed as watchmen outside embassies and offices. It is not a very pleasant sight to see soldiers on guard duties with cell phones in one hand and a rifle in the other. It would be useful to restore the reputation of the Frontier Constabulary by improving their training and upgrading their equipment. There is little in the shape of specialized training or the motivation to deal with the present challenges. One of the best that the constabulary saw after Independence was Sifat Ghayyur, the young, brave, and dashing commandant who died honourably in the line of duty. Were there more officers like him, the districts would have seen greater security from the criminals.

Khyber, like the other agencies had, and has, many a tough and interesting *maliks*. Political Officers know that they can only maintain peace if they can keep the *malik* in good humour. His support is important. Similarly, it is prudent for the *malik* not to unnecessarily quarrel or clash with the administration. One of the wisest and most farsighted *malik* in Khyber was Inayat Khan Kukikhel, who gained riches and renown only because he never tried to cross swords with the Political Agent. There were two other *maliks* in the Khyber who deserve a mention. Firstly, there was the honourable Malik Wali Khan Kukikhel, who was often at odds with the government and in the process suffered financial losses and exile for long. His village in Tirah was bombarded soon after the creation of Pakistan and decades later his house in Jamrud was also blown-up. Wali Khan was short-tempered but was an honest man who never associated with criminals and smugglers. Unfortunately, at times his temperament got the better of him.

He did not request respect but demanded it as a right. As Political Agent Khyber, I had a tiff with him, which we soon resolved, and thereafter the honourable Malik Wali Khan would fully support the administration. Such was his commitment that his detractors cynically observed that Malik Wali Khan was functioning not as a *malik* but like an Additional Political Agent. Once the governor, General Fazle Haq, relying on his fanciful secret diaries, was very critical of Malik Wali Khan in a conference. This was unfortunate and I decided to clear all misunderstandings. The governor was requested to meet the *malik* to form his own judgment and fortuitously he agreed. The meeting was arranged but Malik Wali Khan was informed of the purpose only when his car reached the governor's house, because stubborn as he was, he would never have agreed to the meeting with the governor. After discussions lasting an hour, the governor had a change of heart and a better opinion of him. The other notable *malik* was the fine gentleman, Malik Nadir Khan Zakkakhel, an orator par excellence and a mature and wise tribal leader. He was a great host and was always willing to help the administration. He lived most of his adult life as an exile in Afghanistan but never amassed any wealth, dying in an accident while travelling in a small Suzuki car.

The Khyber Agency has its share of problems. Most people associate it with guns and violence, narcotics and smuggling, and extortion and kidnapping. Unfortunately, much of this is true. In the Khyber Agency, heroin manufacturing was introduced during the early 1980s after the French Connection around the Mediterranean was dismantled. The illegal heroin laboratories consisted of a few pots, pans, and chemicals, soon erupted in the Landikotal area inhabited by the Shinwari tribe. They utilized the opium poppy grown extensively in the Frontier Province, Tribal Areas, and Afghanistan and then smuggled the heroin to other parts of Pakistan and traded it through Central Asia to Europe and beyond. The profits were amazingly high although quite modest compared to the street value of the drug in the West. There was great pressure from the United Nations drug control agency and the Americans, to eliminate drug manufacturing. Actually, the worst sufferers from heroin use, were the Pakistanis, over a million of people were addicted to its use. Governor Fazle Haq decided to appoint me as the Political Agent with strict orders to stamp out the manufacture and trade of heroin. This was the period when William French Smith, the American Attorney General, on a visit to Pakistan, actually set foot in Landikotal bazaar to convey his concern about the manufacture, sale, and smuggling of heroin from the Khyber Agency. Accompanying him was Doug Wankel, the drug control officer in the US Embassy, who very rudely, though quite truthfully, informed the visitor that heroin was being 'sold by the kilos' in the bazaar. I took severe umbrage at his public outburst, and informed the visitors that such rude conduct was unacceptable. For the next month, the American drug control officials were barred from entering the Khyber. After an apology by the good fellow the ban was rescinded. Firm measures were then undertaken, resulting in arrests and destruction of a large number of the illegal laboratories. The Zakkakhel Afridi tribe, whose territory lay next to the Shinwaris, decided to support the administration in the effort which led to a serious clash between the two tribes, resulting in a number of deaths. The drugs were controlled to a large extent.

It was during this period that a common Shinwari tribesman by the name of Tilla assumed leadership of his tribe, pushing the established *maliks* into the background. 'Tillo' was a simple and a genuine person, with a great sense of humour. With his large following, he soon started challenging the administration. When summoned by the administration, he refused to present himself stating that since he was the 'king' of the Agency, it did not behove him to visit the *wazir* (Political Agent). As he continued crossing the acceptable limits, the Khyber Rifles were dispatched to arrest him. After an exchange of a few rounds of ammunition fire, Tillo handed himself over. When questioned how the 'king' felt now that he was in custody of the *wazir*, he chided the local officers for their 'lack of humour', *Taso pa gup na poaigai*. He was released in good time and became a friend of the administration. During those days, some Shinwari *maliks* devised an ingenious scheme to embarrass the Political Agent by deciding to burn the house of his close friend Saida Jan Shinwari for allegedly conspiring against the tribe. Such intra-tribal events remain outside the mandate of the government but since the Political Agent can never be seen to lose face, the Khyber Rifles were ordered to demolish the house of one prominent *malik* if Saida Jan's house was torched. The tribe quickly understood the game and nothing untoward occurred.

Car thefts and kidnapping were also rife in the Khyber Agency and on one occasion, two smart young girls, were arrested with a stolen car. They had duped a young man in a hotel in Lahore. Two policemen from Punjab were also arrested and jailed for three years each. They had made it a habit of recovering stolen cars by pocketing a commission for themselves. In those days, the Khyber Rifles and the Masud Scouts from Fort Salop, were regularly employed for armed intervention, the *baramta*, to recover kidnapped persons and to arrest criminals. Once the target village was cordoned off by the Scouts, a local *jirga* of tribesmen was sent with an ultimatum to accept the administration's demands within half an hour or face the consequences. The ultimatum almost always succeeded but one had to be prepared for any eventuality. Once a risky eventuality arose when Ataullah Toru, the Assistant Political Agent, was supervising a *baramta* dressed in his Friday-best white *shalwar-kamiz*, which provided a very tempting target. Fortunately, no harm came his way except for a verbal outburst from his superior officer. Another Assistant Political Agent was even more relaxed and once decided to keep in his safe custody the recovered *case property*, consisting of a few cartons of scotch whisky. For very explicable reasons, the quantum of the case property continued to decrease every evening. It soon transpired that the only item that remained was the recovery voucher, which showed clearly the number of cartons initially seized, and what was later available. The officer spiritedly informed that the case property was put to good use!

No mention of the Khyber Agency can be complete without a mention of Amir Hamza Shinwari from Landikotal, whose verses and Sufi propensities were acknowledged during his lifetime. As often happens in Pakistan, the true hero is ignored when alive but showered with laurels when he is no more. It was sad that little attention was paid to him by the state when he needed it during his illness. Landikotal also produced the country's 100-metre sprinting champion, Iqbal Shinwari, who once confided that he could not practice sprinting in his hometown because sprinting made some think that he had gone insane.

ii. North Waziristan Agency

The North Waziristan Agency consists of the Uthmankhel Wazir and the Daur tribes who, incidentally, have no love lost between them. Two very charismatic *maliks* belonged to the area and they have become a subject of folklore. The Political Agent in Miramshah was bound to keep both Malik Khandan Maddakhel and Malik Darya Khan in good humour, at all times. Darya Khan was also the master of repartee and of tribal wisdom. During the Soviet invasion of Afghanistan, he was once asked by a senior functionary how the invader could best be evicted from Afghanistan. Like most tribesmen who often speak in riddles or through anecdotes, Darya Khan recounted a story of jackals in a jungle who got tired of the lion and discussed various options for throwing him out. Finally, the chief of the jackals spoke solemnly by stating that he knew of a hundred and one ways of evicting the lion from the jungle but under the circumstances, it would be best that the two of them never came face to face. Darya Khan in effect, was saying that it was not for him to evict the Soviets and this question should only be addressed to those who could deal with it. He would often say that in order to preserve themselves they tolerated the British for sixty years and could do the same with the Soviets for the equivalent period. In the end, the Soviets only stayed for a decade.

The other grand Malik was Khandan, from the Maddakhel sub-section of the Wazir tribe. In 1898, this was the tribe who invited Political Officer Herbert Walter Gee, with a small contingent of British troops, to demarcate the area after which they were served lunch at Maizar. Soon after feeding the guests, they attacked the party, leaving three British officers and two dozen Indian soldiers dead. During the gun battle, over one hundred of the *Malik's* men were also killed. To have attacked the guests, was a criminal act and this left a deep stigma on the local people from the area. The reason for the killing was not important but the breach of *Pukhtunwali*, or the code of Pakhtun conduct, certainly was. No deception is permissible once a *jiba* or word is given by the officials or the tribesmen. This remains a cardinal principle of tribal administration. No wise tribal elder ever tries to take on the government head-on because there is nothing to gain from it. A sagacious Wazir or *malik* always said that the government was the biggest tribe in the Agency and the Political Agent was the most prominent *malik.* Every effort should be made to avoid a confrontation with the Government *tribe.*

Both North and South Waziristan remained resentful and turbulent during the period the British ruled but a working arrangement had evolved, allowing everyone some room to manoeuvre. The British success was due to their developing, strategic roads deep inside the area which led to the creation of a rudimentary system of tribal administration and recognition of the rights and responsibilities of the tribes. The rights were emphasized at all times but the responsibilities were ignored, whenever deemed convenient by the tribe. Apart from the Tochi Scouts, an Army Division was positioned in the area to display strength and thwart any unwholesome ideas. The area saw much action and military operations in the 1930s and 1940s when the Faqir of Ipi was waging his struggle, but times having changed he could not attract much support once the British left. Anyway, the British had a love-hate relationship with Waziristan. A military cantonment was established in the alpine environment of Razmak, in the central highlands, complete with an airport and bomber planes to readily counter any attempt to dislocate the British. Even the footprints of the visit of the first English ladies to Razmak were preserved in cement in the governor's cottage. If the British had more time and peaceful conditions, Razmak would have developed into a hill resort like Simla or Murree, for the area. Sadly, that was not to be.

The Tribal Areas are rich in mineral and water resources which are waiting to be tapped. There is considerable mineral wealth like copper, iron, oil, and gas reserves in North Waziristan and with water available from the Kurram Tangi Dam, the area could become an exporter of agricultural produce as well. There is another geographical advantage available to the people of the region as the new trade route to Afghanistan through the border post of Ghulam Khan is located in this agency. In the course of time, a bustling service industry would develop the area placing Miramshah on the logistical route of the region. A new railway line from Karachi or Gwadar on the right bank of the Indus River, would also be a bonus for the area.

In the decades following Partition, one near-permanent feature in the domain of the Political and Scout officials of North Waziristan was an interesting tribesman nicknamed George, by an English officer. He could be seen loitering around the Scouts soldiers' mess area, the *langar.* Ever since the British era, George was suspected by his tribe of spying for the administration while the administration thought he was conveying secrets to the tribe. In truth, no administration worth its salt would depend upon a simple and harmless bloke like him! The administration merely humoured him and his sole interest in life lay in securing two free meals a day from the troops' mess. This practice continued well into the 1970s.

Another anecdote from the area, relates to the kidnapping of Ajmal Khan, the Vice Chancellor of Islamia College University, Peshawar by the militants in 2010. The kidnappers, who treated him well, nevertheless demanded a large ransom and the release of some of their colleagues who had been arrested by the government before setting the Vice Chancellor free. As the negotiations were not fruitful, his captivity was prolonged and in the process he became friendly with the local persons whose children he would often teach. An old woman from the tribe, was so disturbed to see him in captivity that she once offered to sell her few sheep to raise money to pay for his ransom!

iii. SOUTH WAZIRISTAN AGENCY

The South Waziristan Agency is inhabited by the fierce Mehsud, the industrious Ahmedzai Wazirs, the migrant Sulemankhels, and the educated Burki tribe, who have all done well in different ways. If there was one matter all of these tribes would never compromise upon, it was *nikat*, the tribal rights defined by the ancestors. The essence of *nikat* entailed that no deviation, no matter how trivial, was permissible and an armed struggle is the logical consequence, in a case of deviation. This area has seen continuous violence since time immemorial and there seems to be no respite in the future. The tribes were a thorn to the Mughal's empire while the British were always on their guard. Once, when the stringent Standard Operating Procedures relaxed, there was an immediate ambush. This occurred in the Shahur Tangi defile in 1937, where the Mehsuds under the leadership of Koniakhel, ambushed an Army column, claiming the lives of nearly a hundred military and scouts personnel. The British, however, retained their fascination with Mehsud but also found him and his tribe the most treacherous. During the time when conditions were unstable, incidents like the Shahur-Tangi continued to occur. After the British left, a Baloch Infantry unit of the Pakistan Army was also ambushed in 2007, during the operations.

The dependence of the Ahmadzai Wazir tribe on the Mehsud tribe remained constant and was very visible for most of their history. The former were not even permitted a road of their own from Wana to Tank. This only became possible once Water and Power Development Authority (WAPDA) decided to construct the Gomal Zam Dam south of Wana, the Agency headquarters. The dam was built a hundred years after the British first occupied Waziristan, and interestingly the site was first proposed by British military engineers in the 1880s. Today the Gomal Dam stores nearly a million acre feet of water and generates enough electricity for the surrounding areas. During the construction of the dam, security of the foreign engineers and the workers, remained a serious concern. Soon after construction started, a couple of Chinese workers were kidnapped for ransom and freed by military commandos, but not before one of them was killed during the ensuing firefight. All work was immediately stopped and was started only after complete security arrangements were put in place. There was another accident soon thereafter. A Chinese worker died while fishing when the dynamite he was using exploded prematurely. His colleagues unsuccessfully tried to alter the tragedy to the financial advantage of the deceased's family by claiming that the death had occurred due to militants' actions, which would have qualified his family for higher compensation. A clever attempt!

All through history, conquerors and administrators have noted the importance of Waziristan because of its insularity, topography, and the martial bravery of its inhabitants. After the First World War, a very charismatic character suddenly appeared like a comet in Miranshah and Jandola known by the name of T. E. Lawrence, known to history as Lawrence of Arabia. Although he fought the Turks during the First World War, which resulted in independence for the Arabs, he felt the British and the French had seriously betrayed the Arabs who were made to fight for a falsehood by abetting in the establishment of a Jewish homeland in their territory. He will forever be remembered by the South Waziristan Scouts for presenting to their Mess one of his manuscripts, in which he described in his own hand: 'This disgraceful looking book was written by me but it's squalid type, degraded blocks and quite untruthful introduction are the responsibilities of the publisher.' The presentation was the 'only one I can offer the South Waziristan Scouts in memory of a very good day and night stay,' that he had in Jandola.

Sadly, for the area, violence did not leave Waziristan even seventy years after the British left. Shortly after 9/11, the Pakistan Army moved into the tribal Agencies in an effort to thwart the militants. This was the period when a large number of loyal tribal *maliks* were killed by the militants in order to eliminate traditional tribal leadership. Low-level operations began against the militants without any overall strategic planning. One evening, the army and South Waziristan scouts planned a *baramta* (a raid) on a hostile foreigner known to be residing in the Agency. A Major called the Assistant Political Agent in Wana and asked him to accompany his contingent to a place he did not wish to identify. In accordance with tribal convention, the civil officer enquired whether he should bring along a few tribal *maliks* in case negotiations were required. The Major, who was not familiar with the traditions of the place, was not pleased at the suggestion and retorted that they were going to conduct an operation and were not seeking votes. By evening, the convoy stopped outside a small village with the Major announcing that they would search the village which he then named. The Assistant Political Agent was aghast and told him that they were in the wrong village. The convoy turned around and after locating the targeted village, disembarked. The inmate of the house informed the raiding team that there were women inside, one of whom was in the family way and that they should not enter. Undeterred, the team proceeded forward and soon a firefight ensued, resulting in the death of a number of Army and Scouts personnel. The contingent retreated thereafter, having broken every rule in the Frontier Warfare Manual. The operation was conducted at dusk instead of first light, the political officers were not consulted, and local tribal elders were not associated with the *baramta*.

The killing of the troops caused serious concern in the military hierarchy. The General Officer Commanding, was furious and threatened to arrest the Political Agent Mian Sufaid Shah and burn the Agency. The Political Agent was obviously thoroughly shaken and called me late at night, as I was serving as the Chief Secretary of Frontier province, apprising me of the facts. I telephoned the Inspector General Frontier Corps, Major General Tajul Haq who meanwhile, had been informed of what had transpired involving his outfit. I then spoke to General Ali Jan Orakzai, the Corps Commander and General Iftikhar Shah, the Governor requesting prompt action as it appeared that the Major General in South Waziristan had panicked, which could not be tolerated in a theatre of war. Fortunately, the army had an effective accountability system that addressed any infringement of procedures quickly. The high command having corroborated the correct sequence of events, exactly as narrated by me, relieved the Commandant of the Scouts, the Brigade Commander, and the Major General of their command immediately. The Political Agent, who was not even informed of the botched raid, remained a happy man. A couple of years earlier, following General Musharraf's coup of October 1999, the same officer monitored civil affairs as a Brigadier in the Corps Headquarter in Peshawar and dealt rather harshly with the senior civil officers. One of his favourite quotes was the perennial Army refrain *'Tum log kam nahi kartay. Ab dheko kam kaisay hota hai,'* which meant that the civil officers tend to shirk duty while his performance in South Waziristan was there for everyone to see.

Since 2001, the residents of North Waziristan and South Waziristan Agencies, alongside those in the other five agencies, have seen much death and destruction in the ongoing operations against the militants. The writ of the state has now been largely established but this hold remains tenuous. The main motivations of the insurgents need to be analyzed and policies determined to respond to the militants in the future. Could militancy be neutralized through a combination of political, as in tribal parlance, and through other means? Could the tribesmen have been supported more resolutely in neutralizing the militants themselves as was done by the Wana Wazirs against the Uzbeks? Was there an alternate strategy for dealing with the militants without evacuating the entire civilian population from their homes? Could the military leadership of the time have adopted a different grand strategy with all parties to the conflict including the Americans and the Talibans? Was there an alternative to the US-led invasion of Afghanistan? It is well-known that negotiations are successful when conducted from a position of strength but other options can at times be explored. There was one approach initiated by the Corps Commander of Peshawar which was bound to fail. He struck a hasty peace deal with the insurgents in South Waziristan against the better advice of the Political Agent Azam Khan. When the former insisted that the Political Agent accompany him to the signing ceremony, the latter is reported to have quipped that he did not want to be part of another Paltan Maidan, a reference to the ground in Dhaka where General Niazi signed the infamous instrument of surrender in East Pakistan, was unacceptable to him. The peace deal soon fell through.

Maulvi Noor Muhammad Wazir, an enlightened man, founded a modern religious school, a *madrasah*, for both boys and girls in Wana. Here, computer science, natural science, and English were taught along with the Quran and Shariat. Many years earlier, in the mid-1970s, Noor Muhammad, in his youthful exuberance, imagined he could assume sovereign control of his part of the Agency. He decided to wage war against the state. When words of wisdom did not dissuade him, Brigadier Naseerullah Babar, the Inspector General of Frontier Corps, and Abdullah, the Political Agent, were compelled to chastise him with a few rounds of artillery fire! Since then, he remained loyal but was killed in a bomb blast, some years later.

iv. KURRAM AGENCY

The Kurram Agency was different in many ways from other Tribal Areas because one of the major communities, the Shia Turis, invited the British in 1893 to take over their area as they were tired of the sectarian divide. The high altitude and alpine climate in most of the Agency was very appealing and the British relished their stay. This was complemented by abundant partridge, *chakor*, and water-fowl hunting, and *masheer* fish angling. It is said that a few British Officers actually considered settling here after retirement. The government at the time also had the good sense to measure and demarcate the land and undertake a Land Settlement to establish the rights of the land owners and tenants.

Unfortunately, following the Soviet invasion of Afghanistan, the problems for the Kurram Agency multiplied. The easy availability of weaponry, the ample provision of outside money, and the increased upheaval among the religious sects contributed to violence. The area was also the main supply line for the war logistics inviting much outside interest in the local conditions. There were elaborate bunkers and supply bases cut deep into the mountains on the border which were often the target of Soviet bomber raids. Cross-border shelling was a daily routine. Once, on a visit as the Commissioner Kohat, while taking rest in the garden of the Governor's Cottage, I was startled to witness 32 Soviet aircraft raid on the Mujahideen arms dump some miles away. The heavier bombs could be somewhat identified, but the tracks of the Stinger anti-aircraft missiles were clearly marked. Here was a live war. The Soviet fighter aircraft would often fly into the area but it was the helicopter gunships that were more dangerous. On one occasion when the helicopters' rockets started hitting the outskirts of Parachinar, the Vice Chief of the Army, General K. M. Arif, came to check why the ground-to-air missiles were not hitting enemy helicopters. In a meeting with the witty Political Agent, Sahibzada Yunas, the general said that to raise the morale of the civilians they must be told that the Army also hits back with missiles. Yunas replied that when the people are informed their morale plummets further as the missiles miss their targets! Although, the attacking helicopters were not hit by ground fire, over a dozen Soviet fighter jets were shot down by the Pakistan Air Force (PAF) during this period. In one case, while on Combat Air Patrol mission, a PAF jet located on radar an enemy plane in the Kurram Agency and was ordered to shoot it down. To the PAF pilot's eternal regret, as soon as he released the missile, he realized that it was a transport plane with women and children, aboard which had strayed from its route. The PAF pilot was a gentleman par excellence and an ace pilot, but he died some years later in a transport aircraft crash which also took the life of the Air Chief. It was during those days that a Pakistani aircraft shot down one of the two intruding Russian jets near Sadda. The General Officer Commanding Kohat, Major General Alam Jan, and I, visited the site a day later where the Pakhtun *Subedar* of the Kurram Militia explained the aerial action, in graphic detail. He said as the two planes appeared, 'Our jet immediately shot down one while the other bolted, looking very sad indeed.' *'Dher khapa khapa lar o'* were his exact words.

The Kurram Agency's foremost problem remained the sectarian strife between Shia and Sunni factions. It was seen that the influx of Afghan refugees to Kurram following the Soviet invasion of Afghanistan, swayed the population balance towards the Sunni group and hostilities increased appreciably, often triggered by minor events. In 1986, a major operation was conducted to separate the warring factions when fighting that had started in Bushera village in Upper Kurram, spread to Sadda and then to nearly the entire Agency. A tribal *lashkar* was also reported to be moving in from Miramshah to stake claim on all types of war spoils expected. From Thall, the 73 Brigade was requisitioned under the command of the newly arrived Brigadier Ghaziuddin Rana. The force comprised 5 Punjab, 1 Sindh, a Frontier Force infantry regiment, and the 90 Medium Artillery regiment, along with 12 wings of the Frontier Corps. The force began its operations from Arawali Fort, where the artillery began the 'three-round gun fire' to great effect. Arawali Fort, incidentally, had an airfield of its own since the days of the British. The overall command of the operations was in the hands of the Inspector General Frontier Corps Major General Shafique, a quiet and sensible soldier. The troops, well supported by the guns of Colonel Shaukat Usman, covered the distance to Parachinar in just one day, occasionally using force to remove any resistance. In Sadda, there were two very brave and conscientious Assistant Political Agents, Khizr Hayat and Fazle Karim Khattak, who did not leave their post despite being under constant fire for days. Similarly, Karim Kusuria the Political Agent and Colonel Inam Khan, the Commandant of Kurram Militia remained steadfast. There was only one setback at Sadda as the operation started, when the 5 Punjab Regiment was fording the river, two *jawans* lost their rifles in the river much to the annoyance of Brigadier Farook. It took an hour to recover these, which delayed the march. Peace was soon restored and the writ of the government effectively extended so much so that no one including the most powerful of *maliks* were allowed to carry even a small pistol. A couple of days into the operations, reports were received that one Sardar of Peiwar, a known offender, accused of many heinous crimes, was present in a specified house. The Brigade Commander ordered the Commanding Officer of 5 Punjab Regiment to surround the house and arrest the accused. The Commanding Officer undertook the operation rather casually and surrounded the house from three sides and on the fourth deployed a young levy soldier. The vigilant Sardar found the arrangement most convenient. After promptly shooting the levy man dead, he escaped. The colonel was relieved of his command immediately.

The sectarian problem forecloses the possibility of peace in the area and every few years serious firefights occur. No one has been able to suggest an appropriate solution, over the past centuries, until the Federal

THE SEVEN TRIBAL AGENCIES, NOW THE MERGED DISTRICTS   203

Interior Minister from Gujranwala, offered a lasting solution at a meeting presided over by Prime Minister Muhammad Khan Junejo. He proposed withdrawing all state forces from the Agency and to let the adversaries fight it out till the end. He was dead serious. This reflects the thinking of some Pakistani politicians. There was one other minister in Ziaul Haq's cabinet who had an issue with the local administration. During those stressful days, the amiable federal minister, who was also a serving Lieutenant General, arrived in Kurram on a private visit. He was known to the officials as he was also the head of a prominent subsect of the Shias. As soon as he arrived at the Chapri check post, he was requested to hand over the two automatic rifles he was carrying. The Minister-General was incensed that his official car with Pakistan's flag was stopped by the lowly levy men. The matter was reported to me as Commissioner and although I knew the Minister-General well, he was compelled to hand over his weapons to the levy's *Subedar*. The Minister, in accordance with the protocol requirements, was provided with an impressive mobile escort during his stay in the Agency but no personal weapons were permitted. In a similar case, a member of the National Assembly, the well-groomed Malik Saleh Khan, was not permitted to carry even a small pistol with him. When such persons of note are not shown extra consideration, ordinary people get the message. Much to the surprise of the local officials and the military officers, the tribesmen extended full support to the Army and the administration, as they were convinced that they were impartial and meant business.

Malik Saleh Khan had a really bad case of amnesia. He normally forgot what he had to say to the politicals. He was always accompanied by his friend and companion, Lal Khan, who would constantly remind him of what he wanted to say. Once, Lal Khan was not present in the meeting and that left Saleh Khan speechless, quite literally. Saleh Khan, totally bewildered, told an officer he had called to discuss two points. He promptly forgot the first point and then suggested that he would discuss the second one. Seconds later, Saleh Khan admitted he had forgotten the second point as well. For the future, Lal Khan was told never to be absent. The same Malik once brought a Rolex wristwatch as a gift for me, but my refusal to accept it, greatly annoyed him. He became angry and seriously vowed never to see me again for this public insult as his friends knew he was to gift it. Fortunately, the matter was resolved amicably but I was not destined to retain the watch for long. A friend, Harun Khan, was convinced that the watch would look better on his wrist!

v. Orakzai Agency

Created in 1973, the Orakzai Agency is the only one that does not border Afghanistan and initially, escaped much of the security troubles associated with other Agencies. This was the area which saw action during the Tirah Expedition of 1897 when Samana, Dargai, and Chargukotal were scaled and captured by the Gordon Highlanders, the Gurkhas, and the Guides and other famous battalions. A bagpiper, Sergeant George Frederick Findlater of the Gordon Highlanders won the Victoria Cross for his valour in the Tirah Expedition as he continued playing bagpipes while he was wounded. Sadly, for the aficionados, the particular 'Findlater' single malt is not named after this hero. For the Scots perhaps, a name on the product may have been an honour greater than a war medal! The British dead were buried in a cemetery near Shinawari at the base of the ridge but some decades later, such was the need of the local people for building stones that no trace of any carved stone or marble epitaph was left. Only one piece of dressed granite was found which was placed in the wall of the nearby check post at Yakho Kandao. This also was the route taken by the young English girl Mollie Ellis, while being brought back following her kidnapping from Kohat cantonment in 1923. The return was made possible by the efforts of the Political Officers Sheikh Mehboob Ali, Quli Khan, and Mughalbaz Khan through the influence of the spiritual leader Akhunzada Mahmud Mumuzai.

The Orakzais are law-abiding people and their first job preference was to join the para-military forces until job opportunities surfaced in the Gulf States in the early 1970s. Thereafter, they opted for manual employment generated by the oil boom in the Gulf region. Having saved most of what they earned, they spent it not on business but non-productively on building houses. During the early days, manual workers who had barely ventured far from their villages travelled to the Gulf and brought back all kinds of gifts and gadgets for the folks back home. Many brought electrical appliances when there was no electricity available. Some even carried back empty juice bottles. One brought fancy but fused light bulbs for decoration purposes.

These hardy workers, who earned foreign exchange for the country, unfortunately were subjected to constant extortion by everyone concerned. The airlines, customs, immigration department, and even embassies, all felt they were entitled to a share in these workers' earnings. Closer to home, the police and *tehsildars* pounced on them at first sight. These hardworking people had toiled hard under the Arab sun but wasted their savings in marriage festivities and building cake-like houses. A decade later, they did not have much to show for their labours. The government had failed the people again.

The Orakzais were friendly partners with the administration in developing roads to open up the interior of the Agency. In the early days, the condition of the track was so basic that the Political Agent's jeep had to be pushed, pulled, and actually lifted at places to reach its destination. The objective was to pierce the barrier against the road for the first time. This was achieved only after the full support of tribal *maliks* was secured. No force was employed during or after construction, ingress being totally peaceful.

In mid-1973, the decision to open up the non-protected or inaccessible parts of the Federally Administered Tribal Areas (FATA) was taken by the Federal Government. The primary areas of focus were the Salarzai and Mamund pockets in Bajaur Agency, the Safis beyond the Nahaqi and Mamadghat passes in Mohmand Agency, the Khyber and Orakzai Tirah, the Alisherzai and Mussozai in Kurram Agency, and the Maddakhel-Shawal belt in Waziristan. Incidentally, these were the only areas that were not opened through roads before Partition. It was an avowed policy of the government that the construction of roads, schools, colleges, dispensaries, and hospitals would also be established to bring the region into the twentieth century.

I was posted to the Orakzai Agency and at that time I had a total service of less than three years which included one-and-a-half-years as an under-training officer. The tasks were assigned to all concerned and the progress monitored weekly and even bi-weekly in Peshawar, often at the highest level. There were no constraints on financial resources and the political agents were permitted to select their subordinate officers.

The road to Tirah started from Shinawari Fort and the initial climb to the Dargai Heights and Yakho Kandao was uneventful, with the nominated tribal contractors performing reasonably well. We all knew that *political* problems would arise once we crossed the rim into the difficult tribal Agency and we were not wrong. The use of force was not an option and *jirga* parleys would continue for days and weeks to resolve minor matters. The *maliks* knew fully well that this was their only opportunity to extract their maximum entitlement from the administration. Haggling over petty issues would delay progress and the *high ups* in Peshawar would not brook any delays, come what may. In one small section of a tribe, ten *khassadars* or tribal police were sanctioned for the sub-tribe concerned, consisting of one Junior Commissioned Officer, the *naib subedar*, and nine sepoys. Trouble arose when all ten insisted that *naib subedari* be granted to each one of them. All officers and no sepoys! After long negotiations, it was resolved that they would all be *naib subedars* and wear the badge of *naib subedar* rank but would be paid the wages of a sepoy. The issue was amicably resolved and the construction of the road progressed smoothly. At another place, Zakria Khan, the *naib tehsildar*, acted as a smart pharmacist. To deal with a particularly combative tribesman, he managed to get a supply of sleeping pills to him with the result that there were no arguments as the protesting tribesman slept peacefully throughout the *jirga*. Sleeping pills are so very agreeable! The administration was, however, very liberal with granting developmental assistance for water supplies and other small projects under the rural development head.

Having successfully crossed Rabia Khel and Akhel areas, a nucleus was created in the Ghiljo village. The plan was that in the future Ghiljo would become a *tehsil* headquarter that would have a college, a hospital, and bazaars. The main difficulties being faced were both physical and political in the Sampagna Kandao area as we were nearing towards Daburi. Snow and rain did not help either and servicing the bulldozers was the big challenge. Jeeps could transport only a couple of barrels of diesel for the bulldozers which consumed the fuel in an hour. Carving out the road and maintaining the supply line was an arduous task but somehow because of the determination of the Assistant Political Agent Israr Ullah Shah, the *Tehsildars* Zakria, Ghulam Habib and Munzur, and the Executive Engineer Nawab Khan, the task was accomplished.

Once across the Pass, one had to keep the Mullakhel tribe, particularly its chief cleric Mullah Azim, in good humour day after day. This was no child's play since virtually every one had a demand or a request to make. I felt great sympathy for them and felt that it was proper to construct the road for their own good. When Mullah Azim refused to allow the road to progress any further, a useful ploy was employed to win him over. A small lorry converted into a bus, called *ghattu* locally, was provided to him as an incentive for transporting people and more importantly for a profit to him. Azim was most agreeable to the proposal. It was agreed that for two years, he would have the monopoly over road use. This turned out to be the appropriate incentive as it was a major boon for people in the area. Today, there are hundreds of vehicles using the roads and this would not have been possible had this incentive not been provided. One should not forget Mullah Azim's contribution.

A rather sensitive issue cropped up on the day that I was to travel as the Political Agent to the terminal point in Daburi for the inauguration of the road. The tribe which had arranged a lunch for the occasion for the *political* officers was adamant that the sitting Federal Minister, himself a Mullakhel Malik, would not accompany me, as they were unhappy with him allegedly, for failing to fulfill his promises to them. Efforts were made to convince the minister to travel to his tribe on his own but he absolutely insisted that he would only travel with the Political Agent. Ultimately, the tribe agreed upon my request for him. The visit was a great success, with much celebratory aerial firing and rejoicing. We prayed at the Duburi Jamia masjid and thanked the Almighty for the success provided to the tribe and the administration.

Some years later, while in England, I wrote a note on the construction of this road to Sir Olaf Caroe, a former Governor of NWFP, who had earlier served in Kohat as Deputy Commissioner and was now living in retirement in Steyning. He was most pleased at the road construction that he had started in 1928–29 from Kachai-Marai into the Orakzai territory. I was amazed that he remembered names of all those places clearly after more than half a century. Today, nearly forty years later, all those who were associated with the Daburi road project feel elated for a job well accomplished, in quick time. The vision of those who planned the venture needs to be saluted and to those who executed the works, including the *pultikals*, the engineers, the *khassadars*, and the tribal contractors will forever be remembered for a difficult job done under the most adverse conditions. It would be unfair not to acknowledge the contributions of the tribal *maliks* without whom this noble venture could never be achieved. Above all, this was their success. Once a road has been constructed and opened in an inaccessible area, there are numerous employment and economic opportunities generated for the local people. In addition, it results in extending the writ of the state. The greatest joy I experienced in the construction of the Daburi road came decades after the event, when I came across an elderly Orakzai tribesman in Islamabad who happened to be a Mullakhel tribesman. When I informed him that I had contributed to the road effort in the 1970s, he asked if I was Shakil Durrani? Indeed, there is nothing sweeter than hearing one's own name associated with a worthy cause! For me this was the biggest reward.

During this period of road construction, the security situation in the Tribal Areas would often deteriorate on account of the activities of the tribal *hostiles* who were armed and abetted by Afghanistan's secret service. As a contingency plan the Thal Scouts and the 73 Brigade in Thal cantonment were placed on alert to protect the gains. A briefing in the Brigade's Operation Room was arranged for the Political Agent by the inimical Brigadier Nawaz fondly called *Titch*. The local Brigade Major (BM) however, had other ideas. He enquired of his boss, 'Sir, are you sure it would be appropriate to let the civilian Political Agent Orakzai inside the OPS Room?' The Brigadier assured the BM to trust his word and that no harm would come.

Some tribesmen, through habit, ususally bring a gift for the Political Officers when they visit them. The gift could be a live chicken, a packet of cigarettes, or even a few eggs properly wrapped. On one occasion, an Orakzai tribesman who felt obliged for some official work, offered me, a small emerald (*zammurad*) gemstone wrapped in four layers of cloth. I declined to accept the gemstone and thanked him all the same. The tribesman informed me, as he was unwrapping the gemstone, that he had found the stone while digging in his courtyard. The stone looked less like an emerald and more like a chip from a broken Seven-Up bottle. Some months later, the man returned on some official business and on enquiry stated that he had sold the stone for a staggering sum of money. It was a joy to hear about his newfound riches but his earlier generous offer itself was a treasure.

vi. MOHMAND AGENCY

The Mohmand Agency is bone-dry inspite of the fact that the Kabul and Swat rivers flow on either side of it. The people are industrious and known for their monopoly over two trades. Almost every timber trade in northern India is sure to be Mohmand-owned and so are the restaurants, in Peshawar city. One of the finest Mohmand Maliks, and a close friend, Malik Shahzada Halimzai, was simple man but with a strong muscular physique at seventy years of age. It was said that a minute after he received his *mullaqaat* (meeting) cash from the Political Agent, it was distributed among anyone who happened to be around at the time. Once as the Political Agent, I expressed appreciation for a silver pistol he was carrying and magnanimous as he was, he promptly presented it to me despite my protestations, insisting it was mine. A short while later, Farid Khan, the Assistant Political Agent, entered the office and appreciated the pistol, which a minute later became his property. Generosity is contagious; and at any rate, it should be!

In 1977, after the Political Agent moved his headquarters to Ghallanai, a tribesman by the name of Bacha Kamali Halimzai became friendly with the officials because of his hospitality, there being no hotel or mess in the area. In the course of time, Bacha built some commercial property outside Ghallanai and started living comfortably. He then became a target of jealousy of Halimzai Maliks in the area, who suggested to Malik Shahzada to deal with him appropriately. Now Malik Shahzada, a simple and upright man, informed me as the Political Agent, in a impassive voice that since he could not tolerate Bacha Kamali Halimzai any longer, he planned to eliminate him. I was appalled because I didn't want a law and order situation right next to the Headquarters and more so because Bacha was a personal friend. Malik Shahzada was told in no uncertain words that his suggestion was unacceptable and would ensure the wrath of the government, if he persisted.

The honourable Malik gave his word with a firm handshake, committing that he would not cause any injury and kept his word, while I remained the Political Agent. However, soon after my transfer and the arrival of the new officer, Bacha was killed in his house by Malik Shahzada's relatives. It could be that some official gave a nod to this heinous act. This started a vicious enmity between the two sides, which continued for a long time. In the process, Malik Shahzada was also killed in Rawalpindi when he was a member of *Majlis Shura*, the parliament nominated by General Ziaul Haq. Thereafter, the enmity subsided but only after killing of two of my iconic friends. When will the Pakhtuns learn tolerance and live in peace?

It was in the Mohmand Agency that the government tried for long, to build the Khapakh road toward the Khwazai tribe leading to Baizai and the border with Afghanistan, but could not succeed. In 1978, the road was finally completed and this would never have been possible were it not for the support of Bacha Kamali Halimzai and Malik Abdul Manan. Such were the dynamics of friendship in the Tribal Areas. Bacha became a friend of the government because the Political Agent accepted his hospitality; his mother had presented a traditional shawl to my wife after our marriage which cemented the bonds further. As a bond of friendship had been created, the tribesman could never turn down any request—adverse consequences notwithstanding. Forty years down the road, the sons and brothers of Bacha never fail to visit me on Eid day!

During the mid-1970s, the most important development in the Mohmand Agency after Independence, was the construction of the road from Yusafkhel to Lakaro and Nawagai. This opened up the Safi tribal area and, subsequently, assisted in developing the road network in Upper Mohmand and the Baizai areas as well. The main credit for this and the related developments go to Brigadier Naseerullah Babar, the Inspector General Frontier Corps, and Mohibur Rahman Kiyani, the Political Agent. Just as the construction of the Karakoram Highway to Gilgit and Skardu changed the lives of the people, similarly the road beyond Nahakki Kandau brought education and health facilities to the people. There were many tribesmen who supported the government in constructing this road, without the use of force but none more so than Malik Yarbadshah of Kamali Halimzai. It was supreme irony that some years later, he was killed by mistake during a scouts operation nearby.

The Mohmand Agency also had its share of infamy. In Shaheeda Banda, kidnapped or runaway women were bought and sold. This practice refused to die out despite the numerous actions undertaken against it. These unfortunate women were often sold in marriage, by their poor parents, to strangers or were victims of incest, rape, or kidnapping. It remained a perpetual shame for the *land of the pure*. Some people thought that Shaheeda Banda was merely a symptom of the larger problem regarding the low status and position of women in the country, particularly in the Tribal Areas. These people were certainly right.

The Agency was a rough place and it was essential to follow the rules of the game as any deviation could cause problems. In the mid 1970s, soon after my appointment as Political Agent, I decided to spend a few days at Lakaro in Upper Mohmand to meet the people and monitor the development works. The only government building available for my stay and our meetings was the Rest House in Lakaro. Individual and group meetings with the tribes continued in the open throughout the day, lasting beyond last light. This was a serious departure from the Tribal Areas' standard operating procedures at that time as no meeting was held, especially in the open, after *asar* (late afternoon) prayers. There remained a lone tribesman who had not been able to meet me the whole day and felt he would lose face if he returned home without a meeting. When Fateh, the orderly on duty, finally told him that no meeting was possible he fired at him from near point-blank range. Fortunately, he missed and ran away in the dark. My personal bodyguard, Gulab Sher, grabbed a rifle, aimed it in the general direction of the person fleeing, and fired. In the dark, he got him between the ear and the head. The assailant staggered and fell, but was safe as the bullet had only grazed his head. Next day, his tribesmen were summoned and agreed to burn his house for the offence. The accused, later appeared before the subordinate officer with an offering of a cow to express his remorse. He was allowed to leave with the cow, as the act of apologizing in person compensated for the offence under the circumstances. It was considered appropriate to end the matter then and there so that in future the government's development programme in the area was not affected. Gulab Sher, my bodyguard, was a huge man having served in the Karachi Police some years earlier but had to leave the force for some unexplained reasons. As a gunman he had few equals.

The Mohmands like the Safis, Shinwaris, Mangals, and Waziris live on both sides of the Durand Line. They move across quite freely and engage in trade and the restaurant business. After the Soviet invasion of Afghanistan, they moved to Pakistan in droves. One of them was the polished and proud Malik Firdaus, the Khan of Goshta, who despite his standing in his tribe did not find much comfort from the provincial refugee organization. Only after he was introduced to the governor, was he able to get some assistance for the people of his tribe.

vii. BAJAUR AGENCY

The Bajaur Agency, for the purist, is not a tribal agency but a Khanate as the affairs were controlled by the Khans of Khar, Nawagai, and Pashat. It is perhaps the greenest and most fertile agency with opium poppy as its main cash crop, until the government destroyed the entire crop. After Bajaur's upgradation to an Agency in 1973, Nawagai was linked by road to Lakaro and Yusafkhel to Peshawar. The people of Bajaur and particularly those from the Mamund tribe are considered to be the most handsome in the Tribal Areas and equally hardworking. Many legends, songs, and ballads are associated with the greenery, mustard fields, and the flowing streams of Bajaur, including the tragic ballad of Durkhanai and Adam. The young Winston Churchill spoke highly of the valour of the local Mamund tribe during the military operations of the 1890s and also commented upon the good looks of the inhabitants. For the 'politicals' and the Scouts, nothing brought greater joy than the water-fowl hunting season outside Khar. This was a delight; one could step out of a jeep right into the shooting trench with the *Tehsildar* having ensured complete comfort with cushions, sofas, and Persian rugs in the shooting butt. There were always arguments among the visitors as to which was more pleasurable, the shoot or the food served afterwards. With much of the Tribal Areas suffering from serious insecurity issues, that time was another age and another environment.

Service in the Tribal Areas was never all sport and no stress as both alternated. During the mid-1970s, a contingent of Scouts based in Mohmand Agency entered an area inhabited by the modest Sagi Shinwari tribe, who in retaliation surrounded the Scouts and seized their weapons. This was as serious incident. Everyone, except one very young Mahsud soldier, almost a boy, surrendered but he reportedly started firing back at the tribesman saying that his mother told him never to hand over the weapon to anyone. He was killed. A Scouts installation should have been named after him, but apparently we did not fully appreciate his sacrifice. Like most other tribal Agencies, Bajaur has suffered much material and human losses, following the events of 9/11. American bombings and drone strikes have occurred here on a number of occasions, as in Waziristan, and in an attack on a madrasah in Damadola, nearly forty children were killed. Later it was reported that the telephone conversation of a senior jihadi commander had been monitored from the scene.

The Bajaur Agency was also the scene of a bizarre kidnapping case during the early 1990s. An Uthmankhel tribesman, serving as the driver to a family in Charsadda, decided to try and get rich quickly, by kidnapping the infant child of a family that was visiting from England. The development was serious and the Political Agent was not available; the Additional Commissioner, Aslam Khan was told to ensure the prompt recovery of the child. He was unable to make any headway, having had no previous experience in tribal areas. There was then no option left for me as the Commissioner of Malakand Division but to take charge personally. Before moving to the area, I had two medium artillery guns deployed pointing towards the Uthmankhel hills. A local *jirga* was sent to bring back the infant before nightfall. How effective the *jirga* was, remained a moot point but it appeared that the artillery guns were more persuasive. The child was back with the family sooner than expected!

Part 3

Falling Standards

7

Who Watches the Watchman?

History tells us that in early Islam, the Caliph considered himself responsible for the safety and well-being of everyone in his realm. It was an accepted tenet that even if an animal was found starving on the banks of the Euphrates River, the Caliph would be held accountable. In India, during the reign of Emperor Sher Shah Suri, women travelled alone from village to village in all their gold and finery in complete security. These are two examples of good governance. In present times, we have seen serious crime and narcotics eliminated in countries when an effective government decides to root out this evil. For developing countries, there indeed is a shortcut to quick material progress and physical development. It is called good governance. Unfortunately, it has a reverse side too. Good governance demands altruism. It does not benefit those who wield power and do not wish to be answerable to law but love to exercise unbridled discretion. Those not interested in good governance are adept, as an English peer stated, at creating obstacles for every solution and stay to reap personal benefit. Most of the people who have ruled Pakistan fall into the latter category.

The essence of law and justice was bequeathed to the Muslims during the early years of Islam. Personal, social, or political positions did not prevent anyone from being answerable before the law. The level of accountability displayed by Caliphs like Hazrat Umar ibn Khattab (RA) remains unmatched in history. The Caliph once needed to explain publicly how he could sew a garment from a small piece of cloth acquired from the spoils of war which was to be equally distributed among all. Since the Caliph did not have the discretion to take more than his share of the cloth, he explained that he had taken his son's share as well. Here was an example where accountability was demonstrated at the highest level. The Caliph's good sense did not allow him to take more than his share but the fact that he was questioned by a commonner speaks very highly of the principle of public accountability. Compare the Caliph's integrity with the current Third World rulers, many of them billionaires, whose sources of wealth remains a mystery, judging by their negligible income tax returns. Their properties within and outside the country are vulgarly extensive. They have no qualms in openly operating their personal businesses while holding public office. They operate on the principle of 'ask what my country can do for me!'

In short good governance consists of 'fair rules fairly implemented'. The objectives and priorities of responsible societies today, should only be focused on the people. Goals are determined by leadership within objective conditions. How well these are accomplished, determines the level of good governance. In the days gone by, what is now called good governance was called effective administration; officers were taught to be firm, fair, and friendly. There are many examples of countries where good governance and sound management practices have led societies to quick material progress even when natural resources are scarce; More important was the proper allocation of the available resources of a society, supported by effective management practices. Good governance then, is a function of fair and efficient utilization of the state's resources.

However, good governance assumes the presence of dedicated leadership. Honesty of purpose and firm execution of policy, are key qualities in a leader. In developing countries, the leader has to make a choice. Deciding between building grandiose concrete and asphalt projects that suit individual preferences and preference for human resource development? Most rulers, especially in the Arab world and Pakistan, opted for the former. More mature leaders in South-East Asia remained focused on human development. Investment in human beings can propel societies to growth, which provides large-scale employment opportunities and reduces poverty. For obvious reasons, Third World countries such as Bangladesh, which invested massively in health, education, and family planning outperformed those who invested public money in steel and concrete infrastructure. Multi-lateral donors, quite rightly insist on programme management in development rather than investing their money in brick and mortar project development. Successful development models, seeking quick progress from a low base often demand an element of sacrifice in providing basic rights and material comfort, for a specified period of time. This can lead to adverse social consequences but in the long-term the economic returns are optimized.

Investment in human beings yields the greatest financial and social returns to any society. It more than substitutes for any deficiencies in mineral and material resources for getting out of the poverty trap. Professor Jeffrey Sachs, formerly of Harvard and Columbia Universities, reminds us that resource-rich countries like Indonesia, Venezuela, Libya, Nigeria, and some Arab nations have stumbled because of their reliance on abundant oil, gas, and mineral wealth, to the neglect of human resource development. On the other hand, by concentrating on human resource development, a society gains both in economic development and more importantly, greater equality is ensured. Japan, South Korea, Taiwan, Singapore, Malaysia, and Turkey have shown how countries with a low resource base can progress economically with visionary and courageous leaders. Even in a country like India, states like Kerala and Gujarat have surged ahead because of investment in human beings. It is clear that good governance is not about mega projects but about adherence to rules and equity.

i. THE LEADERSHIP BLIGHT

The real issue here is how to ensure the availability of leadership which could provide good governance in developing societies. There are no easy answers. Political philosophers have grappled with the issue of how best to hold leaders accountable for thousands of years. Dr Phil Edmonds of Edwardes College, Peshawar, felt that modern political thought revolved around the question of *who watches the watchman*? For reasons of survival, man remains predominantly committed to the self, the family, and the tribe; public spiritedness comes sparingly. For every Abdul Sattar Edhi, the philanthropist, there are millions of amoral people. Devoted leadership is the exception and, therefore, very rare. Corrupt and self-centred leadership on the other hand remained the norm in the Third World especially in the Muslim countries which witnessed widespread poverty, ignorance, and malnourishment. The quality of governance, thus, has a linear relationship with the level of development. It is clear why some countries transformed themselves into South Korea and Malaysia while others like Pakistan and Nigeria, stumbled and stagnated.

Holding leadership to account is not easy. It takes a long-drawn political struggle to keep the ruler in check. The effort could last hundreds, if not thousands, of years. In England, the mother of parliaments, the process began with the Magna Carta, 800 years ago. It was supported by milestone events like the Bill of Rights in the late seventeenth century. Unfortunately, the Asian and the African continents, because of their geographical location and historical experience, remained outside the change in the mindset that was brought about by the Renaissance and the Reformation movements. The Muslims, Arabs, and non-Arab lived in a socio-political milieu where tolerance, scepticism, truth, and the spirit of inquiry were discouraged with damaging results for posterity. Without knowledge, science, and technology, it was only a matter of time before they succumbed to more vibrant and progressive forces. One *alam-panah* (sovereign), a Mughal Emperor, reportedly scorned at the offer of installing a printing press by the Europeans insisting that his court calligraphers, the *khattaat*, did a better job by hand. Lord Macaulay may have only slightly exaggerated when he mocked Indian culture as containing little more than 'medieval doctrines that would disgrace an English farrier, astronomy which would be laughed at by girls at an English boarding school, history abounding with kings' thirty-feet high and reigning thirty thousand years long, and geography as little more than treacle and butter.' At a few places in our country, this remains the standard fare even today. There are *nau-gaza*, literally twenty-seven feet long graves at many places in Pakistan today.

The depths to which public officials can fall is best illustrated by the conduct of a senior official of the Small Industries Development Board in the former Frontier province some decades back. The Government having decided to establish a small pilot project for developing ceramic industry in Shaidu-Akora Khattak sought open competitive bids for the supply of the plant equipment. The top-class Japanese bid amounted to ten million rupees but since they were not willing to pay an illegal commission to the official the latter connived with the rival bidder and reduced their bid by a small amount. The Japanese were aghast at the duplicity and offered to gift the plant free of cost but this was not acceptable to the official as they could not get a share of the bribe. The rivals thereafter, supplied poor quality equipment which was soon scrapped. Thus the province lost an opportunity to develop a world-class ceramic industry!

As late as the twentieth century, countries like Pakistan, created in the name of Islam, ignored the essence of the spiritual texts or the need of scientific enquiry. The real meaning of the Charter of Medina, which enshrined public accountability and basic human rights a thousand years before Europe became aware of these standards, were blithely ignored. In most developing states, where accountability was not institutionalized, it was left to chance or the fair conscience of the ruler to deliver good governance. Only once in a long while were some countries fortunate enough to experience strong and charismatic leaders. Most were un-elected like Ataturk, Zhou En Lai, Deng Xiaoping, Park Chung-Hee, and Fidel Castro who were exceptional and they left their imprint. To this list, one can add a few elected rulers like Lee Kuan Yew, Mahathir Mohamad, and Turgut Ozal, who understood their times and circumstances better and produced impressive results. These leaders were visionaries, who faced tough opposition but they sustained public pressure and were able to prevail in the end. This could only be possible by selflessness of character and a combination of dedication and energy. Leaders always have to face an ethical dilemma. There is a human cost to bear, to achieve rapid material development. Representative governments seeking consensual support, often find it difficult to overcome dissent or assuage competing pressure groups. This leads to an inability to take affirmative, quick, and bold decisions on divisive issues. The truth is that autocratic leadership has generally shown better results than most elected ones, in developing countries.

Where leadership is weak or confused, issues continue to multiply because timely decisions cannot be taken as happens in the Third World. In countries like Pakistan, there remain too many unresolved matters; too many 'Kalabagh dams' waiting to be built! Matters like the extent of provincial autonomy permissible, the role of religion in society, the level of the involvement of the state in the economy, and the choice of developing large infrastructural projects have remained contentious and, therefore, remain unresolved for far too long. There is controversy over technical issues such as the construction of certain dams and water reservoirs, alignments for new roads and railways, the place of secular and spiritual education, the desirability of anti-polio vaccinations, the benefits of family planning, and so on. In more fortunate developing countries such matters did not take long to get resolved. In such countries, strong-willed leaders tackled contentious issues decisively but in countries like Pakistan, most rulers were found wanting in audacity. One needed a dictator to get things moving but the uncomfortable truth is that for every effective public-spirited dictator in the world, there have been dozens of vicious and greedy tyrants who failed their countries. There have been too many tyrannical Mobutus, Marcoses, Mubaraks and Bokassas and too few Lee Kuan Yew, Castros, Mahathir, and Zhou En Lai.

One Pathan tribesman with amazing foresight had anticipated what the conditions in the subcontinent would be, once the British left India. In 1947, just before Partition, the Governor of North West Frontier Province (NWFP) made a farewell call on the tribes of the Khyber Agency. A tribal elder, reportedly, Malik Adam Khan Mullagori, wanted to know why the British were leaving India merely on the demand of two *dhoti-clad* Hindus, Gandhi and Nehru. He reminded the Governor that it was important to remain strong on the ground and that he had imagined the English would quit, only when the Khyber Pass would be covered with spent bullets, half a foot deep. In any case, he suggested that if they still wanted to leave, 'don't go too far away because soon we would need you'. He was convinced that the new Pakistani leaders would not be up to the task of governance.

The absence of dedicated leadership explains why most developing countries failed to utilize their potential. This further begs the question about why quality leadership does not emerge easily in their sterile soils. Could this be attributed to intolerance of temper based on their peculiar social, cultural, and historical experience, or could such experiences be the result of the extremely hot climate, forbidding geography, and scarce water resources and so the primary issue remained competing for mere survival. The survival-gene remains dominant in such an environment; no one wants to emerge second-best and that explained their fierce and intolerant nature. Where the environment was favourable, the results were more promising as in much of Europe and for a while in temperate Muslim Spain, the fertile Nile Delta, the rich plains of Baghdad of the Abbasids, and also fleetingly in pockets, in ancient India. It was unfortunate that the Muslim world remained outside the temperate and intellectual current of knowledge emanating from Europe for a variety of reasons. While Europe benefited from the academic and scientific achievements of the Muslims and the Hindus to emerge out of their Dark Ages, the reverse flow of ideas unfortunately did not take place. The knowledge flow never materialized. It was left to colonial powers to kick-start modernity.

In the case of Pakistan, the leadership void continued far to long a period and with pernicious results. Amazingly, dictators here were as incompetent and corrupt as representative leaders. Society remained basically non-functional, even under all four of our dictators. Most constitutional institutions of the state such as the parliament, judiciary, and the bureaucracy have become largely irrelevant for the majority of the people. What actually mattered were personal agendas of a small minority of oligarchs who are wholly out of step with the needs of the country. Elected leaders have remained demagogues, pursuing their own aims and most have turned out to be more tyrannical than the dictators. The inimitable Khwaja Ghaffar of Srinagar found a considerable wisdom deficit in Pakistani leadership which did not hold much hope for the people. Unlike developing countries, the West was more fortunate at the corresponding stage of economic development in dealing with their issues because of their greater tolerance, smaller populations, and more abundant natural resources. They had more time, opportunity, and the right social structures to adjust to the economic and technological change. The expectations of their people were lower, following their exhaustion in constant religious wars. Such an environment was not afforded to most of the developing countries, burdened as they were, with large populations and hugely polarized polities but with very little time available. Good governance was a pressing necessity from the very beginning. So great were the problems associated with the emergence of Pakistan that without ensuring effective rule-based governance, the future looked bleak. Absence of rules meant total exercise of discretion by those in authority, or as Sheikh Rashid the politician would say, law was less important than the face behind the case. The greater the exercise of discretion, the poorer the governance. Justice William Douglas of the US Supreme Court was right when he said that the law has reached its finest moments when it has freed men from the unlimited discretion of some ruler, some civil or military official, or some bureaucrat. Where discretion is absolute, man has always suffered.

Good governance entails two prerequisites; honest leadership and effective writ of the state in all parts of the country. Without the power and capacity of making the state's authority felt in every nook and corner of the country, good governance is not possible. For much of its history, Pakistan neither saw dedicated leadership, nor was the writ of the state extended throughout its territory. If large tracts of land remain as no-go areas, there is a serious problem at hand. It is not surprising that insurgencies are based in these inaccessible areas, often at the behest of hostile forces, who continue to wage war against the state for decades on end. Pakistan has been a failing state and one so soft that both its own citizens and foreigners violate its laws with near impunity. The powerful and affluent do not fear authority and almost everyone finds a way to avoid the inconvenience of law. In such a situation it appears that the assumed duty of state institutions remains confined to protecting the position and privilege of the well-entrenched few. Almost the entire political and military leadership since Independence is guilty of not establishing the writ of the state over its entire geographical area.

The writ of the state, in terms of securing all its territories, never really existed. Large tracts of territories in the Tribal Areas and Balochistan did not acknowledge the presence or the authority of the state. The Tirah area of the Khyber and Orakzai, Shawal, and Maddakhel belt in Waziristan and the Baizai in Mohmand Agencies/Districts have only very recently seen some form of the writ of the state. Similar pockets existed in southern Punjab, Balochistan, and in Karachi as well. The writ is even weaker when viewed against the responsibility of the state to provide basic needs of the people. The army, one would have thought, with its resources, influence, and supposed vision would have recognized this potential threat, but it too was blissfully ignorant of its responsibility. So weak is the state today that in many areas it cannot even recover electricity and gas bills, let alone be able to project its presence.

The region all along the border of the Tribal Areas with the settled areas saw the emergence of *de facto* Tribal Areas. Here, neither government departments operated nor was the police allowed entry. As the Districts shrank in size, Pakistan's sovereignty withered. All rulers from General Ayub onwards were culpable for this failure. Zulfikar Ali Bhutto, to his credit, was the only Prime Minister who had the vision to open up the Tribal Areas and Balochistan to ensure effective presence of the state that could initiate economic and social development. The rest of the leadership would not even visit the Tribal Areas. This vacuum cost the country dearly in the years that followed, all the more because of the developments in Iran and Afghanistan. It was reported by a military aide to Zulfikar Ali Bhutto that while addressing the American Congressional Foreign Affairs Committee in the early 1970s, he had predicted that Soviets would soon make a move towards Afghanistan and that the Shah of Iran would face serious difficulties. These may have been the reasons for his efforts to open up the Tribal Areas and Balochistan as well. Were others not aware of this threat?

In Pakistan today, the core governance issue is, how best to address the security and material needs of the people within the resources available. The common man is patient, silent, and helpless and does not demand much. He is denied even the bare minimum. He is harried in the *thana* (police station), the *patwar* (land administration office), and the *kuchery* (courts). These three agencies of the state are responsible for providing him the rights to life, liberty, and property. The services he ought to get from the government-run school, college, hospital, and dispensary are not available on ground even though the teachers and doctors are getting paid. Municipal amenities like piped drinking water, sewerage disposal, and garbage removal barely exist, except in more affluent localities. Due to a lack of urban planning, slums have developed around all the major cities in the country including Islamabad, Lahore, Karachi, and Peshawar. There is little or no concept of Land Use Planning. Green agricultural land and forests are being converted to Brown use with no consideration for the future generations. The hill stations developed with great care and planning by the British in Murree, Kaghan, and Galliat have also been converted into overbuilt slums with no regard for the conservation of ecology. These areas have become more like warrens of the rodents breeding crime. Wildlife has been decimated. Electricity and gas are woefully deficient and drinking water is often unavailable, even at high prices. Investments required for the future needs of the society in areas such as human resource development, technical training, provision of micro-credit, population planning, and the conservation of water, land, and forests, are ignored. The more immediate priorities of the rulers are personal and pecuniary; the self and the pelf alone are important. The late Major Geoffrey Langlands formerly of Aitchison

College and of Chitral, after a lifetime spent in Pakistan, is reported to have said that if Pakistani leaders were made responsible for the Sahara desert there would soon be a shortage of sand there!

ii. GOOD GOVERNANCE IN PRACTICE

There was a time in Pakistan when good governance norms were actually practiced even at the cost of annoying the top hierarchy. A subordinate police officer, Abdul Hameed, posted as the Petrol Rationing Inspector in the NWFP once refused to sanction petrol for the official vehicle of the Chief Minister, Abdul Qaiyum Khan, because his quota for the month had been exhausted. A distraught Chief Minister, a terror in his own right but now helpless in view of the rules, telephoned the Inspector requesting him to provide the required petrol on loan from another minister and to adjust it against his quota the following month. This was done and everyone understood that the law was there to be obeyed and that no discretion was permissible. Here was as good example of good governance as any. As the competent authority, acting within the law, the Inspector denied the fuel but in the interest of state duty he then used limited discretion in allowing, on loan, the petrol required for the tour. He could have lawfully denied the Chief Minister's wish but that could have aborted the latter's tour to Dera Ismail Khan, which would have been unhelpful. Incidentally, this strict Inspector Hameed Khan joined the police as an Assistant Sub Inspector, the same rank his colleague Mian Bashir Ahmad was appointed to. Mian Bashir rose through the ranks and became the Inspector General Police of West Pakistan through hard work and a more practical approach to service while Hameed retired as an Inspector, mainly because of his habit of speaking his mind openly and rather loudly. Ruling politicians in those days were also more considerate.

One rare example of good governance was seen in Azad Jammu and Kashmir during the first couple of years of the new millennium. The Prime Minister was Barrister Sultan Mehmood, a decent and well-meaning person, while the Army Commander 12th Infantry Division was Major General Parvez Kayani, later the Army Chief. General Kayani was bright, a 'thinking General', and very thorough in the implementation of decisions, which was why the administration remained effective. The Prime Minister of Azad

Kashmir, the Garrison Commander, and the Chief Secretary were primarily responsible for proper execution and monitoring of officials' conduct in ensuring sound administration. With no pressure from any source and no personal stakes involved, policy formulation and administrative decision was taken objectively. There was never any arbitrary or pernicious influence, manipulating from behind the scene. No one could recall any case where decisions were not merit-based.

Barrister Sultan Mehmood was also a relaxed individual, genuinely amiable, and one who supposedly laid great stress on punctuality. Quoting a Law Professor from one of the London Inns, he would say that it was better to be an hour early for an engagement than a minute late. However, once at the highest level, he almost missed an important appointment. General Musharraf was then in power after the coup which he called 'the events of 12th October' and in keeping with the spirit of the times he styled himself as the Chief Executive of Pakistan. He had decided to visit Kashmir House in Islamabad. Until the moment the presidential motorcade entered the premises, which was around midday, the Prime Minister of Azad Kashmir was nowhere to be seen. His servants and even the valet were under instructions to remind him every fifteen minutes post-sunrise to get him ready for the event but apparently without success. The Chief Secretary was obviously distraught to find the Prime Minister missing. Then miraculously the Prime Minister emerged in the reception line not more than five seconds before the President alighted from his car. To his credit, he was on time! He was then requested to rephrase his favourite adage every time he overslept, 'better to be five seconds early than five seconds late'!

In Azad Kashmir, during this period, the government undertook a number of positive initiatives. One initiative, was the establishment of an Endowment Fund for Health. It entitled every person from Azad Kashmir, in proportion to his means, to claim expenses for heart and kidney surgery in the best hospitals, in the country. This was certainly a novel undertaking. It was a great help to those who could not afford the costs. The capital for the Fund was generated by transferring the interest payments deducted on *zakat*, the obligatory tax paid by Muslims for the poor, which was deposited in banks. Previously, this informal account was known as the Zakat Munafa Fund; the rationale being that since interest was prohibited in Islam, it

My paternal grandfather, Khan Bahadur
Juma Khan Nurzai Durrani, Extra Assistant
Commissioner, Quetta, 1919.

My maternal grandfather, Khan Bahadur
Abdul Hakim Khan, Superintendent of Police,
Peshawar, 1936.

My brother, Dr Sohail Durrani in his
clinic in the US.

Major Jafar Hussain of Village Chuhan in
Chakwal (left) with Abdul Wahab Aurakzai.

A British officer in Pathan attire.
One could get the Brits out of the Frontier but not the Frontier out of the Brits!

My father, Colonel Shafi Durrani in retirement with his grandchildren.

My mother, Zaib Durrani with my brother Sohail, myself, and my sisters,
Huma, and Shehla in Upper Topa, Murree, 1956.

Siblings: Shakil, Huma, and Sohail in Rawalpindi, 1951.

Siblings: 63 years later; Shakil, Huma, and Sohail in Washington, 2014.

Princess Salimah Aga Khan, Ambassador for Children, SOS Children's Villages International with the author and his family at the Chief Secretary's House in Peshawar in 2002.

Memories of the Fishing Hut, Chakdara on the Swat River, 1990.
(Left to Right) Sabrina, Shakil, Danial, Shamoun, and Arslaan.

The first ibex culled through the Trophy Hunting Programme in Markhun, Hunza, 10 January 1994.

In the company of fabulous friends from Kohat.
From left: Shakil Durrani,Commissioner, Jalaluddin Katu Khan, Mohabat Ali Zafar, Harun Khan, Danial, Shamoun, and Professor Iqbal Awan on extreme right.

A Kalash lady in all her finery
Photo courtesy: Rashid Zia Cheema

The mesmerizing diva: the Frontier's very own Mumtaz Jehan, known
to the cinema and world as Madhubala.
Photo courtesy: Getty Images

could not be lawfully paid to the poor as *zakat* or alms. It was, therefore, put to better use for the wants, needs, and desires of the persons with influence. Then there was another source of unaudited spending called the Kashmir Liberation Fund, also available with the Prime Minister of Azad Kashmir. Most of the time, money from these funds was spent on keeping the friendly and not so friendly politicians in good humour, especially by sending them to Europe in the summers—less to liberate Kashmir and more to liberate their bodily frustrations. It was to the credit of Barrister Sultan Mehmood that he allowed transfer of part of the money, for the medical treatment of the poor.

Another useful initiative taken up, was the immediate provision of financial relief to the victims of Indian ground, firing through creating a Revolving Relief Fund placed in the Brigade Headquarters. The army was authorized to distribute cash immediately and not later than twenty-four hours to the families of the dead and those injured or whose properties were damaged. Additional funds were transferred to the army as soon as these were disbursed. This measure was a great relief to those affected by the Indian action because previously it took many months and at times years, to receive this relief called compensation unjustly.

One remarkable feature of governance in Azad Kashmir was the regularity with which elections were held and power transferred, without much fuss, to the winning party. On the oath-taking day, both the outgoing and the incoming Prime Ministers would be seated on the dais for the formal ceremonies. The outgoing Prime Minister would arrive with the flag fluttering on his car but would leave without the flag. Pretty civilized conduct!

Among the few examples of relatively better governance seen in the recent past was the short tenure of Chief Minister Sardar Mehtab Ahmed in NWFP, during 1997–99. He was in office for just three years and had barely initiated his reforms when the government changed. His greatest achievement was the construction of the Pehur high level canal which brought immense benefits to many areas and in developing medical and technical education. Then there was Shahbaz Sharif, the bold and dynamic Chief Minister of Punjab, whose party remained in power for nearly two decades during which many large projects were developed though some remained controversial. In the Khyber province, Amir Haider Hoti notably focussed on developing hydro-power projects to raise provincial revenues and generate employment. Sadly, Sindh and Balochistan have remained backwaters because decision-making over there is often predicated upon different terms. There is little doubt that major projects like hydropower dams, motorways, and railway lines are a national requirement but more important than these is ensuring better governance in hospitals, schools, police stations, courts, and revenue administration. To be truthful, governance all over Pakistan, has remained indifferent and has largely failed to address the basic issues of the people.

Shortly after the creation of Pakistan, the Chief Minister of the then NWFP, Khan Abdul Qaiyum Khan, was perhaps the only one who realised that the highest priority should be on improving the administration of police, schools, hospitals, and in encouraging industrialization through cheap provision of electricity.

There have been dozens of other chief ministers, most of whom brought nothing but shame to themselves, while occupying seats of power. Rather than accepting power as a trust from the Almighty, they utilized it for personal profit and party aggrandizement. In Sindh, surprisingly, the tenure of Ghulam Mustafa Jatoi as Chief Minister was fondly remembered by those who worked with him. He was not only said to be considerate but would support his senior officers to the hilt. Chaudhry Pervez Elahi from Punjab, was another Chief Minister, who sought frank opinions in developing consensus of policy issues. His contributions in creating the emergency rescue service, 'Rescue 1122', has been widely acknowledged.

Good governance, as already mentioned, is not a function of money and resources; actually, it may improve with scarcity. It is budgetary neutral as its central concern is with implementing the law fairly. Initiating major development projects is a small part of governance. Project construction is important but putting to good use, what has already been built, is more important. The former is a function of resource availability but the latter is a determined effort to ensure the rule of law and an efficient and impartial administration. Good governance must take decentralization of authority for granted. It is also most essential that power be exercised through objective criteria and the rules alone be given primacy. There should be no room for political vindictiveness or discretion. Priorities need to be so determined that the present and future requirements of the society, are recognized.

A primary and sole example of reasonable good governance at the federal level, in Pakistani politics, was the year-long tenure of Prime Minister Huseyn Shaheed Suhrawardy. He was a remarkable man and without him the eastern wing of the country may never have been part of Pakistan. There was also the shortened but better managed tenure of Prime Minister Muhammad Khan Junejo, during the mid-1980s. Junejo's stint was free of major scandals and he cut the ministers, the generals, and the bureaucrats to size, literally, by reducing the size of their official cars, the ultimate status symbol. The decision was symbolic but did not go well with generals and federal secretaries. The order was reversed, after his departure. To be fair, Nawaz Sharif as Prime Minister, acquitted himself better than others by developing infrastructure and power projects and it is hoped that the recent initiation of major works through the China-Pakistan Economic Corridor (CPEC), lifts the country's economy. The arrival of Imran Khan as Prime Minister in 2018 was widely celebrated both by the youth and those concerned with the deterioration in the country's fortunes over the years. Though the performance of his political party, the Pakistan Tehreek-e-Insaf, was noticeably lacklustre during the period 2013–2018 it remained in power in Khyber Pukhtunkhwa province and there is hope that he would deliver at the federal level. Time would tell.

Apart from a few random examples, good governance has been the exception to the rule in the country. There was an alternate native system, tried and tested for a thousand years of *sifarish* (recommendation) and *baksheesh* (monetary tip), which is most convenient for those in power. Where there is *sifarish* and *baksheesh*, *khushamad* (sycophancy) cannot be far behind. Flattery, as Shakespeare reminded us, is a constant human failing but in Pakistan it has assumed an art form. Seemingly normal politicians and officials go to extraordinary lengths to endear themselves to the rulers. In one case, the car of a prime minister was physically lifted the last few yards, to please him, as he visited a Punjab district! Another time a very amiable colonel of the Frontier Corps—to please Governor Fazle Haq in his presence—insisted that a particular structure was built on the orders of the governor. When the young deputy commissioner corrected the Colonel, the latter quietly advised him to '*do in Rome as the Romans do*',

'*da chalunah izda ka*', 'learn the art of government service'. To the credit of
the governor, he was well pleased with the deputy commissioner. Later in
the evening, when the same Colonel tried sycophancy again, the governor
cut him off saying that he was the biggest *khushamadgar* he had known.
Sycophancy and obsequiousness are the trademarks of our politicians and
bureaucrats. Most of them would stoop to any depth to please the boss.
General Ziaul Haq reportedly once confided to General Afzaal that his
television address to the nation the previous evening, was 'really poor'.
Moments later, a clutch of generals who were present for a meeting, tried
to ingratiate themselves with the President, by greatly lauding the same
speech. The President and his confidante were left speechless. A governor
of the Frontier Province, went a step further. Reviewing administrative
arrangements for a visit of the Prime Minister, he checked every item,
including the toilet seat and flushed it personally to see if it worked. The
story appeared unbelievable but an official swears to its veracity.

The indigenous governance model, developed by the Mughals, was
overhauled by the British after they set foot in India. But soon after
Independence, the native system regained its lost ground and won
acceptability. The environmental and cultural conditions in Pakistan, for
obvious reasons, were not conducive to fair and objective governance. There
were the bullying few, who won all favours while condemning the patient
majority to suffer in silence. Three examples of poor governance may be
in order. They involve an inspector general of police, a federal secretary,
and a minister to show how millions of ordinary citizens suffer constantly.
The police officer, after his retirement, could not get a First Information
Report (FIR) registered of a crime till the deputy commissioner Islamabad
stepped in and had it registered for him. A federal secretary from the
Secretariat Service, after retirement, refused to vacate an official house
allocated to another federal secretary, producing a stay order from a friendly
but obviously biased subordinate court. The order was as open-ended as
ever, stating that till the government provides a suitable plot of land, on
which the retired officer could build a house, he may not be dislodged.
The federal secretary, who was allotted the house, had to get the order
quashed by a superior court, arrange for the police and the magistrate
and even some armed persons of his own, to get possession of his lawfully
allotted house. Then there was an acclaimed and educated federal minister

who forced himself through the police, to requisition a private house in Islamabad because his wife really liked the place. Where the most senior, and supposedly educated, and law-abiding authorities of the state fall to such depths, there is something seriously wrong.

In short, good governance is in inverse proportion to the exercise of discretion, but discretion was what the game was all about in the Third World. Many years ago, it was rumoured that a Pakistani dignitary, on a visit to England, startled his host by announcing a sizable cash award to a charity he also attended. Truthful as ever, the British Prime Minister appreciated the generosity of the guest, admitting that he did not have the authority to grant such an amount. The point to ponder was that the per capita wealth of an average Englishman was fifty times that of a Pakistani but then discretion was only available with the head of the poorly governed country!

Good governance must guarantee the security of life, liberty, and property for all and ensures that the basic needs of the people such as the right to education, access to health care, and the right to work under equitable and satisfactory conditions, are available. Where the state is unable to provide these basic rights to its people, it becomes a failed state. What are the related conditions in Pakistan today? For example, just in one week in the recent past, three heart-rending tragedies occurred in the country and no one was taken to account for these. A young Christian couple in Kot Radhakrishan in Punjab was bludgeoned to death and the bodies burnt in a brick kiln by a large crowd led by the local *maulvi* (prayer leader), ostensibly for making derogatory remarks against Islam. The woman who was the mother of three small children was expecting her fourth child. The police remained silent spectators. In another incident in the industrial city of Faisalabad, also in Punjab, dozens of babies died because the ventilators in the public sector hospital were not working. Finally, in Tharparkhar, Sindh, a famine which had been ongoing for five years, claimed the lives of sixty-five babies because of severe malnourishment and disease. All in one week! A couple of years later in Mardan, a young university student was bludgeoned to death by fellow students in the presence of the police on religious grounds. Who else but our rulers, few of whom have been in power longer than many African dictators, are to be blamed for these tragedies?

iii. CORRUPTION AND INCOMPETENCE

Corruption (*rishwat*) and incompetence (*naehli*), thrive in Pakistan as never before. The easiest and most risk-free method of extracting bribes and abusing the system, is by doing nothing. Withholding or sitting on a pending file, attracts the prey. It was said that in the infamous Rental Power Producers scandal, less than a decade ago, bribe money reportedly changed hands not for approving illegal contracts but in expediting the legitimate ones so that no body just 'sits' on the files. Once the palms were greased, files start moving. The politicians and the officials, reportedly at five levels, were said to have benefited from this arrangement. Yet it did not bring relief to electricity consumers. When the sponsors were asked privately why they paid bribes as they had not violated the law, they replied that their losses would have been many times greater, had the government just 'sat' on their cases. This was speed-money which left no finger prints and no admissible evidence. Many officials with impeccable reputations, like a particular member of the Water and Power Development Authority (WAPDA), however, faced difficulties. They were the meek ones who actually signed the documents which helped others make their millions. And that too in dollars! It is, therefore, important that decisions in all cases be recorded in writing and signed by the minister and the prime minister personally and within a given timeline to pre-empt any mischief. Any delay beyond the determined period, should automatically trigger the transfer of the pending case to the appellate tier while simultaneously sensitizing the watchers of what was afoot. Similarly, all officials should serve their full tenure to prevent them from being victimized and coerced into acting unlawfully. No premature transfer would mean fewer unlawful decisions and should a premature transfer of an official occur, that should attract the attention of the ombudsperson immediately. The government should at all times, encourage bold decision-making and not penalise those who act energetically, in the interest of the state. Corruption can be checked, when honest and professionally qualified persons are placed in important positions to take decisions in accordance with the rules such as ensuring open competitive bidding and complying with the given stipulations. It would be useful to place representatives of the National Accountability Bureau and the Auditor General of Pakistan, which effectively is the secretariat of the Public Account Committee of Parliament, in decision-making boards to ensure compliance of rules, at the contract approval stage rather than waiting for years and decades before initiating enquiries and investigations. It is also important that in the accountability process, after the enquiry stage, an impartial and independent forum consisting of credible persons should decide whether the case should be forwarded for investigation and a reference be filed. The views of decision-takers, whether a board or an individual, should be recorded in writing and those who do not agree with the decision must mention their dissent.

The politicians over the years have become very astute and seldom issue illegal or improper orders under their own signatures, to avoid later technical hitches. Their directives are verbal and it is the official who signs the illegal orders who are held responsible even though the Rules of Business explicitly state that verbal orders have to be followed by written instruction within twenty-four hours. One of the few positions where tenure was protected by law was the position of the Chairman of WAPDA. Time and again it helped check infringements of law. A Federal Minister for Water and Power, during recent times, asked to approve jobs for twenty graduate engineers at his discretion out of the 130 selected by WAPDA on merit. The Chairman did not submit to the open and veiled threats of the minister, and he was told in no uncertain terms that the matter would go to the High Court, if he continued to apply pressure. The open market price for the appointment of one engineer in the public sector was nearly Rs. 2 million. Removing the non-pliant Chairman of WAPDA could have been the easy way out. Fortunately, the WAPDA Act stood in his way. Any other officer would have been replaced prematurely to secure illegitimate compliance. The same minister was able to peremptorily remove a federal secretary when the latter refused to oblige him in a case where he wanted to pay the entire tariff amount received to just one favoured Independent Electric Power Producer.

There have been very few political individuals during the past six decades, who denied themselves personal benefits. Powerful and well-connected politicians and officials, adapt very well to the second oldest profession of seeking bribes, which in many ways, is not much different from the oldest profession. Someday, someone would need to explain why WAPDA and the federal government side-tracked rules and tried to award two large contracts in violation of Rules. In one instance, relating to the civil works of Tarbela Four Power Project, the contract was not awarded to the lowest bidder but to another Chinese company whose bid was higher by nearly Rs. 2 billion or US$20 million. The lowest bidder was then advised by a pro bono lawyer to petition against the wrong done to the World Bank, the project's sponsors. The World Bank, in an excellent display of transparency, immediately thwarted the attempted mischief and provided the country some relief. As if one failed attempt was not enough, WAPDA then tried to award the contract of the transmission lines of the Neelum Jhelum project without competitive bidding to the same foreign company, at enhanced costs. This attempt was aborted by a very tough and honourable lady member of finance in WAPDA, Arfa Saboohi, who refused to budge under official pressure. Her note of dissent found its way to the press, prompting Sheikh Rashid Ahmad, as a concerned citizen, to take the matter to court. Thereafter, the award was cancelled, saving the country a sizable amount of money. Saving millions of dollars in two cases was no mean feat! The question to ponder was why did WAPDA allow and approve two improper and illegal acts in the first place? There was not enough accountability. Lord Acton was right when he said power tends to corrupt; he could also be speaking of electric power!

There are too many opportunities for wrongdoing when those in power try to cut corners. Over the last quarter century, it was estimated that a particular political government recruited nearly 100,000 persons to government jobs without following due processes. They were selected either because of their political and family connections or because they paid the ruling politicians the right amounts of money. The exchequer was emptied of billions of rupees, annually, in wasteful salaries and allowances, paid at a time when development projects like the Mangla Dam Raising Work and Neelum Jhelum hydel power station were starved for funds. In another case, a senior *jiyala*, a Pakistan Peoples Party loyalist, working in a hydel power project, recruited well over 100 persons on the recommendations of federal ministers. He was also able to enrich himself, in the process. Fortunately, the mischief was undone but at the cost of seriously annoying the ministers. Good governance demands that rules must remain sacrosanct. These need to be vigorously implemented by those responsible and then held to account. Difficulties emerge, when the rules conflict with the real forces on ground.

The pressures for infringement of rules by the rulers, both political and administrative, are always intense. Very often the lonely and unprotected official, finds the pressure difficult to resist. Layers of accountability by watchmen are required to deal with the powerful forces bent upon circumventing the law. The accountability structure should effectively check the misuse of power. Custodians should include departmental hierarchies, ombudsman, the public accounts committee, parliamentary committees, the judiciary, the media, and anti-corruption agencies like the National Accountability Bureau. These agencies, in turn, would need to be watched, just as carefully. Since corrupt practices are not performed in public view, proving corruption in a court of law, is very difficult. In fact, acquittal by courts is the norm and so the corrupt get a clean chit. They are then ready to step into the arena again, having been judicially cleansed. The only means of identifying and checking corruption and abuse of power is through explaining the sources of wealth and the lavish consumption of the corrupt. Liaqat Ali Khan of Battal, one of the most honourable officers of the Income Tax Department, would say that Al Capone was jailed only once and that too by the Inland Revenue Department of the United States. The source of income and wealth should be explained by all. It would not be enough for a federal minister to claim that the four million pounds sterling apartment in Europe was not purchased by him but was gifted by a Pakistani friend living abroad. Why is it that the corrupt have such generous friends? A very famous politician, when in power, was reportedly gifted a palatial house, complete with helipads and five conference rooms by a friend, and another had unknown friends who deposited huge amounts of cash in his bank account. Recently, politicians and officials, have fallen to such depths of corruption that they demand a share, even from death compensation and relief amounts paid to the victims of natural calamities and terrorist acts. It really takes some gall to pocket part of the meagre relief, granted to someone who lies prostrate at your feet.

It is reported that less than one per cent of adults in Pakistan pay tax on their incomes and among parliamentarians seventy per cent did not pay any income tax. Even an influential lady politician, who sported a million rupee Birkin bag, is said to be below the tax threshold limit. Free electricity and free irrigation water is deemed a birth right for the rich and the influential. Government functionaries are known to have been beaten, if they showed the temerity to ask for payment of bills. It is estimated that corrupt practices amounting to Rs. 7 billion takes place in the country every day. In such a milieu, it is hardly surprising that finances are not available for raising the literacy rate and health care.

The country has seen better days in the past, even as the seeds of violence and instability were being planted. Political environment has changed as time moves. The change, mostly, is for the worse. Administrative structures have deteriorated and then almost collapsed. Politicians and officials increasingly feel that they were entitled to hold on to power and protocol. In the past, there was a sense of honour that came with public service and the meagre salaries were not grudged. These days, duplicity and greed, largely motivates public service. This coupled with low emoluments and poor governance has enervated the system. Decades ago, only lower-ranked officials were known for petty thievery and that too to make ends meet. When presidents and prime ministers, governors and ministers, judges and generals, bureaucrats and journalists, and a whole lot in between lose conscience and ignore their oath of office, society is well on its way to decline. Apart from kickbacks and commissions, even some governors have been known to walk away with pianos from the governor's houses, others carried off carpets, paintings, and antique weaponry. Someone even took away the earthen flower pots. Deputy Commissioners have no qualms in taking away antique carpets and crockery. Commandants of the Scouts pilfered Persian rugs and furniture from the mess. One colonel apparently thought that a brass trench-warfare periscope, which was presented to the Thal Scouts Mess by the author when serving as Political Agent Orakzai Agency in 1974, would adorn his private house better; it is still missing, forty years later. Could the conscience of the officer who pilfered the binoculars pinch him enough to return the gift to his Unit? Unlikely! If he had the conscience, he would not have stolen it in the first place. Amazingly, a senior bureaucrat tried to gift himself a billiard table from Dera Ghazi Khan.

How the much-abused colonials behaved is revealed in an anecdote from the files. In the small rest house in Mirkhani, Chitral, a water jug and six glasses were found missing during the British days. An enquiry was ordered to fix blame for recovery of the costs. The Enquiry Officer, a *tehsildar*, made four trips to the place on horse-back, thoroughly investigated the theft and affixed blame for the recovery of one rupee and fourteen *annas*, from the guilty party. The amount of time and money spent by the state on the case, may have been ten times greater. The principle of accountability, however, had to be established.

Now compare this with a more recent example. During the visit of the top constitutional office holder to China, a Memorandum of Understanding (MoU), was to be signed for the construction of the Bunji Dam, in Gilgit-Baltistan. The dam had the capacity to generate nearly seven thousand megawatts of electricity annually, with a construction cost of nearly US$15 billion. The annual profits on the project after catering for the interest, loan, and the operating costs, were about US$500 million. As Chairman of WAPDA, I was told to sign it although the Federal Cabinet had not approved it, as was required under the Rules of Business and there was no competitive bidding for the project either. No approval in black and white meant that those pushing for the deal did not want to be held personally responsible. Responsibility would lie only with the bureaucrat signing it, who would face the music. By then the politician would be safe in Europe, America, or the Gulf and the money ensconced, in a Swiss Bank. Half a billion dollars means two thousand new high schools, twenty thousand primary schools, ten thousand tube wells, two standard oil refineries, or a hydel power project generating two hundred megawatts of electricity. Why would a poor country like Pakistan with a per capita income of about US$1500 gift such an amount to a developed country? As for the proposed Bunji Dam, the detailed engineering studies and design of the dam were still not complete but there appeared to be indecent hurry to sign the MoU and the sacrificial lamb selected for the purpose, was the author. The Ambassador in China and an Adviser to the Government insisted that this Memorandum be signed and that is when I emphatically declined to do so, and told the Ambassador to sign it himself. I was then asked to explain my refusal personally to the powerful office holder. Accordingly, I was ushered in to his suite, where I informed him that I could not sign the document as the rules did not permit it, in a meeting that lasted fifteen seconds. This would surely be a record for brief meetings. Thereafter, the Memorandum was signed by a politician, who was placed in the Board of Investment. After my refusal to sign, I was convinced that I would be sacked from my position as Chairman WAPDA, on return to Pakistan but the top office holder had a kind word for me and mentioned to a close associate that at least, I was not a *munafik* (hypocrite).

Earlier, a similar project, the Kohala Hydel Power in Azad Kashmir, designed for 1,100 megawatts by WAPDA, was granted to a Chinese company without any bidding which was an infringement of the law. My objections, both verbal and in writing, were ignored. Five years after this MoU was signed, the company was still demanding better terms. If serious corrupt practices were restricted only to the politicians and the bureaucrats, the ship of the state may have moved or at least drifted towards its destination. However, once the so called superior judiciary gets sullied there is little hope, as Churchill once reminded his listeners. They have a dual responsibility in that they have to decide matters honourably and more importantly they have to ensure that all subordinate courts and offices function honestly and promptly as well. This is generally not the case in Pakistan. In district courts, many cases are said to be decided through exerting influence or employing money, with the result that frustration continues to build up. High courts are better but hundreds of thousands of cases remain pending with them including those where young people become overage, waiting for court decisions for years on end. This is most unfair and it matters little if the judge considers himself honest. A senator quite recently is said to have completed his full senate term of six years, but because of a temporary injunction provided by a High Court, even though he was not qualified to retain the seat he held. There is also this story of a very senior judge, who was reportedly paid one million dollars through a Frenchman in Europe, to decide an election appeal in favour of a fabulously wealthy person. If the story were true, there is little hope for the country.

Only with good governance, is public welfare possible. In the subcontinent, Sher Shah Suri would have been a good model for governance, judging by his public works in the sixteenth century. Henry George Keene was probably right when he observed that 'no government, not even the British, showed as much wisdom as this Pathan'. Most of the other rulers concentrated on marriages, mausoleum, and mosques. In a sense, one should be grateful for that too, because we are at least left with the Taj Mahal and the Badshahi Mosque! This money too could also have been frittered away in wine, opium, and dancing girls or in their wars to kill and blind their brothers. However, the penchant of Pakistani leaders, after a stint in power, to build their own Taj Mahals in Paris, Dubai, London, New York, Kuala Lumpur, and Barcelona continues. The British Raj is justifiably missed because it brought order, integrity, and progress. The British were known for their quality administration. They built large infrastructural works which not only generated income and employment, but also alleviated the common peoples' problems. It was nothing short of a miracle that the British started building the Amandara Headworks and the Benton Tunnel in Malakand, for the diversion of the Swat River, less than a decade after first occupying the area. Today, over a century later, the government found it difficult merely to rehabilitate the same Jabban hydel power project. No wonder local people would remember that such was the power of the *Pairangai Bacha*, the foreign king, that they could bore a hole in the massive Malakand Mountain for diverting waters through the Benton Tunnel. The second tunnel incidentally was built a hundred years later but again by foreign consultants. The construction of the Sukkur Barrage, on the River Indus in Sindh in 1930s, led to irrigating almost eight million acres of barren land. It was another marvel which only dynamic rulers could conceive. The colonials, unlike the Pakistani rulers who replaced them, utilized the public resources wisely and economically. This is what good governance is all about. To be truthful, it must also be mentioned that there were scarcely any other European colonial powers, apart from the British, whose performance in the colonized territories was better. There was one exception, the Russians, both the Czars and the communists had amazing foresight in the Central Asian Republics which they had colonized in the nineteenth century. The developments of railways, the underground mass transit, the roads, the dams, and the power stations were no mean feats either. To this may be added the almost 100 per cent literacy rate and universal healthcare introduced, not to mention patronizing operas and ballets. In the old Soviet Union, the cost of a ticket to an opera or a ballet was no more than the price of a bottle of a soft drink served in the interval. Such levels of state patronage, were almost unheard of anywhere. Under a different environment, Afghanistan could have also have benefited from the Russians and emerged a modern state with socio-economic indicators, matching those of its neighbours like Uzbekistan and

Kazakhstan. That was not to be because international power politics were based on other considerations.

At over seventy, governance in Pakistan leaves much to be desired. Organizations and think-tanks dealing with governance, transparency, and corruption issues constantly place the country among the worst performers. Discussions on whether it is a failing or failed state, therefore, remain topical. Is the deterioration the result of the system's inability to remain relevant? Or is it because those entrusted with responsibility are not held accountable? It may be a bit of both. There appears to be a need for studying another model of political governance. A former Chief Minister of Khyber Pukhtunkhwa province (NWFP), after a few years in office is reported to have said that the easiest job in the world was his. He had to issue orders and the work was done. He could allocate hundreds of millions to any project he wished, appoint and transfer officials virtually without check, and use discretion to suit his whims. What he could not fathom was that his job was one of the most difficult in the world, if he had considered fulfilling all his obligations as well as abiding, by the text of his oath. He just saw one side of the picture, the easier one, relating to his rights and powers. Had he taken up the responsibilities his oath ordained, he would have found the job difficult to undertake.

Over the centuries, and especially after the British conquered India, common people slowly and gradually realized that it was in their long-term interest to vest powers in a legitimate government and to obey it. They obeyed the government because they felt this was the only way to ensure peace and stability. Only an organized and efficiently run society could ensure dispute resolution, among people. This, in turn, allowed business and industry to flourish. If the rulers act on personal whims and exercise subjective discretion to benefit themselves, the people would resist and revolt sooner or later. In the case of NWFP province for instance, the resistance started even earlier than expected because the government, the police, the courts, and the administration had ceased to become relevant to the people. The resistance to the state started in the Malakand Division first because the people were dissatisfied with the status quo. It then spread elsewhere. It is important to understand the situation in the correct context. The situation in parts of Balochistan and in other provinces is not much different. The parliament, provincial assemblies, the prime minister, the chief ministers, the supreme court, the high courts, the district courts, the election commission, and the government's secretariat have almost ceased to address the concerns of the people in the country. The system is rigged in favour of the one per cent or less of the people who control the affairs of the state. It is they, who enjoy, the fruits of Independence at the cost of the rest. Pakistan is indeed an explosion-prone chemicals laboratory for experiments, as Arbab Sikander, the former Governor of the NWFP province said. One of the biggest embarrassments ever experienced by any self respecting Pakistani, was during a meeting of a Prime Minister of Pakistan with the Ameer of Qatar, a few years back. The Prime Minister, who had requested the Ameer to invest in Pakistan, was in for a surprise. Every Pakistani in the palace appeared to melt in shame when the Ameer, looking the Prime Minister in the eye, responded that he would do so provided there were no kickbacks and commissions at your end. The Prime Minister of the Islamic Republic of two hundred million people, boasting nuclear weapons, was speechless. For the Prime Minister to be spoken to like this was poetic justice because of his tainted reputation.

There are two types of sins relating to governance—the sins of omission and the sins of commission. The former is much more serious as the country stands to lose in colossal terms by not focusing on the highest needs and the greatest priorities. Not building the Kalabagh Dam, cost the country billions of dollars annually in lost water and electricity. Similarly, delaying construction of the important multiple-purpose Diamer Basha Dam on the Indus River, was fraught with serious economic consequences. Work on this dam should have started in 2013 but was delayed by nearly seven years due to the rulers' indifference. There was no need to simultaneously build the run of the river Dasu Dam while constructing the Diamer Basha Dam. The annual loss, in the non-accrual of water and power benefits, would be nearly five billion dollars and even larger after adding the economic multiplier. All functionaries of the state would need to see things in the correct perspective and get their priorities corrected. Similarly, the failure to construct the Munda-Mohmand Dam on the Swat River, during the last thirty years, the state has lost about twenty billion rupees annually in electricity not generated. The benefits accruing from flood control measures would be in addition to this. The losses suffered for the monumental failure in developing a consensus over the construction of irrigation storages and hydel power projects are too massive to estimate. Hopefully, work on the dam is set to start now. The losses are much greater because of our neglect of the education, health, and family planning sectors. These are some serious examples of acts of omission which are glossed over by the rulers. The bottom line is the absence of good governance and the need to focus on it. Public money is a trust to be spent as the General Financial Rules say just as one would spend one's own money. In Pakistan, the rulers act like Arab potentates who do not differentiate between the state and the self. They routinely travel for Hajj and Umra to Makkah, in an attempt to wash their sins, with scores of friends and relatives at the state's expense. Some of our Presidents and Prime Ministers have visited Ajmer Sharif in India, seeking the saint's blessings, but used special planes at the expense of the taxpayers. The blessings were apparently withheld and their prayers not answered as they all were forced out from power, soon afterwards or were routed in elections. Then there was a President who once counselled the importance of water conservation at a seminar by insisting that the water tap be closed while brushing teeth. He conveniently ignored conserving the expenses of the state, when he utilized public finances by officially attending his son's graduation in America. There is a saying attributed to an observant Pathan who said that 'unfortunate is the person who does not fast during the short winter days and unfortunate is the person who does not indulge in corruption when the Peoples Party is in power'!

It is often said by people exposed to officialdom that the performance of most officers today is quite unsatisfactory. Most operate one or two steps below their positions and spend time devising means to avoid decision making. No decision means that nothing has been done and no enquiries to follow. This is hardly surprising because none are held accountable for such acts of omissions. They are the ones who easily manage promotions, due mainly to sycophancy and connections. There is little regard for merit in services today. Monitoring and supervising junior officials and writing objective Annual Confidential Reports (ACR) are no longer fashionable. Even so, two senior officers, one from the police and the other from the elite Administrative Service, reportedly had their records manipulated in the Establishment Division. Many officers, mainly those who had served only in Sindh, felt that accepting bribes, altering personal records, and shamelessly obliging the politicians was the essence of service because they had never seen anything better. It must be admitted that salaries these days are not commensurate with the cost of living. Adherence to the rules does become difficult when one has to make ends meet. Two very honest Frontier Service field officers were compelled into corrupt ways at the tail-end of their careers. On being questioned for the changed outlook, they replied that they required the money to build their own houses and marry off their children. Society shares part of the blame because these officers served honourably for most of their careers. Later they felt they had no other option but to indulge in some money-making. Salaries of the government officials are indeed paltry. There is a need to provide them a 'living wage', perhaps by reducing the number of government officials. Incentives through honoraria and bonuses, is another way of recognizing merit. Till that happens, officials will continue to cut corners.

8

The Long Wait for Good Governance

The Constitution guarantees the security of life, liberty, and property for all citizens of Pakistan. The functioning of the civil administration and of the justice system all the way from the police, the prosecution, and the courts' hierarchy is marked by delays, mismanagement, and corruption. Personal discretion in decision-making in all major agencies of the state, is a norm. Those most adversely affected, are naturally the poor and the weak, since they need the state's help the most. It is a sad reflection on the working of the state that often serious crime is seldom taken cognizance of, or where reported, rarely leads to conviction of the accused. Provision of relief or compensation to victims, barely exists. It is clear that in the past few decades, all the way from Peshawar to Karachi, heinous crimes like murder, extortion, kidnapping for ransom, rape, and robbery have soared and this has happened despite the attention paid to the financial and personnel needs of the police and judiciary. Quite clearly, there is a failure on the part of the state in checking crime and ensuring effective measures being taken which are long overdue in order to save the situation.

After the collapse of the Mughal Empire, much of India degenerated into lawlessness and chaos, with warlords establishing their suzerainty in different pockets. It took the courage and discipline of the British rule to rein in the chaos and establish order and security. In Bannu for instance, during the years immediately preceding the Indian Mutiny, serious crime was rampant, which made life intolerable for the people. The young John Nicholson, as Deputy Commissioner, spent four years fighting crime and criminals. The measures he undertook were tough and at times severe, but most effective as well. It transpired that during his last two years, serious crime was almost non-existant. It was reported, not that it should be repeated, that once Nicholson resorted to unconventional means to instil fear; he had the severed head of a recently-killed desperado placed on his side-table, while advising notables of the area to cooperate with the British. The message communicated was loud and clear and serious crime ceased, for a while. Pakistan too had its tough law enforcers and their efforts could be seen in their areas of responsibilities. Sadly, there were too few of them. Most officers strive to get field postings but once there, they remain tied to their desks. Often for them, powerpoint presentations substitute for courageous action in the field. Crime data is most easily manipulated or misinterpreted; most police presentations are doctored to show a reduction in crime statistics. Had these figures been true, crime would have been eliminated years ago. Tariq Khosa, a respected police officer, was right when he said that a superficial approach to releasing crime data is part of a hackneyed police mentality that sweeps the crime under the carpet and eliminates the criminal to appease the politicians who want quick-fix solutions. It is the responsibility of the police command not to buckle under political pressure or employ military means to eliminate adversaries. The *thana* (police), *patwari* (land administration) and the *kacheri* (courts) between them, have inflicted great grief among the people of Pakistan. The country's rulers ensure that the police pre-empt any socio-political disequilibrium that interferes with their authority; the *patwari* and the *kuchery* likewise perform their assumed role to protect the status quo. Few are bothered by their nonprofessional and corrupt conduct. The police are geared more towards protest control and physically protecting dignitaries than in providing community-policing and investigating and prosecuting criminals.

i. The Right to Life and Property: The Police and the *Patwari*

The initial recording of a crime in a police station sets in motion a long process which ends in the conviction or acquittal of the accused. The security of the individual and by implication the society is dependent on this initial report. This is the FIR, or First Information Report, and this is where the first problem emerges. Since the police stations are not closely managed, the police use their personal discretion when registering a FIR, either not registering, or incorrectly recording the report. The police are normally hesitant in lodging an FIR because it then becomes a duty

to arrest those charged, determine the motive, solve the crime, and get
the accused convicted. In practice, and contrary to the rules, very often
informal prior permission of the Superintendent of Police or his deputy is
sought to register an offence. No FIR means no crime record in the books
and, thus, no police responsibility. An example from Kohat District during
the 1980s is revealing. The people on the Kohat-Hangu road had grown
tired of kidnapping and robberies. They put up a formal complaint to the
Commissioner which listed thirty-six cases of serious crimes committed on
the road. Enquiries revealed that the police had registered only ten of these,
while the others had been concealed under various pretexts. In another
incident, some criminals posing as passengers booked a taxi, packed the
driver in the boot of the vehicle, and made off with the kidnapped person
and the vehicle. They were later apprehended and ingeniously charged for
the offence of cheating rather than for the very heinous crime of kidnapping
and robbery. When confronted, the Station House Officer of the police
gamely explained that the criminals had actually cheated the taxi driver
by not informing him of their actual intent. Another Superintendent of
Police, in all sincerity, suggested that highway robberies in Kaccha Pakkha
near Jozara, on the Hangu road, could only be prevented by chopping
down the adjacent forest. Today, the fact on ground is that most victims of
crimes, both person and property related, are unable to freely lodge FIRs
in police stations. To get the police to lodge an FIR, is a very daunting
task requiring executive power, social influence, or pecuniary resources. A
former Inspector General of Police, Asad Jehangir Khan, one of the most
respected police officers in the country, felt that only one-third (or even
fewer) of the crimes committed, were actually registered by the police as
FIRs. Even where FIRs are registered and cases are taken up by the courts,
the conviction rate after appeals is barely five per cent. When only one in
twenty accused is punished, there is little possibility of controlling crime.
Some of the criminals arrested in Karachi were reported to have committed
or connived to commit dozens, even hundreds of murders, but the police,
the prosecution, and the lower courts either for fear or gain did not convict
them. Such is the state of affairs as far as constitutionally guaranteed rights
of life, liberty, and property are concerned. Perhaps General Ziaul Haq
was right about the sanctity of the constitution. He once declared that
the constitution was like the Army Regimental Orders—these could be

altered or torn to shreds whenever the commander so wished. Were there an effective monitoring system in place, every crime would have been reported and prosecuted. Only a small minority can get an FIR registered. Included in that small minority was Salma Ataullah Jan, originally from Mardan, and lately a senator from the upper house of parliament, in Canada. Early in 2017, she was robbed at gunpoint outside a well frequented restaurant in Islamabad about a mile away from the President's House, the Supreme Court, and the Federal Secretariat. As a foreign celebrity her police report was registered immediately although a telephone call from the minister helped. Within thirty-six hours the accused were arrested and the valuables recovered. Now there are two options available to everyone. Either they become a celebrity or make the police accountable to a quasi-judicial supervisory body. The accused turned out to be hardened criminals, known to the police, who had been released from prison, a week earlier. The prison system is another big failure. You enter as a novice and exit as a hardened criminal, bent on repeating offences. Parole and probation services need to be extended to all but a handful of the most serious offenders. Microchip implantation, regular police monitoring, and provision of surety from immediate families, and community elders would help create much needed space in most prisons and rehabilitate prisoners into the community.

The police are not alone in committing excesses without checks. The land revenue administration in districts, which comprises the infamous trio of the *patwari* (one who maintains land records of a local area), *girdawar* (petty land revenue official), *and tehsildar* (a senior revenue officer) holds tyrannical power over the rural areas and is a lasting shame. They are the face of a corrupt state. The small farmer and the impoverished tenant lives a life of bare subsistence, surviving from crop to crop, with this trio mandated to pocket any surpluses available. The farmer pays them a percentage for the crops he sells, the inputs he buys, the entries he makes in the revenue record, the copies of documents he requires, and the fertilizers and bank loans he contracts. Solely breathing is free, at least for the moment! It is said that even President Ayub Khan and the Nawab of Kalabagh, a former Governor of West Pakistan would pay customary dues to the *patwari* to keep him in good humour and to prevent long-term loss through sleight of hand mischief. This is all the more probable as none but he can decipher the handwriting in the revenue record. In Charsadda, a *girdawar* who I once helped out of a difficult situation, which could have led to trouble, had no qualms trying to appropriate a small piece of his benefactor's land. Actually, all *patwaris* have influential benefactors as the benefits flow both ways. Chief ministers, ministers, officials, and landlords go to extraordinary limits to ensure that their *patwari* is not disturbed. None, however, could surpass *Maama patwari* from Rush Circle in Abbottabad when it came to influence-peddling in the 1970s. As a young Assistant Commissioner, I decided to post out (transfer) *Maama* since he had spent several tenures in the same circle. Immediately, all hell broke loose as the high and the mighty used their resources to get the orders cancelled and were it not for the personal intervention of the Commissioner, Salim Abbas Jilani, it is likely *Maama* may still have been on that post today.

The police and the *patwari*, one controlling life and liberty, and the other land and property, have an iron grip in rural areas, especially. The third agency of the state, the *kacheri* (courts of law) are just as distant. These three are also state monopolies but in actual fact are not accountable to anyone. The *patwari* can manipulate revenue records at will, the police remain the lords and masters of their domains and the courts, which are responsible for dispensing justice, perpetually fail the citizen.

This criticism of the police, however, cannot detract from the bravery and the sacrifices many police officials have rendered, especially during the present campaign against militancy in Karachi, the Khyber province, and the Tribal Areas. Thousands of personnel of the police, along with those from the Army, Scouts, Rangers, Constabulary, and *Khassadars*, have all laid down their lives in the line of duty. The police force lost some of its best officers such as Chaudhry Aslam Khan, Malik Saad, Siffat Ghayur, Hukam Khan, and Abid Ali, who were all killed in the line of duty. Just as there are no bad armies, similarly, there is no bad police force. It is the police officers who are honourable or otherwise. The fault always lies with the leadership. Devoted political leadership is also of supreme importance because only devoted rulers can get the best out of the police; the right officers must be posted to critically important positions. A single superintendent of police in a district can alter the status quo and show results, often within weeks, by providing inspiring leadership. Most police officers these days, much like their colleagues from other services, are more concerned with lucrative postings and perks than in effectively discharging their duties.

Duties are clearly laid down in manuals and it is for the officers to ensure that the police perform its duties, effectively. The police officer should not be servile; one superintendent of police from the elite Police Service of Pakistan posted in the Frontier made it a habit to be present whereever the Chief Minister went. On one occasion, he remained on duty for hours at night outside in the cold, while the Chief Minister was busy *officially* watching a *mujra* of dancing girls at a wedding. Upbraiding by a colleague for acting in an obsequious manner, had no effect on him.

There was a time when police officers felt honour-bound to take on criminals. Now, there is scant incentive to remain honest because financially lucrative positions are easily provided to those who can oblige politicians in power. Those, who do not follow the whims of the ruler's, are removed from posts. Going after dangerous criminals is risky but what saps the morale of our brave officers is the quick acquittal of a large number of the accused in courts of law. Many a politician and prosecutor, for one reason or another, wishes to see criminals out of jail and often want to keep themselves in the good books of these criminals. When courage and hard work remain unrewarded, the majority of the police force naturally start looking after their own immediate interests. They start supporting the political bosses and the media. They trumpet any police success for their own self promotion and ensure that their names appear prominently in the press. A senior police officer in the Frontier would find laudatory mention of himself almost every day in the local press. It later transpired that a newspaper reporter was merely reciprocating the favour in return for getting a resourceful *thanedar* (a sub inspector incharge of a police station), posted to a lucrative post. I saw for myself that during the democratic rule in Karachi, the Inspector General's day normally began with the receipt of faxed orders from the Minister or Adviser of the Home Department for the transfers of key personnel to the choicest slots. These orders would be issued after resourceful police officials had finalized their midnight deals with politicians.

It may sound unbelievable but police stations are not provided their annual budget requirements and each police station has to collect an additional few hundred thousand rupees per month, 'off the ground', to cover expenses of utilities, fuel, and even investigation. How much they collect for themselves can be imagined; how could service improve under such conditions?

There remain police officers who are conscientious, competent, and courageous but there are many more incompetent officers at all levels. Transactional corruption at lower tiers has been known to occur all along, but over the last few decades' integrity, drive, and ability amongst police officers at the district, range, and provincial levels has fallen. Some very wealthy Inspectors General of the police in the Khyber Pakhtunkhwa province, for instance, stooped down to despicable depths in amassing personal fortunes. It was painful to hear that the serious security situation due to militancy did not deter some officers in procuring substandard weapons at very high costs. There is little hope for the country when, in the midst of the present militancy, senior police officers were reported to have sold high-yielding positions to bidders. In such an environment, it is unsurprising that lower-level policemen resort to extortion and bribes. A well-heeled person in Islamabad, reportedly paid Rs. 250,000, to the police to save his reputation after two bottles of alcohol were found in his car. Another policeman on checkpoint duty at Barakahu Police Station rummaged through the personal baggage of a young couple and on being questioned by a government officer, who happened to be around, insisted that he was looking for a terrorist whose sketch he held in his hand. A terrorist hiding in a suitcase must surely be a first! The police can be brutal and rapacious whenever they have a reasonable chance of not being held to account. A young college girl walking in a park, in Islamabad, with a male friend and with no one else around, was subjected to the kind of harassment by policemen that none would wish for a daughter, wife, or a sister. Serious crime and insecurity have become major threats all over the country. Almost anyone, anywhere, anytime, could be robbed, kidnapped, raped, or murdered with no redress by those in authority. Often the media reports that the chief ministers have taken notice of grievous crimes, resulting in visits to the families of victims of rape, which unnecessarily humiliates the hapless people a second time. It is not for the chief minister to take notice because that is the responsibility of the head of the police station or the district superintendent of police. Chief ministers, ministers, chief secretaries, and above all, the inspector generals of police need to take notice of whether the accused has been convicted adequately and in good time. If this does not happen, all those responsible need to be cautioned or punished for dereliction of duties. The persistent failure of the police can be gauged from the fact that in just one week, Islamabad, Lahore, and Karachi High Courts made damning observations about police failures. The Islamabad Police was found guilty of cowardice and inefficiency, while those in Lahore and Karachi were responsible for poor investigations and deliberately obstructing justice, resulting in the acquittals of hardened criminals.

The police need to greatly improve their performance to ensure peace and stability. Increase in numbers will not be enough to tackle crime. For police performance to improve, greater stress will need to be placed on professional training in crime prevention, forensic investigations, riot control, effective prosecution, as well as providing adequate resources. No organization can function efficiently if there are no checks placed upon it. In the case of the police, effective monitoring cannot be ensured through departmental action alone, but through extra-departmental accountability and supervision. What little restraint existed on the police from the era of British rule, is no longer in evidence, especially after the introduction of the calamitous new Police Order in 2002. This has allowed and encouraged standards to fall precipitously. Pretending to hold a force and authority like the police accountable merely through facile devices such as the Public Safety Commission or the Police Complaint Authority is a disservice to the people. The police force must be watched by judicial and quasi-judicial officials around the clock to check violations of law and procedure and only then will the improvements emerge. Experienced Police officers like former Inspectors General Nawaz Khan of Malakand and Yusaf Orakzai from Peshawar were aware that efficiency in the police was only possible through proper accountability. The Criminal Procedure Code, the Police Act, and the Police Rules laid emphasis on these accountability devices which the police today find irksome. No one wants any restraints on themselves. The framers of the original Police Act and the Police Rules had provided enormous power to the Superintendent Police and the Station House Officer in the Police Station, but they too were held to supervision and accountability. Meaningful supervision and accountability is possible only by a magistrate who can pass judicial orders under the Criminal Procedure Code if the police avoid it. The Public Safety Commission

model in our environment, therefore, has been a non-starter and more of
a Trojan Horse to safeguard police interests rather than a vehicle to hold
the force to account.

In the absence of executive magistrates, law and order situations get
dangerously out of control because the police is neither trained nor trusted
to resolve matters through dialogue. In Swat, in 2002, the Governor of
the Frontier province decided, on a whim, to shift the head office of
the Board of Intermediate Education out of the district despite advice
to the contrary. There erupted a district-wide strike and all roads were
blocked. The police was helpless while the district coordination officer
had no powers to deal with such matters. When the elected *nazim* tried to
negotiate with the demonstrators, he was ridiculed and accused of treachery
against locals; he too then joined the strike. This stalemate continued for
a couple of days after which the chief secretary, a former commissioner of
the Malakand Division, had no other option but to intervene personally
to resolve the issue.

Any discussion on the competence and integrity of the police must keep
sight of the central truth that there are actually two quite distinct police
forces in the country; senior officers, all very highly educated and well-
groomed, who generally are from affluent backgrounds but comprise about
one per cent of the police; and there is another police force, comprising the
other ninety-nine per cent, which actually interacts with the common man
in the police station and on the roads. The former deals with the political
leadership and makes laptop presentations; the latter is the oppressive
instrument that ordinary people know. However, when people complain
about police high-handedness, rapacity, and corruption, they are generally
referring to subordinate police personnel like station house officers whose
motivations are different. The police force today needs some restructuring
to deal with different types of crime. Terror, kidnapping for ransom,
extortion, and narcotics are specialized subjects that need to be dealt with,
by specialized personnel at the level of the district and not at the police
station. Overall, police numbers appear sufficient today but the force
deployment in the specialized branches is clearly insufficient. The *thana*
(police station) should have its full complement of officers, equipment,
vehicles, and an operational budget. Unfortunately, too many police
personnel are tied to providing security and protocol to political leaders

and their families, parliamentarians, and high ranking police officers, both serving and retired. Further, watch and ward duties and what is called the maintenance of law and order, takes obvious priority out of the remaining police resources. The painstaking work of making arrests, investigating, and prosecuting gets little attention and resources. Limited resources and poor monitoring during the investigation stage, results in complainants bribing the police regularly and adequately to complete the process. Amazingly, it is the victim of the crime who is made to pay for investigation costs, which includes transport, food, and even office stationery because these costs are not budgeted by the government. It goes without saying that crimes such as smuggling, gambling, prostitution, illegal drugs use, car thefts, extortion, and increasingly kidnapping for ransom are seldom possible without some complicity or laxity by the police. Similarly, the police routinely encourage bribes from those whose cars have been stolen, or who have reported kidnappings, to ensure recovery. A car stolen from Mardan many years ago, was recovered in the Khyber Agency and was handed back to the owner after he produced a police report and identity papers. The owner, thereafter requested that the police station cancel the report, but he was detained till he had paid a suitable amount of money for all the efforts made by the police. For the police, the Pushto proverb that every mischief is a blessing has some substance!

While dealing with serious crime, the government should also be generous in providing cash rewards for the police's notable successes. Likewise, the police must also be protected from revenge killings, as happened in Karachi, where two hundred police officials were killed in retaliation for lawfully conducted operations. Finally, it is amazing to note that the most effective intelligence outfit in the country, the Special Branch of the police, has declined over the years and the best officers shun it. The Special Branch, which consists of police personnel who serve in the field also, have intimate knowledge of their area and people. Much is heard about the reformed role and responsibility of the police in the postcolonial era. The fact is that during the colonial period, police performance was adequate, as far as crime control was concerned. Excesses were committed when the sovereignty of British rule was threatened, as happened during the Indian Mutiny of 1857 or during the Frontier disturbances of the 1930s and 1940s. An account titled *The Frontier Tragedy* preserved by Ali Sayyad of Peshawar contains a medical certificate issued by Dr Khan Sahib of the Indian Medical Service which states the following:

> This is to certify that I admitted eighty patients to a special hospital which was arranged by public subscription at Peshawar. These were the Khudai Khidmatgars from Charsadda Tehsil who were beaten by the Police at picketing at a liquor shop in Charsadda. Several of them were very cruelly treated; most of them had more than thirty marks on their body caused by *lathis*. The majority of them could not lie straight in bed, their buttocks being a mass of bleeding red flesh. I was surprised by those cases specially, those who suffered from swelling of the testicles which were squeezed and twisted by a British Officer according to the statements of the patients. In my opinion these poor people were treated even more cruelly than the wild beasts.

The times, for the poor in Pakistan, have not changed!

ii. The Right to Liberty: The Courts and *Kacheri*

There are three main organs of the state that remain dysfunctional in practice. Harried people lie at their mercy. The rights of a common citizen are first violated by the accused and then infringed by these three agencies. Just like the police and the *patwari*, there is little respite from the judges of district courts; many of them have little credibility and they do not even care. Few stand up for the citizen. Whereas superior courts have in the immediate past largely vindicated themselves after decades of servility, thanks to the likes of the Justices Iftikhar Chaudhry and Jawwad Khawaja, the judiciary at the lower level remains pathetically incompetent, corrupt, and unaccountable. Could it be that the best students are not attracted to the legal profession? Better law graduates choose to work as professional advocates rather than seek jobs in the judiciary for the sake of higher monetary compensation. There was this interesting anecdote relating to a bright student being denied admission in a medical college, in Peshawar. The High Court judge, Bahadur Sher of Bannu, on hearing the arguments, immediately accepted the plea of the student against the state, observing that medical students were the brightest ones in class and needed support. He remarked that during his days in college, those students who could not enter professional institutions or executive government positions 'became lawyers and subsequently judges like me'!

For the country to prosper, the judiciary needs to ensure that citizens' rights are guaranteed in practice and not only confined to words. It is for the judiciary to affirm these.

A higher standard of propriety is demanded from judges of the superior courts who should not be susceptible to executive pressure or financial inducement. It was sad to read that two Lahore High Court Judges were accused in the press for being in league with the government of the day in a case against Benazir Bhutto. The deviations from fair play and justice started as soon as the judiciary in Pakistan replaced the robes of the colonial judges. The stigma of subservience dates back to Justice Munir of the Federal Court in the Maulvi Tameezuddin case. Many others like Justices Anwar ul Haq, Nasim Hassan Shah, Irshad Ahmad, Riaz Ahmad, and Hameed Dogar were similarly criticised for unjustly supporting the rulers of the day. Many of them belonged to the Kakaizai caste though it must be mentioned that the Kakaizai caste has also produced some remarkable scientists and administrators! Four times the Supreme Court legitimized military coups in Pakistan through the *Doctrine of Necessity* and since all four juntas failed to deliver, it was only fitting that the judiciary delegitimized them but only after they were ousted. Hopes were raised again when the lawyers, through a year-long campaign against President Musharraf, succeeded in restoring the legitimacy of the superior courts by reinstating Chief Justice Iftikhar Chaudhry. Shortly after the restoration of the judiciary, its credibility was lost again in the eyes of the people because it appeared that the lawyer were more concerned with their privileges and powers. Much effort would need to be made to make the courts look respectable as the people are now tired and frustrated. The failure of the judiciary to ensure the supremacy of law may well have been the most important factor leading to the failed state syndrome in Pakistan. Churchill was right when he said as long as there was a functioning judiciary, no country could be destroyed.

The first sign of decay and withering in the state becomes evident during the rise in crimes like extortion, kidnapping, and murder. The displacement of the writ of the state by other non-state actors who wield power on the ground then follows naturally. The elite continue to live in islands of decadent affluence and those in power live on borrowed time. Until very recently, the authority of the state was mostly absent in Karachi, Quetta, rural Sindh, large parts of the Khyber Pakhtunkhwa, Balochistan, and in the Tribal Areas. Even in south Punjab the absence of the state was apparent. What was worse was that the leadership appeared unaware of it or was not concerned enough to address the situation. The command has actually devolved to 'men of straw' and there remains a fear that over time, many parts of the country will meet the same fate. No fort, after civilized fort, should be allowed to fall to anarchy. Was British rule really an aberration that it has now given way to conditions similar to what prevailed before their arrival?

The proceedings in courts have become farcical and roll out for years without providing justice. Justice Kayani summed up the farce well when he pithily remarked that our courts dispense law and not justice. Frequent adjournments in court hearings are the root cause of the delay and corruption in the judiciary. As the commissioner in Malakand, I was responsible for much appellate judicial work and made it a point not to grant adjournments in court proceedings. When lawyers requested adjournments stating that they had to argue cases in different courts of law, I would end the argument by informing them that they could appear before all other courts during the day and appear in my court later in the evening. That would give me time to play golf or tennis after which I would hear their cases. Soon, lawyers stopped requesting extensions and the backlog fell. Today, legal proceedings do not inspire much confidence as it is very rare for the accused to be suitably punished in criminal cases. The low conviction rate is a severe indictment against the police, the prosecution, and the judiciary. No retribution for the guilty and no redress for the aggrieved, make a mockery of the system. On this yardstick alone, the state has failed. No wonder there is such clamour for introducing military courts for trying serious criminal cases.

Even when cases are finally settled in courts, having the decree executed, remains a problem. There was this civil case which soon turned criminal in the vicinity of Islamabad. Here, local roughnecks supported by a prominent politician forcibly took possession of someone's land. It took the Supreme Court to order the eviction of the land mafia. The judicial proceedings for implementation of the order alone, lasted fifteen years and the mere recording of the evidence of three key witnesses, took seven years. In the case of forcible possession of agricultural lands in Malakand Agency belonging to one Gulistan, it took the judiciary nearly twenty years to affirm the ownership of a person. The matter did not end because the administration would not evict those in possession for fear of creating a law and order situation. One Chief Minister frankly conceded that rural peasants were his vote bank and he would not allow their eviction. Fortunately, for the owner, the next Chief Minister Mir Afzal Khan, had a different outlook. It took Pirzada Khan, the Assistant Political Agent, only an hour to dispossess the land grabbers. The mere sight of a platoon of the Frontier Constabulary helped 'persuade' those in illegal possession of the land to vacate it without much fuss.

The absence of security and the prevalence of serious crime in the country can be controlled within prevalent laws and existing institutions at the district level. The institutions only need to be allowed to work in accordance with the rules as laid down in the books, without any political influence or pressure. All crime, big or small, must be taken note of whether it is car-snatching, pickpocketing, extortion, kidnapping for ransom, or sectarian and ethnic killing. It needs to be understood that police and rangers by themselves cannot control crime through the use of force alone. Kiran Bedi, the remarkable Indian police chief, was right when she said that the local police should not be exclusively held responsible for crime in an area as this would only encourage *burking* or not registering the crime actually committed. Crime can only be controlled by the collective efforts of the police, prosecution, and the courts; if one were to point out the most important of these three agencies in checking crime, it would be the courts. Without effective retribution by courts there would be no deterrence for criminals. This has been the case in Karachi for decades and crime continues to soar. Crime control does not necessarily lie in the severity of punishment awarded but in the consistency in awarding it. No one should think he might get away with crime. During the 1980s in the tribal Kurram Agency, there was prohibition against carrying firearms in public areas. The penalty was just a week in jail, a fine of Rs. 5,000 (US$50), and the confiscation of their weapon for repeat offenders. No one was shown leniency, not even a parliamentarian or a serving lieutenant general. The results were startling. This was possible only because the law applied equally to both the meek and the mighty.

To remedy the poor performance of the judiciary, the government once availed a US$300 million loan, on interest, from international donors to 'access to justice' for the people. A decade and a half later, all that the judiciary, as the implementing agency, could show for the 'access to justice' were poorly designed court rooms, new office furniture, numerous computers, and vehicles, but no relief for the litigants. In our country, most of those who get an opportunity to put their hand in the till, do not shrink from grabbing the benefits. Much greater resolve and integrity is required from superior courts to show real performance. Lawyers also need to be regulated so that they do not become an end to themselves. Closing courts in the name of protests must be stopped as courts are established to dispense prompt justice. The number of court days lost because of lawyers' strikes in Pakistan must hold some kind of record. Lawyers cannot be above the law as they very often seem to think. In some subordinate courts the Prosecutor and Reader of the court, often acting on behalf of the presiding judge, demand financial gratification merely for keeping the case alive. Where the plaintiff or the victim is a helpless poor young woman, the heavens weep at her plight. All kinds of demands are made by the police, lawyers, and even the court officials and nothing remains inviolable to her. It is, therefore, important that the presiding judge in all cases under Family Laws, where issues of dissolution of marriage, maintenance, custody of children, and inheritance are concerned, should be women.

iii. THE *Jirga* AND THE ALTERNATE DISPUTE RESOLUTION

Who can litigants complain to about the delays and the corruption in courts? The judiciary has little or no impact on punishing or deterring violations of law. Those in authority, are the only ones actually responsible but have little to show for redressing ills. An extreme example would reveal how matters could improve. During the rule of the Wali of Swat, a person murdered his uncle late in the afternoon and was arrested while trying to flee. The local *Qazis* met immediately, gathered evidence, and after having recorded statements of the witnesses and the accused, announced the verdict. The murderer was sentenced to *qisas* (death), and the relatives of the murdered were given the first option to execute the murderer. The sentence was executed and the funerals of both the murdered person and that of the murderer after a judicial trial, took place simultaneously. Such promptness is not possible of course, but justice delayed, we are told repeatedly, is justice denied. A prominent cleric in Malakand Division was once asked for his interpretation of Shariah, or the Islamic law, and without wasting a breath he replied that it lay in deciding all cases under law, within a weeks. A very pithy observation!

The judiciary in Pakistan does not cater to dispute resolution or the redressal of grievances; it actually denies justice as delays and costs are beyond the reach of the ordinary litigant. Both petitioner and respondent are impoverished by the time the case is finally decided. I remember a case from the Malakand Division where I was serving as the commissioner. A land pre-emption case in Bajaur Agency was decided by an official *jirga* under the Frontier Crimes Regulation, in a few sittings lasting about three months. An appeal, actually a judicial revision, was preferred which was disposed of in another two months following which the decree was implemented. About the same time, my father had lodged a private pre-emption petition in a court in Peshawar and fifteen years later, the case was still in courts. Meanwhile, my father had passed away.

The measured pace of a civil case in a Charsadda court, as a local landowner, the inimitable Fazle Ghafur Khan of Prang, would often joke, needs to be recorded in the judicial hall of shame. During a hearing when the name of the plaintiff was called for attendance, a person present informed the court that the announced person who was his grandfather had died, a decade earlier. Not just him, the court further learned, even his father had since died and now he was present as the third generation heir. In societies like these, even delayed justice would be a boon for some. When the wheels of justice move so slowly and it takes generations for routine cases to be decided, the people get frustrated and take the law in their own hands.

The inability of the state to deliver speedy justice to the people is not so much a failure of the system as it is a failure of personnel where bias and bribe hold sway. There is little merit and accountability left in the system. The Evidence Act and the Procedural Codes, demand a level of integrity and character that was standard during the British Raj, but in the present times this absence is noticeable.

The Alternate Dispute Resolution mechanism could be a practical alternative. The traditional Frontier Crime Regulation (FCR) *jirga* as practised in the erstwhile Tribal Areas could be the effective option but it must remain under the watchful eye of the state. The vanity of the judges and the turf considerations prevent the introduction of a more informal but effective system of dispute resolution. There is little difference between the American jury and the traditional FCR *jirga*, both in functioning and in its structure. Both make recommendations to the presiding judge for approval while the sentencing of the accused is the responsibility of the judge. The FCR *jirga*, however, has one difference: the members are free to produce evidence themselves being men of considerable local influence. There is also a basic difference in the philosophy of *jirga* trials and those under the Criminal Procedure Code. In *jirga(s)*, the effort is more to assuage the anger and the hurt of the complainant and less to punish the accused. So once the verdict is announced, further vendetta is not pursued, as the following example shows.

During the early 1990s, a transactional dispute cropped up following the sale of a pickup truck between two persons from the Buner and Dir Districts of the Malakand Division. To exert pressure on their opponents, the parties started seizing vehicles from the other side and soon afterwards took hostages. Each crime was reported to the police. Before a long serious stand-off developed between the two districts, there were two options available to the administration. The first was to register dozens of criminal cases, investigate these and then pursue multiple cases in the courts of law; the second was to have a *jirga* of elders well-versed in the transport business to resolve the main issues outside the courts. The parties agreed to the second option. Within forty-eight hours, the entire matter was settled to the satisfaction of both contestants and the local administration. Had this alternate system of adjudication not been available, ordinary courts would have taken forty-eight months, or maybe that many years, to resolve the protracted issues involved. Interestingly, there actually was a case in the court of the Commissioner Malakand Division, during the early 1990s that had been instituted forty-eight years earlier. This case was once resolved before the merger of Swat with Pakistan but was remanded after a revision was allowed by the appellant court and the proceeding started again. If and when this case was resolved, I am not aware. Where mediocre judges are presiding in courts, complicated cases are promptly remanded on the flimsiest of reasons to lower courts, which adds a few more years to the life of litigation. The answer lies in adjudicating some classes of cases through state-sponsored *jirga(s)*. Private village *jirga(s)* and *panchayats* of course cannot be allowed as these are mere vigilante outfits. Authorized *jirga* justice is codified both in terms of procedures adopted and penalties imposed under the penal laws of the state. The ends of justice are met especially where the accused are dangerous and hardened criminals. Lawyers and judges are opposed to the *jirga* system more because of turf considerations rather than for any other reason. It may be proper for them to be involved in the *jirga* process directly. An Islamic welfare state needs to ensure that prompt and accessible justice is provided to the people; the personal interests of any professional group should not be allowed to hinder this process. In the Larkana district for instance, a land ownership dispute between the Lashari and Kalharo tribes led to the killing of almost thirty people from both sides. Every time violence erupted and people were murdered, the police would routinely register cases leading to judicial proceedings to the financial benefit of the lawyers but to the detriment of the parties. Over the decades, many lives were lost and money expended but the underlying dispute could not be resolved through the conventional judicial system. The opposing groups were so tired of their heavy losses that they agreed to the award of an independent *Jirga* of the elders of the area. The elders understood the issues comprehensively and they displayed the intention to resolve the dispute. There, however, is one serious problem even with the state's *jirga* members; they are open to bribery and influence-peddling from the parties. The selection of members has to be undertaken very carefully. It should, however, be noted that Alternate Dispute Resolution system or state sponsored jirgas perform judicial or quasi-judicial functions and cannot be placed under the police as has unfortunately been done in the KPK province.

iv. THE RIGHT TO EDUCATION AND HEALTH

The most beautiful sight in life, in my view, is that of two children, a brother and sister, hand in hand, going to school in the morning. They are sleepy and their school bags heavy but their small steps move towards hope. In Pakistan, nothing depicts poor governance more than seeing half the population illiterate, nearly seventy years after Independence. The new state was created so that the people could live their lives according to Islamic tenets. Islam places great emphasis on education and the acquiring of knowledge. Unfortunately, we do not have much to show for our promise of universalizing education in the country. It requires a firm commitment which has been absent. Education has received lip service while matters that enrich the rulers, hold real attention. Today, in most parts of Pakistan, a typical government primary school has five classes (nursery to fourth grade), but there are normally only two rooms. More often than not there is just one teacher for five classes. Even when there is more than one teacher, they are seldom physically present to teach. In return for pocketing a portion of the teacher's salary, the supervisory officers allow them to remain absent from school for weeks and months. The teacher is free to earn a second salary by moonlighting in other jobs. They can scarcely be blamed because they have limited facilities and have to live off the ground in far-flung areas and remain at the mercy of local influential persons. Boarding and lodging, especially for women officials in education and health sectors, is an even more serious problem which the city dwellers cannot even imagine. School buildings are poorly built, floor mats or broken chairs pass for furniture, electricity or piped water is generally non-existent, and books and stationery are always hard to find. There are no toilets for the students or for the teachers. Proposals to establish hostels for teachers, especially female teachers, in the rural areas of every district have not been given priority. Regretfully, these deficiencies are not the result of any financial constraints. The only constraints are those of the absence of political will, a commitment and competent management. How else could one explain the thousands of 'ghost schools' in every province while the literacy rate remains shamelessly low. Billions of rupees are being spent annually by the government on these non-existent schools, yet few of those responsible have been held to account. To check the absence of teachers and ensure basic educational standards, better administrative management and greater supervision through the concept of Parent Teacher Association for schools, needs to be in place.

The condition of schools for ordinary children is poor enough but the schools for children with special needs is heart-rending. Sheer neglect of children with physical and mental challenges, shames not only the government but also the conscience of the society that neglects these children. The bureaucrat, the spiritual leader, the affluent landlord, the businessman, and the judge are all responsible in one way or another for the neglect. Even in the animal world, elephants and gorillas, to name just two species, try and assist the frail and the seriously injured, but Pakistani society does not do so. The following example reveals how low the high decision-makers can stoop. In Sindh in 2007, the Provincial Secretary of Education, once forwarded the most wretched summary ever to the Chief Secretary, with the approval of the Minister, no less. He recommended the diversion of the total sum of Rs. 15 million from the development budget earmarked for Special Education to purchase two top-of-the-line Toyota Land Cruiser and Mitsubishi Pajero luxury vehicles, for official use. The meagre sum was meant for purchase of basic furniture, wheelchairs, special toilet kits, and teaching aids for children with disabilities. Fortunately, this particular desire for luxury vehicles was rejected by the Chief Secretary of Sindh. Pitifully, one rejection would not change the warped mindset of the politicians and the bureaucrats of the country!

If anything explains low literacy levels, look no further than the village school. Many years ago on a partridge shoot in upper Sindh, near Nara Canal, a hunting party spent two nights in a canopied wooden structure that appeared to be built for a public purpose. On enquiry it turned out that this was a government school where the children were given two days off to provide for the needs of the *shikaris* (hunters) who were all affluent officials and landlords of the area. They did not care if someone was missing school. Governments in Pakistan, with few exceptions, behave no differently from the Sikh Khalsa rulers of the nineteenth century whose sole objective in conquered areas was to extort taxes and levies from the hapless inhabitants. (An exception, of course, was the elegant Khalsa High School the Sikhs built in Peshawar city during the nineteenth century). The needs and requirements of the ruled subjects do not really matter to the rulers. Were it not for the arrival of the British in India, most of the local people would still be paying extortion money to the rulers. Much of the physical and social infrastructure that exists is owed to the colonial rulers. The foremost duty of any government is to provide the basic needs of the people. Functioning schools and colleges with classrooms, furniture, books, and teachers must be the prime requirement. Healthcare units such as hospitals or dispensaries are not complete without the available services of doctors, paramedics, diagnostic laboratories, and medicines. To these deficiencies, maybe added the near-absence of municipal services, sewerage disposal, and garbage removal. In actual practice, even routine municipal functions are rarely performed.

Increasingly for the more affluent sections of the community, the state is no longer required to provide the basic needs as the private sector has moved into the health, education, water, public transport, and telecommunication sectors. For the private sector, even more than for the government, the presence of an effective 'regulator' is a prerequisite. Without such regulation, there is little chance for the successful functioning of all institutions. The private school operator, like the government school teacher or supervisor, has too many incentives to cut corners and violate the rules. It is, therefore, not surprising that the educational standards of schools remain very poor. What is worse is the fact that to cover up poor educational standards, cheating in examinations is widely encouraged. Cheating in examinations has become a thriving business in itself, especially in Sindh and Balochistan. Attempts at thwarting it, meets with a strong reaction. In the Swat District of the Frontier province, for example, during the late 1980s, the administration decided to crack down on examination cheating. Students, however, never used the word 'cheating', but insisted that 'UFM' or 'unfair means' cases in the examinations not be penalized. Over the years, they were largely successful in their endeavours. The decisive measures taken against such practices did not sit well with some students; and sure enough a delegation of students called upon the Commissioner Malakand Division, demanding the removal of Naveed Cheema, the Deputy Commissioner, who was a straightforward and tough officer from Punjab, for his 'anti-Pathan prejudice in not permitting them to use UFM' and pass examinations! The students were rebuked harshly.

The abject conditions of the education and health sectors would remain so, as long as the rules are not followed and merit is disregarded. The convoluted thinking of one chief minister from Sindh, was revealing. He was adamant in breaking every rule in the book so that his partisans could sell the posts of school teachers, during 2007. The World Bank, having provided nearly US$200 million in soft credit for a project to improve schools, rehabilitate buildings, and recruit about 15,000 new teachers, naturally insisted on a merit-based selection criterion. The chief minister was, however, determined to oblige his ministers, assembly members, and political cronies and had earmarked a numerical quota for each of them. It was rumoured that a teacher's post in those days would sell for over Rs. 300,000 each. The World Bank quite sanely proposed that a written examination be conducted amongst the candidates, carrying 80 per cent marks and the remaining 20 per cent marks be based on the interview. That was not acceptable to the Chief Minister, who wanted the marking done the other way round to preserve his discretion in selecting thousands of party loyalists and friends just a few months before the upcoming general elections. He told the donor plainly that if he did not have arbitrary authority in the selection process, Sindh would not accept World Bank financing. The chief secretary reminded the chief minister that while a Swiss canton may not need finances for literacy, Sindh certainly did. Such was the commitment to primary education.

Countries like Cuba, Venezuela, Turkey, and Iran have raised their literacy rates to near universal levels within a decade or two. Given the political will, this task is achievable. In the Gilgit-Baltistan region during the early 1990s, the concept of community schools was introduced under which the government provided an endowment of Rs.100,000, later doubled, to any village or urban pocket that did not have a school. The community was to provide two rooms during the day for teaching and it was left to them to select a trained or untrained teacher from the area at a stipend equal to the profit accruing from the endowment fund placed in a bank. The idea was to place all children in school. The concept caught the imagination of the people. In two years, 700 schools were established in an area where only 1,000 schools had been established in the previous fifty years. These schools are still functioning efficiently, two decades later. The current Prime Minister of Pakistan, Imran Khan greatly appreciated the working of these community schools and also praised the concept in a newspaper article. Yet after two years in office and seven years since his party first formed the government in the KPK province, the number of out of school children in the country remains alarmingly high.

There is an even greater need to involve the tens of thousands of *madrassas*, Islamic seminaries, into the mainstream of modern education in Pakistan. Besides teaching the Holy Quran, Sunnat and Sharia, other subjects such as English, Mathematics, Natural Sciences, Computers, and Business Management should also be taught. This process does not need to be a 'command and control' effort as the ulema and Islamic scholars want to expand the frontiers of knowledge. An attempt to modernize *madrassa* education in Pakistan, during the last military regime stalled because of the turf war between the Education and the Religious Affairs Ministries. In India, many *madrassas* in routine teach modern and scientific subjects so much so that many have non-Muslim students on their rolls. In some of those in West Bengal, over half the students are from other religious communities. Shaista Amber, President of the All India Muslim Women's Personal Law Board, correctly observed there was the need for 'a fusion between faith and modern systems of knowledge, especially science'. Many *madrassas* in Pakistan, and even in the Tribal Areas, have already incorporated English and Natural Sciences as subjects in their curriculum. This would not only make them more competitive, but would raise the literacy and education levels as well. In Azad Kashmir, there was an *Uloom-i-Deenia* Department which, with the support of the district administration, recruited teachers in English and Natural Sciences in about 100 *madrassas* who were paid by the government some years back. Selecting new teachers was left to sponsors to provide them with an incentive. It did not matter if those selected were the relatives or friends of those managing these *madrassas*.

The poor quality of healthcare available in Pakistan is as dismal as is the condition of education. The widespread prevalence of malnutrition in children, tuberculosis, anaemia, and liver diseases are endemic. In the twenty-first century, the fact that polio and measles are making a comeback while conditions such as iodine deficiency and arsenic poisoning remain prevalent, should shame our leaders. The infant mortality rate for children under five and under maternal mortality in childbirth are among the highest in the world. The high fertility rate for women and the low contraception prevalence ratio has led to an unacceptable population growth rate. This neglect would cost the country dearly. These unsavoury statistics could easily be redressed once the political will for affirmative action is in place. In life, most constraints experienced are not related to money but are to be found in poor planning and limited commitment to good management. A confused mindset, rather than a shortage of funds, is often the main cause of inaction, as the following example shows.

The Christian Mission Hospital in Tank, in the Khyber Pakhtunkhwa Province which has been serving the people for over a century, is an excellent example of pure dedication, on a limited budget. Typically, there are about five foreign doctors, mostly women, working in a very risky area and a hostile environment. Quite unlike the Pakistani doctors posted to far-flung areas, none from among the missionaries is ever absent from duty. The extent of their dedication can be judged by the presence of the daughter of the Archbishop of Canterbury in one of the mission hospitals near the Tribal Areas. Such dedication among the sons and daughters of the soil may have been common, half a century back but is conspicuously absent today. Among the missionaries, the spirit of service survives and not just in providing health and education needs. One of the founders of the mission hospital, was Dr William whose offspring were equally distinguished in their service of Pakistan.

The missionaries of Tank were a very special category as far as dedication and service to humankind was concerned. One afternoon, a bus fell down a ravine in Waziristan, killing and injuring a large number of passengers. Over a dozen wounded or dying persons were brought to the government hospital in Tank. True to form, there were no doctors or emergency staff to attend to them. A request was made to the Mission Hospital to accept the more seriously injured patients. This request was immediately honoured and their treatment commenced. Some hours later, with still no relief available in the government hospital, another request was made on behalf of the remaining patients for moving them to the Mission Hospital as well. Such a humanitarian request could not be denied. To make room for the injured, offices and verandas were emptied so that they could be treated. The budget of the government hospital must have been many times more than that of the Mission Hospital but what good was it when no government doctor was present to provide relief. What mattered most was commitment! Similarly, early in 2017, ninety persons were killed in a bomb explosion in a shrine in Sehwan in Sindh and it transpired that only a couple of doctors were present against the dozen posted there. Many years ago, as the Additional Chief Secretary of NWFP, while on a visit to the Mission Hospital, I enquired if the mission required any financial assistance. I was surprised to learn that they needed nothing. On my insistence, they reluctantly asked that an additional ward may be built in view of the increased number of patients.

In all districts, as in Tank, the quality of care and service delivered by the state schools and hospitals remains very basic. Outside the provincial headquarters in rural areas, the health and education units barely justify their existence. Even at the tertiary level, effective hospital care is rare. In Swat, during the 1990s, not one doctor out of the twenty-two posted was available in the main hospital one afternoon, to attend to an emergency patient from Karachi. An anecdote from the government's Lady Reading Hospital in Peshawar depicts the level of devotion of the doctors. The West Indies cricket team was in town and there was no shortage of government doctors watching the match during the morning session when they should have been in the hospital, attending to their patients. Surprisingly, these same doctors were absent from the match in the afternoon when the world's best batsman, Sir Vivian Richards, was at the crease. It transpired that the doctors in the afternoon had gone to their private clinics. Money obviously was a higher priority than Viv! People are compelled to reach out to the private sector due to the poor availability of services in government institutions, at the district level. This is why there is such congestion in schools and hospitals at the provincial level. Some years back, a proposal was mooted to transfer the management of some high schools and district hospitals along with their staff and budget in the Sindh province to the Aga Khan Development Network (AKDN) and some other reputable NGOs. The NGOs offered to manage these and to make good the deficiencies. The proposal seemed too good to be true and could have provided the services required. At that time, the politicians and government doctors, teachers, and their subordinate staff did not allow the proposal to materialize. The corruption of the officials and the discretion they enjoyed in making staff appointments, and in procurement and purchases, would have ceased, had the transfer taken place. There is always a very strong lobby for greed and incompetence.

On the contrary, there seldom is a lobby for positive initiatives. Decades back, a retired senior bureaucrat visited the Staff College, Lahore to deliver a lecture. This bureaucrat, who during his career was posted as Chief Secretary in the Provinces and held top positions in the federal government was asked why more was not done by people like him to raise literacy levels in the country. His shocking reply was that literacy levels were low because of the absence of a lobby for primary education, in the country. He may have been right but one would have thought that senior officers like him would lobby for poor children. One does not come across too many little boys and girls protesting with placards in their hands, demanding education.

v. THOSE WERE THE DAYS!

Pakistan has seen nearly fifty governments at the federal and provincial levels, during the past seventy years. Only two or three passed the good governance test. One of the better examples of governance was set in the early 1950s, by the provincial government in NWFP, now Khyber Pakhtunkhwa. (Actually, Abasin or the Khyber province would have been more elegant and linguistically acceptable names). The first chief minister was Abdul Qaiyum Khan, who originally was from Kashmir. He was said to be effective, impartial, and very tough. Most importantly, he was not corrupt and no detractor has ever accused him of corruption. True, he was loath to remain in the opposition camp and had reportedly apologized, in writing, to President Ayub Khan to escape jail but that did not detract from his administrative abilities. In the early years of Pakistan, because of the imprint of the erstwhile British administrators, few politicians or officials were known to line their pockets and bribery was not a major issue. Foreign bank accounts or off-shore properties were not even heard of. The quality of governance soon changed for the worse as greater *Pakistaniat* took hold.

Khan Qaiyum, as he was popularly known, was responsible for a number of reforms in land revenue administration, introduction of compulsory primary education, development of professional colleges, and the facilitation of industrial development. He lived a simple life and was never accused of amassing wealth, even after holding power for long stretches of time. Ghulam Ishaq Khan, later the President of Pakistan, remembered that such was Abdul Qaiyum Khan's devotion to public service that on an official visit to Lahore, he took time off to travel to Badami Bagh to persuade a local mechanic to go to Takhtbhai Sugar Mills to repair a piece of machinery. The sugar mill was not his own and was not even owned by the government, yet he chose to spend his energies on a noble cause, related to his province.

In those days, governors, chief ministers, ministers, and senior officials remained subservient to the rules and accordingly, junior officials also followed them. A Commissioner in Karachi survived in office despite refusing to provide a choice piece of land to a relative of President Ayub Khan because it was earmarked for a public purpose. However, years later, the gift of state property in Karachi and other places to a few favourites did not raise eyebrows. An affable chief minister from NWFP almost made it a habit of gifting huge bungalows in Nathiagali to close friends in important positions. People remembered the first chief minister of the province, Abdul Qaiyum Khan, who did not even have the discretion to see a patient outside the visiting hours in the Lady Reading Hospital. As soon as Sister Alexandra found out that the Chief Minister had not left the ward, she chased him out. More credit was due to him than even the matron!

Such honourable leaders became rare as the country grew older. The likes of Abdul Qaiyum Khan were followed by some very incompetent and untruthful ones. Consider the case of an almost Saraiki Prime Minister. Though nominated by his party, he was not destined to be notified as Prime Minister because of an alleged narcotic substance charge against him. He enjoyed the Prime Ministerial protocol for only forty-five minutes. During these brief minutes, he ran into a common friend who made an unsolicited request for my retention in an important position in government. The 'would be Prime Minister' declined the request saying that he had already, within less than an hour, promised that position to someone else. Lying through their teeth, comes easy to our politicians. Pakistan's plight is depressing, most unfortunately, as there are few gentlemen left in politics. The poet Newbolt had correctly noted for countries like ours 'and what you are, the race shall be'.

During the initial days of Pakistan, rules reigned supreme in matters big and small. For example, as late as the mid-1970s, all the top functionaries who stayed in a circuit house or a rest house, including the governor and the chief secretary paid their bills for boarding and lodging. Their staff insisted on taking the receipts with them to claim the reimbursements. Only a few years later, no room rents or food expenses were charged and it was left to district heads of departments to cater for the lavish expenditures of the visiting dignitaries. Ultimately, all such costs are extracted from ordinary people, in many underhanded ways.

The leaders in the early years lived simple lives; arrogance and extravagance were a later addition as leaders converted politics into business. Hardly any ruler escaped been tainted. The Chinese Premier Zhou En Lai and the Indian President Abdul Kalam would purchase their groceries personally and so would some Pakistani Federal Secretaries such as A. G. N. Kazi. This is a far cry from present times. Today, there is no profession in Pakistan that yields greater pecuniary returns than a stint or two in government. There was Mian Jaffar Shah from the Frontier who continued to sell his property to finance his political career. Decades later, his son would jokingly narrate with pride that all he inherited from his father was diabetes! There were but a few of his ilk, the most notable being Nawabzada Nasrullah, the perpetual political negotiator; however, others who followed him, were said to be more practical, once in power and made up for his restraint. Today, Pakistani politics has become fully amoral. Even a supposedly rebel politician from south Punjab would want the people to believe in his integrity and forget that he had ditched more political parties than one can count on one hand. After a long stint in power, he increased his land holdings from the inherited few acres to hundreds and hundreds of acres and continued to acquire more land. Compare this politician with Mian Jamal Shah! The wealth of those who occupied higher positions in Pakistani politics becomes truly mind-boggling. It is said that some top office-holders own wealth in billions of dollars within and outside the country.

Those responsible for governance knew all along that good administration required a balanced structure, a judicious environment, and dedicated leadership. In the absence of good leadership, the wielders of power use it for personal benefit. To ensure good governance, there is no option but to ensure strict adherence, on pain of punishment, of legitimately framed laws. That no one is above the law, is a dictum which few publicly practice. Pakistan has, however, been fortunate in securing a galaxy of officers who were gentlemen and thank God for them. The peoples' ordeal would have been even worse without them. The Public Service Commission should be thanked for generally selecting honourable officers. Of course, there has never been a shortage of incompetent and crooked officers in the country. Right from the very beginning, senior officers responsible for administering the properties of the departing Hindu refugees amassed personal fortunes. There were others who allotted agricultural land and urban properties to themselves by depriving the deserving ones. During the first martial law in the country the art and science of corrupt practices thrived. For example, to induct a favoured persons in the Central Superior Services, a handpicked retired officer from the Civil Service, known to be rather pliable, was selected chairman of the Central Public Service Commission. On the directions of the President Ayub Khan, the officer, unfortunately for the country, selected some undeserving officials and once awarded almost 100 per cent marks in the interview to ensure that a well-known Begum's son was selected to the top service. Another Begum's son was given a near perfect score in the interview to find a place in the Civil Service of Pakistan. This Chairman, like some others later, that included retired generals, indulged themselves by selecting some poor specimens of bureaucrats. Compare them to the God-fearing and honourable Abdullah, who as the Chairman of the Frontier Public Service Commission never accepted anyone's intercession and actually delayed his son's application for a position till after he had completed his tenure.

To be truthful, virtually every president and prime minister and many services chiefs too, selected some very undeserving lateral entrants to the top three civil services in Pakistan.

India has been more fortunate as far as leadership was concerned. Lal Bahadur Shastri, while Minister of Railways in India, resigned following a major train accident. He accepted moral and political responsibility for a mishap for which he was not personally responsible. Years later, when there was a similar serious train accident in Pakistan, the Pakhtun Minister of Railways refused to resign. When reminded that Shastri had quit, he blithely stated 'walay zha dartay Hindu khaarum', Pashto for 'you think I am a Hindu?' Decades later, a railway minister from Lahore almost prostrated before the chairman of the railways, in an effort to award the contract for poor-quality signalling equipment. The amount on offer was US$5 million; unfortunately, for the minister, the deal didn't go through.

Pakistan, nevertheless, was heir to an envious governance model. It is said that a Governor of NWFP, Sir George Cunningham, while traveling to Nathiagali Hills, found himself stranded as only one-way traffic was allowed for some hours, on the narrow road. Rather than delaying the governor for two hours, a police officer decided to suspend the traffic out of turn to allow the governor's vehicle to proceed. He was promptly reprimanded by the governor, for trying to break the rules. The governor waited out the two-hour enforced halt on the road. These days, the rulers and the ministers' convoys routinely, and at great risk to other commuters, violate red traffic lights with sirens blaring as if heavens would fall if they were delayed a minute. It was always pleasant to see Prime Minister Margaret Thatcher of Great Britain, being driven like any other person. Sir George Cunningham and Mrs Thatcher were from a foreign country, while our leaders are bonafide citizens of the Islamic Republic of Pakistan. For service in the government, courage and character, which are essentially the same values, are crucial. Brilliance and financial honesty no doubt remain important ingredients but there is nothing like the courage of conviction. A British governor of a province once called the commanding officer of his son's battalion requesting for an extension of his leave. The commanding officer queried if he was speaking as the governor or a father? On hearing that he was speaking as a father, he was told that for the army all fathers are equal and the leave would not be extended. Not in Pakistan though!

Lady Cunningham, the wife of the Governor of NWFP, would make sure that there was no pilferage or wastage in the Governor's House because public money was involved. Once when two visitors called on the governor in Nathiagali, the head waiter informed Lady Cunningham of the guests' arrival who then personally unlocked the storeroom and gave him two spoons of sugar, telling the waiter that the Governor need not be served because he had already had his tea. In the early years of Pakistan, the leadership adhered to all rules and adopted frugal habits. A young Captain Shafi Durrani, (my father), recounted that on being named on a panel for selection as aide-de-camp to the Governor General, the Quaid-i-Azam, spent a few days being introduced to the new setting. Mrs Knowles, wife of the Military Secretary, Colonel Knowles of 6 Lancers, told the captains that the budget of the Governor General's House being limited, only one dish would be served at the daily meals and for fruit, only two pieces were to be bought, as there were only two occupants, the Quaid and his sister, Fatima Jinnah. No one would believe this today. A personal example is infectious, especially when it emerges from the top. One of the few governors who led a very simple life was Arbab Sikander Khalil in the Frontier province, reduced food expenditure substantially. Hospitable as he was, he would invite his friend, Colonel Shafi Durrani, to dinner rather frequently but the modest meal soon became a chore for the guest. After the first few occasions, the Governor was told in good humour to expand the menu on the table because one expected more than plain okra and gourd, *bindai torai*, in the Governor's House larder!

Those were the days. Now times have changed. Angelina Jolie, the devoted actor and United Nations Ambassador, after a visit to flood victims reported that she 'was feeling awful at that time to see so much food at the table, suffice for hundreds of flood victims who were fighting like crazy to get a small bag of flour and a small bottle of water'. She was ill at ease when she saw the interior of lavish Premier House and the chartered planes and other luxuries when there was so much misery outside. She recommended to the United Nations that Pakistan reduce its luxuries before asking for foreign aid. These are the times we live in!

The Army Chief and President, General Ziaul Haq was to visit the Hangu-Thal area to witness a field exercise. For weeks and months before his arrival, the 9 'Fort' Division in Kohat remained occupied with all kinds of administrative planning down to every conceivable detail. There were predetermined fall-back positions which were followed by further step-back contingency planning. Nothing was to be left to chance or the fickleness of the human mind. A colonel in the divisional headquarters was so busy that he could not return the telephone call of the author, then Commissioner Kohat. When he finally did call back, he regretted the delay, which he explained was occasioned by the chief's forthcoming visit and revealed that he was in charge of a very important set of plans. I was suitably impressed with the dedication of the officer and by way of sympathy, enquired about the nature of planning the officer was entrusted with. 'I am responsible for finalizing the field lunch menu', he confided but then they say an army marches to its stomach! The trials and tribulations of the Commander of the Lunch Menu brigade paled into insignificance when compared with those of the officer responsible for making a field mosque where the General was to say his prayers. A camouflaged underground wood structure with *maizerai* (the local dwarf palm) was created and the foot path was marked on both sides with three rows of coloured pebbles and every rock nearby properly whitewashed. It was apparent to any one that lunch and prayer arrangements were the centrepiece of the planners; the operational requirements of the exercise appeared to be a side-show. The General arrived, was given a short briefing, ate his lunch, said his prayers, and left. Ten thousand pairs of eyes saw him do all that; the exercise was over!

With the British, the priorities were slightly different. A Khyber tribesman once narrated details of an inspection tour of the underground defence works by the Commander-in-Chief of the British Indian Army, during the Second World War. After the inspection, the Commander-in-Chief's driver parked the car ahead on the road so that the ADC could bring out sandwiches and a tea flask from the boot of the car. The two officers then ate their field lunch. No pomp, no protocol. It takes a great effort to rise to the top of one's profession and as Mahatma Gandhi advocated, simplicity as a virtue!

Fortunately, even when the roots, trunk, and branches of the tree of the state were diseased, there were some individuals who upheld the norms of frugality and integrity. One such gentleman was President Ghulam Ishaq Khan, with a strict countenance but with unparalleled integrity. He was thought to be 'khushk' (dry and irritable) but as someone pointed out, anyone with a mastery over the Urdu poet Ghalib could never ever be dry. He spent most of his life in the arcane world of the finance ministry, where cutting expenditures was a core value. It is said that when he assumed office after the death of General Ziaul Haq, he was asked about the food requirements of the Presidency and it did not take him long to point out that under the rules only the immediate family member of the President was authorized to dine. The quantity of mutton bought was reportedly brought down from a hundred kilograms per day to just one kilogram per day. This tale may or may not be true but it well-reflected the outlook of a thrifty president. Rules were framed to be followed. Years after his retirement, he was heard arguing in vain with his ten-year old grandchild who insisted on celebrating his birthday party at the nearby

Chief Burger restaurant in Peshawar. The former President and Finance Minister marshalled impressive arguments for holding the birthday party at home on the grounds of cost and cleanliness, to no avail. He rounded off his brief by mentioning that for the cost incurred in the restaurant, five times as many friends, could be served at home. Yet he failed to convince the youngster. GIK was out of the finance ministry but the finance ministry was never out of him!

Times indeed have changed now. The British imperialists treated public service as a sacred trust and followed the law diligently. All public money was spent with great care as they would spend their own money. All petty bills were checked carefully and the rules were followed meticulously. An Inspector General of the Frontier Police, Mr Gilbert Grace, on being mistakenly summoned by a lower civil court, obeyed the law and appeared in uniform before the civil sub-judge. The summons was actually meant for a police constable and since his address was not known, the process server sent it to the IGP to forward it to the concerned policeman. Having being summoned by law, for whatever reason, he promptly appeared to acknowledge the dignity of the court much to the embarrassment of the junior judge. The law had to be obeyed. The same Gilbert Grace once had the trouser pockets of a policeman sown up because of his habit of putting his hands, and money, in his pockets.

Another governor who left his mark was General Fazle Haq, a very colourful person indeed. He was strict, witty, and kind. Most officials dreaded his meetings, correctly called 'conferences' by the military. He remained an honest man contrary to his opponents charges. The one officer who was most subjected to tongue lashing in a 'conference' was named the 'man of the match' and one's success lay in avoiding this honour that day. A political agent of Khyber who had to excuse himself, midway in a meeting to attend to some serious security issue, was allowed to leave with the remark that he could go and 'sit in his mother-in-law's lap'. Another time in a formal dinner for an American delegation, led by Lawrence Eagleburger, the Deputy Secretary of State, the Governor had no qualms in informing the diners, which included a number of women, about the sexual preferences of the Sikh ruler Ranjit Singh. That, of course, was before the era of same-sex marriages in the West! The Governor only once met his match in Princess Anne of the United Kingdom who was appalled by a rather crude joke made by the Governor that she glared at him to chasten him for the evening. The Governor, who was visibly embarrassed, excused himself for a while and murmured an expletive describing her as a female pet, once he was comfortable distance away from her! The Princess Royal could be curt when she wanted to. On her departure from Peshawar a local artisan, Ali who barely spoke English presented her a 'small' gift of an engraved brass metal plaque which was about a foot and a half in diameter. She received the gift and remarked rather tongue in cheek 'it could not have been any bigger'. This was hardly surprising as she was the daughter of Prince Philip, who was also known for his clangers. On being introduced to a group of aborigines clad in their traditional dress, the Duke famously enquired if they still threw spears at each other!

There used to be ripples galore in all the meetings which General Fazle Haq attended. Once the stocky Political Agent of Bajaur, Malik Abdur Rahim sauntered in dressed in a black sherwani, wrongly assuming that was the official dress code when it actually was the national dress. General Fazle Haq would not let such an opportunity pass and enquired from Rahim who his tailor was, hastening to add that 'I am asking so that we don't go to him'! The Governor would frequently take liberties with foreign guests as well, enquiring of a Foreign Minister, 'Mr Peacock', why he did not bring the peahen with him! On another occasion, he was very appreciative of the lady partner of an American, probably the Congressman Charlie Wilson, who was a great supporter of the Afghan Mujahideen. The visitor was equally witty and with a straight face asked the Governor, 'How many camels would you give me for her?'

The late Syed Faridullah Shah, the consummate field officer, would often recall the earlier days, when most bureaucrats and politicians remained dedicated to the cause of good administration. He was untiring and tough; he was also unconventional. As deputy commissioner, he was once approached by an old woman who had complaints against her son. The son was summoned and an earthen pitcher full of water was tied to his stomach, for a few hours. When the pain became unbearable, he was told that his mother had carried him for nine months without complaining but that he had started crying within hours. The message was loud and clear. On another occasion, he was told to acquire land under the land acquisition law, for setting up industries near Nowshera. Since the law ordained a three-month period to acquire land compulsorily, he initiated the process but only a week later, the Chief Minister Abdul Qaiyum Khan enquired if the land was taken over. When Faridullah Shah replied that under law it would take three months, the Chief Minister reminded him that as a barrister he knew the law well but he expected a deputy commissioner to be trusted by the people that they would never doubt his word. The acquisition process under law could proceed unhindered and a fair price paid to the people but in the meanwhile the land could be surveyed for planning purposes so that time was not lost. Only those officers who behave honourably are trusted!

There was one Frontier provincial service officer, who was no paragon of virtue or cleanliness, but was well-known for his wit and riposte. He was Sahibzada Yunis, an untidy and unkempt individual, but very sharp and bright. During President Ayub Khan's re-election campaign, he was Assistant Commissioner Charsadda and like other district officers, he was told to collect a sizeable crowd for the public meeting the President was to address in Peshawar. On the appointed day, Yunis failed to assemble the convoy or the crowd in Charsadda but imperturbable as he was, he was not concerned. He merely asked the police to stop all traffic by placing a barrier on the Naguman Bridge ostensibly, to check the bridge structure. When scores of private cars and buses had gathered, the assistant commissioner calmly arrived, to lead the so called convoy in support of the President. The Special Branch reported that his was the longest convoy! In Peshawar, the crowd quite expectedly, went about their own business and as such his Charsadda assemblage appeared the thinnest in the public meeting. Sahibzada was not one to worry. When told that the Nowshera crowd was the largest, he quietly but assuredly had his confidantes place Charsadda's welcoming banners, right in front of the Nowshera crowd. Again the Special Branch Daily Situation Report mentioned that the largest crowd came from Sahibzada's sub division. His seniors were most impressed! Sahibzada Yunis was not the most handsome of men and was rather dirty in dress and disposition but humorous to the extreme. In an official meeting, he made some suggestion before the Governor, General Fazle Haq which the latter did not like and blurted out that the suggestion was 'as ugly as Yunis himself'. An expert at repartee, he told the Governor 'in that case you should look at the handsome face of Secretary Aftab, but listen to my words'. On another occasion, when the Governor commented on his 'dark face and awful looks' Yunis had the perfect retort ready. 'Sir, it was not my fault that the British never stayed in our area for long,' insinuating the obvious for the Governor from Mardan which drew loud laughter. Then there was Islam Bahadur Khan, a very heavy but a well-meaning, kind, and affable officer who would make it a point to sleep and snore loudly in formal meetings to the great amusement of others.

Such has been the impact of the administrative structures inherited by Pakistan that after decades of manipulation by politicians and bureaucrats, there remain officials, though not many politicians, who still follow the dictate of conscience and the correct path. The British administrators, the Paladins, of Sir Olaf Caroe, need to be remembered, who, through their manuals, codes, and practices bequeathed a functional and progressive system to us. The competent and honest leadership provided by the British, may not be possible to replicate in our *biradri* (brotherhood) and *baksheesh* riddled culture, but their guiding principles should remain a model for us. Amazingly, there still are officials who do not infringe rules. Tahir Mahmood, a Custom Service Collector, was dubbed an *angraiz* (Englishman) in Peshawar for not heeding *sifarish* (intercessions) against the rules. The good conduct of officers was the norm in the distant past, both because the emoluments received, were sufficient for their needs and secondly, standards were maintained in the recruitment and the selection system. Abdul Rashid Khan of Matta, was said to be so strict that as Deputy Commissioner of Peshawar, he once forbade his father from visiting him because he was interceding on someone's behalf. Major Abdul Rauf Durrani of Charsadda as City Magistrate always tried to look stern, despite his mild temperament so that no one could approach him.

There were also some interesting officers like Zafar Ali Khan of the Frontier Provincial Civil Service. He was witty and a thorough gentleman and had his office table crammed with coloured golf balls and miniature cars. He did not lay claims to intellectual brilliance but more than made up for it by recounting absorbing tales and anecdotes. He was once appointed chairman of a committee to recommend the distribution of forest royalty proceeds in Chitral, which was a sensitive issue. To ensure that recommendations conformed with ground realities, the author, then the Deputy Commissioner Chitral, offered to write a first draft of the findings knowing fully well that it would become the final report as well.

The chairman happily agreed as it saved him a lot of hard work. When the recommendations were presented to the chairman, he returned the report a few days later, stating that he had made the necessary changes in it. On hearing this, the Deputy Commissioner's heart skipped a beat because any changes made by the chairman could spell problems. Scrutinizing the first draft, now the final report, revealed no changes whatsoever and not even a comma was altered. This was perplexing. It then transpired that the chairman had merely altered the title, by adding the definite article and nothing else. The heart resumed its regular beating!

There was also the friendly Khalid Mansoor who, as Assistant Commissioner, once avoided police action upon students demonstrating against serving food during Ramzan, the Islamic month of fasting. Having decided to enforce the religious tenets themselves, the crowd started breaking the windowpanes and then the crockery of Jan's and Green restaurants and nearby shops. An undertraining assistant commissioner accompanying him, stressed on *lathi-charging* the demonstrators in vain. Young and brash as he was, he soon got an opportunity for the initiative when a demonstrator was seen whisking away, a bottle of Dimple whisky after damaging a liquor store. He gave him a chase, recovered the bottle, and handed it over to the Gharbi police station 'as case property for further legal action'. Mysteriously, the bottle disappeared during the night and truly, there was only one use of it!

Also, on the lighter side, there was a petty misdemeanour involving the Assistant Commissioner Iskander Mirza, later the President of Pakistan, and the Assistant Superintendent Police Rana Taleh Muhammad, posted in Nowshera during the pre-partition days. On a particularly hot evening, the two could not find ice, to cool their drinks while sitting in a Rest House, near Kund and so decided to stop and 'inspect under law' the dining car of the Frontier Mail train, travelling to Bombay for any contraband that may be on board. The only contraband they found was what they were looking for and there was enough ice to last them for the evening. Unluckily for them, there was a senior officer from Bombay, travelling by train who reported the matter to the authorities. An enquiry was held but these two were let off, with a light slap on the wrist. Accountability was seen to be in place.

vi. OUR PAKISTANI VALUES

Truth, compassion, and justice are valued across humanity; these alone make communal living possible. These values in the public services' motto in Pakistan of *sadaqat, adalat,* and *imamat* incorporate them succinctly. Indeed, without the recognition of basic rights and access to justice, public service is not possible. One of the most remarkable leaders of the twentieth century, the late Lee Kuan Yew of Singapore often spoke of core Asian values such as thrift, charity, and filial obligations towards parents and family. These values, alongside truth and integrity, contribute to societal stability and benign governance. Among Pakistanis, some of these core values are very much in evidence, albeit in different measures, while others are conspicuously absent. Thriftiness is notably absent but hospitality is widespread. Hard work and friendship bonds are extensive but lying and cheating even more so. Filial responsibility is like an article of faith but so is extreme extravagance. The level of caste, class, and colour prejudice amongst Pakistanis would put the Ku Klux Klan to shame.

The real or imagined differences in cultural or social traits amongst ethnicities in Pakistan are narrowing and may soon be gone. Until that happens, the opinion of an expatriate from Punjab, living in Holland, is worth recalling. He thought that the best amongst the Pakistani people were properly educated Pakhtuns. 'Properly educated only,' he insisted. He further thought that many affluent Punjabi judges, bureaucrats, businessmen, and politicians, needed some detoxification. There was often a *Punjabi-cunning* among some of those mentioned, although to be truthful, it must be stated that this conniving streak permeates smaller ethnicities as well, if perhaps to a lesser extent. How else could one simultaneously explain the gross servitude to the power and arrogance towards the weak? How else could one explain the mass desertion of almost all Muslim League members in the Punjab Assembly in 1993 from the Chief Minister, Ghulam Haider Wyne, to an opposition politician, to form a new government in the middle of the night? Old timers reminded that something similar happened at the creation of Pakistan when the well-entrenched Unionists decided to join the Muslim League with indecent haste. In the past, some judges mostly from Punjab that belonged to the superior courts carried the reputation of being rather pliable towards the government of the day.

Fortunately, the trends are changing fast. On the other hand, even fearsome dictators like Generals Ziaul Haq and Pervez Musharraf, found it very difficult to win over opposition politicians from Sindh, Balochistan, and the Khyber Pakhtunkhwa province.

Sadly, some people from the smaller provinces feel that consistency and loyalty cannot always be taken for granted, in the Punjab. Admittedly, selfish and self-serving human traits are found all over our blessed land, perhaps in varying proportions. I, for one, would never be unduly critical of the Punjab to which I owe much gratitude for the love of friends and generosity of associates over the years before, during and after my service career. However, there is a general perception that after retirement from service, the conduct of some colleagues and 'close friends' changes even if they owed some favours. They ostensibly remain friendly but only while they need persons in important executive positions. A former judge of the Lahore High Court, quite soft spoken but very callous when it came to his personal interests, turned out to be very disappointing; he was from Punjab. Another time, there was this service colleague who borrowed some fishing tackles but forgot to return them even after two years. The matter was petty but as a point of principle he was requested to return the items. He had the temerity to remark that he did not remember if he had returned these to me or had given these to someone else. His domicile was Lahore. The case of the banker, among others, in Islamabad takes the cake, almost literally. He was social in the extreme and his frequent parties drew only one kind of guests; the very senior officials, top bankers, and affluent businessmen. He invited, and then deleted my name from the dinner invitees' list, on learning that I was to retire a week later as Federal Secretary to the Government of Pakistan. The next day, as luck would have it, I was appointed as Chairman, WAPDA, the most sought after position in the country, for a five-year term. Without any qualms, he immediately re-sent the same invitation card for the same dinner at the same place and time. Lahore was his permanent address. There was this Punjabi engineer, responsible for water issues, who I always thought, was most friendly and who would insist on hosting a dinner every week but since my retirement, he had apparently developed amnesia. As mentioned, Punjab does not have a monopoly on such crass individuals. Interestingly, five very affectionate friends that I made, close to my retirement from service were all non-

Pakhtuns; two Punjabis and one each from rural Sindh, Azad Kashmir, and Karachi.

Actually, it may be true to say that human behaviour is not always consistent and people behave according to the demands of the occasion. There may be an unpleasant characteristic in a person as there is loyalty and amiability.

Here, a small anecdote may be in order. An official team from Gilgit Baltistan travelled by road to the Chinese province of Xinjiang via Khunjerab Pass some decades back. As Chief Commissioner, I led the delegation and invited a close friend to accompany me which he joyfully accepted. He in turn requested that a person we both knew from Lahore be also accommodated and I agreed. The evening before the visit however, I was quite disturbed to learn that these two had brought another two of their friends, a doctor and a businessman from Lahore, without my permission for the free trip to China. I was getting worried about the increasing numbers of dominos. Somehow I just did not have the heart to refuse the new party, now numbering four, including the two uninvited ones because they supposedly were guests. The correct course was to send them back. The visit proceeded well, especially, for the 'free riders' except when I was informed that the budget of the hosts was surpassed because of the higher expenses and that the excess was being paid by the host officials from their pockets. Sardar Ameenullah, the respected Development Commissioner, thought this was improper and we decided that all team members would contribute to pay the excess amount directly to the cashier, without informing the hosts. Every member of the delegation paid from their pockets, except the four 'non-officials' from Lahore who did not pay despite being requested. I was upset. Some years later, the two friends of mine redeemed themselves by paying their shares; the retrieved amount was given to charity.

It may be irreverent to mention that Sher Shah Suri, the greatest and most versatile of local Indian rulers—bearing in mind that most of our heroes have been from outside the subcontinent—made two pithy observations on his life and rule. The first was a historical fact and the other a very subjective opinion. He greatly regretted being 'enthroned at the time of the setting sun', which did not provide him enough time to build a Grand Trunk Road to Makkah. He also held an unsavoury opinion about the dominant classes of Lahore of his times, finding them untrustworthy, and pledging to treat the city and these people differently, if he had another life.

During my career, I met many Pakistanis who put up false pretences to show off. They would like people to believe that they have a noble lineage, even if it had been lately contrived, or wish to be acknowledged as pious, no matter how evil their ways. Showing off and saving face, comes very naturally to many, as they apply layers of gloss to conceal the truth. I was told the story of this senator who, accompanied by a European lady, found himself at dinner hosted by a rather affluent person, in Islamabad. The first, and then the second bottle of wine offered to him were deemed unacceptable, after he had sampled them. He then enquired, if a particularly expensive wine was available and on learning that it was, tasted it. To the great embarrassment of the host, he did not approve of it either. The crude senator then asked for Johnnie Walker Blue Label which was poured for him. Next, he startled everyone around by emptying a can of 7 Up in his drink. Nothing beats such pretentious conduct! Another countryman would take great pains to display, albeit discreetly, the designer labels of his suits and neckties, and one prime minister would lovingly check the brand name of neck ties of close friends. Then there was this detestable feudal lord in Sindh, also an elected representative of the area, who persuaded a well-known professional dancer to perform in his village, in return for a gift of a Toyota Land Cruiser vehicle. She gave a performance but only to regret it later. After the *mujra* (courtesan's dance) ended at three in the morning, the vehicle was formally gifted to her only to be hijacked, two miles down the road, by his henchmen. Later, the unfortunate dancer, travelled by bus to Karachi while the Toyota Land Cruiser, found its way back to the landlord's *dera* (camp).

Perhaps the most despicable trait amongst Pakistanis and one which refuses to be mollified is prejudice against colour and caste. Skin whitening creams sell very well in the country as beauty is equated with fair skin. No one thinks of banning these creams and soaps. Colour prejudice is a flaw that appears to be ingrained amongst Pakistanis, despite all the pious sermons of equality among Muslims, and is stratified as the caste system, among Hindus, in India. Fair-skinned people are considered more beautiful and looked up to! At a cricket match in Lahore against the West

Indies, a Lahori youngster was heard calling an opposing fielder *kalia* or dark skinned, and one look at the face of the heckler revealed, that he was within a shade of the colour of the player. Only one person from the crowd had the sense to upbraid the boorish conduct. Unfortunately, the educated and the more affluent people are not immune to this trait. In the prestigious Aitchison College in Lahore, some decades back, most of the boys, who were supposedly from the elite sections of the society, left the swimming pool in haste after the son of an Afro-American diplomat, jumped in. One particularly offensive habit amongst Pakistanis relates to publically ridiculing those with physical disabilities for general light-relief. This takes an even more grotesque form in films and the country's television programmes, where anchors routinely poke fun at transgender people, the eunuchs, for instance. The two Pakistani television programmes, cover themselves with shame every time they make fun at these 'unfortunate specimens of humanity' as described Justice Ameer Ali. The media are not concerned that they are contaminating the minds of their viewers with such programmes but as long as their commercial ratings rise, they do not care.

Over the centuries past, peculiar characteristics have been attributed to different ethnic groups, in the country. The Pakhtun supposedly, is hardy, courageous, hospitable but also spiteful and vain. Many have stereotyped him as the daft watchman, stupid, and incapable of learning; however, there is little doubt that the Pakhtun is at his best when he works and lives outside his own Frontier province. In foreign lands, he is unequalled in hard work and generosity. The circumstances and the conventions within the province consumes him in jealousy and revenge, making life difficult for him. The Punjabi generally, has a reputation of being bright, disciplined, and industrious but he may also be too selfish and an *ibnal waqt* or a 'ward of the moment'. He, generally, is said to be very adaptable to times and does not stick to principles, when opportunities beckon. The Sindhi is seen as lazy and prone to perpetual pleasures and pelf while others, of late, find a new ferment in him. The Baloch is said to be honourable, but too tradition bound, and with limited capacity for adaptability and industriousness. The Saraiki and the Sindhi-speaking Baloch are now indistinguishable from the people of the areas they have migrated to. Some Saraiki speakers, in the opinion of those from central Punjab, apparently are sweet-tongued but often undependable. The Frontier's tribesmen, the history books insist, are treacherous and full of intrigue while others recount their hard work, courage, and sacrifice. That leaves us with the Kashmiris, who are generally refined and educated, notable for their cuisine and fine arts but some think they are not trustworthy. Before their freedom struggle erupted in the Srinagar valley in 1989, they were thought to be cowardly and the infamous *'dup charsi tai tus karsi'* label stuck to them. It is said that a group of Kashmiris sent to battle placed their rifles in the direction of the enemy and waited for the warmth of sun to trigger the bullets. Their sacrifices in Occupied Kashmir, in India, over the last two decades have been truly astounding and have laid to rest, all uncharitable opinions. That said, there are scarcely a friendlier and more generous and hospitable people, than those from the Mirpur area in Azad Kashmir.

With the passage of time, all over Pakistan, basic decency norms and an adherence to scruples and civility are being substituted increasingly by greed, rudeness, and craftiness. The years ahead, will give shape and direction to our value systems. Will we be like the Germans or will we become more like Italians in thought, word, and deeds? Some of our countrymen living in Europe and America actually wish to pass off as Italians, mainly for reasons of physical similarities, when they should actually pass because they share other Italian traits as well. The former Italian Prime Minister Berlusconi, for instance, would find himself perfectly at home, in Pakistan, as would most of our politicians, save a few, in Italy. Our politicians and businessmen appear to have developed typical Pakistani characteristics, deemed financially convenient, even if these are morally repugnant and legally prohibited. Politicians in particular, have learnt to be amoral and where the politician treads, others follow. In due course, bureaucrats, journalists, generals, and judges are also veering in this direction while businessmen were already comfortably ensconced there. The less said about the ecclesiastical class the better. Corruption and lack of scruples is the common thread, uniting these six dominant groups, and this unfortunately constitutes our leadership. The 'common' person, whether a poor labourer or a simple peasant from any province, cannot be blamed for selfish behaviour; he barely ekes out a living.

The truth is that human trait and behaviour are shaped by the political and the natural environment that people are subject to. Over time, these become character traits. Allama Iqbal felt that destiny of a people, like those in central Asia, lay in the hands of the audacious men from the mountains or those from the deserts. William Blake agreed when he said that 'great things are done when men and mountains meet', and not 'by jostling in the street'. The characteristics attributed to an ethnic group are often based on the experiences and perceptions of informed outsiders, over an extended period of time. There often is empirical substantiation for it. A German, when in a relaxed frame of mind, makes contemptuous and supercilious observations about Italian discipline, English food, and French courage. Such arrogance has equal application in Pakistan.

The Pakhtun, arrogant to the extreme, is convinced that he sits at the apex of the society for any number of real or imagined reasons. He also feels entitled to casting aspersions and passing adverse comments on others 'down his pecking order', as he sees it. The Punjabi and the Muhajir, the new Pakistani, on the other hand, ridicule Pakhtuns for their crude manners and alleged intellectual shortcomings. In a further twist, the Pakhtuns from the Peshawar valley have quite unfairly arrogated to themselves the leadership role in the province and therefore the right to ridicule the southern Pakhtuns and others alike. This friendly banter starts early from school and college. No one from outside the Peshawar valley is spared ridicule and disparage. The Chitrali, the Swati, the Bunerwal, the Hazarawal, the city-dwelling Peshawaris, the Kohatis, and Bunnuchies, the Derawals and even the tribesmen get their share of light-hearted barbs and sharp epithets. Even the soft Pashto speakers from the southern districts are disparaged and laughed at, forgetting that a majority of Pakhtuns speak these dialects. One reason for this behaviour, is the fact that the Peshawar valley has provided political and intellectual leadership for a very long time. The other factor is the productive land-holding and affluence of these people. A third factor may be the public perception of other people, whether or not based on empirical considerations. There may be some truth attached to widely-held opinions about different traits amongst people, hallowed over the centuries, but then are the Pakhtuns or the inhabitants of the Peshawar valley above reproach?

My favourite tribe in the subcontinent is the Rajputs, who live on both sides of the India-Pakistan border. In terms of bravery, honour, friendship, and sacrifice, they are said to be the last word and this is true among those living east of our border. It is said that during the Partition riots, the conduct

of the Hindu Rajputs was more sympathetic to the Muslims than those of
the Sikhs and the Hindus. They assisted the migrating Muslim refugees,
safely across the new border. Some Rajputs may have given honour, a newer
meaning. It is said, that the Rajput wife of Captain Skinner, of Skinner
Horse, reportedly killed herself the first day her daughter went out of the
house to attend school on the child's father's insistence, as she saw in this
a humiliation of her status. There are exceptions, however, even among
the Rajputs. The son of a prominent Rajput politician from Punjab while
studying in America, once could not pay his fees in time as the amount was
delayed. A Pakhtun friend gladly lent him US$2,000, when so requested.
Ten years later, he had still not repaid the full loan!

The Rajputs may be the top-drawer tribe but some people from India
I encountered in different parts of the world always wished to score small
points in arguments and insisted on having the last word. While watching
the cricket World Cup match in Chandigarh between Pakistan and India,
as guests of some incredibly hospitable Sikh friends in 2011, it hurt when
many from the Indian crowd used abusive language against the Pakistani
cricketers. There were only two of us older Pakistanis, waving our flag, and
propriety demanded that generosity be shown by the hosts. Fortunately,
generosity was shown by the hosts later in the day when Wahab Riaz, the
Pakistani fast bowler, who got five Indian wickets, visited the stand to see
his parents. The crowd gave him a rousing round of applause. There was
another public display of affection from a person in the crowd and our
personal atmosphere brightened, despite the poor showing of our cricketers.
This was the match where Shahid Afridi, the Pakistani captain, apparently
forgot to use his Power Play overs! During the game, we wished to buy
snacks and drinks from a vendor, who happened to be far away from us,
and contact having been established, the items were relayed to us through
a dozen hands. As we passed the money back through the same route, a
distinguished senior Sikh doctor seated midway, returned the amount to us
and paid for our snacks himself. He was most magnanimous and any grouse
that existed, vanished. Sikhs, in any case, are friendly and a hospitable
lot, as one saw in London and Chandigarh. Here, I may also add, that
an acquaintance, who spent a long time in London, was convinced that
Sikh women were also amongst the most beautiful! As for their generosity,
once upon a time in a small seaside restaurant in Malacca, a local Sikh

gentleman, hearing four of us speak a strange language, he had never heard before, Pashto of course, became friendly immediately. Moments after he left, the waitress brought a gift of a bottle of the choicest Scotch and also informed us that our bill was already paid by the Sikh gentleman. It took much persuasion to make him defer his generosity for another day. In how many countries in the world would a stranger offer, to spend a hundred dollars on persons he had met, only five minutes earlier? No where!

The British mentioned that one or two of the Frontier tribes were known for extreme cruelty, intrigue, and treachery and likened them to scorpions. The same was said about some of the Mirs of Hunza-Nagar and the Mehtars of Chitral. The ordinary people in these areas of course were and remain honest, diligent and friendly. It is however most unfair of writers to have condemned the scorpion and snake, two strikingly beautiful and efficient life-forms of nature, to describe human depravity. The snake would never be guilty of what innumerable people in history have done. Seemingly, normal men and women, commit hideous excesses almost in routine and no human class is exempt from this evil. Often kings, soldiers, merchants, and even pious priests act not as animals do but as humans do. It is humans, not animals, who are actually the 'beasts'! The recent excesses, committed by the Burmese Buddhists, are an example. It may also be interesting to hear more about the traits of the Afghans, our next door neighbours, many of whom lived in Pakistan for a long time. Amongst the historians and the strategists, the Afghans over time have earned a name for courage, hospitality, and independence. There are others like John Nicholson, the Deputy Commissioner Bannu district, who in 1854 conveyed his assessment of the Afghan character to Sir Herbert Edwardes, the Commissioner Peshawar. He wrote: 'I hope you will never forget that the Afghan's name is faithlessness, even among themselves…In Afghanistan, son betrays father, and brother brother, without remorse…Even the most experienced and astute of our political officers in Afghanistan were deceived by the winning and imposing frankness of manner, which it has pleased Providence to give to the Afghans, as it did to the first serpent.' Where does the truth lie? A few Afghan Pakhtun friends of mine, Firdaus Khan of Ghostha and his son Chandan and the brothers Latifullah and Tahir from Logar, however remained steadfast. They never forgot the small favours!

It may be too early for a common Pakistani culture or ethos, to fully take shape, but for good or bad, it would be based upon the conduct of the dominant ethnic class. This may not be surprising, as the people have been subjected to similar political, social, and historical experiences. It may be true, that different ethnic groups in some ways are still distinguishable from each other but if this is so, it could only be a transient phase as the people race towards a common identity. One socio-economic society would lead to one set of national values, in the long run. These in turn, would be shaped by the economically dominant ethnic group. Some positive human values such as loyalty to the family, friendship, courage, and hospitality are an integral part of the Pakistani character. These values are generally common to all ethnicities and provinces in the country. Yet Pakistani ethnicities, in some respects, are said to be different from each other. Wali Khan, the politician, would often say that he was a Pakistani for half a century, a Muslim for about fifteen hundred years and a Pakhtun for a few thousand years. *Pakhtunwali* or the Pathan code of conduct, for instance, consists of hospitality or *melmastia*, alongside *nang*, *badal*, and *nanawatai* meaning honour, revenge, and asylum. Many of these traits are common to all Pakistanis. Some Pakhtun officers are known to have provided false alibis to personal staff to avenge the loss of a son or a brother thereby saving them from the law. Where the state fails the common people take matters in their own hands.

Many people from the three smaller provinces, and from different walks of life, often complain about the harsh attitude and haughty conduct of some Punjabis, in positions of power and influence. They relate unkind anecdotes about bureaucrats, policemen, judges, and politicians in support of their contentions. Retired officers from the Punjab, often point out that many a Punjabi subordinate would not return a telephone call after the senior had retired from service, let alone provide help. This happens but rarely with Pakhtuns, Sindhis, and Balochis. There are very honourable exceptions of course to the rule and these exceptions are many.

Among some of the best officials I came across in the country, apart from the local officers, were those from Punjab and Sindh who had spent a part of their careers in the Frontier province. These 'frontiersmen' from different service groups were less aloof and more responsive to the needs of the common man perhaps due to the environment they served in. In service and after retirement, they remained more considerate, conscientious, and caring and won the admiration of those who came in contact with them. On the lighter side, the moral of the story is that to placate pride, officers from other provinces be sent early in their careers to the Frontier province where equality and dignity is demanded as of right by the common people.

It is painful to note that in social interaction, most people in Pakistan do not disapprove of lying, thieving, and cheating. These traits are almost a second nature with the more established and affluent sections of the society. The political leadership, as in most societies, sets the example and shows the way for others. Most in the wealthier socio-economic bracket do not pay the national or local taxes or bills actually due from them. This defiance reaches the very top. One prime minister even retained, for family use, the necklace gifted by the wife of a foreign prime minister for the flood-affected families. He returned it two years later when he was threatened with a criminal case.

There may be historical reasons for the development of our distasteful habits which developed in our economically deprived and hostile security environment. Over millennia, people had to adapt to the climate and the invader, both very unforgiving, merely to survive. Life would have been difficult if not impossible without prostrating to the rising sun and therefore the more obsequious the conduct, the greater the reward in position, politics, and property. Those who adapted to the times, were successful and those below, imitated them. It is, therefore, no longer surprising to see the ostensibly better-educated and well-heeled people lie, pilfer, and cheat unabashedly. These were traits that brought glory to their fathers and grandfathers. Adherence to principle and convictions become serious obstacles to this kind of progress. There is little sanctity of the spoken word amongst Pakistanis, unlike in the West. The Pashto adage *zanawar pa paray tarey au banyadum pa jibay*, means that *one ties an animal with a rope but a man to his word*, means little in our environment. In fact, the ideal of constancy should be valued as a mission statement. A word in the West is as good as a bond for all, except perhaps for many of their politicians! The unsavoury attributes of dominant classes in Pakistan feed on each other and tend to be mutually reinforcing. In the short run, it would be very difficult to remedy these traits, as they are now part of our gene pool. Those who dominate the country's power structure, will not let go of their hold easily.

For ages, outsiders have admired the hospitality of the people from this area. Hospitality, however, is different from philanthropy as many Jews, Christians, and Hindus have exhibited. Economically, life is difficult for the majority of Pakistanis and as such charity is confined to giving alms and food to the village mosque. Until recently, the more affluent people shied away from philanthropy with the honourable exception of the Memons, Bohras, Parsis, and Ismailis, based mostly in Karachi. They have most distinguished themselves in philanthropy. They share their wealth through established institutions much like Bill Gates and Warren Buffet do in the West. There were many in India of the past, such as Sir Ganga Ram and Gulab Devi who established hospitals and schools for the poor and few of them were Muslims. Then there was Rai Bahadur Udhaw Das Tara Chand who 'personifying sacrifice, surrendered his soul for the hospital' in Shikarpur Sindh, in 1933.

The attitude of some affluent Pakistanis may be set to change in a positive manner. Over the last couple of decades, a very helpful trend is at work and at great speed. This relates to philanthropy. Times are changing because increasingly hospitals, dispensaries, schools, colleges, and food kitchens for the poor are being established by richer Muslims. This is some relief in a country, where there is no social security. Many affluent people from businessmen to people from the service industries, and those from sports to showbiz, especially from Punjab and Karachi, are taking to philanthropy. For the present, at least among the Pakhtuns, Baloch, and the Sindhis, charity consists in giving away left-over food and some spare cash to beggars by way of *zakat*. Philanthropy is a gift from God and He does not bless everyone with this attribute. It consists in more than just providing basic food to the *mulla and cherayn*, the prayer leader, and his understudy in the local mosque. It is the realization that those more fortunate, must share their wealth with those who have none. No wonder, there is great emphasis on *zakat*, the obligatory tenet of Islam, which enjoins the provision of resources for the less fortunate.

Surprisingly, Pakistan boasts of some of the biggest philanthropists and charities in the world. Abdul Sattar Edhi of Karachi had the largest private ambulance service in the world and Imran Khan, the cricketer-politician, established the Shaukat Khanum Memorial Cancer Hospital and Research Centre in Lahore. Another such hospital has since been built in Peshawar and one is planned for Karachi. There is also the Indus Hospital in Karachi, founded by Dr Abdul Bari, where patients are treated free. There are renowned humanists like Dr Adeeb Rizvi, Shamsh Kassim Lakha and families like the Dawoods and the Dewans and many more who try to mitigate the miseries of the common people. The main passion of the brilliant scientist Dr Abdus Salam, the Nobel Prize winner in Physics, was to expand the study of sciences in Pakistan. Amongst the most generous philanthropists today is the industrialist, Syed Babar Ali from Lahore. He has been involved in wildlife conservation, keeping alive the art of calligraphy, teacher training and offering quality higher education as manifested by the institution of Lahore University of Management Sciences (LUMS), which now has engineering and law departments. I once suggested to a very wealthy Chief Minister of the Frontier Province, to become the 'Babar Ali' of his province, but he curtly brushed the suggestion aside, remarking that '*zma da zdra zoar nishta*', literally meaning that he did not have the strength or the heart for philanthropy. Of late, or as Harun Khan of Bannu would say, 'of lately', a few Pakhtuns have also taken up the initiative to serve humanity, and notable amongst them is Maulana Idris of Swabi who has set up impressive orphanages and schools in Nowshera and Wana, through his Umma Welfare Trust.

The Pakistani-Canadian businessman, Bilal Chapti, who travelled to the Frontier province, once made an offer of US$200,000, as assistance for orphans. He confided that his mother had told him to help the people of the Frontier province, who she thought were good Muslims. Mr Chapti was frankly informed that under government rules, the orphanage would have to be built by the thoroughly corrupt Provincial Works Department and operated by the equally disreputable Social Welfare Department. A more useful investment, it was proposed to him, would be the establishment of a university of science and technology, in the province. On hearing about the proposal for a science university, he left everyone speechless by offering to contribute about US$4 million, in phases for the purpose. A site was selected for the university near Havelian, in close proximity to science universities in Topi, Taxila, and Islamabad with the help of the famed Dr Abdul Qadeer Khan and the gifted Dr Naseer Khan. Sadly, for science and technology, after the military coup in 1999, the Governor Frontier province preferred to establish an ordinary general university with the conventional faculties in a far-away place. This was a big loss to the people of the province but it is hoped that the generous Bilal Chapti would renew his offer, some day.

Despite all charity efforts in Pakistan, the conditions of the orphans remain pathetic. Those orphanages, run by the government, are pitiable and in any case are withering away. The vacuum has partly been filled by internationally sponsored SOS homes which have emerged in many parts of the country thanks to the dedicated efforts of Begum Salima Aga Khan, Suraiya Anwar, and Safia Awan. There are other committed volunteers like Shahnaz Wazir Ali and Zamurad Khan, the sponsor of Sweet Homes, who provide practical support for the poor and orphans. Lately, some people of Mirpur in Azad Kashmir, living in UK have set up a large orphanage, through donations. Apart from charity for the poor, the treatment by most Pakistani towards the *bayzubaan* (mute), uncomplaining animals, both wild and domestic, is shameful. The conditions of government-owned zoos, are worse. There are only a few devoted people, who provide good care for injured cats, dogs, donkeys, and camels. Non-governmental organisations, such as the World Wildlife Fund and the International Fund for the Conservation of Nature continue to assist inspite of the fact that the staff of the dormant Society for the Prevention of Cruelty to Animals, do not receive their salaries regularly.

Philanthropy for a while was synonymous with the name of another Pakistani, Agha Hasan Abidi. As a banker, he was much reviled by the West for some alleged sins but one who was spoken of in glowing terms by those who knew him well. Consumer banking graduated to new levels of personal consideration, during his stewardship of the bank. It was said that in return for the grant of permission to his Bank for Credit and Commerce International, to operate in Pakistan, he was prepared to transfer the initial years' profits to philanthropy. The Finance Minister at that time was Ghulam Ishaq Khan, who later became the President of Pakistan, suggested establishing an Institute of Science and Technology and that was how the country's top centre of excellence was established. With the determined efforts of Dr A. Q. Khan, H. U. Baig, Shams ul Mulk, and Jehangir Bashar, the Ghulam Ishaq Khan (GIK) Institute in

Topi has matured into a world class institute of science and technology. While many Pakistani industrialists, bankers, and politicians have invested in luxury villas, diamonds, paintings, and dubious offshore accounts, Abidi was content to invest in higher education which has benefited thousands of the bright students in Pakistan. The citation for the second highest civil award, the Hilal-e-Imtiaz, which was awarded by the Government of Pakistan to Agha Hasan Abidi in 2014, was proposed appropriately by the Society for the Promotion of Engineering Sciences and Technology for him. Fortunately, there are many positive sides to Pakistani people.

Personal and societal traits, change over time. The catalyst is provided by prevalent political leadership and the socio-economic conditions in the country. French President Charles De Gaulle once mentioned some unsavoury attributes of French people. Despite that, today France is the world leader in business, science, defence technology, arts, culture, and above all in humanism. A country may suffer defeats in diverse fields but could gather itself to win epic victories, with a change of stewards. Times and circumstances do change and the hope is that shameful traits evident amongst the Pakistanis, would also change for the better one day. A day will come, when the Pakistanis will be known for their better attributes which presently are the preserve of a minority. That would be the day, politicians would stop lying and cheating, government officials would stop fleecing people, and there would be no need to chain drinking metal cups to public water containers for fear of being stolen. As someone said there would also be greater devotion in praying in mosques, knowing that one's shoes would not be stolen by fellow believers!

For the present, however, we have to bear with the tainted reputation of our people and more so of our political leadership. Some offensive habits associated with Pakistanis transcend time and continents, as is evident by the conduct of quite a few of the immigrants to the West. Claiming bogus social welfare grants, not paying taxes and rates due, and small-time cheating, is associated with many immigrants from Pakistan and Asia. Such behaviour obviously irritates those who generally respect the law. There are exceptions though. A Pakistani visitor, while buying a packet of cigarettes outside a tube station in London, reminded the English vendor that he had not included the recent tax increase in the price. 'Oh no this was the old stock', replied the honest vendor. Both of them were gentlemen!

At the other end of the spectrum, many shortcomings of Pakistanis are compensated by the strong traits of friendship and hospitality. These are highly regarded by most people in Pakistan, although not often by those in business and public service, where hospitality and friendship are confined to self-interest only. A story from the Tribal Areas tells of a person of modest means, who was the house guest of a rich friend where he was served with the choicest food and care. Sometime later, the rich friend returned the visit but the modest host was too poor to afford a goat or even a chicken for the guest. All he had was a work donkey, his lone source of livelihood, which he promptly shot and killed, in the presence of the guest. His explanation was that friendship was all about generosity and the spirit of sacrifice called 'tawaan'. The guest had showed his friendship for him by serving him with lamb, chicken, and pulao and since he could not reciprocate the expenses likewise, he would gladly bear the tawaan by shooting his only treasure, the precious donkey. Philosophically, they became equal!

Most Pakistanis carry hospitality to a fault, delving into their scarce savings and what economists call, investible surplus. This may be an important reason for their inability to climb the economic ladder easily as capital is squandered, so as not to lose face. A dozen different food items are a common sight on feasts; quite unnecessary but then, no one wishes to lose face amongst relatives and friends. Westerners are more practical and therefore more secure financially. Once at a dinner given by a professor in the UK, after the customary slaking of the throat, the host announced food which consisted of roast beef with bread and butter. The Asian first-timers in England, were totally nonplussed. One from India, quietly enquired, if that indeed was dinner! Europeans would suffer a cardiac arrest were they to experience the hospitality of the likes of Malik Shahzada Mohmand, Nawab Subhan Khan of Khar in Bajaur, Samsamudin Bangash of Kurram, Ali Baksh Mahar of Sukkur, Ghazal Usmani of Karachi and of Gulzar Khan and Naveed Cheema of the Civil Service of Pakistan. A lavish spread in Pakistan is meant both to honour the guest but also to emphasize the host's status. If ten guests are invited, food is prepared for five or ten times the number of guests.

Equally extravagant is the hospitality of Sindhi waderas (feudal landlords), during a partridge or duck shoot; the ten o'clock breakfast could consist of a dozen items, while the lunch served a few hours later, would be more generous. Huge expenditure on food and festivities is unnecessary and does not reflect well on our sense of propriety except when the purpose is to impress. Actually there might be an inverse relationship between economic and social development of a society and the size of the *dastarkhwan*, the food menu. The larger the one, the smaller the other! Emma Duncan has been quite precise in her description of the hospitality of affluent Pakistanis, the mistakenly-called upper class, in her book *Breaking the Curfew*, 'the quality of the parties and the liquor matter; the more extravagant the dinner, the greater the host's justification for asking something in return. A Red Label will not command so many favours as a Black Label party.' 'Johnnie Walker is the currency of exchange'.

There were, however, some people whose food requirements were enormous and they made no bones about it and in any case bare bones were all that was left, after they descended on the food. The captain of this team in the Frontier province was one Attal Khan, a provincial service officer, well recognized by his girth. Once, while on a tour, he stopped around noon time at a *chappli kebab* shop and asked his driver to get one *seer*, about a kilogramme of beef kebab with two *tandoori naans* for him. He consumed these quickly and having appreciated the contents, announced to his bewildered driver that in view of the rich quality of kebabs, 'he would now have his lunch there'.

The social reformer in Abdul Ghaffar Khan, Bacha Khan, was more reflective on extravagance as he would insist on frugality whether or not it blended with Pakhtun code of hospitality. On Eid day, he would invite stern comments by encouraging his visitors to leave early to go back to their homes to eat but a real leader does not have to follow empty convention. He must do what is best for his people. Bacha Khan was interned by Prime Minister Zulfikar Ali Bhutto in 1977, at the Michni Rest House near Warsak, where I was serving as Political Agent of Mohmand Agency. Due to cold weather Bacha Khan asked for a blanket and the staff was directed to get a 'pair of blankets' for the Rest House. Hearing this Bacha Khan said he had asked for only one blanket and were two bought some one would steal the other as *'dha da loot mar watan dai'*, a society where loot and pilferage is the norm. All the same, two blankets were bought but some months later only one was accounted for and Bacha Khan turned out to be right. Bacha Khan also carried thrift to the limits of miserliness.

The day he was released from house arrest, he gifted me a watermelon to the great astonishment of every one because he was not known for such generosity. Hurriedly, a photograph was taken to preserve the moment for posterity but cynics insisted that the fruit would be rotten. A short prayer was said and the melon was cut open; it turned out to be rotten! One further thought about Bacha Khan. He greatly craved for independence but remained objectively reflective on other matters of life. On a visit to Windsor in UK, he was delighted to see the relaxed environment with people basking in the sun, a book in hand, others were picnicking or strolling and he regretted that such serenity was sadly missing, in Pakistan. After Partition, whenever he would recall the fair attitude of the British officials, compared to oppressive approach of the current politicians, police, and jail authorities, he was harshly upbraided by a long-time associate from the Khudai Khidmatgars, 'the servants of the Almighty'. 'You richly deserve this harsh treatment because it was people like you, who pushed the British out of India,' he was told unequivocally.

Over the past few decades, however, Pakistanis with all their faults have been unjustly vilified by the Western press. Our association with endemic poverty, our untrustworthy politicians, and more recently the extremist violence may have been the cause for this stereotyping. Poverty compels people to adopt desperate means to emigrate to the West, the politicians' corrupt practices draws world attention towards us, while our geographic location compels outsiders to blame us for terror. The American attorney who spoke disparagingly of the Pakistani attitude towards their parents, probably borrowed the stereotype from his own country. He was totally wrong describing our alleged disregard towards our parents. Whatever their other shortcomings, Pakistanis show more respect for their parents than most people in the world. The attorney may well be describing the callous attitude of most Westerners towards their old parents when they are no longer of much use to them. Objectivity for journalists and for lawyers, often fails when an argument needs to be won. The commissioner in the Frontier province responsible for rehabilitation of refugees from Afghanistan once seriously scolded a Western aid official who in a heated argument used abusive language against a subordinate staff member. 'Now calling someone a bastard in the West may not evoke a violent reprimand because most of you are born outside wedlock anyway but here it is a very serious matter,' was the commissioner's exact response.

There is one amusing trait about Pakistanis which concerns their interpretation of traffic rules. When turning right, they switch on the right indicator and on turning left, they turn on the left, as most people do the world over. In addition to this, Pakistanis use the indicator lights for other purposes as well. When they wish to allow a vehicle behind them to overtake, they switch on the right indicator and when they feel it is not safe to do so, they switch on the left indicator. This is not all! When they wish to travel straight on a cross-road, many of the drivers put on the double hazard lights and traffic policemen have been known to upbraid drivers for not doing so. 'Why else did the clever Japanese install double lights on your vehicle if not for travelling straight?' Another equally amusing but more dangerous interpretation of the rules concerns the flashing of head lights repeatedly, to inform the oncoming driver to stop and let you pass first as you demand the right of way. In civilized countries flashing of headlights is a courtesy shown to the other driver, allowing him to move first. A Pakistani visitor to England once learnt to his cost what the incorrect interpretation could result in. He flashed his headlights on a single lane road bridge in the countryside and sped along, thinking the road was now his 'father's own', when he saw a bigger vehicle from the other side, travelling towards him at speed. The driver managed to apply brakes just in time to avoid a serious collision but the visitor's face soon collided with the right fist of the driver. They had both survived. One punch on the face was better than two dead men.

To be fair to our countrymen, an element of duplicity in conduct runs across all people of the world. Our misfortune may lie in the fact that a large proportion of our people fall in this category. For sometime to come, our past reputation and even our present conduct will unfortunately, continue to haunt us and we will only be able to shed our unhappy traits when those in the country who control matters decide to stand up to higher principles themselves. The state will only start functioning effectively when the leaders take a firm and honourable stand on principles. That is when the arrogance of the politician will be tamed, the timidity of the judges transformed, and the dishonourable deeds of the bureaucrats, reversed. Much remains to be done. Lastly, the words of the outgoing Country Director of the

United Nations Development Programme (UNDP), Marc-Andre Franche, published in the press, can be quoted here in the hope for change:

> The only way a critical change will happen in Pakistan is when the elite of this country, the politicians and the wealthy sections of the society, sacrifice their short-term individual and family interests in the benefit of the nation. You cannot have a political class in this country that uses its power to enrich itself, and to favour its friends and families. This fundamental flaw needs to be corrected if Pakistan is to transform into a modern, progressive developed country. The political and economic elite must also try to build consensus. Pakistan will not be able to survive with gated communities where you are completely isolated from the societies, where you are creating ghettoes at one end and big huge walls at the other end.

Part 4

Critical Issues

9

Endangered Wildlife

i. *MAHSEER* and *MARKHOR*

Some years ago, at a dinner, given by the Vice Chancellors of Australian Universities in Sydney, for the visiting delegation from the Frontier province, the ambiance and the mood was most pleasant until I was asked about my hobbies. The moment they heard the word hunting among my many other hobbies, absolute silence descended around the dining table. For the rest of the evening, the guests may well have been invisible and the only sound audible on our table was the sound of the cutlery. The Australians have come a long way from the violence of temperament, displayed by them against the aborigines, the original settlers, and the unique wildlife they decimated. Attitudes change over time. Most people today resent hunting, some castigating it as 'a blood sport', while the majority does not consider it a sport at all. Attitudes to smoking are similar! Hunting for food may be acceptable but deriving pleasure from killing is not. The Hunt Saboteurs Association of England is convinced that 'people who torment animals for fun are bound to be bullies and thugs'. For many observers, hunting is the display and perpetuation of class barriers, especially in England and Europe, where there is a grand protocol associated with it. Attire, horses, support staff, not to mention guns and rifles, costs a fortune. A pair each of James Purdey, Holland & Holland, or Boss hunting guns, costs the equivalent of a house in a choice location or in other words, an arm and a leg. Aristocratic hunters point out that blaming them is unfair because a great majority of huntsmen are actually middle-class folks, increasingly from business and industry, especially in America and Asia.

It has been said that 'over the course of history, hunting has been steadily evolving along more ethical lines in tandem with the rest of western society

302

and that it is natural for this process to continue'. Sadly, our oriental society remains unaffected by these ethics. There is the view, that pressure on the hunters, has made them more 'ethical' and 'compassionate' but others argue that how could one be more compassionate in killing? If one has ever heard the terminal shrieks of the *chikor* as it is shot or the sad eyes of a duck, moments before its life ends, one would throw the gun away. The politicians Abul Kalam Azad and Wali Khan said that they stopped hunting when they saw the tears in the eyes of a mortally wounded deer. Most politicians and officials in the subcontinent, have never seen human tears. If hunting is immoral, hunter-killers retort, then in principle, the killing of all life forms, cockroaches and flies to tigers and whales, is equally reprehensible. In both cases, life is being snuffed out deliberately. Clearly, this argument appears flawed. There may be two opinions about the ethics of hunting but there is little doubt that the sport is increasingly being frowned upon.

There are those among the hunters who are convinced that without their efforts, wildlife would have vanished through the process of 'development'. They feel they are among the foremost conservationists because they, more than anyone else, recognize the value of wildlife. In the United Kingdom, United States, and many other places, tens of millions of acres of wilderness or 'semis' is managed and planted with trees and bushes by gamekeepers. During the last few years, the numbers of waterfowl in America has increased appreciably due to additional land conservation. Maintaining wildlife reserves parks for the benefit of both visitors and wildlife is a gift for posterity. Where else could one see the Battle of Kruger, a three-way mortal struggle between a pride of lions, two crocodiles, and a herd of buffalos, in September 2004, except in a wildlife park. In this battle, a few lions managed to grab a buffalo calf, which fell into a river only to be seized by crocodiles, but miraculously the calf walked free for a while before being attacked again by the lions. This was when the alpha male buffalo charged the lions, ensuring that the calf would live. This was a truly amazing battle scene. In an equivalent man-made battle, the male buffalo would have been awarded the highest gallantry award!

Animals are truly amazing. What is even more amazing, is the tenderness they can display, and this is not confined to pet dogs alone. Pet dogs are incapable of frowning or grumbling at you, no matter 'how late you arrive home at night' as they say. They may bite for a purpose but never backbite and thankfully they have not learnt any hypocrisy. Even the largest of animals, the elephant, can be gentle and very sociable, and all things being equal, have been trained to watch over infants while their parents are at work. During the Mutiny of 1857, Lieutenant Robert Biddulph of the Indian Army, may have said the kindest words ever for elephants. He thought they were 'the nicest creature in the world...so strong, so sagacious and yet very gentle'. They followed their mahouts like faithful fat old gentlemen. They sometimes break a branch off a tree with their trunks, to use as a fly whisk. All life forms serve a natural purpose and even the humble frog and mouse are important and interesting in their own way. The incredible story of the hero frog needs to be retold. A snake catches a frog near a pond but has trouble swallowing it fully and decides to move into shallow waters to complete its meal. Another frog, the hero frog, seeing the plight of its mate decides to go to battle and lunges at the predator snake which leads to the release of the frog. Freedom always demands sacrifice and the frog proved it. This one was also worthy of a gallantry award!

Hunters defend their interests on grounds of it being 'natural' to hunt, shoot, and fish, as it involves getting in touch with nature. Killing to eat in the food chain certainly is natural since without it life on earth, may not be sustainable. Man has adapted and converted these instincts into conventions and in the process, these get 'humanised' to an extent. One of the facts of life is its uncertainty and nature by definition, is very cruel and uncertain. Tens of thousands of humans die in earthquakes and tsunamis while in the animal world many more are decimated by starvation, disease, sudden snowstorms, and other natural phenomena. Unseasonal summer snows once killed the entire stock of *urial* sheep on Deosai plateau in Pakistan, for instance. Even the restraint of the king cobra wrestling with an intruding male for turf is for a purpose. The rule is that they do not bite each other in the struggle as both could be injected with fatal poison but once mastery is established the king promptly kills and actually eats any female which has already conceived with a different male. Nature then is both unfair and arbitrary. Similarly, a male lion dutifully kills all offspring's of another.

Hunters at their end, also feel that 'factory rearing and fattening of cattle and poultry is unethical in the extreme and people who decry hunting have no qualms in eating beef, fish, or chicken raised in very small cages'. They also point to the millions of people who find employment through hunting and fishing industries and to areas conserved and managed by hunters and gamekeepers.

The debate may continue endlessly, as on many other issues, and both sides remain unconvinced. There are those who oppose hydropower dams because they find them unfriendly ecologically or view high-rise buildings visually polluting. No one would seriously advocate not building high dams and it is important that mitigating measures be taken to ensure that animals are 'protected' and the ecology 'conserved'. In every extreme argument the truth lies some place in between the opposite arguments. Are cricket test matches a waste of time and is ice hockey a sport or a battle? Proponents and critics, cling to their positions. A common strand which is emerging, until the final victor emerges, is for greater regulation of hunting, shooting, and fishing and the need for retention of wilderness and breeding habitats on a much larger scale.

One form of sport in Pakistan which draws huge crowds is bear-baiting and its equally brutal version of hare-disembowelment. Why these are called sports no one knows, but looking at their wealthy and so-called educated patrons, one can only feel sorry for the country and countrymen. For the sport of bear-baiting, you require a defanged bear with claws clipped, and the animal tethered firmly to the ground by rope. Then three or more ferocious dogs are unleashed on the helpless animal. One hears much grunting and snarling and sees a lot more blood and raw flesh, adding to the delight of the crowd and the bulging pockets of the organizers. The practice is officially banned in Pakistan. Hounds tearing apart a captive wild hare in an enclosed space with spectators all around, salivating at the sight of the hare being disembowelled, is an insult to humanity. The hungry and dehydrated hare, having spent hours inside a dark sack is dazed and has difficulty adjusting to light when it is targeted by the hounds and all in the name of sport. There is a sadistic pleasure derived by people, who with some exception, are thrilled at the sight of blood and aggression. Bullock fights, dog fights, rooster fights, and even tiny quails are made to fight to satisfy lust and passion of the goons. In 2010, during the massive floods in Pakistan, wildlife near the River Indus was greatly affected. Many bears in the Kund wildlife park were carried away by the waters and drowned; those that did not drown were mercilessly clubbed to death by local people. The same happened to the thousands of hog deer, the 'paras', along the length of the river.

Without effective regulation of hunting and protection of wildlife, animals have absolutely no chance of survival, let alone any chance of multiplying. Pakistan's population has increased six times since Independence and is set to double again, in thirty years. There is little space left, except in the most inhospitable deserts and mountains, where some form of wildlife can survive; the black buck, *chinkara* deer, urial, hog deer, pangolin, wild hare, monkey, jackal, iguana, and even the wolf and the leopard numbered in tens of thousands across Pakistan till some decades back. Partridge and mongoose could be seen on the road side a few miles out of most cities of the country. Even the ibex, *markhor*, alligator, and Marco Polo sheep were in abundance because the habitat was extensive and human population was not in competition with wildlife. With little respect of laws and with habitats shrinking, it was only a question of time before wildlife took a severe beating. The Pakistani *chakor* or *chukker* was introduced to America some decades back from Shilman and *Koh* Sulaiman areas and has thrived in its new habitat while it is near extinction here. Similarly, the original black buck was sent to Texas from Thall and Tharparkar, where it multiplied to such an extent that it was sent back to Pakistan for ensuring its sustainability here. The sisi partridge thrived in huge flocks in the Balochistan and the Khyber Pakhtunkhwa provinces of Pakistan until a few decades back. Since its flesh is the most tender of white meats, city dwellers here and Arabs from the Middle East have taken fancy to it. The next thing one heard was that these were being trapped by the thousand through recorded bird calls and their numbers had been severely depleted. Many years ago, while hunting imperial sand grouse near Fort Sandeman in Balochistan, we came across over a hundred sisi partridges feeding at a wheat-threshing yard. Colonel Farhatullah, the Piffer, begged to be allowed to fire only two cartridge shots simultaneously, at the feeding birds so he could collect nearly fifty of these. His request was declined and the birds flew away to the great delight of some, though not of all, in the group.

ii. Wildlife Culling through Trophy Hunting

Under certain ground conditions, the Trophy Hunting Programme was initiated in Pakistan to provide relief to the falling numbers of wildlife. It was a positive innovation, in the direction of greater regulation of hunting, which has not only led to great increase in numbers of wildlife but has protected habitats as well. In 1993, as Chief Commissioner of the Northern Areas, now called Gilgit-Baltistan, I sent a proposal for initiating trophy hunting to Prime Minister Benazir Bhutto. A recommendation was made to allow the culling of six male ibexes annually with licensed hunting fees to foreigners and locals. Foreigners were to pay 4000 dollars while for the locals the fee was Rs. 20,000 each. The most important recommendation in the proposal was that 80 per cent of the money from the license fees be given to the villagers where the ibex had been culled from, so that there was an incentive for them to conserve rather than shoot for food. When the letter reached the Prime Minister, she was 'livid with anger' in the words of Ahmed Sadik, her principal secretary. She told him that she wanted wildlife conserved rather than being hunted as the chief commissioner was recommending. The details of the proposal were then explained to the Principal Secretary to convince the Prime Minister that there was no better way to increase the population of these mountain goats except through this programme. The Prime Minister agreed.

The *markhor* and the ibex life span is ten to twelve years and it is best to make use of this resource before they die of old age or severe climate kills them. After the Prime Minister approved the proposal, applications were invited from hunters and outfitters, licenses were issued, and the rest is history. The programme has been a resounding success as the animal population has increased massively. Eighty per cent of the fees are paid to the community of the area to provide them with an incentive for conservation with the remaining twenty per cent spent on developing similar hunting reserves elsewhere. The culling programme has turned around the threatened urial, ibex and most importantly, the *markhor* numbers, which have increased exponentially. In some areas, especially during harsh winters, there are too many animals to be sustained by scarce food supply. In such cases, license fees need to be lowered so that more of these are culled for greater profits for the local people, otherwise animals would be lost to glaciers and snows.

The Chief Commissioner of Gilgit-Baltistan, (yes me, as charity begins at home), shot the first ibex under the new programme on 10 January, 1994 in the Sust Markoon area after buying the permit at the prescribed rate. It was an easy shot and as soon as the ibex had been retrieved and the throat drained of blood, the local guide removed the animal's heart and promptly grilled it over coal as this was the hunter's 'first animal' so to speak. The permit fee from the first ibex shot was paid to the village elders by the local *Tehsildar*, immediately afterwards. It was used to buy shoes, sweaters, and other needy items for village children. The stakes of the local people were thus well established, which was the very purpose of the programme. The total number of ibex counted by Ashiq Ahmad, the world famous conservationist, before the Trophy Hunting programme was introduced, was estimated at fifty, which rose to over one thousand a decade later due to the involvement of the community. The same success story was repeated in Chitral, Duregi, Kirthar, Torghar, and Chakwal which has led to an amazing increase in the populations of the ibex, *markhor* and urial.

Currently, a *markhor* hunting permit fetches US$100,000, whereas the outfitter charges the foreign hunters an additional amount. A permit for ibex hunting sells for over Rs. 300,000 for Pakistanis and for almost US$10,000 for foreigners. Sadly, there is no rebate for Pakistanis for shooting *markhors*.

On learning of the Trophy Hunting programme, the then Army Chief, General Waheed Kakar, planned a visit to Gilgit for the shoot. He was asked to first pay Rs. 20,000 and the gentleman that he was, he paid the fee. Ordinarily, the high and mighty are never asked to pay license fees in Pakistan. It is no surprise that seventy per cent of our parliamentarians do not file income tax returns, let alone pay hunting fees. General Waheed, permit in hand, then decided to plan a hunting visit in late March that year, in view of his commitments before that date. I informed him gamely that the ibex would not wait for him since it was unaware that he was the Army Chief and by the month of March it would have climbed to very high mountains making stalking impossible. In the event, the general did not visit and the fee was returned. There have been several generals and senior air force officers who have shot randomly from helicopters using automatic weapons but here was a decent general with a difference. In another case, a general and his friends, all uncouth and perhaps uneducated as well, fired at a herd of urial in Traki Hills with army supplied G3 automatic rifles. Their bag included half a dozen dead and dying urial females and plenty of injured young ones as well. Someone needed to tell the general that a urial is only brought down by a single rifle shot through the shoulders for quick results and that alone would pass for a hunt. Who would educate brutes anyway?

After the introduction of Trophy Hunting, no civil and military officers or other influential people will be permitted to shoot their resource for free; it is like pinching thousands of dollars from their pockets. So intense was the watch by the villagers that once while returning from Tashkurgan in China by road, I stopped to see a light single-ply tent pitched by the village watchmen. One of the two watchers on duty was suffering from pneumonia and had he not been evacuated to the hospital in Gilgit, he may not have survived.

The government has failed completely in controlling poaching and the community is the only hope for wildlife conservation. There are two types of poachers prowling around; those who are affluent and influential, and those that are poor and starving, who live in the vicinity of wildlife. The few underpaid wildlife watchers find it virtually impossible to deal with both categories of poachers but for different reasons. In the few instances where cases are registered against the poachers, prosecuting the cases in court and providing judicial evidence is never sufficient to deal with the issue. The powerful, force their way through, while the meek ones are pitied and acquitted. In Chitral district during the martial law days of 1981, a poacher who had shot an ibex was booked, both the point two-two rifle used, and wet skin were recovered from the accused. The military court, amazingly, acquitted the accused for insufficient evidence. The rumour was that money played the dominant role in the acquittal.

The need now is to expand the trophy hunting programme to the other areas and to include winged wildlife and *mahseer* and other fish in community managed reserves. The number of heads that need to be culled should be estimated taking into account the feed and the proportion of older males available. Too few heads culled, could result in the area not being able to feed larger stocks leading to weakening of the animals and early deaths. The licence fee could be reduced in such cases as older males need to be culled because of their greater fatality rate due to the heavy weight of their horns and weaker legs. Such animals often fall while crossing glaciers or steep slopes and ought to be culled. The record for a Astore *Markhor*, now looking down at the diners in the dining room of Drosh Mess of Chitral Scouts, is sixty-four inches and this one was not shot but was recovered from a glacier.

From a great abundance of wildlife in the subcontinent a century ago, wildlife numbers are fighting a losing battle in Pakistan today. Shrinking and unprotected habitats, soaring population pressures, and a contempt for wildlife laws has decimated it in the *shamilaat* or commons and on state land. Presently wildlife thrives only in private preserves and who knows what will happen there tomorrow! Sardar Muhammad Alam of Kot Najeebullah, a former political agent in the Khyber Agency, recalled his posting before Partition to the Rajputana State of Alwar. Once he had to wait for nearly half an hour near a jungle to let a herd of deer cross the jeep tract. Deer was plentiful in Cholistan, Tharparkar, Thall, and Toi Banda; ibex in Kirther and Gilgit; urial in Skardu, Jhelum, and Attock; while the hills of Islamabad abounded with goral and barking deer. Unfortunately, in some of these places they are extinct and in others no longer does one find them in great numbers. The brown bear is threatened in Deosai; the black bear extinct in Galliat, Kaghan, and Swat. The Ibex and *markhor* are no longer available in Tirah, Malakand, and Sheikh Badin, and the black buck was shot to near extinction in the desert, and were it not for the Ruler of Abu Dhabi it would not have been reintroduced. The crocodile survives tenuously but the Indus dolphin may not survive long. The humble jackal, a scavenger with a call as poignant as it is melodious, has almost run out of cover; it was a talisman symbol of good hunting for the hunters, *shikaris*. Foxes, iguanas, lizards, snakes, pythons, and armadillos are losing their habitat and breeding areas. Wild boar and stray dogs alone face no immediate threat.

The Mughal Emperor Babar hunted rhinoceros in the Hangu valley 500 years ago. Thousands of years ago, there were giraffes in the Potohar. The last tiger was killed in the Panjnad area in the early nineteenth century and the Asian lion was finally eliminated in Khairpur by the middle of the nineteenth century. Leopards were common around Peshawar until the late nineteenth century and jackals and foxes till a couple of decades back. A project feasibility study to reintroduce both the tiger from Bangladesh and lion from Indian Gujarat was prepared in Sindh, in June 2007 by me as chief secretary of the province, but was shelved later perhaps due to lack of a sponsor. There would have been no shortage of sponsors if there were proposals on offer to construct petrol stations or residential plots for influential persons.

Pakistan being a subtropical country has more than its share of wildlife, compared to many of the Arab countries where one only sees pigeons. In the past, winged wildlife was unimaginably abundant. During Jim Corbett's days, the estimated number of waterfowl migrating to India and Pakistan was approximately 30 million annually. During the last few years, fewer than a million, and at times, just half a million have been sojourning during winters in Pakistan. Chakors, red-legged, grey and sisi partridges were shot by the hundreds, in a day's shoot in Dir, Swat, Chitral, and Buner and much of the country. The Wali of Swat's annual duck shoot would bag more than 500 a day; once the figure rose to 990, but try as they may, the last ten birds remained elusive. Some duck shoots in Sindh and Balochistan still score in the hundreds. This is an additional reason for decline in numbers as fewer and fewer breeding females are left because more of these are shot as they migrate later in the springs. The habitat for migratory birds is also decreasing rapidly. Waterfowl and geese are harried all the way from the flyways of Kurram, Kabul, Bajaur, and Hunza right down to the coast. When these are not shot they are being trapped. Sanctuaries and reserves do not restrain influential people and clandestine poachers. One President of Pakistan was said to have a Wildlife Reserve denotified for a day to make it legal for him to shoot and then afterwards, it was renotified.

Our Arab brothers give no respite to the bustard during their winter sojourn and each Sheikh's party return home with their falcons with an average of a thousand or more birds. It has been estimated that each bustard killed, costs the Arabs over a 100,000 riyals after all costs are included. They have bags of money, but the bustards population has sharply decreased. These birds will soon be decimated but Pakistani *miskeens* and local sponsors do not seem to mind as long as their pockets are being filled with riyals and dinars. There are local culprits as well. Educated and influential people like doctors, businessmen, and those from defense and civil service are known to have shot over 300 geese on a single outing. They then have the gall to post pictures on Facebook knowing well that laws are only for the poor in Pakistan.

Fifty years ago, my maternal uncle Abdul Rahim Ahmad, a Deputy Superintendent of Rangers, shot eleven black bucks in one day in the desert. Then, that was the norm but even recently a Brigadier shot eighteen *chinkara* deer in Cholistan while another general officer shot many *paras* or hog deer in one day. 'Oh it was great fun', he said. Early in the season, the fishing contractor at Chashma Barrage routinely nets 300–400 ducks daily and sells these. Today, a pair of mallards sell for nearly Rs. 1,500. In an effort to eliminate netting ducks, the support of the chief ministers was solicited but nothing came of it. Later, a local subordinate judge actually threatened to initiate legal proceeding against officials trying to enforce wildlife laws. A partridge in 2018 sold for Rs. 600 at retail with wildlife, police, rangers, and netter all sharing in the loot. Arabs have now taken a liking for partridge after the Houbara bustard population started decreasing, making trapping and netting quite profitable. May God preserve the wildlife. In Karachi, Lahore, and many other cities, partridges and other wild birds are openly available for sale and are the main dish in elite receptions.

Civilized societies develop mechanisms for regulating wildlife conservation, and culling, when required. Without these regulations wildlife cannot be sustained. As George Schaller correctly pointed out many years ago, if we continue to kill wildlife indiscriminately all we would be left with, are empty hills and the stones of silence. We need love and care, and a little compassion for wildlife. We cannot act like an Arab hunter who wrung the neck of a pigeon with his hands to feed his falcon in Dera Ismail Khan. Then there was this other Arab seen on a video screen, who after chasing a deer in a jeep, let loose a tame *cheetah* on the exhausted prey. This hunt lasted fifteen seconds and he would have gone home satisfied with his *shikar*. These are despicable and wicked acts of cruelty and do not fall under the head of civilized conduct. Hunting at best should be restricted to culling only. Large uninhabited areas need to be set aside as Reserves and Wilderness parks as a start.

In 1993, during my tenure as Chief Commissioner, Northern Areas, the ecological-rich Deosai plateau at 12,000–14,000 feet above sea level was declared a Wilderness Park, where no human construction such as paved roads or buildings would be allowed. This followed the conservation efforts of Anis Rehman and Viqar Zakriya who wished to conserve the brown bear which had almost become extinct in the country. The Deosai plateau extends over a thousand square kilometer area and is a natural marvel covered in wild flowers, during the late summer. Brown bears, urials, marmots, and the occasional Kashmir stag are its inhabitants. The water has a particular kind of local fish. At the time of the construction of Satpara Dam near Skardu, it was with great difficulty that a proposal by some local leaders to divert this stream through a tunnel to add to Satpara's irrigation water was prevented. Fortunately, better sense prevailed then and that better sense continues. Unfortunately, state wildlife reserves are meant for a privileged few only, who are loath to pay for the pleasure they seek at the taxpayer's expense. In the Khyber and Sindh provinces, there are a number of wildlife reserves for governors and chief ministers, but unlike Sir George Cunningham, the British Governor of the Frontier province, Pakistani leaders never pay permit fees from their own pockets.

The variety of snakes, reptiles, butterflies, and insects in Pakistan is equally amazing and they all need protection. This is only possible if their habitat is not encroached upon. The pythons in Bhimber, in particular, need their space near the river and streams before they are all captured and smuggled abroad. The cobra and other snakes, the mongoose and iguana, the grand toad and the flying fox, the pine marten and porcupine, all need protection and the only effective way to do so is by notifying separate habitats by law, by provincial governments. The World Wildlife Fund and the International Union Conservation of Nature need to keep pressure on the government to ensure that this is done.

The Indus crocodile and the blind dolphin can be more easily protected by prohibiting netting in their reaches for it is licensed fishermen who do the most damage. Some Rajput tribes near the Indian forests and other indigenous communities have learnt to co-exist with wildlife to their mutual advantage. Not so in Pakistan! We spare no opportunity to strike or deprive the helpless regardless of the species or the season. The Governor's House in Peshawar had its own resident jackal pack till the mid-1980s, whose inimitable calls and cries in such surroundings were not acceptable to the staff. A military aide to then Governor Fazle Haq decided to remove these 'encroachers' physically. He had the bamboo clump near the front gate, cut and burnt, and the emerging poor jackals shot, clubbed, and killed. The ignoramus did not know that these animals had lived in the area before the Governor occupied the estate, before the British had taken possession of the surroundings, before the Sikhs and the Mughals had colonized the Frontier and, in fact, before man had set foot on this soil. Jackals not only bring good luck for the hunters but cheer despondent souls by their melodious wails in the dead of the night. The Governor House jackals need to be reintroduced!

The harsh and callous attitude of Pakistanis towards wildlife and pets is known the world over. Raja Kamal of Dudial in Azad Kashmir once ordered and paid in advance for a pair of English pointers for me from a kennel near London. On the delivery day, the owner of the kennel learnt to his shock that his pointers were destined for Pakistan and decided to annul the contract unilaterally. He offered to pay back the cost with penalty and was even prepared to face litigation but his 'lovely dogs' would never be allowed to set paws in a country that does not value animals. He had a valid point!

Such is the reputation of Pakistanis towards wildlife even as this land is an abundant and pure ground for its variety of fauna and flora. Our national tree is the statuesque *chinar* which is well-endowed in elegance and stature, which 'even a king cannot provide' as the powerful Mughal Emperor Aurangzeb rued. The country's national flower is Jasmine, which is deeply alluring, if not enduring. The national animal is the incomparable *Sulaiman Markhor*, regal with its majestic crown of horns. The word *markhor* literally means 'snake-like horns', not that it eats snakes! It is a wonder how it thrives in such dry and harsh conditions. The national bird should have been Iqbal's inspirational eagle, the *shaheen*, which holds both children and the adults spellbound, but due to a large number of competitors, it could not be a national bird. Instead, Pakistan's national bird is the *chikor* also called *chukker*. It may have been more appropriate, though if the common crow was also recognized as our national bird because of its utility in consuming garbage and in keeping cities clean. The thousands of municipal cleaners and sweepers cannot ensure cleanliness without the devoted contribution of the crow. Similarly, the cow could do as the national animal for its humble effort in keeping a family above the poverty line. The milk provides protein, its sale earns a few rupees, the dung is fuel for cooking, calves for future sustainability, and most importantly because the cow lives cheaply off the ground. Long may live the cow-crow combination.

Nature has also been very kind to Pakistan in the grant of physical landmarks starting with its lifeblood, the mighty lion river, the Indus. Not for nothing is it called *Abasin*, the father of rivers, but the other rivers like Jhelum, Chenab, and Kabul remain just as beautiful; there are the glacial lakes like Saif-ul-Malook, Satpara, and Maho Dand with waters so clear and pristine that legend believes only fairies lived there. Then there are the mountains: Godwin Austen, Tirich Mir, and Nanga Parbat, covered with silver during the day and embroidered in gold in the setting sun. The Deosai plateau, Fairy Meadows, the Lalazar heights and the Tharparkar desert are all different landscapes except that their allure is equally bewitching. What more could Pakistanis wish for?

The potential we have, provides hope and inspiration that all is not lost. There is still time to salvage most of the lost wildlife. Through community involvement and the profit motive Pakistan's national animal, the *Sulaiman Markhor* and other trophy wildlife, are growing in numbers. The Western Tragopan pheasant in Kohistan District has survived mainly because of its isolation but like the Monal pheasant and Himalayan snowcock, it needs protection. Wilderness parks, community reserves, scrub land, wetlands and water reservoirs, saline ponds, jungles, forests, and the hills and mountains need to be identified and conserved with human activity either prohibited or greatly regulated. Urban wildlife is a blessing and can be saved; habitat is important for them so that they find food and shelter. The two requirements that need to be met are a restricted core area for resting and breeding, and safe passages for movement are essential. Walls and barriers should have openings for free movements in the urban areas. Birds in urban areas can thrive but pollution and harmful ingredients in petroleum products, causes organ malfunction and sterility and a reason to shift the Lahore Zoo from the center of the city. In most cities in Pakistan which boast tree and bush cover, one can still hear the chirping of at least half a dozen different kinds of birds, early in the morning. One event which provides me with great joy, even twenty five years later, was the return to the original habitat of a pair of Himalayan snowcocks presented to me by the local headmen!

Rudyard Kipling, the most famous poet who lived in India and author of
the Raj books, had much to say about diverse topics but none as affectionate
as about the lion fish, known as the *mahseer*. There 'he met the *mahseer* of
the Poonch beside whom the tarpon is as a herring and he who lands him
can say he is a fisherman'. Angling for *mahseer* is like angling for gold as
someone said and there is much more. Even a small-sized *mahseer* will keep
one occupied for quite a while but the heavyweights would take one hour
to land, if the line does not snap in the meantime. The record for a *mahseer*
is 120 pounds from the River Cauvery in Southern India and is held by
the fancifully named deWet van Ingen in 1946; a less fancied name could
not have landed the most fancied fighting fish in the world. On the status
and qualities of the *mahseer*, at the very top, there can be no compromise
though there could be discussions on about the second greatest. The record
for the largest *mahseer* is 86 pounds in what is now Pakistan and probably
held by Colonel Cobb, the Political Agent of Malakand Agency who landed
it near Chakdarra. Then there is the unverified claim of the diminutive
old *Pir* from Toi Banda in Kohat who swore that he split the head of a
gargantuan *mahseer* with an axe in very shallow waters. It was said to be as
large as him and had to be carried on a cot. Having known the *Pir*, I could
vouch for his truthful nature although not for the size of the *mahseer*.
Perhaps a 100 pounds! However, what cannot be confirmed is the claim
of Ghulam Habib, the late *Tehsildar* from Malakand, that having lost a
metallic snuff box in the Swat River, he recovered it from the stomach of a
large *mahseer*, he landed a year later. A fisherman's tale probably!

Sadly, the *mahseer* is on the brink of extinction today all over Pakistan,
just as many positive human values are similarly threatened. We show
scant care, concern, and consideration for our surroundings. The *mahseer*
habitat is being polluted by oily vehicles, industrial runoffs, and domestic
sewerage. The streams running into Rawal Lake in Islamabad were teeming
with *mahseer* half a century back but that was before we had 'progressed'.
The spawning grounds of this mighty fish were checked by the construction
of Tarbela and Mangla Dams, none of which had fish ladders; amazingly
the Canadians, the Americans, and Europeans did not give much thought
to the environment. Our government and WAPDA could not have cared
less at that time. Hopefully for the new dam and reservoir projects under
construction such as the Munda-Mohmand Dam on the Swat River and

the Tarbela Four on the Indus, there is still a chance to cater for fish ladders. There may still be a little hope for the queen of the fish. In Srinagar and southern India, river stretches have been left undisturbed for *mahseer* spawning and for 'catch and release' angling, and the hope is that in Kotli-Mirpur in Azad Kashmir and in the Khyber and Balochistan provinces, community fish reserves will be developed with all financial benefits going to the local people.

It has been said that wildlife if given habitat cover and some protection, the animal and bird populations grow exponentially. It is theoretically possible, although practically not so, for a pair of tigers to multiply and to nearly 6,000 in thirty years, if optimum conditions exist. The community's environment is the key constituent as the Trophy Hunting Program in Pakistan and Campfire Programme in Zimbabwe, have proved. Wildlife security is built around the profit incentive and needs to be vigorously pursued. Wildlife remains loyal to its surroundings and even to those who wield the gun. With only a little care and concern, there is great future for wildlife and hunting in Pakistan. Millions of dollars could be raised by and for those living near wildlife but only if the rules are followed earnestly. In 1975, Zulfikar Ali Bhutto, Prime Minister of Pakistan, prohibited the hunting of Marco Polo sheep when he was told that only seventy-five were left in Kilik and Mintika areas to the west of the Khunjerab pass. The ban had no effect and the numbers further dwindled since local people had no incentive to conserve. In the winter, they would shoot them for meat and the opportunity cost was hundreds of dollars per kilogramme of meat. His daughter, Benazir Bhutto, as Prime Minister, adopted the Trophy Hunting Programme which augurs well for wildlife as *markhor*, ibex, and urial have increased in numbers. Currently, Aslam Bhotani and Saleh Bhotani sponsor the trophy hunting in Duregi in Lasbela where the animal population has grown to thousands, providing livelihood and local prosperity. The Torghar and Chitral *markhor* thrives today for the same reason. Salman Warraich's efforts in Jhelum may similarly add to the numbers and diversity of wildlife. For winged wildlife, community reserves with partridge breeding farms need encouragement. In other parts of the world, notably in Hungary and Spain, controlled breeding has led to growth in numbers and there is great incentive for the people. Sporting fish like the *mahseer* carp in India earns a US$100 a day for 'catch and release' alone. Seriously, there is more money in wildlife than in the cultivation of the opium poppy crop. Command and control means of enforcement by the state would not yield the best results and what is required is to give way to incentives of the private enterprise.

iii. Hunter's Tales

Hunting is one pastime where the pleasure is derived multiple times. Firstly, before even setting out for the hunt, there are preparations to be made. Secondly, the thrill on the day of the hunt and later in the recollection of the successes and regrets. In later years, one recalls a particularly good shot, and even a missed one, knowing that the bird escaped and hopefully, its numbers will multiply. I recall seeing a whistling curlew fly past me gently once and such was the joy of its sight and sound that shooting it was not an option. This non-shot was worth a hundred kills. Similarly, perhaps the greatest hunting pleasure I can remember was in Aqib Jatoi's reserve in Sindh. Someone else fired and injured a partridge which was seen falling into thorny bushes, some distance away. A group, including myself, set out to find and retrieved the bird after a twenty-minute search. The pleasure of finding it was a real Eureka! In those days, the lawful bag limit of birds was five and since that number was shot early in the day, the gun was packed and it was time to watch the others shoot. The combined total bag that day was in disregard of the law as one hundred and thirty partridges were collected, with Hafeez Pirzada, the top gun bagging thirty-five, followed closely by Danial. This number was very high even though unfortunately, in Sindh hunting parties are known to shoot five hundred or more in one outing.

Shikar anecdotes run into the hundreds with most being fictional but then bragging, to be sure, is an integral part of hunting. The story must begin with the doyen of Frontier hunters, the inimitable Aziz *shikari* of Kabuli descent, who was both, uneducated and unemployed. He excelled with the gun and the rod. President Ayub Khan, Governor Fazle Haq, Commissioner Nawabzada Sher Afzal, and hundreds of others were spellbound by his *shikar* narratives, his wit, and his bombast. When he was not hunting or fishing, he was found gambling small time and that often got him into trouble with the law. Fittingly, he died hunting partridge

in Toi Banda Reserve and was buried there. The tombstone inscription
was provided by a fellow hunter, Karim Hazeen aka Khan Bahadur Sahib.

Hunting tales are many but only a few are true. Khwaja Nazimuddin,
Governor General of Pakistan in the early fifties, was insistent on shooting
a bear in the Kaghan valley. The deputy commissioner of Hazara made all
arrangements but was frankly informed that it required much stalking over
high mountains. Now the Governor General's other claim to fame was his
appetite and so his girth and size made stalking that much more difficult.
A solution was soon conjured by the deputy commissioner and the local
Tehsildar. A performing bear was bought and tethered behind a distant rock
as the beaters with drums started the hunt. The affable bear was no stranger
to the drums and as soon as the Governor General, rifle in hand, came
close it started dancing to the beat of the drum. The *Tehsildar*, who had
bought the performing bear, must have come up with an explanation for
the behaviour of the bear as *Tehsildars* always do but the boss had his day.
In *shikar*, as in life, some are more special than others. In Communist Soviet
Union, President Brezhnev, who was not known as an accomplished angler,
nevertheless always baited the biggest fish, much to his delight. It transpired
that actually naval frogmen were deployed deep in the lake who would
dutifully hook the fish to the President's bait. The Communist boss was
most pleased. There were similar Standard Operating Procedures in other
countries, notably in General Franco's Spain. When President Iskandar
Mirza was invited for a driven partridge shoot in Spain, he was perplexed
to find a thick iron sheet placed by the side of his shooting bunker. On his
protesting, the Hunt Master explained that it was not to shield Franco but
to protect Iskandar Mirza from Franco's wild shots.

For much of his decade-long governorship of the Frontier province,
General Fazle Haq would not miss his partridge shoots and many an
officer or an attendant got a verbal lashing merely for fun that day. On
one occasion as the *shikar* began, Fazle Haq enquired if there were any
pointer dogs available. Two obliging ministers, reportedly Jamal Shah and
Mohsin, quickly blurted out: 'we are here, Sir'. What they meant to say was
that if no pointer were available, they would do the beating. A while later, a
shot rang out and a partridge dropped; an obsequious officer immediately
shouted 'good shot, Sir'. The Governor launched at him with a four-letter
word informing him that he had not even fired.

Another time, General Fazle Haq's anger knew no bounds after he gifted
a basket with four each of the recently shot *chakors*, black, grey, and sisi
partridges to President Ziaul Haq. Sometime later, the President thanked
the Governor for the gift of *batkhain* or ducks that he had sent him and this
was what made Fazle Haq livid with anger. General Zia could not tell the
difference between duck and partridge any better than he could between
democracy and dictatorship. All the same, hunting is a convention, a ritual,
a social occasion, an exercise to keep fit and much more. It has its own lore
and style, and the best stylists are those who know the limits. Most Sindhis,
Baloch, Pukhtun, and Punjabis are uncouth and brutal in *shikar*. Angling
was not a favoured sport in this region but after Partition the people took
to it in a big way. Even so the collection of fish, not through angling but
through the use of the net, electric current, explosives or laxatives became the
standard form of killing. The hunters and fishermen have only one criterion
for the day which is their total size of the bag. The more the better. General
Fazle Haq classified hunters into two categories, the gentlemen *hunter
shikaris* and the *khansama (cook) shikaris*. The latter filled up deep freezers.

Due to an absence of effective regulation coupled with poor state of
governance in Pakistan, hunting has been the cause of many an altercation,
leading to quarrels, fights, and murders. In one case, dozens of people
from both sides were killed over a decade, with the dispute originating
from poaching a deer, in the Mianwali district of Punjab. The vendetta
ended only when all the leading men had lost their lives. Such was and is
the level of violence in the country! The finesse, convention, and the style
of the hunt has evaporated into the air as we become more *Pakistanised*.
Honorary Captain Fazalur Rehman Rabiakhel Orakzai of the Frontier
Force Regiment, as my security officer in Orakzai Agency, was among the
last of the stylists. Every shot invoked a comment from him. If the shot
dropped a partridge, Fazal's voice would ring out 'good shot, Sir'. If you
missed then to save the officer public embarrassment, he would announce
'out of range, out of range'.

A *shikar* outing everyone enjoyed was in the Nara Canal area not
for the number of partridge shot but for the company. Professor Iqbal
Awan of Kohat had written a pamphlet *Teetar ba Qamand Awar* on this
partridge shoot with focus on many a detail. His verse and writ was edifying
mentioning Mohabat Ali Zafar also from Kohat who had never touched a

gun in life and General Ghazi Rana who could never let it go. There was no mention made in the book however, of the plight of Jalaluddin Katu Khan running naked after being confronted by a snake just as he was answering nature's call, his trousers left hanging on a tree. Imagine Katu Khan, about 300 pounds in mass, unable to return to his trousers.

Then there was a unique and most unforgettable partridge shoot, even if shoot is the inappropriate word to describe it. General Salim, being six feet six inches tall, Additional Commissioner Aslam six feet two inches tall, and Jalalud Din Katu Khan, once decided to go hunting in the Toi Banda Governor's Reserve in Kohat but without official permission. As soon as the wildlife watcher saw the grandees with guns but with no permits, he was thoroughly shaken and pleaded with the mighty three against shooting. The two tall ones nevertheless started their hunt, firing with abandon, and each shot the watcher heard appeared to be striking at his heart. Meanwhile, as Katu Khan and the watcher started strolling in the reserve they heard a shuffling sound in a nearby bush. They approached the bush from opposite sides and getting very close, surprised a partridge which entered the *shalwar*, the loose baggy trousers of Katu Khan. Immediately, Katu sealed off the escape route by tightly holding the lower portion of the *shalwar* and soon they had a live bird in their hand. An hour later, the two tall hunters arrived having fired over forty shots but without bagging even a single partridge. Forty shots and no game bird while Katu got one in a gamely manner, without firing a single shot! There was an ecstatic Katu, a relieved wildlife watcher, and two very embarrassed tall hunters. This record was beaten only by four senior officers, posted in Hangu, in the mid-1970s; a Political Agent (Khalid Aziz), a District Officer Frontier Constabulary (Aziz Khan), an Assistant Superintendent Police (Mazhar Sher) and an Assistant Commissioner (myself). We had gone partridge shooting in the Shinawari Reserve but after firing sixty cartridges, we were still looking for our first bird. Perhaps in a previous life, we were conservationists!

Then there were two phenomenal hunters from Gilgit, Jalalud Din and Farman Reza. They had most trusting and remarkable eyes and could spot *markhors* and ibexes almost a mile away in the dark recesses of the mountains. Jalal could point to an orphan ibex from a distance when others could not even spot the big ones. He could not only see the animal but had noticed that its horns were thinner than usual because of not drinking the mother's milk. Another time, Farman pointed to mallards, distinguishing the males from the females nearly half a kilometer away below in a pond.

As the Commissioner Kohat Division, I remember a 'non-hunting' outing one day. I had decided not to go for *shikar* and instead enjoy a picnic lunch with a gun in hand and a pointer just in case. There were five family members and we travelled five miles from Kohat and laid out a picnic lunch about five hundred yards from the main road. Soon Camy, the pointer got scent of partridge. In five minutes, I fired five shots, dropping five partridges. The picnic lunch followed but I cannot recall if there were five items on the menu! The most unforgettable part of my *shikar* was my dog. Camy, a female pointer, who was gifted to me by Colonel Wahid Jan. She was an amazing companion and remained matchless in picking up game scent. When she fell ill because of old age as her knees gave up. She was examined by a pioneering American heart transplant surgeon, a Dr Allen perhaps that was his name, who was visiting Swat as a house guest. The surgeon first sought permission to examine the 'patient' and having examined Camy suggested some medication but insisted that his opinion be confirmed by a veterinary doctor. Sadly, she died and was buried just outside the commissioner's bungalow. Chief, the German short haired pointer, will be remembered as an extraordinary dog whose ability to pick up scent seldom failed him. The Black Labrador, Caesar, who could spend hours patiently looking at his master, died early in Lahore and was buried in the compound of the WAPDA Chairman's House. The arrival of dachshunds, Leksi and Cleo, and Stella the pointer, were only partial compensation.

There are two absorbing stories of loyalty, one about a pet and the other about wildlife, which are being told strictly as narrated. *Darogh ba gardanay raavi!* Those who love dogs would have heard the oft-proffered advice that when looking for a friend, get a dog. A pointer dog belonging to a keen hunter started behaving strangely to the extent that people thought it had gone mad. All diagnoses and treatments failed. The grey beards in the profession recommended putting it to sleep to avoid any untoward incident. The owner was not convinced, and looking into the dog's eyes, found nothing alarming. He thought it was a case of temporary glandular or hormonal imbalance but that the dog did not appear mad. The greybeards had the last word and on an appointed day the pointer was brought to the garden to be shot to forestall a larger tragedy in the community. This at a time when hundreds of homo sapiens in the country should have been punished for their crimes but who walked free. A single shot at close range rang out, the dog staggered, looked around for its master, recognized him, crawled to his feet, and died. Its last thoughts may have been that actually the master had gone mad to shoot it, because in happier days, he would only shoot at partridge for game; who was mad, no one would ever know, but the dog had proved its loyalty till its last breath. The tale about a lively dancing horse of Bahadur Khan of Baghdada Mardan, who always fed it personally, was equally poignant. Three days after the owner died, the horse also lost the will to live and died peacefully!

The second story of loyalty was narrated by an inebriated person and has to be taken with a pinch of salt or at least a sip of brew. A genial soul, short and stocky, but with a generous heart and supreme self-confidence (they call me Farooqi was how he introduced himself!) decided to take his first trip to England, (or was it Ireland), many decades ago. He lived close to a pub but had little idea why people went there in the early evenings quite sober and returned late, very boisterous. One evening, he weighed the pros and cons and entered the place. He sat down in a corner below an amateur painting of a lovely goose and of an elegant fox in a tweed jacket with leather elbow patches. The pair that gave the name 'Fox and Goose' to the pub, the inscription read, used to visit the meadows adjacent to it long ago. They got to know each other well and soon there was a stirring in their hearts but they were prohibited by the village pastor from any closer arrangement. The grief was quite unbearable but what made it worse was the attitude of the village folk who accused one of stealing their chickens and the other of damaging the agriculture produce. The pair decided to migrate to the promised land of kinder people but just as they were ready to depart, the foreleg of the fox got caught in an iron trap. As the villagers closed in to club the Fox to the hereafter, the Goose barely made it to the air, tipped its wings in salute and flew off some say to the Cape of Good Hope. Were her hopes well rewarded? *Nadeshda*! Having read the story of how the pub got its name, our stocky friend slowly moved to the bar. When the bartender enquired about his preference for the evening, he had no idea what he should order. He had heard people order 'a pint of' something unfamiliar for he had never heard the word lager. He was familiar with only one item from his homeland and so confidently ordered a 'pint of whisky'. There was much laughter. He, however, managed to get out of the embarrassment rather easily because of his self-confidence. 'Abay tu kya bechta hai' or who do you think you are! What he was not able to explain once back home was the cock and bull story or more accurately the Fox and Goose happening. He apparently had ordered his pint before he read or misread the story under the painting but was not even sure of this sequence. A pint after all could jumble up the story of the species of the two characters and the sequence of events. Loyalty was explained though.

The loyalty of birds and animals to those who love and care for them, is immense. The love for the mate in some species is even more sublime. The Brahminy ducks(ruddy shelduck) known as *surkhab,* are partners for life, like the cranes, and when one is shot by vile hunters, the survivor keeps circling the fallen mate till the hunter shoots it too. The saddest *shikar* story that I often recount, relates to my shooting a *surkhab,* at Borith lake in Hunza whose wailing mate continued to return to its fallen companion till it was shot by someone. Never again have I ever fired at a *surkhab* or a crane but could other species be shot? The Red List of threatened wildlife of the World Conservation Union means very little to hunters in Pakistan and most of them remain shamefully inconsiderate.

One tale with a joyful ending, relates to a pair of goral sheep who lived happily ever after. There was once a solitary male goral sheep sulking in a wildlife department pen in the Frontier province while about the same time the chief secretary Azad Kashmir found a depressed and lonely female goral in Pateeka Reserve, in Azad Kashmir. Marriage terms were soon settled across provincial borders and the bride was dispatched to the eager bridegroom. And yes they lived happily ever after!

At the other end, there is that chilling story of a British colonel who was to catch the evening train out of Multan for home in England on the eve of the Partition of India. He reportedly had his servants bathe and groom his two horses and six pedigree dogs and after a swig of cognac perhaps, shot each animal in the head. Then he explained that he could not find any 'native' who could have cared enough for his beloved pets and did not want them to suffer neglect, once he was gone. Having seen how pets are treated in our dear land he had a valid point. There is another story in the same vein. The Anti-Narcotics Force's request to the Germans for providing sniffer dogs was declined on grounds that Pakistani personnel had previously treated the dogs sent, inhumanely. The donors were prepared to offer Mercedes vehicles to the yahoos of the force, but not dogs. With Pakistanis, it is common for the handlers of zoo animals to divert part of food and maintenance costs to their pockets as these animals never complain and stay loyal forever even when you steal from them, their food.

The tale of two leopards is even more absorbing. A snow leopard was reportedly trapped in a house in Torkho, in Chitral, while stalking domestic goats. The owner locked the door from outside and then did not know what to do next. When this was reported to a European lady, perhaps Linda Bernard living in Karachi, she travelled to Chitral at her own cost, reached the distant village, rescued the confounded animal and released it in the wild. I give full marks to the lady. About the same time a common leopard cub, having lost its mother and the way from Margalla hills found itself near Satellite Town, in Rawalpindi, where it hid in a garage. The area was soon surrounded by the brave and bold Punjab police armed with automatic rifles and as the door was opened a dozen blazing rifles fired at the helpless cub. It is not known for sure if medals of shame were pinned on their chests but they certainly deserved them.

The story of the pair of *murghe zarin* or monal pheasants gifted while I was the Commissioner, Kohat Division during the 1980s, needs to be told for posterity. These pheasants are about the most beautiful birds in nature but are regularly trapped for sale in the snow-capped mountains of the Kurram Agency. I was not pleased with the gift and was annoyed at receiving the caged birds much to the consternation of the tribesman who brought it. Moments after the tribesman left, the birds were sent with an escort who were told to walk up the same mountains as far as their legs could carry them and release the birds there. This was accomplished and a written report submitted by the guards.

This chapter cannot end without an anecdote about two queens, one from Pakistan and the other from Hollywood. The famous Aziz Shikari once hooked a large *mahseer* fish 'the queen' from Toi Banda in Kohat and appreciating the size of the catch, decided to gift it to someone very special. He handed it over to the Commissioner, Peshawar Division, Nawabzada Sher Afzal Khan, a *mahseer* enthusiast. The Commissioner was amazed to see the fish and decided not to eat it but to send it to someone very special, who happened to be President Ayub Khan. Now the President, an angler himself, was most pleased to see the *mahseer* but wanted to gift it to someone very special. That evening, he was travelling to Iran, and presented the game fish to the Shah, who was a sportsman himself and who greatly appreciated the gift. The above narrative is the verified truth but the next paragraph is a fisherman's tale and so take it with a bite. The Shah of Iran thought that he ought to gift the *mahseer* fish to someone very special and since he was travelling to the United States he presented it to President Kennedy. Now Jack Kennedy was forever on the lookout for fish of one kind or another. He thought of giving it to someone very special and that is how it landed in Marilyn Monroe's lap or was it Kennedy's lap! One *mahseer* all the way from Kohat to the United States of America!

Similarly, once in Swat an angler sent a thirty-five pound *mahseer* to the author. The very sight was inspiring and there was no way it would find its way to the kitchen and instead was gifted to Air Chief Marshal Hakimullah Khan, then heading the Pakistan Air Force, and a quality angler himself. For a fortnight, there was no response from him but then at six o'clock one morning, there was a telephone call. Holding the handset, I thought something really serious like an enemy attack had occurred for the Air Chief to call but all he said excitedly in Pashto was that *'da mahseer dai'*. He then explained that when his staff told him earlier that a very big fish was sent by the Commissioner, he assumed it would be a china carp but was amazed to find the queen instead. Thanks to our polluted rivers and streams, unchecked netting, and also the failure to breed in hatcheries, the *mahseer* carp might not survive long. (Just for the record it may be mentioned here that Hakimullah Khan, as a young pilot flying his F104 Starfighter interceptor during the Indo-Pak war in 1965, forced an Indian Gnat fighter, piloted by Brigpal Sikand, to make a forced landing on a landing strip in Pasrur out of sheer fright). On the subject of fighter aircrafts, I cannot forget the tipping salute for the *shikaris* by four MIG fighters of the Pakistan Air Force, early one morning in Chashma. The pilots had spent some time with us the previous evening!

Finally, there is the heart-rending story containing two characters, one a crooked hunter-poacher, and the other a compassionate man of religion. A Hindu priest in an *ashram* in India would lovingly throw an unleavened wheat *paratha* bread every morning for a big *mahseer* in a stream close by, which would thankfully accept it. This continued for years, till a Muslim mendicant saw what was happening which resulted in tragic consequences. One day just before the priest fed the *mahseer*, the mendicant threw a *'paratha'* of his own but with a hook and line attached to it which the unsuspecting fish swallowed hook, line, and sinker. An hour later, the priest was at his wit's end when he noted with concern that the life-sustaining *paratha* flowed slowly down with no *mahseer* to bite it. An act most foul, but then there have always been two types of people on earth! Those who trump, and those who get trumped. The former ruled the roost, normally!

Let this chapter end with a word of caution on hunting as it is also one of the most dangerous of sports. In 1902, Mark Beaufoy of Coombe House, Shaftesbury, Dorset, England provided safety instructions on presenting his eldest son with his first gun:

> If a sportsman true you'd be
> Listen carefully to me…
>
> Never, never let your gun
> Pointed be at anyone.
> That it may unloaded be
> Matters not the least to me.
>
> When a hedge or fence you cross
> Though of time it cause a loss
> From your gun the cartridge take
> For the greater safety's sake.
>
> If twixt you and neighbouring gun
> Bird shall fly or beast may run
> Let this maxim ere be thine
> "Follow not across the line."
>
> Stops and beaters oft unseen
> Lurk behind some leafy screen.
> Calm and steady always be
> "Never shoot where you can't see."

You may kill or you may miss
But at all times think this:
"All the pheasants ever bred
Won't repay for one man dead."

Keep your place and silent be;
Game can hear, and game can see;
Don't be greedy, better spared
Is a pheasant, than one shared.

10

Water and Power Issues: *Na Bijli, Na Pani*

It is an accepted fact that there is not enough water or electricity in Pakistan today. The timely development of both sectors should have provided the main engine for economic growth in the country. For seventy years, the country has failed to address critical shortages of both water and electricity. This scarcity in the midst of much potential, is deeply disturbing. The lapse has led to poverty, under-employment, and stunted economic development. With the exceptions of President Ayub Khan, General Musharraf, and Prime Minister Shaukat Aziz's team, the performance of other leaders has been unsatisfactory. Some politicians and water bureaucrats, owe many explanations to the country. This need not have been the case.

Initially, there had been some success. Following the loss of the three eastern rivers to India in 1960 under the Indus Basin Treaty, a number of water storages, link canals, and hydel-power projects were completed with international assistance. With a potential greater than all but a few countries, it appeared that nothing would stop Pakistan from attaining a developed economy status based on water and power. Five decades after independence, the per capita electricity consumption in the country only remained around five hundred units per year while water storage capacity per person fell below a thousand cubic metres annually from a high of nearly five thousand cubic metres after Partition. This loss in water availability is explained by the failure to check rapid population growth and the inability to increase water storage. A number of rivers originate in the high northern mountains of the country, providing nearly one hundred and fifty million acre-feet of water. This could easily generate 100,000 megawatts of hydel power. Pakistan could feed a population twice its size if land and water resources were utilized to the optimum. Apart from hydel power, Pakistan also has considerable lignite and coal deposits which could generate surplus amounts of power. In addition, solar, and wind power, theoretically, could generate power in terawatts. The country's economic growth and development and its capacity to overcome the poverty trap would have been easily accomplished but for its failure to tap its resources effectively. Where did the failure lie? The political leadership must share the blame with the bureaucracy, for its lack of vision. It also did not have the political will to implement the decisions taken on water and power issues. Many myopic experts in the planning commission, the ministries of Finance, Water & Power and Petroleum, and in the Water and Power Development Authority (WAPDA) were responsible in varying degrees for this neglect. Pakistanis argued endlessly and quarreled over specific projects while the real Asian tigers, quietly developed their resources. The bold ones became the tigers. Only President Ayub Khan of all our leaders had the vision and the will to move ahead decisively. Others merely planned on paper, leading to an analysis paralysis. The Gomal and Kurram Tangi dams were placed on the priority list, early on and then abandoned in the 1960s; the Kalabagh and Munda dam reservoirs were discussed for nearly half a century but to no avail and just when resources were available for the Diamer Basha storage dam, the Government preferred the Dasu Dam which was only a run-of-the-river dam, with no water storage capacity.

At Partition, Pakistan inherited the largest continuous developed irrigation system in the world. The British, wasted no time in furthering the development process, wherever they went. By 1910, barely a decade after occupying the Malakand Heights, they laid the foundation of the Amandara Headworks and dug the Upper and Lower Swat canal systems. The boring of the Benton Tunnel was an engineering feat, bringing waters to the Jabban Hydropower project. The powerhouse, with its turbines, generated hydel power for nearly seventy years before a fire led to its replacement with a new project with generous French Government assistance. Such was the quality of the British equipment that the old mechanized trolley in the project, continues to function stoically even today and has completed an uninterrupted eighty years in service; there would not be many mechanical machines that are still working after so many years. The only other comparable engineering feats in the country, were the building of the Khojak Railway Tunnel in Balochistan in the 1880s, the 'couplings to the Khyber', and the Railway line to Landikotal, which is still operational. The Swat canal system added tens of thousands of acres of barren land into quality irrigated agriculture in Malakand, Charsadda, Mardan, and Swabi areas. When the officials of the Finance Department in New Delhi objected to the limited economic feasibility of these canals, the Viceroy is reported to have snubbed them, by stating that the political and strategic benefits of the project far outweighed their financial costs. In today's jargon this is called social cost-benefit analysis. The purpose then was to 'tie' the Pakhtun people to their land so that their energies were not spent fighting the British. The canal colonies in Lyallpur, Montgomery, Bahawalpur, and Multan and the development of the Sukkur Barrage, similarly, led to irrigating tens of millions of acres. Food security, rural employment, social stability, and burgeoning textile industries were the real benefits accruing to the society. Some imperialists like the British in India, the Russians in Central Asia, and the Moors in Spain were known for developing infrastructure projects to provide benefits to the local people.

After the signing of the Indus Basin Treaty with India in 1960 when there was an imminent threat of the diversion of the waters of the Ravi, Sutlej, and Bias rivers, the Pakistani leadership for once did not remain lethargic as they did later. The Mangla and Tarbela Dams, with their huge water reservoirs along with a number of connecting barrages, were promptly constructed, within fifteen years. This success was credited to the Water and Power Development Authority (WAPDA) and its first four Chairmen, during the *ghulamaan* (slaves) period, comprising Ghulam Ahmad, Ghulam Farooq, Ghulam Ishaq, and Abdul Ghulam Kazi. They were *ghulamaans* indeed but slaves only in the service of the people. WAPDA's corporate structure was molded on the private sector model because a need arose to create an autonomous organization that 'combined the authority and credibility of the Government with the initiative and flexibility of the private sector' to undertake the gigantic hydro power and canal projects in the country. The new organization did not let the people down during the first two decades of its existence and used its expertise wisely. Actually the ethos of Pakistan's 'political eleven' mirrors its cricket eleven which at times is capable of amazing feats but otherwise remains pretty indolent. The people of Pakistan similarly display vigour, courage, and sacrifice but only in emergencies after which they return to their slumber, mainly because of their supine and greedy leaders. This was in evidence during the 1965 war with India, the 2005 earthquake in Azad Kashmir and Mansehra, and the forced Swat internal migration in 2009 which quickly cast the people into a nation during difficult times. When normalcy is restored, they become their real selves again and revert to their quarrelsome, greedy, and selfish habits. An old army doctor in Kakul would often quote: 'God and the doctor all men adore, when sickness comes and not before; when health returns and things are righted, God is forgotten and the doctor slighted!'

In the years ahead, Pakistan would face further challenges, none more severe than the imminent shortage of water. The decision to sign the World Bank-sponsored Indus Basin Treaty with India in 1960 which denied Pakistan all water flows from the three eastern rivers of Ravi, Sutlej, and Bias has been dogged with controversy. Many in Pakistan felt that India got more water than what it was entitled to, while others were convinced that under the circumstances, the country got what it possibly could. It is said that Eugene Black, then President of the World Bank, told President Ayub Khan that the best option for Pakistan to get more waters was 'to go to war with India and win it' but short of that, the Treaty in hand was his best deal. Since India was to get the waters of the three eastern rivers, corresponding waters needed to be diverted for irrigated agriculture from Indus, Jhelum, and Chenab rivers to offset the loss. This was a gargantuan effort which was financed by the World Bank, major donors, and curiously by India as well. During those days, Ghulam Farooq Khan, as Chairman of WAPDA, went to America in search of quality consultants to undertake the replacement works. He reportedly enquired about which amongst the top consultants knew Ike well. When he was informed that Davis, the boss of Harza, would often play golf with President Eisenhower of the United States, his firm was chosen without demur. In those days, ministers and bureaucrats could be trusted to take the best decision for the country. Golf incidentally, is one of the better ways of improving networking and networking is what drives business. (Half a century later while attending the Top Management Programme in Baguio, Philippines I was part of a mandatory four-ball for golf in the evening. I disappointed the hosts by informing them that I had never played golf. A concerned senior executive from Motorola Corporation asked me how I 'cultivated' my boss if I did not play golf. I have since taken to golf but not to cultivate my bosses). The game of golf, therefore, served WAPDA well over the years!

Even before WAPDA was created, a major hydropower project was initiated by the government of NWFP under the Colombo Plan. This was the Warsak Dam on the Kabul River, the site which was first identified by pre-Partition British engineers. The dam was completed by WAPDA in 1960, at a cost of about US$10 million but during its fifty years of operation it contributed over US$6 billion at current costs to the national exchequer. With the successful completion of Warsak Dam, Pakistani engineers gained the expertise to undertake storage projects, the first of which was the replacement storage of Mangla Dam on the Jhelum river. This contributed to the development of new engineering skills for officials and contractors in the country. The first time a Tunnel Boring Machine, the Mole, was employed anywhere in the world was at the Mangla Dam and it took another half a century before such a machine was used again in Pakistan for boring the twin tunnels of the Neelum-Jhelum project. President Ayub was at hand to inaugurate Mangla Dam and it is said that Ghulam Ishaq Khan, the Chairman of WAPDA after a brief Pashto-accented English speech invited the President to kindly 'open the dame'.

The next mega project constructed by WAPDA was the Tarbela Dam and then for decades thereafter, nothing much was done because WAPDA and the various governments focused only on building the Kalabagh Dam to the exclusion of other potential storages. Unfortunately, for the country in the process, not only was the Kalabagh controversy un-resolved but other water storage projects were put on the back-burner. WAPDA, it would appear, deliberately did not undertake consultancy studies for other sites because it felt that this could have led to delaying or shelving the proposed Kalabagh Dam, the apple of its eye. The controversy over Kalabagh Dam construction continues half a century later, despite a wealth of data supporting its utility. In the process, Pakistan might well have compromised its rights to the 'historic use' of Kabul River waters in the future because once Warsak Dam was fully silted, the waters from the Kabul River cannot be stored. In actual fact, no province suffers more from the construction of the Kalabagh Dam, certainly not Sindh, which would add another two million acres of irrigated land because of the increased flows. Similarly, there is absolutely no chance of the inundation of Peshawar, Charsadda, and Nowshera in the Khyber Pakhtunkhwa province as these areas would be at least forty feet higher than the maximum water elevation of Kalabagh. Shams ul Mulk, the former Chairman of WAPDA and all those who understand the country's hydrology, have been pleading its cause, but to no avail. It appears that the real reason for Sindh's aversion to Kalabagh Dam is its apprehension that in the future, with an expanding population, Punjab may divert Sindh's share of waters. That is why Sindh wants not a constitutional but a 'geographical guarantee' so that such an eventuality never occurs. The 'geographical guarantee' that Sindh prefers consists in not creating any storage in the Punjab from which a canal can divert water someday. This argument appears faulty because even today, except for the three months of floods, all waters of the Indus can be diverted easily, but why would Punjab want to do that? I believe that in another twenty years when the populations of the provinces will nearly double and there will be a severe shortage of food and water, Sindh and the Khyber Pakhtunkhwa provinces would actually demand the construction of the Kalabagh Dam. Time will tell!

A country that could build the Tarbela Dam, which was an engineering marvel of its time, should have been capable of undertaking a similar project quite easily. It was said that because of its sheer size, the technical and engineering dimensions of Tarbela Dam stretched the frontiers of science and technology. Dr Cassagrande, the legendary guru of dam geology felt that such were the innovations and techniques employed in the construction of Tarbela Dam and its power house that he could offer a hundred PhDs from Harvard University to engineers and experts, employed in the project. Unfortunately, WAPDA went into hibernation after building the Tarbela Dam and wasted precious time dithering over the choice of projects. Even if a consensus was not possible on building the Kalabagh Dam why did WAPDA not initiate the feasibility, engineering, and design studies of alternate sites such as Diamer Basha, Dasu, Pattan, Thakot, Shyok, or Akhori Dams? It reflected poorly on WAPDA and the federal government that feasible projects like the Munda, Gomal, Kuram Tangi, Tank, and Potwar Dams were similarly placed on the back-burner for decades. Many engineers, perhaps because of their focused technical training, often lack the vision to provide viable options to the policy makers. The construction of an additional underground powerhouse at Warsak to utilize flood waters was in fact suggested by a non-engineer and not by WAPDA's engineers.

Under the circumstances, it was creditable for General Musharraf and the Prime Minister Shaukat Aziz that they initiated work on the Mangla Dam Raising Project, the three Khwar Hydel Power projects in the Frontier province, and also on the Gomal Zam Dam in South Waziristan. In addition, they initiated contracts for the detailed engineering studies of the Diamer Basha Dam. On its part after the initial period of activity, WAPDA was only able to develop the 1450 megawatt Ghazi Barotha, run-of-the-river project, during the 1980s even though this was dogged by controversies. Earlier at one stage, Prime Minister Benazir Bhutto pushed WAPDA to construct a smaller capacity project at this site, which would be completed earlier and earn her some political mileage. As a mature politician she accepted the advice of Chairman WAPDA, Shamsul Mulk, to wait another couple of years so that the project site could be optimally developed and the benefits maximized. The limited project development in the country, also showed the waning influence of the 'frontiersmen' on the decision-makers in Islamabad as in the past many of the federal ministers and chairmen of WAPDA were from the North West Frontier Province (NWFP, now called Khyber Pakhtunkhwa).

It is hoped that in the years ahead not only would Pakistan be in a position to develop all its water reservoirs but would also assist Afghanistan in developing the Kunar-Kabul River basin resources for effective land utilization. A water utilization treaty on common rivers is required between Pakistan and Afghanistan on the pattern of the Indus Basin Treaty, signed with India.

All of President Ayub Khan's shortcomings can be ignored, except the the War of September 1965, because of his foresight in developing the water and power sectors. Gratitude is due to him also for introducing the family planning programme in the country because there would never be enough waters, if the Pakistani population continues to grow at its present rate. Pakistan would survive all other dangers except for the steep growth of its population. Ayub Khan was a visionary, as far as water issues were concerned. He had set eyes on other projects too. He inaugurated the small Khanpur Dam with a beautiful rest house, and the suite he often used now, bears a plaque to commemorate his visits. The 1965 war with India may have shelved plans to construct the Gomal and the Kurram Tangi dams.

Since then only the Ghazi Barotha and the Chashma Hydropower projects were established in the country. These were too few and far between.

There was one other achievement of the Pakistani leadership in the water sector since then. The unanimous signing of the Water Apportionment Accord of 1991 was no small feat and the credit for this goes to former Prime Minister Mian Nawaz Sharif, and the four Chief Ministers. The disputed water claims of the provinces over the preceding thirty years, had prevented the development of water resources. The Accord, which became possible because of Punjab agreeing to reduce it share of water while realizing its full potential if additional storage is constructed.

One of the first irrigation projects undertaken after the Water Accord was the Pehur High Level Canal in the Frontier or the Khyber Pukhtunkhwa province. The finances were provided by the Asian Development Bank to the Province but the execution was quite correctly left to WAPDA which alone had the expertise required to develop major works. A problem arose in constructing the project because WAPDA had twice rejected the construction bids solicited on account of the high costs offered. After the bids were called for the third time in 1997, WAPDA still remained unwilling to commence work for reason of the higher costs stating that its own project contractors would also demand similar rates. With WAPDA refusing to undertake the work and the donor threatening to withdraw the finances because of the inordinate delays, the additional chief secretary (Development) in the Frontier province, proposed that the provincial cabinet and not WAPDA, as a special measure, approve the escalated rates. This proposal was acceptable to WAPDA because the rates were approved not by it but by another forum and the work was started soon started. The benefits accruing to the province have been enormous. It was Sardar Mehtab, the Chief Minister NWFP, who took the bold decision in 1997 to actually build the Pehur High level canal, to provide irrigation water. All chief ministers before him, studiously avoided committing the counterpart funds for this work because they thought they will not reap major political capital from it.

Apart from this, the only projects WAPDA developed during this lean interregnum were soil conservation and reclamation ones, the SCARPS, and the two Outfall Drains in Sindh. The Right Bank Outfall Drain (RBOD) and the Left Bank Outfall Drain (LBOD) were meant to carry high saline and toxic flows fed by water logging to the sea. These have met their objectives to an extent but a better alternative was experimented on, in 2010, by WAPDA to desalinate the contaminated water and use it for agriculture rather than wasting it and returning to the sea. Should it succeed, nearly three million acre-feet of saline water could be put to agricultural use.

i. How Not to Manage the Power Sector

A project planning expert, while studying the Mallam Jabba Ski Resort established in Swat during the 1960s, arrived at the unhappy conclusion that here was a good example of how not to develop a project. The concept of the resort was too exclusive, the slope too steep, the hotel design too archaic, and the costs too high. The power sector in Pakistan after the bifurcation of WAPDA, would compete for a similar description. Forty years after its establishment, WAPDA had developed into a mammoth organization, dealing with water and power sectors. From generating a few hundred megawatts capacity, it had an installed capacity of over 25,000 megawatts of power. The number of consumers rose to twenty million, making it difficult to control technical losses and theft, which when added to the low recovery of electricity dues meant that nearly half the generated revenues were lost. Any addition to generation meant more losses for which the government had to provide additional subsidies. Under these circumstances and on the continuous pleading of foreign donors, the government agreed by 1998 to bifurcate WAPDA into two independent entities for power and water.

However, WAPDA continued to dither and the actual separation was delayed till October 2007. The former Prime Minister, Shaukat Aziz, having notified me as the chairman of WAPDA and Munawar Baseer as Managing Director, Pakistan Electric Power Corporation (PEPCO), asked how long it would take to actually bifurcate WAPDA. I informed him that it would take two weeks. The Prime Minister smiled wryly and retorted that for the past fifteen years despite the government's policy-decision, WAPDA could not be separated and that it could not be done in two weeks. I was of the view that it was the privilege and mandate of the government alone to take policy decisions and the bureaucrats, having given their input, were expected to obey these decisions. In case they did not agree with the decision, they ought to resign or ask for a posting elsewhere in service. Within the allotted two weeks, WAPDA was physically bifurcated but through a clever arrangement the Ministry of Water and Power ensured that the new Distribution Company called the Pakistan Electric Power Company, or PEPCO, would not be independent but would be directly placed under it. To further increase its patronage, PEPCO also took control of thermal power generation and all power transmission as well. The so-called 'Gencos', and the National Transmission and Distribution Company, comprised the ministry's empire which totaled over a hundred thousand personnel. The minister and the secretary had more personnel under their command than three Army Corps Commanders put together but the principal purpose of bifurcation was lost. The collapse of the new power sector was predicted and it did not take long in crashing. The connivance of the ministry of Water and Power to the new arrangements in the early days spelled long-term trouble. It was physically not possible for the ministry of Water and Power to operate and supervise ten distribution companies, the DISCOs. Rather than streamlining the Distribution and Thermal Power companies for privatizing or leasing, PEPCO saw itself as a new but smaller version of WAPDA, in the power sector. The losses multiplied, pilferages increased, and the subsidies soared as a result of the circular debt amongst the entities that had emerged due to poor cash flows of the DISCOs.

The direction of the post-bifurcation PEPCO, as a temporary arrangement, went horribly wrong from the very beginning. Instead of granting full autonomy to the DISCOs, the new chief executives of DISCOs, with the support of politicians became totally unaccountable. The new setup did not work because two opposite strands were at play. Would the DISCOs be working as private companies under the Securities and Exchange Commission or would PEPCO be a new public sector corporation? The new management did not want to forego the authority and the discretion of awarding huge contracts, making appointments by the tens of thousands and patronizing individuals and private companies, financially. It was an open secret that some frontmen of influential energy sector businessmen and politicians were placed in management positions, for the benefit of their benefactors. The era of unchecked corruption, mismanagement, and circular debt had arrived. Most people in the supposed 'land of the pure' do not consider electricity theft as a crime or a sin much like businessmen and wealthy 'patriots' who shy away from paying taxes. A very prominent politician from a religious party once publicly announced that the charge of stealing electricity cannot be laid on power thieves because only an item that was visible could be 'pilfered' and clearly no one had seen electricity. Someone should have asked him to place his finger in a high voltage socket to check if there was any electricity.

The rulers in the country have devised ingenious means of accommodating thefts. One such bizarre drama was enacted by influential players just before WAPDA was bifurcated in seeking bids for operating Rental Power Projects. A foreign company, having quoted the lowest tariff, was approved for establishing a rental power plant but in an effort to reduce the rent further, WAPDA officials got the lowest bidder to lower the tariff even further, which he agreed to do. An influential investor from Lahore, who was the losing bidder, then decided to scuttle the project completely by complaining that he too should have been asked to similarly negotiate a lowering of rent. This, of course, was against the rules and he was not allowed to do so which led to quite a ruckus. After his efforts to buy off the concerned officials failed, he initiated a mudslinging campaign to achieve his ends, and much to his later regret, succeeded in having his way. This happened, because by then PEPCO had been bifurcated from WAPDA as a fully independent entity; almost the first decision the new management took was to cancel the previous bids and call for fresh tenders. This time, the favoured businessman won the bid but the process was cancelled later by the Supreme Court on grounds of lack of transparency.

The new PEPCO, with the support of the Private Power and Infrastructure Board (PPIB), an entity under the Ministry of Water and Power, then decided to add increased thermal power capacity. In 2008, bids were called for yet more Rental Power plants, Independent Power plants, and two new Thermal Power projects in the public sector. The combined capacity of these was over three thousand megawatts to add to the existing seven thousand megawatts, in the private capacity. This policy was ill-conceived as the issue those days was not that of deficient installed capacity but of reducing line losses and improving bill recoveries. The new programme was unprofessionally but deliberately designed by PPIB, which was favoured in high power corridors. There was no objective criteria for comparing the cost and the output of the proposed plants and different bidders were allowed. It was clear that the rates were very high and had to be reduced, and in my capacity as Chairman, WAPDA, I protested against these high tariffs. I was vehemently opposed by the Managing Director, PPIB on grounds that no negotiations were possible under the rules. However, Salman Farooqi, then Deputy Chairman of the Planning Commission agreed with me that the rates were indeed very high and to have these reduced to bring them closer to the lower rates that the un-bifurcated WAPDA had secured six months earlier. Unbelievable as it may sound, a senior official of PPIB, actually whispered to the bidders not to agree to any reduction in the rates.

A year earlier, the process for establishing two thermal power plants in the public sector were started by the federal government. Midway through the project it was decided that the plant at Chichoki Mallian would not be established by WAPDA but it would be transferred to the Government of Qatar so that foreign investment could be encouraged. This was done by General Musharraf and Prime Minister Shaukat Aziz to improve relations with Qatar, which were at a historic low because of the coup that had ousted Nawaz Sharif. The Qataris also gifted an Airbus commercial plane, reportedly valued at US$60 million, to Pakistan. The transfer of Chichoki Malian was a grievous mistake as the cost of the plant negotiated by the undivided WAPDA with a French firm was nearly US$150 million less than the price which Qatar later finalized. Something appeared to be cooking. Unfortunately, for reasons unknown, Qatar then walked away from the deal, causing a massive loss to Pakistan as the costs by then had risen steeply.

The other thermal plant at Nandipur also stalled for different reasons. Of all conceivable reasons for projects to be delayed in Pakistan, a new one was added. The government refused to provide the legal opinion for a project effectively killing it for years and it was left to the Supreme Court to take notice of the lapse. NEPRA, the national electric power regulator, had put on record, in one of its determinations, that during the tenure of the Pakistan Peoples Party government, the Law and Justice ministry was responsible for delaying the project for two years during which period, the project cost increased by about 160 per cent, from US$329 million to US$574 million. The people of Pakistan need to ask why they should end up paying the extra billions. Incompetence and corruption reigned supreme, during those times.

The performance of PEPCO and the power sector entities established after the bifurcation of WAPDA, continued to deteriorate. Over five years, there were five ministers, six secretaries, and seven management directors of the company and the downhill trend continued. The fact that there was a gap of up to Rs. 4 per unit between the power sector regulator's determined tariff and the one actually charged, added to the total losses which reached a figure of nearly Rs. 500 billion, annually. This was the infamous circular debt for which a matching subsidy was repeatedly being paid by the Government. This amount was almost equal to the Army's budget at that time . The resolution of circular debt and reduction of losses were very serious issues, capable of crashing the budget and with it, the country's economy. The payable circular debt was cleared by the finance ministry a number of times through procuring loans from banks but it would re-emerge because the underlying losses, pilferages, and receivables issues were not resolved. The problem of electricity shortage can be resolved but only through better professional management, leading to the privatizing or leasing of the power distribution and thermal power generating units. Until that is done, competent, honest, and innovative officers are required to be selected from the private or public sectors. Today, most of the top management of the PEPCO, DISCOs, and GENCOs owe their positions to different patrons. One chief executive officer in a Punjab DISCO, soon after bifurcation, reportedly paid Rs. 180 million to a top politician to be allowed to stay on for another year. Another reportedly reimbursed the Rs. 10 million, lost in gambling by the son of a minister, in return for his new position. Virtually, every official from the chief engineer down to the superintendent, the meter reader and the linesman received and paid gratification money. Non-payment of bribes resulted in immediate transfers out of 'lucrative' positions. The contracts at the National Transmission and Despatch Company and the routine operation and maintenance works in GENCOs or thermal power generating companies were often given for monetary considerations as well. Even installation of authorized electricity meters meant paying under the table costs by the consumers and this was apart from the licensed fees applicable. Fresh tube well connections were first banned following which the minister granted hundreds of 'rule relaxations' for a cost which was pocketed by the kin or major political supporters of different ministers, assembly members and party activists. Connections for factories, hotels, commercial businesses, or shopping plazas fetched money in six and seven figures. It was said, during this period, there were only five honest officials amongst the 100,000 people working in the Distribution companies. The integrity levels of officials in the National Transmission and Dispatch Company, responsible for power transmission and GENCO, the public sector thermal generating units, remained just as low. The few competent professionals in the PPIB, like N. A. Zuberi, were the only ones to suffer.

The introduction of independent power plants and the rental power plants, added further opportunities for corruption. A senior official in the PPIB once unabashedly 'enquired' from the sponsor of a new power project about the size of his proposed plant. When told that it was a hundred megawatts, the official reminded the investor that it was less because one megawatt belonged to him while the sponsor had the balance of ninety nine megawatts. The one megawatt 'gift' cost about a million dollars. The concerned technical staff at National Transmission and Dispatch Company and their related entities had also developed ingenious ways of extracting money. The heat rate of the plant, the thermal efficiency ratios, the continuous running of generators before commercial operation, the plant factor permissible, the exemptions from load shedding, and many other issues were 'adjusted' by the officials for a cost. This 'adjustment' was developed into a fine art which left no fingerprints. The payables to the independent power producers and rental power producers for the power supplied could be expedited and reprioritized also for a price. A federal secretary was prematurely transferred, when he refused to oblige the Minister of Water and Power, who demanded that he pay the entire money provided by the Finance Division for a certain period, to the minister's favourite private sector plant. During this period, a particularly demanding political party leader with a few seats in Parliament, was won over politically by getting his nominee appointed to a top position. This done, he asked for nothing more, at least for a while. Honest and effective management and being free of political influence could have reformed the situation but where the intensions were crooked, nothing could be done.

Very rarely were honest and effective CEOs appointed. In Sindh, during this period, an honourable officer, Sheikh Nazir, was appointed only to be removed within a few months on the collective demand of all political parties. He would not tolerate undue *'sifarish'* or the illegal intercession by the politicians. It was alarming to see some very corrupt and incompetent ministers appointed to the Ministry of Water and Power by the Pakistan Peoples Party government, following their victory in 2008. There was minimal interest in the job but the purpose seemed to be to amass fortunes and they achieved great success in doing so. Despite the fact that all were aware that the power sector was by far the most sensitive ministry, the Government handed the charge to the most incompetent ministers with dubious reputations. There was, a method to the madness although. Every decision had a price and there was no other care in the world. A better arrangement would have been to create a Holding Company, as a parent company in Islamabad, with effective supervisory and executive powers over the DISCOs till these were privatised. The contrived arrangements were not sustainable and how could they be, when the daily losses rose to more than one billion rupees. President Zardari was perhaps right when he admitted that the power sector was mainly responsible for their loss of the elections in 2013.

Why incompetent and corrupt, ministers with poor reputations were appointed in the Ministry of Water and Power which defies imagination. Their interests were confined to lining their pockets rather than in improving the water and power sectors. More competent persons with integrity could have made a difference. Corruption, technical and line losses, pilferage, and low revenue collection continued to plague the power sector, costing the country untold losses. By way of contrast, the water sector, by and large, performed better as most of the senior officials were known for their competence and honesty. It was rare for an official of the level of a member or the chairman to be involved in corrupt or improper practices. There were exceptions. However, once a member (Water) from WAPDA, mentioned almost in a whisper, that the Minister of Water and Power wanted 'commission money'. This is the 'cut' which corrupt engineers and others are known to charge the projects' contractors. I was aghast at hearing this and told the officer that this was most shameful and that it should be avoided but if someone still wished to blacken his face, *mu kala karna*, he alone would be responsible. It was sad that a politician earned the sobriquet of *Raja Rental*, relating to his alleged role in the rental power contract award. The conduct of some senior officials, was just as odious!

ii. WAPDA's Water Vision 2020

In the water sector, after a twenty-year slumber, WAPDA finally woke up in 2002 by unveiling the Vision 2020, which consisted of many useful projects but by then precious time had been lost. Under instructions of President Musharraf, the Chairman WAPDA, General Zulfiqar, who was appointed four years earlier, planned a slew of water storage and hydel power projects. Three large irrigation projects for the provinces were started. The first was the Kachhi Canal off taking from River Indus at Taunsa Barrage meant to irrigate nearly 700,000 acres in the Dera Bugti, Bolan, and Naseerabad districts in Balochistan. The next was the Rainee Canal, meant for irrigating Ghotki District and the left bank area of Sindh, while the Greater Thall Canal was to provide water for Bhakkar and Thall in the Punjab. Since General Musharraf and Prime Minister Shaukat Aziz were enthusiastic supporters of these three canals, sizable budgetary allotments were provided during their tenure. Unfortunately, after their departure, the budgetary allocations were reduced appreciably with the result that these strategic projects were considerably delayed. Although, the Greater Thall Canal was made operational by 2010, the other two canals, Kachhi and Rainee, took years to construct owing mainly to inadequate budget allocations. Failure to provide adequate financing for the Kachhi Canal by the Pakistan Peoples Party government, coupled with the local security issues, deprived the Baloch people of the resources that would lift them out of poverty. Kachhi Canal was completed in 2016. The irrigation canal for Khyber Pakhtunkhwa province called the Chashma Right Bank Lift Canal could not be started as the annual operational and maintenance cost per acre after completion was calculated at nearly Rs. 6,000 per acre. This was a huge sum of money in a country where farmers refuse to pay Rs. 500 as *abiana* or water charges per acre. Until more water storages are constructed, the Khyber Pakhtunkhwa, Sindh, and Balochistan provinces will remain deprived of their water needs.

During this period, WAPDA started work on six medium-sized hydro power projects at Sadpara in Skardu Baltistan, Khan Khwar, Alai Khwar, Dubair Khwar, Gomal Zam, and Jinnah on the existing Kalabagh Barrage for a total generation of nearly 500 MW. These were largely completed by 2012 and although this capacity was modest compared to over 6,500 megawatts of hydel power already installed yet it signified a new determination for action. All these projects however, were delayed for a variety of reasons the most important being that WAPDA, under orders from the top, started work without first conducting detailed engineering studies of these projects. This was uncalled for and led to major cost increase. Further stoppage of works due to floods, earthquakes, civil strife, judicial intervention, and of course, shortage of resources all contributed to the delays. In some of the projects in the Swat and Kohistan region all Chinese workers were once evacuated on account of the civil disturbances emerging from the operations against the militants. There were security issues in Gomal Zam Dam in South Waziristan Agency also as two Chinese personnel were kidnapped, one of whom lost his life in the rescue operation. Work was resumed a year later with the deployment of a Wing of the Frontier Corps and at four times the original cost of the project. Human life is precious and security had to be ensured, especially for all the Chinese who came from a one-child family.

During the next five years, WAPDA rebuilt the small Jaban hydro power project in Malakand Agency. This project was first commissioned by the dynamic British engineers in 1935 and some of its components, like the mechanical trolley, is still functioning today. After the departure of the Shaukat Aziz government, financing for this project totally dried up but fortunately the French Development Agency offered to pay for it. They also generously provided financing for the undertaking the engineering design of the 840 Megawatt Munda-Mohmand Hydel power project on the Swat River and assisted in establishing the Mangla Hydel Power Training Institute, besides a few other smaller dams in Gilgit-Baltistan. Such was the state of the apathy in the Pakistani bureaucracy that for years no ministry had accepted the offer of the French Development Agency for funding the approved projects even though their money was available. The best the government did was to present a wish-list of proposals which were neither feasible nor approved. This void was happily filled later by WAPDA as the government of France not only provided the desperately needed funds for projects but they also awarded me the French Order of Merit (Commander Class), merely for facilitating the receipt of official funds to WAPDA. *Ham khurma ham sawaab* or the proverb that eating dates is a divine blessing, besides being nutritious.

During his rule, President Musharraf was determined that as many new projects as possible be started in doubly quick time. The work on a number of these projects was started. During the period 2008–10, two large hydro power projects that were unfortunately awarded to the private sector during General Musharraf's tenure six years earlier, were transferred back to WAPDA, on account of the failure of the private sector to construct these. The 1,450 megawatt Tarbela Four Project, with an internal rate of return of over 30 per cent, was handed back at WAPDA's insistence, thanks to the efforts of the interim Minister of Water and Power, Tariq Hameed. Soon afterwards, the World Bank committed over US$850 million to undertake the work as it was an excellent investment, paying for itself within four years. Then the 840 megawatt Munda-Mohmand Dam on Swat River, which was basically a flood-control project, was also recovered from private entrepreneurs from Lahore who had wasted six years without any development. By not developing this dam, the country annually lost Rs. 20 billion in lost power generation. This recovery of the project from the private sector was made possible through the efforts of Raja Pervez Ashraf, the Minister of Water and Power and the former Chief Justice of Pakistan, Iftikhar Muhammad Chaudhry. The delayed completion of the two projects combined, cost the economy of the country nearly Rs. 50 billion annually in lost power generation alone. For WAPDA, the return of these two projects was truly a crowning achievement. Who would not feel proud of adding Rs. 50 billion to the state's exchequer every year? Tarbela Four project has since been completed but not before the country lost approximately Rs. 100 billion in 2018–19 due to serious infrastructural damages, delays and non-accrual of benefits caused by its unnecessary premature inauguration. The enquiry ordered by Prime Minister Imran Khan revealed that the inauguration was done in March 2018 when the waters in the reservoir were at dead level only to please the previous political leadership. The construction work on the other project, Munda-Mohmand Dam began in 2019 after it was recovered from the private sector sponsors of Lahore. The people of Pakistan would have been poorer by many billions of rupees annually were the private sector allowed to gain the Munda-Mohmand Dam!

It has been rightly said that sins of omission cost the society much more than sins of commission. In 2010, the Punjab government's deliberate omission did just that. For years it has been trying to develop the Taunsa Barrage low-head hydel power project but only on terms that the provincial bureaucrats wanted. International competitive bids were duly called by the officials of the Irrigation and Power Department but with the intent, it so appeared, to award the contract to a particular Chinese company. The bid of a reputable Korean company was not considered although they were ranked first by the technical staff and when their representative visited and enquired into the matter he was told that their documents were not responsive and that they were already informed of the rejection. The Korean asked for a copy of the communication allegedly sent to their company, any receipt, any email copy, or even a telephone number but none was shown by the department. The officers were caught cheating! These facts were brought to the notice of the Chief Secretary Punjab. The Chinese company was awarded the work but they, true to form, balked at the project a few years later as their demand to alter it to their advantage for certain financial terms could not be accepted. Years later, the work had not even started.

There was one project where WAPDA's request for undertaking the work itself was consistently overruled by three highly placed individuals in the government. This was the 1,100 megawatt Kohala Hydel Power Project whose detailed feasibility and design was developed by WAPDA and financing was being arranged. Without inviting competitive bids, the project was handed to a Chinese company by the Ministry of Water and Power against all Public Procurement Regulatory Authority's rules and despite the consistent opposition of the Chairman of WAPDA. This company's intentions were always suspect. Unfortunately, eight years on, the Chinese company had still not started the project work causing Pakistan serious losses totaling billions of dollars. Meanwhile the people of Azad Kashmir started a protest movement because of valid fears that their water supplies and environment would be adversely affected by the construction of this project. Who would be held accountable for this loss? Failure to seek competitive bids under law was the prime reason for this glaring act of corruption. Investments in future should be carefully evaluated by the donor and the recipient. In 2020, the newly established China Pakistan Economic Corridor (CPEC) Authority has taken over the construction of Kohala Hydro Power project under its wing jointly with the Chinese company and as such there is hope that the project would be implemented smoothly.

There was an interesting development in the case of the Satpara Dam near Skardu in Gilgit-Baltistan for which funds were sought from USAID as the government's budgetary allocations had almost ceased. After the Pakistan Peoples Party government assumed power, it had its own priorities and the water sector did not figure very prominently in it. USAID committed the funds but just as the amount was being released they received a complaint of sink holes being formed in the dam basin from a private person. The United States Congressman who received the complaint was understandably concerned and he ensured that the funds were not released until an impartial investigation was conducted. WAPDA's concern was even greater and two of its top experts, Dr Izhar Ahmed and Khaliq Khan, were directed to study the problems mentioned prior to the American experts examining the problems. These two experts opined that the two small sink holes would not impact the dam and would be naturally filled in a short period. WAPDA actually encouraged the inspection by the American experts who on arrival at the site, fully endorsed the report of WAPDA engineers. The withheld amounts were released and the project was completed, adding not only electric power but more importantly, increased WAPDA's credibility as well. This dam would be beneficial for the people of Skardu as the Skardu plains produce non-seasonal potatoes, vegetables, and fruits which is much sought in the rest of the country. Fortunately, for environmental reasons, WAPDA did not allow the lone stream in the Deosai plateau to be drained into Satpara Dam. Thus the wilderness of Deosai would survive!

During the tenures of the Pakistan Peoples Party's, it was sad to see the low priority accorded to the water sector projects. Their priority was always highways, underpasses, and ring roads mostly in their constituencies. In a meeting with the top office holder when it was pointed out that enough allocations were not being provided for the Mangla Dam Raising project, Neelum-Jhelum project, and the Kachhi Canal, he in an off-guarded comment, stated that these were not his priorities as these were 'started before his Government assumed power'. His priorities lay in building smaller but expensive irrigation dams at the cost of the allocations to the larger projects under construction. The initial cost estimate of the Nai Gaaj Dam and irrigation Project in Sindh was nearly Rs. 59 billion (later reduced by WAPDA to Rs. 26 billion) almost equal to the Kurramm Tangi Dam in Waziristan although the latter would generate 84 megawatts of electric power apart from irrigating three times the land as the former. This is the bane of all Pakistani political parties who in power re-order priorities to suit their political preferences and there is no National Development Consensus.

After the 2008 elections, the new government tried to create an association called the 'Friends of Democratic Pakistan' under the impression that a 'democratic dividend' of nearly a US$100 billion would be provided to Pakistan for an unexplained quid pro quo. In the event, the imagined bonanza turned out to be an empty wish and a spectacular failure. Then a visionary idea of conserving water through the use of high efficiency irrigation practices of drip and sprinkler irrigation was considered. The idea was sound but not at the cost of developing larger water reservoir and power projects like Neelum-Jhelum, and Diamer Basha Dams. Unfortunately, there was not enough money available for both ideas!

Soon after Prime Minister Shaukat Aziz left, work on almost all the projects under construction by WAPDA slowed due to the reduction in the budgetary allocation to a fourth of what had been provided earlier. Were it not for Shaukat Aziz none of WAPDA's ten water and power projects would have been completed. With the arrival of the new finance minister, all allocations for hydro power and water sector projects were further reduced to a trickle. In vain, I requested three finance secretaries, in succession, to provide finances for such strategically important projects.

Then two miracles occurred. Firstly, on the request of the Chairman, WAPDA, General Ashfaq Parvez Kayani, the Army Chief, used his influence to get the crucial funds released to complete the Mangla Dam Raising Project. This was fortuitous as the completion of the project generated an additional Rs. 18 billion worth of water and power annually. Secondly, USAID stepped in to fill in the deficiency in finances. This was made possible due to the persistent efforts of Secretary of State, Hillary

Clinton and the dynamic, Richard Holbrooke. Immediate disbursal of
funds came about because of the effort and dedication of a number of
American officials working in the economic and development section of
the Embassy and USAID, led by the redoubtable Robin Rafael and later by
Richard Albright. Financing was quickly provided for the Satpara Dam in
Skardu, the Gomal Zam Dam in South Waziristan, the Kurram Tangi Dam
in North Waziristan, and later promised for the Diamer Basha Dam on
the River Indus. The money was carefully invested in projects to yield the
optimum results and in the case of repairs to a generator in Tarbela, nearly
a hundred megawatts were added at a cost of just US$17 million. USAID
provided free grants but other donors gave loans which have to be repaid.
Many of these loans to Pakistan, over the years, were often squandered in
content-light but jargon-heavy activities in the name of capacity building,
gender sensitization, stakeholder congregation, sustainability processes,
and the like. Then there were the consultants, especially from the social
sectors, most of whom could easily be dispensed with. One consultant
sent by the European Union for drug rehabilitation in the 1990s ended up
spending a third of the total loan of US$6 million on her salary, expenses,
and travels. Fortunately, there were also some very dedicated consultants
available as well. One of them was the ever considerate energy specialist,
Charlie Mosley. In the water sector, WAPDA could never have completed
its projects, were it not for the endeavours of professionals like Charlie
Mosley, Marybeth Goodman, Rosario Chato Calderon, Vinay Chawla,
Roger Garner, and Mian Shahid who worked with complete devotion. A
special mention is also due to Maria Otero, Assistant Under Secretary, and
Tom Nides, Deputy Secretary of State, for their support in the development
of the country's water and power resources.

iii. The Neelum-Jhelum Development Model

It has increasingly been noticed that big projects with the desired economic
impact on the economy are not being undertaken because of political
controversy, weak leadership, fears of accountability or limited technical and
administrative capacity available. Today there are just too many constraints
of different kinds in initiating large hydroelectric projects in the country.
The only way forward is to develop a political and administrative lobby

for a feasible project and start work confidently with one step at a time. An important focal person with a strong lobby is required to develop any big project. If one tries to take too big a step without the requisite lobbying effort, as happened in the case of the proposed Kalabagh and Akhori Dams, the chances of success are remote. The Neelum-Jhelum model was initiated by WAPDA without a complete finance plan because India had started building the competing Kishenganga hydro-electric project. The project was started with small amount of funds available to ensure early completion and to avoid cost escalation. The detailed design and engineering of the 969 megawatt Neelum-Jhelum was completed by 1998, yet it took WAPDA and the Planning Commission another four years to approve the project for construction. Only after the approval of the Planning Commission and the Executive Committee of the National Economic Council (ECNEC) was the project cleared for construction. By 2007, the only amount available with WAPDA was Rs. 5 billion as seed money provided in the federal government's budget, and work was started with this nominal amount. In the meantime, five years were lost which allowed the Indians to move ahead on the Kishenganga hydel project upstream on the same Neelum River in Occupied Kashmir. Those responsible in the Planning Commission and the Water and Power Ministry during that period need to answer for the delay. Had the project been started five years earlier, which was possible, this project would have been completed ahead of the Kishenganga Dam and Pakistan would not have been deprived of the extra waters in the winter months.

To raise part of the funds, a novel idea was initiated, by involving the electricity consumers to contribute in financing this project. This required the approval of the cabinet for a 10 paisa, one tenth of a cent, surcharge per electricity unit on all power billings. In 2007, the cabinet approved the proposal which could generate about Rs. 60 billion for the project, after a presentation was made by the Chairman WAPDA. WAPDA owes gratitude to the support provided by the interim Prime Minister Mohammad Mian Soomro for the new measure while personal lobbying with some of his ministers did the rest. The balance of the financing from foreign donors and international bank loans came much later when the work was in full swing. Had WAPDA waited to fully arrange US$3 billion for the 'financial close' before commencing work, as the Planning Commission and the

352   FRONTIER STATIONS

Finance Ministry were advocating, it would still not have started six years later. By then, costs would have doubled again. This was in essence the 'Neelum-Jhelum model' of expediting project construction and it worked amazingly well.

Starting work on approved projects, with whatever finances were available in order to complete the project quickly so that benefits start accruing, is the only way out. The same process was started in 2010 with the Diamer Basha Dam project when land acquisition and construction of project offices were begun with meager available funds. Even though the federal finance ministry was loath to provide sufficient funding for the Neelum-Jhelum Project to WAPDA, the initiative ensured that work was ongoing inspite of lack of money. Finances were temporarily transferred from other projects where construction was slow and loans obtained at interest from some WAPDA entities. One WAPDA official, the country will always be obliged to, is Mumtaz Rizvi, the Chairman of the Federal Board of Revenue, who allowed WAPDA to defer the payment of billions of rupees in custom duties payable just when the financial crunch was at its worst. His foresight contributed billions of rupees to the country.

The actual construction work on the Neelum-Jhelum Hydro Power Project in Azad Jammu Kashmir, with a capacity of 969 megawatts, was started in 2008. This project draws water from the Neelum River which is called Kishanganga River in Indian Occupied Kashmir and on which Indians were developing their own run-of-the-river hydropower project with a capacity of 330 megawatts. Pakistan disputed the Kishanganga project at International Court of Arbitration in the Hague as it would divert part of the water away from the natural flows in the Neelum River. As usual, the water bureaucrats failed the nation because what should have been done in 2002 was initiated as late as 2010. The final award was announced in 2013 which allowed Pakistan the use of half of the total water flows in the Kishanganga River, during the four dry winter months. This was a small victory for Pakistan since India had been determined to use the entire winter flows of water during these dry months. The Court also accepted Pakistan's legal right to challenge India's diversion of the river at the International Tribunal and disallowed India from any manipulation in the reservoir that would be to Pakistan's disadvantage. It may be mentioned in the passing, that the decision to seek International Arbitration was taken, very unexpectedly and almost casually, in a routine Senate Committee meeting in 2010 by Senators Professor Khurshid, Lashkar Raisani, Nisar Khan, and others. Surprisingly, the experts and concerned officials were not keen on approaching The Hague route early but were compelled by the Senators to do so. Sadly, the physical work was started very late and even then the required financing was not available.

The Planning Commission and the Ministries of Water and Power and Finance were responsible for wasting many years even though during this period, those heading these were well-known names. What they lacked was initiative and courage which remains the bane of Pakistani decision makers. Funds normally are not a major constraint but closed mind-sets are. In another country, a project of such high national priority would have been allocated funds to the exclusion of everything else. This was not to be. The then Deputy Chairman of the Planning Commission would openly say that he would approve the project only after WAPDA arranged the financing. Regretfully, he should have known that it was for the Government of Pakistan to arrange the financing and not for WAPDA to do so.

By September 2007, the China Gezhouba Group Corporation was selected as the contractor for the project as the French Company, did not bid. For some projects, difficulties never end and Neelum-Jhelum was one of these. The Norwegian-led consultants then decided to pull out of Pakistan for security and other concerns and fresh bids were thereafter called. It was encouraging to find another Norwegian company, Norconsult, team up with Montgomery Harza Watson, to make a bid for the consultancy engineering which was found acceptable. This done, it was the turn of the contractors, the China Gezhouba Group, to attempt a retreat for flimsy reasons of their own. They cited the adverse security conditions of the region for wishing to pull out as if they had never known that before; in fact, the main reason was that their bid price was too low. They were clearly told that their security bid amounting to Rs. 2 billion would be forfeited and the company blacklisted if they did not start work immediately. The message was read loud and clear and only then did they agree to mobilize at site. Funding for the project remained the critical issue as the 'seed money' of Rs. 5 billion provided by Planning Commission was soon exhausted. The proposed 10 paisa per electricity unit charged from the consumers, provided limited relief as earlier the Cabinet of Prime

Minister Shaukat Aziz had twice rejected the surcharge for fear of raising the electricity tariff just ahead of the elections.

The problems for the Neelum-Jhelum project still did not end. It took the government of Azad Kashmir over three years to provide the land, even though the land acquisition cost was paid to them very early. There was also a constant shortfall in electricity, provided to the contractor for operating the drilling machines owing to poor voltage and reduced supply which further delayed the project. The contractor also caused a delay of some years by not positioning the five drilling jumbo units. Then there was always a shortage of technical staff. It was once reported that after a Chinese foreman had left, the contractor replaced him with the company's cook! Hardly believable but then facts can be stranger than fiction. There were many other delays and at one stage the project was over two years behind schedule. Constant quarrelling between the South African Project Manager from the consultant's side and the Chinese contractors did not help matters. Design documents were always delayed while the contractor could not recruit the required number of trained technicians. To add to this, was the security threat to foreigners especially to the Chinese after 9/11. At one stage, there were almost three security personnel deployed for every foreigner working in WAPDA's projects. In hindsight, it should be noted, that large works, particularly in the hydropower sector, should always be awarded, after bidding of course, to the most credible contractor and not to the lowest bidder. Selecting the lowest bidder often cost more in delayed completion and late accrual of benefits. One year's delay in completion would deny the country 5 billion units of electricity valued at Rs. 60 billion or almost half a billion dollars. Tarbela Dam works were not awarded to the lowest bidder but to the best construction company, incidentally.

Meanwhile, the operation of Murphy's Law for the project continued without interruption and a host of problems were encountered. Five years later for one reason or another, the loan promised by Chinese Exim Bank of US$448 million for Neelum-Jhelum equipment to be bought in China did not materialize. This was despite the fact that the President of Peoples' Republic of China, committed to the loan in the presence of President Zardari at a formal banquet in the Great Peoples' Hall in 2010. For the future, it is important to note that paperwork for foreign loans should be finalized before the project contracts are signed, since verbal commitments are clearly insufficient. The Chinese Exim Bank had balked, reportedly, because two of their projects, the Safe City Project in Islamabad and Jaglot-Skardu Road had been cancelled because these were contracted to Chinese companies without adhering to public sector procurement rules. It is important that all laws are complied with and foreign companies informed clearly about these. Meanwhile, Abu Dhabi Development Fund's loan of US$100 million was also not disbursed because the Government of Pakistan had not fully delivered on their Etisalat telecommunication company's purchase of Pakistan Telecommunication earlier.

Just when WAPDA thought that no more problems could dog the Neelum-Jhelum project, the project consultants informed WAPDA that all concrete and steel structures such as the fifty-six kilometer tunnels, power house, the dam, the stilling base, and the desander would need to be substantially strengthened. This was necessitated in view of the fact that the huge earthquake of 2005 revealed that a fault line ran right under the project and there were serious risks involved. The consultant also brought about other changes, including the river crossing structure which greatly added to the cost. So not only were two years lost but the cost had also doubled because of basic structural changes in the design, the depreciation of the Pakistani rupee from sixty to nearly a hundred per dollar, and the rise in interest charges.

To recover the time lost, the possibility of purchasing tunnel boring machines was raised. There was initial scepticism but after sustained analysis spread over some months, agreement was reached among the consultants, the China Gezhouba Group, the contractor, the Panel of Experts, and WAPDA that operating two tunnel boring machines would complete the project twelve to eighteen months earlier. The earlier generation of over five billion units per year was valued at nearly Rs. 60 billion per year or six times the basic cost of the tunnel boring machines. When the Planning Commission and the Ministry of Water and Power were approached for advice and orders on employment of these machines, they developed cold feet and directed that WAPDA alone must take the decision. The decision to replace the drill and blast jumbo machines by modern tunnel boring machines was certainly one of the most momentous decisions I have ever taken in my career. When the senior policy-makers in Islamabad shied away from taking a decision, someone had to take the decision and the buck stopped with the Chairman, WAPDA and the Neelum-Jhelum Board of Directors. A German company, Herrenknecht AG, was selected to supply the tunnel boring machines after competitive bidding under the law, over an American company, which saved WAPDA nearly US$37 million. By 2017, both tunnels were successfully bored.

It must be recorded, with regret, that for years afterwards four enquiries and investigations were held to probe the procurement of the equipment. Most Pakistanis cannot imagine that equipment worth Rs. 10 billion could be purchased by public servants without lining their pockets. Fortunately, there were some considerate gentlemen in the investigating agencies who ensured that objectivity and fairness was followed so that there was no witch-hunting of bureaucrats. With most politicians, however, one could not be too sure! There is little doubt that the bold decision to deploy the tunnel boring machine was risky because tunnel boring operations could have gone awry, but then only audacious decisions, as Clausewitz said, ensure victory inspite of the accompanying risks. Years later, with the benefit of hindsight, I am not sure if I would ever take any bold decision again, if I were in a similar position. Not taking this momentous decision could have resulted in Pakistan being permanently denied water by India, apart from the exchequer losing over fifty billion rupees through delayed completion of the tunnels. Strange are the happenings in the 'land of the pure' where decisive decision-making is discouraged!

With the myriad problems financing resolved, it was decided to appoint Lieutenant General Zubair, originally from the Army's Engineering Corps, a dynamic individual with the required expertise and experience as the Project's CEO. He brought the necessary initiative and drive to the project construction, especially the works related to the tunnel boring machines and the river crossing effort. The boring of tunnels and civil construction in the fragile mountain conditions would always be challenging and risky, but then without taking risks any herculean endeavour is not possible.

The Neelum-Jhelum Model may well be cited as a convenient way out of a seemingly intractable situation. Where the project is of supreme national importance, it should be initiated boldly and without loss of time even if financial, technical, and administrative problems remain. The main requirement should be to ensure that the project had been approved by the competent fora of the government and that it was feasible in engineering, technical, and financial terms. Over time, any hindrances remaining, are always resolved. Eight years later when the project was nearly three-fourths complete, the finance ministry had still not approved the financing plan of the project. Not taking this momentous decision could have resulted in Pakistan being permanently denied water by India, apart from the exchequer losing over Rs. 60 billion annually through the delayed completion of the tunnels.

iv. Diamer Basha: To Dam or Not

What WAPDA now needs most is to develop the feasibility and engineering studies of as many large and medium-sized storage and hydel power projects as possible. In 2002, when it became clear that the Kalabagh Dam did not have enough political support, WAPDA did not have the design and engineering studies of any large project in hand. It took WAPDA six years to develop the detailed drawings and related documents for Diamer Basha Dam.

Following the country's failure to build the Kalabagh Dam forty years after it was first mooted, because of some opposition, WAPDA should have started to plan the construction of the Diamer Basha Dam, as the first water storage to be built after the completion of Tarbela Dam, in 1978. This project would store 8 million acre-feet in gross storage and have a power generation of 4500 megawatts. Fortunately, a national consensus exists on the development of the project. In 2010, the Council of Common Interests headed by Prime Minister Yousaf Raza Gillani with all four chief ministers present, unanimously approved the project. Were it not for the Pakistan Peoples Party government and the personal interest shown by Prime Minister Gillani, the reluctance of one province could have blocked the project early on. Gillani may have been a controversial premier but he ensured the unanimous approval for the construction of the Diamer Basha Dam. When the Sindh chief minister requested for more time to evaluate the project, Prime Minister Yousaf Raza Gillani agreed to the suggestion. In a light-hearted comment, he then allowed him an extra sixty minutes to evaluate!

It took WAPDA nearly six years to fully develop the design and engineering studies of Diamer Basha Dam through the German consulting house, Lahmeyer. In 2012, immediately after my tenure ended, the new Chairman of WAPDA decided to support the World Bank contention to build the run-of-the-river Dasu Dam before Diamer Basha. The opposition to Diamer Basha was unfortunate but such events are common in our country. The World Bank, especially the Vice President who was a former Country Head of the Bank in India, vociferously opposed Diamer Basha Dam. This was probably prompted by behind the scene pressure of India, as it deemed Gilgit-Baltistan region a disputed territory. This led to wasting over eight years during which period the cost rose by over US$6 billion. The Asian Development Bank was of the view that by itself, it would not be able to finance the huge project. The World Bank may have thought that if it cannot be a major partner on a large water sector project in Pakistan, it would be better to keep it on the drawing board. Constructing the Dasu Dam, without the availability of the Diamer Basha reservoir of nearly 8 million acre-feet, meant that Dasu would generate electricity at less than half its capacity. Clearly, the altered sequencing for the construction of the two dams would deprive the country of the much needed water storage. If alternate financing for the construction of the Diamer Basha Dam cannot be arranged simultaneously, those responsible would be held to account by posterity for the damage caused. This would be a lasting regret for the people of Pakistan.

The Government would find it very difficult to simultaneously start construction of both Dasu Dam (first phase) at US$6 billion and the Diamer Basha Dam at US$14 billion. The only practical course for the present, consists in earmarking US$ One billion annually (Rs. 150 billion) from the Public Sector Development Programme for the civil works. The electro-mechanical equipment could then be arranged through suppliers' credit and care needs to be taken to procure the best equipment from Western sources so that the quality and operational efficiency are never compromised. The private sector should be kept out of this project because of the easy availability of foreign loans.

If the construction of the Diamer Basha Dam is delayed for whatever reasons, the economy of the country will lose over six billion dollars annually because of the inability to generate nineteen billion units of electric power and store 6 million acre-feet of usable water. Moreover, US$2 billion worth of foreign exchange would be saved due to the reduced import of furnace oil and a host of downstream industries would be set up that would employ millions of people. Whenever the Diamer Basha Dam is finally built, the efforts made by General Musharraf, Prime Ministers Shaukat Aziz and Yousaf Raza Gillani, would always be remembered. Many in the government had other priorities. During the US-Pakistan Strategic Dialogue in Washington in 2010, the Pakistani Ministers for Foreign Affairs and Finance did not even mention the Diamer Basha Dam during their address in the conference, despite being requested a number of times by Chairman WAPDA. Actually, the Americans were more responsive to the water needs of Pakistan than the Pakistanis. Hillary Clinton, US Secretary of State supported 'Chairman Durrani's proposal for creating water storages' in her speech and also spoke of climate change benefits. Maria Oterro, the Under-Secretary of State, agreed to advocate Diamer Basha Dam, during the conference when our own Ministers remained silent. Later, it was the Deputy Secretary of State, Tom Nides who would regularly follow up developments on Diamer Basha Dam while Pakistani ministers and senior water sector officials focused on other matters. Tom Nides once stated that he was baffled when, during his meeting with President Zardari, the latter talked of minor subjects but not once 'did he look me in the eyes and demand the construction of the Diamer Basha Dam'. Who do we complain to?

In the past, Sindh objected to building the Kalabagh and Akhori storage dams and was supported by a few politicians from the Khyber Pakhtunkhwa Province, for no legitimate reason. Later, it appeared that the delay could be caused by insisting on building two large dams, simultaneously. Opposition to reservoirs from the people of Sindh is easily explained as they say quite openly, though unfairly, that they do not trust Punjab with the storage of waters. There is an additional reason as well. If there are no reservoirs in the north all the summer flood waters flow down inundating the state-owned riverine areas called *katcha,* along the banks of the River Indus, totaling hundreds of thousands of acres. These state-lands are under adverse possession of influential landlords and *waderas,* most of whom are politicians, bureaucrats, or dacoits. They cultivate this free land with the free waters that flows down, generating billions of rupees in income, for themselves. For them to support water reservoirs in the north is like turkeys voting for an early Christmas!

Even though, there was little progress on arranging finances for the Diamer Basha Dam, land acquisition measures which were started in 2011, have resumed. The Asian Development Bank had laid a set of four 'safeguards' relating to the development of consensus amongst the provinces in favour of the dam, transparency in award of contracts, maintaining the environmental balance, and most importantly, guaranteeing the rights of the affected people of the project. These have been complied with, fully. The people dislocated by the project, numbering 6000 families, are to be resettled nearby with provision of services and facilities better than what they had, before the dam construction. More than half the land required was state property but the balance of approximately 18,500 acres was to be acquired through negotiations and not compulsorily under the Land Acquisition Act. Ultimately, this transaction was successfully negotiated by the ministerial committee, the Gilgit-Baltistan administration, and local stakeholders, at rates that were higher than those prevailing in the market. The dedicated efforts of the Federal Ministers Manzur Wattoo, Qamaruz Zaman Kaira, Raja Pervez Ashraf, and the Chief Minister of Gilgit-Baltistan, Syed Mehdi Shah, should never be forgotten in resolving the all complicated issues. After all, 'safeguards' were agreed with the donors who initiated the loan processing formalities. USAID provided an initial grant of US$20 million for the due diligence studies to authenticate the consultants' reports. By 2012, a dozen contracts were awarded by WAPDA from their budget for constructing offices, residences and infrastructure related to dam construction. A separate Special Purpose Vehicle, on the lines of Neelum Jhelum Project, was to be created to raise financing from all possible sources. For Diamer Basha Dam to become a reality, the firm and unequivocal support of the Government of the day would be essential. It was therefore quite surprising not to find a mention of Diamer Basha dam, in the CPEC list of infrastructure projects costing US$56 billion which were committed by China to Pakistan.

The story of the ground breaking ceremony of the Diamer Basha Dam in Chilas needs to be told as it was bizarre event, even by byzantine standards. President Zardari, apparently goaded by the those opposed to Prime Minister Gillani, decided to attend as the chief guest, even though the Prime Minister had announced more than once that he would unveil the plaque. This event became tricky verging on the embarrassing, as two top functionaries of the state were in a juvenile contest to perform the ground-breaking ceremony of Pakistan's largest project. President Zardari obviously had the last word and WAPDA had his name engraved on a new plaque, hurriedly prepared for the ceremony. The date was set and all arrangements finalized. The evening before the ceremony, it was learnt that the Intelligence agencies had warned about the likelihood of terrorism incident at the site which led to the cancellation of the President's visit but not that of the Prime Minister. So now there were three plaques: Gillani's, Zardari's, and Gillani's again, to cater to all eventualities!

This was strange and gave rise to many a rumour, on exactly why the President was not attending. One had thought what was sauce for the goose was also sauce for the gander, but that apparently was not the case. The President would not attend for security reasons but the Prime Minister would. Was this manipulation by someone unknown? No one knew. What was clear was that this singular honour was being denied to a controversial President while the Prime Minister was found to be more acceptable. He arrived at the appointed hour and the ceremony was conducted in a safe and secure environment to convey to the donors the importance being accorded to the project. WAPDA officials felt that Gillani's presence at the site, augured well for the inauguration of Diamer Basha Dam, as two smaller dams at Winder and Gabir, where the plaque was unveiled by the President remained incomplete. WAPDA at the time did not want that to happen to Diamer Basha Dam. A couple of years earlier, General Musharraf had also attended a ground-breaking ceremony for the same project but at a different site, when the location of the dam had not been finalized, the project was yet to be approved, and the provincial consensus had not been achieved. The moral of the story for Pakistan remains that form is more important than the substance!

The construction of dams and storages should be the foremost development priority for the country before Pakistan 'runs dry' as the water shortage reaches alarming levels. Agriculture, industry, and infrastructure development will remain stymied in the absence of adequate water for irrigation and municipal use. Already, the per capita availability of water in the country has fallen from 5,000 cubic meters, half a century ago, to under a thousand cubic meters now. The wastage of water must cease and the best way of doing that is to place a price on water in economic terms so that people who are over utilizing a scarce commodity are made to pay for it. The heavy subsidy of irrigation and drinking water has to end immediately if sustainability is to be achieved in water. On average, a land owner is charged under Rs. 500 per year as *abiana* or water tax and even this is not paid, except in Punjab. Additional storages are important but what is even more important, is utilizing the existing waters more productively. The Diamer Basha Dam multi-purpose project needs to be built without further loss of time and this must be followed by a number of other reservoir projects such as Munda-Mohmand, Dasu, Bunji, Shyok, Pattan, Thakot, Akhori, Kalabagh, and a host of smaller projects. The private sector, both from outside the country and from within Pakistan, could be encouraged to finance, build and operate hydropower projects if funding is not available with the government. Fortunately, now that there is no dispute on the sharing of waters of the Indus River basin following the historic Water Accord, amongst the provinces in 1991. Instead there is need for developing additional storages to provide the water requirements of the provinces.

The politicians and the water bureaucracy in the governments of Balochistan and Sindh provinces are equally responsible as WAPDA and the Planning Commission, in their failure to conserve water or develop smaller storages. The five medium-sized irrigation dams identified by WAPDA at Awaran, Kharan, Hingol, Winder, and Naulong in Balochistan, which could have led to sustainable food security in the most neglected districts of the country, were never championed by local rulers and planners. Frequent and fervent requests to three chief ministers, three provincial chief secretaries, three corps commanders, and three deputy chairmen of the Planning Commission brought no interest or results as they had other priorities. Interestingly, although these projects were not started, some Baloch sardars in the districts started demanding kickbacks, conveniently forgetting that they themselves, more than the local people, were the beneficiaries from the projects. Similarly, WAPDA's proposal for conveying piped irrigation waters from the Nara canal to the drought-stricken Thar Desert did not generate much interest either in the Sindh Government. This, if constructed, could have prevented the famines that regularly descend on the poorest in the country. It would appear that the influential people in the state support those projects which benefit them or which fetch them votes. It is, therefore not surprising, that the conditions of the common people remains mired in poverty, disease, and ignorance.

v. Floods: Forever and Ever

In 2010, the most devastating floods in the Indus basin since 1929, were seen. Eighty years earlier, heavy rains and a glacier which had blocked the Shyok River was the cause of the floods. After the water pressure had finally forced the debris out of the glacier, the flood flows reached massive proportions and when the monster floods reached the confluence of River Kabul with the Indus, the huge water wall at Attock compelled the Kabul River to flow backwards. River blockages have previously occurred a number of times on the Indus River and its tributaries. A Sikh army detachment was reportedly swept away near Haripur around 1843, during a particularly massive flood. The 1929 floods in the Kabul and Swat Rivers, flowed at 170,000 cusecs at peak while the high flood in these two rivers in 2010 was over 300,000 cusecs. The basic cause of the 2010 flood was the convergence in Swat area of the summer monsoons from the east and a freak westerly system from the west. The downpour over three days was unparalleled with some areas receiving over 300 millimeters of rain. The swollen waters of the Swat River first burst its banks by devastating houses and hotels, roads, and bridges all along the river embankment in the district. This was to be expected as in the absence of any land use regulations, people had actually been encroaching into the river bed area while common sense and regulation in well-governed societies dictate that nothing be built below the maximum flood level. There was no law in effect before these floods and none following it, to prohibit construction below maximum flood levels. Efforts by the commissioner Malakand division, while exercising the authorized powers of the Wali of Swat, to prevent any encroachment into the river and prohibit effluent flows into it, were declared unlawful by the local courts. No one was held responsible for the massive losses caused by the floods. As they say in Pakistan, *sab chalta hai*. Anything goes!

The floods started with the roaring Swat River which were joined by the waters of Panjkora River in the Malakand Agency near the Munda Headworks above Charsadda. The headworks, built in the late nineteenth century, was designed for a peak flood of 100,000 cusecs and could not handle a flood peak, three times higher. It collapsed. The waters inundated the Charsadda and Peshawar plains before arriving at Nowshera. The gorge upstream of Nowshera caused the river to rise appreciably and soon the entire city and cantonment were under water. The Grand Trunk Road was submerged in six feet of water at places and every house in the cantonment was flooded.

As this flood surged past Nowshera towards the confluence of Kabul River and the River Indus, a super flood was simultaneously moving down the mighty Indus. This flood was even mightier than the 1929 super flood. At its peak, the flows upstream of Tarbela, were over 800,000 cusecs, out of which Tarbela's reservoir was absorbing 200,000 cusecs, allowing the balance to flow downstream. Tarbela's reservoir is designed to store water gradually and the filling criterion does not allow storage of more than 200,000 cusecs for fear of damaging the rims of the reservoir and its infrastructure. Had there been no storage at Tarbela, the water flow downstream at Sukkur Barrage at peak would have been over one and a half million cusecs which would have been catastrophic for the barrage and for the whole of Sindh province. Unfortunately, Sukkur Barrage was very poorly maintained and managed by the corrupt and incompetent Sindh Irrigation Department. Due to heavy siltation, the gates were unable to pass waters at the designed capability. The Almighty, and the Tarbela reservoir, saved Sindh and the Sukkur Barrage with its eight million acres of canal command areas.

It used to be said that Sindh was a desert without the Sukkur Barrage and without the Tarbela Dam it could have become a desert again. Yet, there are ill-informed people who oppose water storages upstream. Had there been other large reservoirs at Diamer Basha, Akhori or Kalabagh, the flood damages would have been minimized. In 2010, the flood damages totaled over US$10 billion and is almost the cost of a new large hydropower dam. We never learn from the past and are therefore, condemned to see a repetition of catastrophic events.

Meanwhile, the flood, after passing Tarbela and Nowshera, next flowed onto the Jinnah Barrage, at Kalabagh managed by the Punjab Government. The Irrigation Department of Punjab was equally guilty of poor maintenance of Jinnah Barrage with many of its gates heavily silted and the left bank embankments protecting Mianwali were in abject state of disrepair. To save the Jinnah Headwalls and Mianwali city, the panicky Punjab administration immediately decided to take the ultimate step. This meant the controlled blasting of the Right Bank embankment to reduce water pressure. There was just enough time to move the Chinese and WAPDA officials working on the Jinnah Hydel Power Station from their camps, before the emergency plugs were breached through mine blasts. Considerable equipment, like turbines and generators which had recently arrived for installing in WAPDA's low head Jinnah hydropower project, were damaged.

From Jinnah Barrage, the waters moved towards the WAPDA-operated Chashma Barrage. For once the authorities in Pakistan, in this case WAPDA officials, were fully prepared to deal with the emergency. Chashma Barrage's maximum flood evacuation capacity was about one million cusecs when newly built. Forty-five years later and thanks to the quality of the barrage's construction and regular maintenance of the structure, the full volume passed safely from the outlet canals and gates. For nearly forty-eight hours, every WAPDA official from the chief engineer to the labourer, guard, and peon worked around the clock to successfully battle the flood and contain it. All Standard Operating Procedures were dutifully followed. Rock and stone were available in reserve and the staff did the rest. It was a close call, although all WAPDA's officials like the Chief Engineer Nazir Afridi, engineers Mahmood and Muhammad Ali Chaddar, and their staff handled the situation most professionally.

The Supreme Court appointed Commission praised WAPDA's officials for their exemplary conduct. WAPDA's technical personnel have over the years, acquired remarkable engineering proficiency owing to the strict standards it has followed. The engineers understood the nature of their work and displayed a professional dedication towards it. There could be few engineers in the country of the calibre of Chaudhry Mushtaq, Muhammad Hanif, Rashid Bangash, Hazrat Umar, Shahid Hameed, Hasnain Afzaal, Amin Khalil, Irshad Ahmad, Wajid Hamid, Brigadier Zarin, and Amer Mughal. It is said that when Justice Mansoor Ali Shah of the Lahore High Court visited Chashma Barrage in connection with the enquiry into the lapses of the Punjab Irrigation Department during the floods, he warmly embraced WAPDA's junior engineers for their skills, in averting a catastrophe. Such encouragement does wonders for the confidence of the staff.

The Chashma Barrage having been saved, the floods reached Taunsa Barrage in Punjab where some embankments in Bhong and Muzaffargarh gave way due to inadequate maintenance. Guddu barely sustained the flood pressure before the battle at Sukkur Barrage began. Of all the departments in the Sindh government, the Irrigation Department is perhaps the worst, ranking well below the revenue, police, and education departments and as a former Chief Secretary of Sindh, I believe, I can testify. The Irrigation Department's top priority always lay in constructing new projects, for obvious reasons, while the funds meant for annual maintenance of barrages and embankments were mostly misused. The right bank embankment below the Guddu Barrage, notably the Tori Bund, was so poorly maintained by the Sindh Irrigation Department that the Army and WAPDA officials were convinced that it would be breached. An embankment loses one inch of its topsoil every year due to natural causes and since there had been no maintenance since 1996, the bund at places was nearly a foot and a half lower than the required height. During an aerial survey and while flying at treetop level a few hours earlier, it was evident that the Tori bund would collapse soon and it did. The embankment overtopped and breached on 7 August 2010. The incompetence of Sindh Irrigation Department was clearly visible. The army had barely enough time to evacuate the infantrymen who were trying to raise the embankment before the deluge.

The total damage and loss in Sindh ran into hundreds of billions of rupees. Chief Minister Qaim Ali Shah and his professional advisers did not consider breaching the left bank of the Sukkur Barrage which would have relieved the water pressure. In such a case there would have been little damage on the right bank of the Indus while on the left bank most of the waters would have passed through the disused Nara canal and the old Indus River bed and in any case flood damages would have been much less. Deliberate breaching would have inundated a smaller area, but politics did not allow the Chief Minister to do so. Without a deliberate cut, losses could only be blamed on nature and not on the chief minister. During the 1970s, Prime Minister Zulfikar Ali Bhutto had agreed to make cuts in the Sukkur Barrage embankments to save other areas. Not this time. There would be more Tori-like disasters in the future because no one was punished for the lapses of 2010 inspite of the enquiries that were conducted. Chief Minister Qaim Ali Shah was also responsible for the losses amounting to billions of dollars that occurred on the right bank of the Indus River following the breach in the Tori embankment.

One very painful sight, witnessed during the floods in Sindh, was the meals served to the provincial government officials. The tables were always vulgarly brimming with food of all varieties while millions of flood-affected people were trying to eke out a living. Gluttony never ceases in our country, especially in circuit houses when chief ministers are on tour. The extravagance in any case was financed by the government in one way or the other, even as the chief minister explained the overflowing food as 'the traditional hospitality of the Sindhi people'. On the contrary, the WAPDA rest house in Sukkur was restricted to a one dish meal only. Three years earlier, during the floods in Larkana and Shahdadkot, meal tables were well stocked for the then chief minister. Politicians are a breed who think of nothing but their perpetuation of power. It was disgusting to overhear the then Chief Minister inform General Musharraf during the flood inspection that his administration was doing its best for flood-affected people and that his prolonged stay in the area has 'benefitted them politically as well before the elections'. To his credit, General Musharraf ignored the second part of the chief minister's inane observation.

The floods of 2010 had one silver lining. The pitiable living condition of the people living around Manchar Lake was brought into focus. The livelihood of the fishermen had been under threat for some years because the fresh water lake was increasingly being polluted by saline waters flowing in through the Right Bank Outfall Drain. Over time, the fish catch decreased and the availability of fresh drinking water ceased. The poor people had to travel great distances to fetch drinking water. WAPDA therefore decided to establish a small desalination plant on an experimental basis. This sorry state of affairs caught the attention of the Chief Justice of Pakistan, Iftikhar Muhammad Chaudhry, who ordered WAPDA and the Sindh government to establish six small desalination plants each for the people. One would have thought that the provincial government's foremost responsibility lay in providing the basic needs of the people, especially water, but our politicians have other priorities. The Supreme Court of Pakistan reminded the Sindh government of its duties. Later, WAPDA started work on a pilot project to convert the saline waters that drain into the sea for use in irrigation. If the experiment succeeds technically, an additional three million acre-feet of water could become available for agricultural use.

After the 1996 floods in Sindh, the Irrigation and Flood Control Manuals were revised to ensure that all embankments would be raised by six feet over the maximum flood levels. This was not done perhaps because there was not enough profit in such small maintenance work. Not only was the recommended remedial and punitive action not taken on the earlier reports, but the lapses and failures of the irrigation departments and of the politicians in power, highlighted by the Flood Commission Report mandated by Supreme Court, were not addressed. The politicians and irrigation departments' officials of Sindh and Punjab remained protected, despite the fact that the provinces suffered losses in hundreds of billions of rupees. There was no alibi for the neglect of the Pakistan Peoples Party and the Pakistan Muslim League (N) politicians because they in turn had been in power for years prior to the floods. Our people have short memories and the same politicians were re-elected again in the elections of 2013, forgetting their past incompetence.

There is little prospect for improvement in the country if the conduct of the defaulting politicians is not taken into account during subsequent elections. The neglect of flood embankments for decades before the 2010 floods by all governments in Sindh, allowed the natural creeks called *doras* to be silted and were encroached on by roads and habitation are criminal acts. Similarly, the failure of the governments in Punjab to implement the recommendations of the Flood Commission Report of 2010, prepared by Justice Syed Mansoor Ali Shah condemned the province to a repetition of the floods. Ultimately, floods can only be averted once additional reservoirs are established at Diamer Basha on the Indus, Munda-Mohmand in Mohmand Agency on the River Swat, Ghanche on the Shyok River, Kurram Tangi on Rivers Kurram-Kaitu, and on Akhori and Kalabagh on the Indus River. The Kalabagh Dam is of particular importance in utilizing the flood waters of both the Indus and Kabul Rivers, thereby creating a historic right to its water as well. Constructing reservoirs in Pakistan is beset with many problems as our argumentative and quarrelsome politicians can seldom act in unanimity, except for personal gains.

The resolution of the problems of both *bijli* and *pani*, electricity and water, lie in the hands of the politicians and the Planning Commission. A little foresight and dedication could achieve much. The political will is mostly absent and only incompetence and corruption thrive. It was said that during the mid-1990s an investor from the Far East decided to set up a coal-based thermal plant on the shore, in Sindh. During a courtesy call on the chief minister, the investor was assured full facilitations but reportedly also told to hand over a sizable share of the project's equity free of cost to him. The investor took the first flight home and was never seen in the country again. The indigenous coal sector was also largely ignored during the last few decades for reasons of corruption and limited vision. Informed estimates, speak of enormous reserves of coal, oil, and gas in the country so much so that the country could become a net exporter of energy. The missed economic opportunities and losses suffered by the people hardly bother the political and administrative leadership. 'O God give wisdom to the leaders of Pakistan,' was an integral part of the morning prayers in Edwardes College, Peshawar. May our prayers be answered. Without 'integrity in politics', the late Maureen Lines from Chitral said, nothing substantive will emerge in Pakistan.

11

Degradation of Environment

i. The Need for Land-Use Planning

Pakistan has been a victim of serious negligence in many areas. The gravest default has been the inability to check its high population growth and the failure to plan land-use. These twin failures have aborted not only material progress but have led to a degraded environment where much of the country is now little better than a slum with a disproportionate number of people. Notably missing is the concern for universal primary education, basic health care, family planning services, clean drinking water, and garbage removal. A society that cannot even remove its garbage or drain its sewerage cannot be expected to progress materially and this in a country which has split the atom. Filth overflows, plastic bags pollute, cesspools remain everywhere, roads conditions are pitiable, and road rage and rudeness is uncontrolled. Such conditions have become our constant companions. When simple obligations are not met, how can complex matters be addressed by a country?

Bizarre as it may appear, no land-use planning is specifically mandated by law in the country except in the few new housing development projects and in the military cantonments. Anyone can build anything, anywhere, and at any time. A century ago, Peshawar, for instance, had very wide roads in the cantonment with gardens and plenty of open spaces. It was a garden city, now transformed into a warren of filth. Today, Pakistan is free, but freer still, to circumvent the rules as there is no law abiding 'colonial' administration or *ferangi* to resist this violation of law. The Jamrud Road in University Town, Peshawar, is an appropriate example. There is an air force base, military installations, a cemetery, hospitals, hotels, shopping plazas, used-car depots, warehouses, retail shops, universities, schools, residential bungalows, apartment complexes, irrigated agriculture, and naturally the ever-present slums. Sadly, there is no public park to break the monotony. What is even sadder is that no one in the government, civil society, or the media is bothered with the absence of land-use regulation.

The residential University Town in Peshawar used to be a small island of greenery but has now been commercialized under pressure by the powerful business interests of the government of Chief Minister Pervez Khattak. People are now free to construct offices, restaurants, and shopping areas. The Ladies Club is all but gone. The army's own properties are not properly planned either. The Defence Colony on the Khyber Road was developed by the army as late as 1972, yet internal roads are only fifteen feet wide much like the narrow city streets of the eighteenth century. No wonder Major Zahinuddin would call it the *Hinduano mohalla.* So much for the planning capabilities of the army! The Ring Road around Peshawar was built for speedy travel but so many exemptions were granted for hotels, restaurants, shops, and residential properties that the limited access road became meaningless, almost immediately. Efforts to implement the rules were repeatedly overruled by the Chief Minister Akram Durrani

Even in the modern capital city of Islamabad, slums have emerged all around, which appear unsightly when seen from the air. Barakahu, Simli, and Bani Gala are new slums in the north; Latrar is the ghetto right up to the airport in the east; Pir Wadhai and Tarnol are particularly congested in the south. Only the western approach was saved and this was only because of the presence of the high mountain obstacle of the Margalla hills. The clever people of the Khyber province have now started building chalets west of the hills to stamp out the remaining trees and wildlife. There is no Justice Iftikhar Chaudhry to take *suo moto* notice to stop them!

In Islamabad, the Master Plan regulations are often flouted both by the state and by influential people, many of whom have built mosques without permission. Green areas appear to be an easy target and a red rag to the high and mighty. General Ziaul Haq would not lose a night's sleep after allotting restricted green areas for constructing houses of the well-connected. Those who followed him were scarcely more circumspect. Along a number of roads of Islamabad, green belts have been used to establish unauthorized religious *madrassa* schools and mosques, knowing well that the weak district administration will find it difficult to raze them down. It appears that unless effective land-use planning is adopted, ultimately the entire country would become a huge built-up slum with a ribbon development of shops and houses along all our roads. Perhaps, Sahibzada Imtiaz, the former Federal Secretary, was right when speaking about the adherence to the bylaws in the capital city, 'Islamabad is an aberration, enjoy it while it lasts.'.

One wonders what would be the future prospects of a society which remains oblivious to its visible needs. No city in Pakistan has a modern or even a functional city transport station like Victoria Terminal in London or New York's Port Authority with a central conclave and bus boarding bays. This is so elementary that anyone with the responsibility for the job should have developed such facilities. Daewoo of South Korea did initiate an efficient intercity bus transport but again the infrastructure required, is missing. The development of motorways is a step in the right direction but what is urgently required is the creation of central bus stations with intra-city and inter-city links. Even the Lahore-Islamabad motorway is badly aligned as it has added an unnecessary extra seventy kilometers to its length, resulting in extra fuel consumption and time. There is a near absence of public toilets and bus stops in our cities and the highways. Some years ago, a thoughtful official had public toilets built on the Kohat-Bannu Highway in the Khyber Pakhtunkhwa province but as soon as the local politicians got an opportunity these were converted into small wayside shops. No one can surpass Pakistanis in building shops; one finds them outside bungalows, below offices, on encroached green fields, and even around mosques, and tombs. There will be a time when half the country's space will be covered by shops. *Bazaristan*, as someone called it. This is already visible along all our intercity roads. Imagination and vision, sadly, are missing with our political and administrative leadership and these are ingredients that cannot be physically implanted in the planners. Why public toilets and road-side bus stops are not being built is baffling because nothing is easier done than this? An official, again in the Frontier province, persuaded the city fathers, actually stepfathers, to build a public toilet on the road just outside Peshawar where a small payment was charged for use by the public. It turned out to be very successful and soon drinking water, soft drinks, soap, and towels were on offer by the minority community contractor.

Adequate functioning of modern high-population density societies is possible only through strict enforcement of regulations developed on sound and professional lines. As far as the rules on environment and land use are concerned, these are conspicuously absent in Pakistan. The British were more considerate and prescient. A hundred years ago environment conservation and pollution control were incorporated in the Forest Act, the Canal and Drainage Act, the Land Settlement and Land Revenue manuals, the various Municipal Acts, the Criminal Procedure Code, and even in the Police Act and Police Rules. In Pakistan, the application of laws is taken very casually; it is the discretion of the officials to take cognizance of an offence or not to do so and since the officials are normally not accountable, no improvement is possible. That is the bane of our administration and the main cause of our drift.

The wooded hills around Murree, Abbottabad, Mansehra and Battagram, among others areas, are being denuded of trees and then levelled to build houses and hotels. Even the Margalla Hills overlooking Islamabad have lost most of their trees. All one sees is human habitation. Similar is the case with the fertile Charsadda-Mardan plains, and unbelievable as it may sound, there is no specific law regulating building on private agriculture land with the result that every time father's inheritance is distributed, the sons build their homes in the middle of their inherited agricultural land. Over time, 'brown use' is expanding at the expense of 'green use'. Thirty years from now when the population will nearly double much of our irrigated land and green hills will have been lost. In the United States, the construction of houses is not allowed on hill slopes if these are visible from the stream below to avoid aesthetic pollution. Our politicians and our planners are not even conscious of the issue.

People cannot be allowed to build in whatever areas they choose, whether these be private green fields or forests. Houses must only be constructed after detailed planning of residential colonies in cities, towns, and now villages as well. In Germany and Kazakhstan for instance, farmers live together in planned and compact housing units even where agricultural lands are extensive. Their homes have small pieces of land adjacent to the houses for poultry, dairy, and kitchen gardening. In the twenty-first century, people need to adapt to the environment and the available constraints; today they cannot live by nineteenth century conditions.

The conditions of the hilly areas of Galliat and Murree are deteriorating, by the day. The roads in the shopping areas are narrowing constantly so

much so that driving through the bazaars has become very difficult. What is
even more painful is to see that hundreds of additional residential plots have
been carved out in the existing townships and the hills to accommodate
the rich and influential people. The result is that virtually every house
looks directly into someone else's and the privacy of the hills has been lost
forever. Fortunately, early in their tenure, the Tehreek-i-Insaf government
of Imran Khan and Pervez Khattak took some remedial steps to limit the
built-up covered area to only one third the size of the plot and also to tax
properties in proportion to the size of the structure. Unfortunately, the
same Tehreek-i-Insaf government soon caved in to the pressure of the
rich and influential persons by undoing the essence of these reforms! This
decision hurt the environment and led to my resignation from the Galliat
Development Authority.

There is only one prized piece of alpine meadow left, known as Lalazar
between Dungagali and Nathiagali on what is colloquially called the *bandar
road* or the monkey tract. A number of influential people have tried their
luck to capture this for personal use but fortunately without success. One
Governor of the province wanted to build a hotel on it while another
important person wanted to convert it into a residential housing. To save
it from prying eyes, Lalazar was converted into a park for bears, musk
deer, and leopard which were once native to this area. It is important that
effective by-laws are developed to regulate all kinds of construction in
townships and villages to save the fragile hills and agriculture land from
soil erosion and the trees from being felled. The forests need a patron just
to survive because of the expansion of population and profiteers' pressures.
The actual forest cover has shrunk rapidly while the promised billion trees
tsunami in the Khyber Pakhtunkhwa province is not really visible. It must
also be understood that poplar and eucalyptus trees do more damage
than good.

Those who love pine forests, people like Rudolf Prybrinski and his wife,
would plant ten conifers for each they harvested, as inputs for making rifle
stocks and furniture. The Buddhists went a step further. They would plant
six saplings at the birth of a child. The people of Pakistan are different;
they cannot resist the temptation of cutting trees. In Kohat cantonment,
an army station commander in the mid-1980s waited only for the garrison
commander to be away on a foreign tour before he ordered the felling of

numerous rosewood or *shisham* trees. The Corps Commander, General Aslam Beg, on the request of the Commissioner Kohat thereafter issued orders that in the future no tree would be cut without his permission. No such orders were on file in the case of WAPDA's Rawal Rest House in Islamabad, so the concerned engineer chopped all three mature trees which had tenderly surrounded a small annex. It was to save these trees in the first place that the architecture of the building was adjusted. The engineer later explained he cut the trees because these 'gave a jungle look' to the place. Some people would never understand. His approach was similar to the genial Superintendent of Police in Chitral, Saeed Ahmed, who wondered why mountaineers risked life and limb to climb high mountains. The Deputy Commissioner advised him to concentrate on other issues.

The government needs to act and act now to save what remains of our green fields, meadows, *shamilaat* or the commons, hills, and mountains and above all the waters in the streams, lakes, and rivers. We should not forget our seas either, or the more limited freshwater brought by rain and our rivers. There are few crimes more heinous than polluting the streams, rivers, lakes, and now the sea. All receive chemical and industrial effluents in the millions of gallons, leading to diseases in both human beings and fish. What does one expect of Federal and Provincial governments which have even failed to control the use of polythene and plastic shopping bags for over two decades? They continue to clog the drains and waterways all over the country. Zar Aslam of the Environment Protection Fund said that hundreds of cattle and goats die every year, especially in the hills because of swallowing polythene scraps which block the intestines of the animals. A research study revealed that most seabirds have already eaten plastic in the oceans and scientists have projected that ninety nine per cent of all sea birds will be affected by 2050.

ii. The Ugly Mile

The British remained in the NWFP for a little less than a hundred years. During this period, they conducted numerous military operations to ensure their control of the province. This, despite the fact that during this period saw their resources diverted towards fighting two World Wars in Europe, Africa, and Asia, apart from the operational demands of the Indian Mutiny,

the Crimean War, Afghanistan, and the Boer Wars. The British were able
to plan and reconfigure Peshawar and a number of other cities in NWFP.
They extended the railways to the major cities and started focusing on
developing roads, schools, colleges, hospitals, and irrigation works. Pakistan
has been in existence for just over seventy years but we have little to show
for our efforts.

The city of Peshawar, during the British Raj, particularly its new western
portion, was remembered as an elegant frontier town. After Partition, the
Pakistani ethos took over, marked as it was by limited vision and an absence
of aesthetic sense. The coup de grace was provided by the influx of Afghan
refugees from the western border. Until then, Peshawar was an architectural
delight. Travelling from the venerable and restored Bala Hisar Fort on the
Khyber Road, the first imposing edifice was the iconic provincial assembly
building where Frontier democracy was born. Close by were the neat and
functionally designed district courts, civil secretariat, Victoria building
housing the museum, the majestic Governor's House, Edwardes College,
Company Bagh, Combined Military Hospital, and the Convent School
leading to the Masonic Lodge and ending at the endearing Peshawar Club.
Before Partition, the Peshawar Saddar bazaar shops looked like they were
extensions straight from Piccadilly Circus in London, with high ceilings
and broad verandas to keep the heat out. The conspicuous merchants of
the bazaar included people like Mehr Chand Khanna, Kirpa Ram, and
Ishwar Das highly esteemed for their business propriety. Unfortunately,
Peshawar's luck did not last long.

These colonial structures reminded everyone of what Peshawar once
was. Much of this has been replaced by some of the ugliest structures man
is capable of building. The provincial assembly building has been more
than doubled in size by adding tasteless concrete mass all around at the
expense of the lawns by the military Governor General Iftikhar Shah. Two
democratic but uncaring chief ministers who followed him added grotesque
elevated highways, adjacent to the structure. If that was not enough, Pervez
Khattak the Chief Minister of Imran Khan's party, made sure that the
front lawn would be replaced by monstrous concrete offices to ensure
that the endearing Assembly building was no longer visible. Vandalism
indeed comes in various shapes! They summarily rejected the more
aesthetically-inclined options to accommodate the modern requirements

of the Assembly. Pervez Khattak would forever be castigated for building the Bus Road Transport corridor in Peshawar ostensibly to streamline urban transportation. This ruined 'metro' besides being ugly in the extreme has clogged road traffic and that too at a phenomenal cost of Rs. 100 billion. Those who planned, approved, and executed this monument to shame, need to be placed in the dock.

It does not end there because the old and graceful offices of the Deputy Commissioner of Peshawar have been torn down to be replaced with concrete shoebox-like structures. Very rectangular and very awkward! The ghosts of British and Hindu architects would be greatly disturbed. The mile ends with a mosque built virtually on the road when a green space could have been retained around the mosque.

Why cannot Pakistanis design more functional and aesthetically appealing structures especially as they claim to be heirs to the Taj Mahal? The Governor's House Peshawar, Governor's Cottage Nathiagali, Cavagnari House in Kohat, Abbot Lodge in Abbottabad, Deputy Commissioner's House in Chitral, Drosh Scouts Mess, Agricultural Research Institute Peshawar, the Bolton block in Lady Reading Hospital, and the many smaller offices and houses built a century ago were more aesthetic and inviting. In the civil officers compound in Peshawar, a dozen houses were built for senior officers during the 1980s. The architect was Nayyar Ali Dada no less. These houses have no verandas to encourage the monsoon rains to flood the premises; there are long French windows to allow the summer heat in and for the public to peep inside; there are sunken Roman lobbies to assist in breaking your limbs and finally there are two dozen pillars built at great cost but for no purpose. The chief secretary and additional chief secretary at that time, brushed away the suggestion for building verandas, saying they were modernizing Peshawar. Their personal houses however, were different with long and deep verandas. The military men were not far behind. One Inspector General of the Frontier Corps allowed the establishment of a petrol station right next to the entrance of the century's old Bala Hisar fort to 'generate money for the welfare of the troops' he pleaded without much conviction. Next someone should build a shopping arcade in the lawns of the Governor's House to raise funds for its maintenance! It was with great difficulty that a more considerate successor of the General in

Bala Hisar had the petrol station removed and relocated at a site provided by the Frontier government.

During 1998, an interesting situation developed relating to the reconstruction of the Secretariat building in Peshawar. A small piece of land belonging to the Governor's House jutted into the Secretariat compound which would have resulted in reducing the size of the front lawns. As additional chief secretary frontier province, I wanted this piece of land to form a part of the chief secretary's block in the secretariat. However, there was a problem. The chief minister had earlier declined to provide an equally small piece of land to the Governor's House which wanted to realign its rear gate. It was clear that the Governor's House would similarly reject the chief minister's request. The two highest functionaries in the province were not on the best of terms for some other reasons as well. This was turning out to be a no-win situation! I decided to take the initiative and 'untruthfully' informed the Chief Minister that the Governor had agreed to provide the land for the Secretariat voluntarily. On hearing this, the Chief Minister revoked his previous decision and ordered that the land required for the Governor's House may be transferred to it. All's well that ends well. Both parties were satisfied thanks to a small 'fib' of the additional chief secretary; the political officers' *pultically* won the day!

There was no such problem in the Governor's House, Nathiagali. This mansion was based on the design of an Italian Count and is unarguably the most majestic and beautiful building in the country. It reportedly cost Rs. 100,000 in 1931, with Samdani Khan as the contractor from Peshawar. Fifty years later, the government built a Governor's cottage in Chitral which appeared to have been designed by a cook. The site selected by the provincial works department misses out the sight of Mount Tirich Mir, the 26,000 feet eye-catching landmark in Chitral. So much for the setting, but ponder the poetic justice delivered. At the inauguration of this building by the Governor, General Fazle Haq, the chandelier in the lobby came crashing down, narrowly missing the Governor's head. The ghosts of the British architects of the nearby Chitral Scouts Mess may have been responsible. There was also an interesting tale relating to the foundation stone of this Mess which was 'well and truly laid' by three young British officers who legend says, placed a bottle of champagne under it as a blessing. Actually there was just concrete.

A final word on Governor's cottages; there is a wood-and-stone structure in Parachinar which is elegance personified with a sensational view of the mountains on three sides. A heavy wooden staircase with solid balustrade makes for a splendid entrance and there are two bathrooms in each suite for 'him' and 'her' as there was no modern flush system at that time. The building was originally meant to be part of the Parachinar Railway Station on the Kohat to Kabul railway line that was never built. Sadly, after the departure of Viceroy Lord Curzon the priorities changed but the railway's loss was the Governor's gain. Parachinar town's Kurram Militia Mess was another small icon emerging from a supposedly fictional past, built around acres of garden. The sitting room had a bar, with the comfort of leather sofas and a wooden mantelpiece over a chimney. The English, novel as always, had dug a well outside the mess which was filled in with the winter snows to provide the right cool beverages in the summers. The billiard room wall was covered with python skin with plenty of prized heads shot which kept one occupied, if one did not spend time in the cards room. The dining room was full of silver and trophy heads and the menu often consisted of the most delectable oven-baked chicken and kidney pie. The *balti gosht* food culture had not yet arrived! A short distance away was the Robert's Garden, named after Lord Robert of Peiwar, which provided fruits that were sent as gifts.

Then there was the old Khyber rifles Mess at Landikotal, built round a stone-and-wood structure with lots of history locked in. Many hundreds of tired and hungry scouts officers restored their balance in its bar after an arduous *gasht* or a skirmish on a border station. When Queen Elizabeth II was informed during her visit in 1961 that the Mess was being pulled down to be replaced by a larger structure, she made a fervent request for its preservation. Alas that was not to be, for we do not want 'foreigners to dictate' to us! It was replaced with a stone and concrete monstrosity with toilets placed right at the entrance; class and finesse continues to elude Pakistanis.

This chapter ends on a happier note as some iconic structures have been conserved by a few concerned persons. The bungalows the British lovingly built in the second half of the nineteenth century in the Frontier province, having outlived their usefulness were ready for demolition. Most fortunately on my request as one who lived in some of these buildings the competent authority agreed to proposals to restore these instead of razing them to the ground and building half a dozen new but tasteless houses. The Deputy Commissioner's House in Chitral, the Roos-Keppel House of the Political Agent Khyber Agency in Peshawar, the Cavagnari House in Kohat, the Gilgit Residency which is the home of the Chief Commissioner, and the Commissioner's House in Peshawar were five buildings that were close to collapse with mud walls crumbling and the roofs disintegrating. All were restored in the original colonial style, indistinguishable from the blueprint, and good for another century to the great delight of Khalid Shah of Leeds. The unbaked brick walls were lined with new bricks supported with steel reinforced beams while the wooden roofs were replaced with steel girders and wide tiles. Most officers desire field posting for the leisure and pleasure of living in the comfort of the bungalows with trained household staff. However, during the renovation of these bungalows, I and my family had to move out and spent nearly a year each time in very cramped conditions. This was a small sacrifice to pay for the joy of extending the life of the building for another hundred years at least. The Nicholson House in Bannu now needs to be restored if for no other reason than because Sir John Nicholson who occupied it in the middle of the nineteenth century had brought peace and stability to an area, which had seldom seen it before and after him.

As far as restoration of structures of the past is concerned, few could compare with the Russians, including the czars, communists, and democrats, for their care and dexterity in restoring these. The mosques, *madrassas*, and tombs dating back to the Amir Taimur era as well as more recent ones have been most delicately conserved. It took them decades to complete because this was a labour of love! Czarist palaces like the Blue and the Catherine Palaces in St Petersburg, which were severely damaged by Nazi bombing during the Second World War, have similarly been lovingly restored. Those who designed and constructed these originally must have been men of stature but those who brought them back from death were even more remarkable people. Walking in the huge palace compounds one came across two massive metallic statues of Greek gods which were pulled out from the palace and taken to Germany for smelting. Only hours before the foul deed was to be committed Russian tanks reached the foundry in Germany and saved these for posterity. To those of us who have rarely come across anything better than cheap box-like concrete structures being built here, the majestic buildings in most European capitals leave us shocked and dismayed. The structures built, are functionally appropriate and aesthetically gracious and were built to suit the local climate.

Few, if any, buildings constructed after Partition match the provincial assemblies of the Punjab, Sindh, and the NWFP. Similarly, the governor houses in Peshawar, Quetta, Lahore, and Karachi are rich architectural monuments. Then there was, and is the 'Journey's End', the deputy commissioner' House in Chilas. Why could we not replicate such structures especially since colossal amounts of money have been spent? The small cottage on the brook in Chilas was where the 'journey ended', having started by ship from London, Southampton or Glasgow across two oceans, thereafter traversing the deserts on camels, Kashmir mountains on horseback, leading to the killer Burzil Pass on yaks till it ended in the sleepy village of Chilas. If there was a Deputy Commissioner like Sohail Rashid, you could be sure that the residence was as well-managed as the Chilas district was. One feels sad when comparing the beautiful structure built with parental care by the British to those constructed after Partition. The President House in Islamabad looks like a nuclear bomb shelter while the Parliament building is similar to a high-rise car park. The capital city is unique in another way too; it has no central square and only an apology for a modern transportation system. Elegance for the British was not enough as the buildings were supposed to be functional and long lasting as well. After a severe earthquake struck Malakand Division in 1991, it transpired that the buildings that were constructed during the British era or those which were constructed by the Wali of Swat escaped serious damage but those built much later by Pakistani engineers either collapsed or developed major cracks. The Railway bridges like the ones in Attock, Khushalgarh, and Sukkur on the River Indus, and the Victoria Bridge in Bahawalpur were built well over a century ago but remain functional long after their useful lives. Fortunately, there is hope for a few classical structures but only a few. One of these is the old Multan Club in the military cantonment with its endearing regal domes which have been conserved thanks to the efforts of a couple of appreciative army officers. The restored structure now competes favourably with the domes of the city's other shrines but it was said that the proposal to conserve or pull down the Club building was carried by just one vote. Thank goodness for democracy in the cantonment! The military, unfortunately, was not considerate towards the old and venerable building of the Command and Staff College Quetta; it was torn down and replaced by an abominable substitute. Someone should have had the good sense to retain the old building's façade at least. This happened in 1971 when the old Pakistan was similarly torn down.

12

The Legacy of the Railways

A mong the greatest legacies of the British rule in India was the establishment of the Railways and the Post Office. The Railways ensured one could travel across the length and breadth of the subcontinent quickly, cheaply, and comfortably. It also meant better control over the territories. Similarly, one was assured that a letter or a money order posted in Gilgit, almost in Central Asia, would arrive in Cape Comorin thousands of miles to the south, some days later. In Pakistan today, these efficiencies cannot be replicated; both the railways and the post office appear to be in decline. During the past forty years only once, in 2004–05, did the railways show an operational surplus, let alone a profit, while the Indian railways routinely earns billions of dollars annually. It was no surprise that Lallu Prasad, the barely literate Indian Minister for Railways, would be invited to speak at Harvard University on management issues! He had shown results. Not so in Pakistan, as the priority the Railways deserves, has seldom been provided by successive governments. It has reflected poorly on the country's leadership that even seventy years after Independence the total operational railway track had actually decreased by about a thousand miles. There were no mainline tracks laid during this period while the percentage of passengers and freight carried decreased sharply.

However, where personal or political priorities so demanded, our leaders saved no effort or expense. An example of this was the disused narrow-gauge line to India that both President Musharraf and Prime Minister Shaukat Aziz were very keen to develop. It later transpired that this was being undertaken at the insistence of the Muttahida Qaumi Movement, from urban Sindh, who often travelled to India to meet their relatives separated since Partition. The Mirpurkhas-to-Khokrapar rail link and onwards to Munabao in India was accordingly laid in record time at a cost of nearly Rs. 1 billion. The railway was given to understand that the track would be used to cater to Indian trade through Karachi which would provide much needed revenues to Pakistan. The line was used only a few times a month and accumulated heavy losses.

To his credit it must be stated that President Musharraf did try to stem the rot in the railways. His efforts were not destined to succeed. As a first step he ordered that new locomotives, coaches, and freight wagons be procured immediately. A trio of Generals, Javed Ashraf Kazi, Minister, Saeed uz Zafar Chairman, and Hamid Butt the General Manager, decided to buy locomotives on a fast-track basis. During those days, economic sanctions were imposed on Pakistan following the nuclear tests the country had conducted, which severely restricted the availability of foreign loans. Only our Chinese friends offered to provide a loan for the purchase the equipment. Sixty-nine Chinese locomotives were accordingly purchased and operated on the tracks. Four years later almost all these had broken down because of the problems with the chassis frame or engine. These locomotives were generally of a poor standard and compared most unfavourably with General Electric and General Motors locomotives which ply on happily even after forty years of service. This loss could have been averted had the railways followed its Standard Operating Procedures which clearly stipulated that every time new equipment was to be procured a limited trial order should first be introduced to evaluate the performance. The Generals later said that the purchases were made in 'good faith' in view of time constraints. Good faith!

Railway operations are expensive. Purchases are even more costly and one has to carefully and honestly evaluate offers before orders are placed. In one case of the procurement of modern signaling equipment, the experience was gruelling. An earlier decision to buy inferior Chinese signaling equipment against the advice of railway professionals needed to be revised. When the suppliers of the Chinese equipment and their local agents learnt that the railways was more focused on quality than the lower costs they started applying excessive political pressure and followed it with financial inducements to finalize the deal. Firstly, they offered to reduce the price by US$5 million but when they were told that it was not the cost but the quality that was the concern they homed in, with monetary offers. There was a most despicable local agent from Karachi who thought he knew how decisions could be manipulated in Pakistan and decided to meet me when I posted as Chairman of the Railways. He came to my office with a briefcase and said that he had cleared the matter with the Minister and was accordingly carrying the first installment of money in a foreign currency. I was outraged and responded to his offer by planting a tight slap across the agent's face and called my staff to throw him out. This stimulus got the right response! Later, fresh bids were called for and quality European equipment procured. In making purchases, what is most important is to assess the life cycle cost of the equipment and not the initial price. As for the Chinese equipment, it transpired subsequently that a number of train accidents on their railways were attributed to their poor signaling equipment.

The Generals in charge of the railways also took the decision of transferring to private management, the poorly managed railways golf course in Lahore. This was a wise decision but they were unjustly pilloried for it. The rules appeared to have been followed in the transaction when the offer was first advertised but the enquiries and investigations against the senior railway officials continued. Today, the Royal Palm Golf Course is the best of its kind in the country. There were a couple of deficiencies in the contract, in that all railway officers were not allowed golf membership and some additional land was also added later, but these were matters that could be settled easily.

Service in the railways was unmatched by any other profession. Senior railway officers after retirement missed two privileges the most. The first was the use of the railway saloon while travelling on duty. Many a minister had ordered their withdrawal to try and win personal plaudits. In truth, the ministers should have focused on generating greater efficiency in the system and in checking corruption, starting with themselves, but such decisions did not make it to headline news. Instead, they opted for the easier path and concentrated on the trivial. The saloon was extensively used by railwaymen to check the working of the signaling equipment and the maintenance of railway track. While 'foot-plating', it could be parked anywhere, even in the wilderness. Most official meetings were also held while on the move. One chairman, more idiosyncratic than others, would board or disembark from the saloon in the deserts of Tharparkar or the hills of Toi Banda in Kohat while on inspection. A partridge shoot, at times, was added to the 'inspection'!

The other privilege most missed related to living in Mayo Gardens in Lahore, the residential colony for senior railway officials. This is prime real estate, located in the heart of the city and quite naturally everyone in authority, in Islamabad grudged the railway officers for living in large houses. They said they wanted to privatize it for raising finances for the railways' expansion. Firstly, Nawaz Sharif and then General Javed Ashraf Kazi ordered the sale of this property but just when the transfer to the private sector was to be actually affected their tenures ended. Later, perhaps fortuitously for railways officials, a newly posted chairman of railways, decided that instead of selling Mayo Gardens dozens of smaller houses for officials would be constructed on the site. The architect, Nayyar Ali Dada, was assigned the task to build four or more houses within each larger compound firstly because the older houses had started falling down but more so to pre-empt any future effort at depriving the railway men of their few rights. It would be a pitiful day for aficionados of the past, if the Mayo Garden rest house, whose municipal registration number was two, Punjab Governor House being one, were to be razed to the ground to make room for commercial plazas.

Somehow railway properties remained open to annexation by all and sundry. In Walton, the railways had developed a number of quality apartments adjacent to a military establishment. A Corps Commander Lahore had his eyes on these and asked for 'renting' a few of the high rise structures. Now a Corps Commander's request is normally complied with and the railway authority was on the verge of 'renting' these when fortune smiled on it again. Sheikh Rashid Ahmad was appointed the minister and because of his stature and eloquence he was able to prevent the railways from losing the apartments that housed scores of junior officers. Rank neutralizes rank! That was not the only time the dynamic Sheikh Rashid, came to the rescue. In Rawalpindi, a retired General, who had earlier headed the railways, could not bear to vacate a Victorian-style house he lived in, perhaps for sentimental reasons. Having occupied the place for years, it was difficult to dislodge him but then the Sheikh from Lal Haveli was equal to the task. The general soon vacated the house.

It was always a delight to see the railway officials at work; they remained professionally engaged, especially in emergencies. Among the best in the railways was Ahmad Nawaz, who left the service early because he could not make ends meet in a corrupt environment. There was Ashfaq Khattak, who as Divisional Superintendent, remained bold and innovative and was the one responsible for establishing the delectable railway museum at Golra Station, at no cost to the state. The doyen of the Pakistan railways was the brilliant General Manager Abul Kalam with Ziaullah, Iqbal Samad, and Aurangzeb Khan not far behind him. Then there was the honest, innovative, and courageous Nur Muhammad Masud who died resisting a robbery. Imtiaz ul Haq, Malik Hayat, Saeed Akhtar, Naeem Malik, and Imtiaz Khan were true professionals who worked hard in difficult circumstances. The Railways would not forget the services of Ahsan Mahmood, who managed to fabricate an inspection trolley locally, at a fraction of the cost of an imported one. Another senior officer was Shafiqullah, who was not only competent but could dance Pakhtun-style for hours, to relieve stress. It was sad to see some of the best railway officers suffer imprisonment because they could not resist the corrupt ways of the ministers. They should have refused to comply with improper orders but in a society where there is no sanctity of an official's tenure some of them find it difficult to resist.

There was one stress that was synonymous with service in the railways. This reached a crescendo if there was a midnight telephone call. The call communicated a major accident on the system. Such a call in 2006, conveyed the staggering news about a three-train accident at the Sarhad station in Sindh, on the border with Punjab, resulting in the deaths of 134 persons. Railway officials often recount that it takes two or more cases of negligence for a serious accident to occur. In this case, the Karachi Express (Down) rammed into the back of the stationary Quetta Passenger train in the station just when the Tez Gam (Up) which was travelling at top speed from the opposite direction hit the doomed trains. Here were two cases of negligence again. The Station Master of Sarhad allowed the Quetta Express to depart and without checking whether it had actually left the station then signaled the Karachi Express to move from the last crossing station. Unfortunately, unknown to the Station Master, the Quetta Express had stalled and stopped because of a mechanical failure. The incoming driver of the Karachi Express, having been permitted to move, did not notice the outer red signal at that hour in the night as he had travelled the route hundreds of times before and assumed that the signal was green. By the time he realized his mistake, it was too late and even though he applied emergency brakes, he did not see day light again. It was then the misfortune of the Tez Gam to crash into the wreckage of the two trains. Had the railways procured the automatic braking system in time, the accident could well have been avoided. There was twisted steel and badly mangled heaps of debris all around but in such depths of gloom, there was one silver-lining that saved scores of additional lives. The silver-lining was the help provided by the local people of the area with the Hindu community in the lead. They removed the dead and took the injured to hospitals, providing vital life support, at a crucial time. Pharmacies and clinics were opened at night to provide immediate relief with people paying from their own pockets. Early the next morning, Edhi aircraft and ambulances started delivering much needed supplies. By then the police, the rangers, and the army had also arrived on the scene but the pivotal assistance was what the villagers had initially provided. It is not known whether a plaque remembering their dedication is in place but then someone said it is important to 'love the game beyond the prize'. Their valiant efforts were in marked contrast to the looting and stealing that the people of Okara in central Punjab indulged in, when a serious train crash took place in the 1950s. They deserve a monument of shame.

The chapter could appropriately close with a rather touching story of railway hospitality of an unknown junior functionary. More than sixty years ago, my father, then a young army Major, travelled to Lahore by bus for some personal errand. He arrived late in the evening and decided to take a horse-drawn *tonga* to the railway colony where a relative, Aslam Salim, lived. There being three railway residential colonies in Lahore, the *tonga* took him to the wrong one. He knocked at the nearest house whose occupant was a Punjabi-speaking junior official. He invited the guest to a cup of tea and then suggested that it being late he may have dinner with him before they decided how he would travel to the relative's house. That was the period when there were no telephones or taxis in the area. The host then insisted that because of the late hour, he would set up a bed in the sitting room, the *baithak*, for the army officer. The next morning, the unknown host escorted my father to the office of the relative and explained that it would have been very inconvenient for both the Major and his relative, had he travelled to Mayo Garden, late in the night. Such was the level of the modest host's concern and consideration; happily, there are tens of millions of such people in Pakistan.

Part 5

The Power Brokers

13

The Battles Within

Aldous Huxley famously said 'that men do not learn very much from history is the most important of all the lessons that history has to teach'. He could be speaking of Pakistan. Despite the heavy cost, we have had to bear we rarely learn. Since Partition in 1947, there have been a number of 'watersheds' and 'defining moments' in the country but these did not lead us towards the desired path. The country was and remains polarized in its varied ethnic, religious, and sectarian divides besides having uneven economic indicators. Quarrels between regions have often led to animosity, which turn violent and culminate in civil strife. We did not learn from the Urdu-Bengali language controversy of 1948 nor from the constitutional crisis sparked by the dismissal of the federal legislative assembly, a few years later. The One Unit administrative setup foisted in West Pakistan shortly afterwards, was not well-received by the smaller provinces. Although the failure to grant more autonomy to East Pakistan had tragic consequences, the economic gap between different regions of Pakistan remained glaringly stark. Political battles have since waged uninterruptedly even on fundamental issues. Were the general elections starting with President Ayub Khan in 1965 onwards fairly conducted, and did the winners adhere to the constitutional necessities? Was religion and ethnicity, on occasions, used for furthering political and personal gain? Why did the state not place the required emphasis upon raising socio-economic indices in the country? What would be the long-term effects of conscious decisions taken to external events on the western borderlands? And finally, are the power elite, comprising formal and informal pillars of the state, being meaningfully held to account? These issues have caused considerable grief and much loss to Pakistan over the years.

These were the 'defining moments', which should have been anticipated and undertaken in accordance with the law and fair conscience. I was directly associated with only one such 'watershed moment' in Karachi and that was on 12 May 2007, while serving as the Chief Secretary of the Sindh province. In the preceding chapters I have often been irreverent in order to focus upon the truth as I saw it. In actuality, I spoke out of pain. Countries with conditions similar to us have left us far behind in areas that mattered. Where does our rainbow lie? When would the series of tragedies that Pakistan experienced finally end? I believe I understand, to a large extent, why and how epochal decisions are taken by the rulers. The short answer is that such decisions are motivated by personal and group benefits at the cost of the country's interests. No opposition is brooked and the bureaucracy along with the other power sources, are expected to follow the rulers' diktat. The judiciary mostly looked the other way. On the face of it, Pakistan is governed in accordance with the law and the Constitution, though the reality is far removed from this perception. Every effort was made and every subterfuge resorted to by the rulers to perpetuate themselves in power and when that was not possible, the law could be ignored. Where whimsical rulers get directly involved in decision-taking, risks increase. Karachi on 12 May 2007, was a text book example. This date would rank as one of the darkest in the country's dark history.

The military government was in power with the Army Chief, General Musharraf having been supposedly legitimized by a farcical referendum as President. Earlier, General Zia had infamously declared that the Constitution was like regimental orders which he could disregard and tear up at any time. The debate on whether the President would take 'his uniform off' was obnoxious, both literally and figuratively. President Musharraf's very dubious first term in office was to end soon and general elections were around the corner. The General desperately wanted another term to complete his reforms and 'resolve the Kashmir dispute' even as Chief Minister of Punjab, Chaudhry Pervaiz Elahi promised him many more terms, with or 'without' his uniform. A year later, the emperor had no clothes!

In such a setting, General Musharraf dressed in full military uniform, summoned the Chief Justice of Pakistan, Iftikhar Muhammad Chaudhry, to his office to persuade him to resign. Upon his refusal, he forwarded a reference to the Supreme Judicial Council containing various charges seeking his removal.

The General feared the Chief Justice, as the latter had steadfastly made clear, would not comply with the General's bidding. The General desperately wanted one final term as President while still in command of the Army. The Chief Justice thought this one term was too much.

The reference having being filed in the Supreme Judicial Council, the Chief Justice was made 'non-functional'. This was yet another judicial device invented by pliable Pakistani lawyers to win General Musharraf's favour and all that comes with it. There was a surprise awaiting these lawyers. As soon as the news spread of the removal of the Chief Justice on 10 March 2007, there were widespread and continuous protests across the country, such that the regime had never anticipated. This was the beginning of the Lawyers' movement, aided and supported, by the media and the people of the country. The spark having being provided, there was no let up. The names of leaders of the Lawyers Movement became household names, in no time. Aitzaz Ahsan, Ali Ahmad Kurd, Muneer Malik, Justice Tariq Mehmood, Justice Wajiuddin, Asma Jehangir, Latif Afridi, Justice Saeed-uz-Zaman Siddiqui, and hundreds of others would be remembered by the people of Pakistan for their commitment to democracy. The Long Marches and convoys led by the deposed Chief Justice, with Aitzaz Ahsan in his new role as chauffeur, were enthusiastically supported by hundreds of thousands of people. In 1970, Aitzaz Ahsan stood first in the Central Superior Service examinations but did not join the civil service because he wanted to serve the country in a more meaningful manner. He got the opportunity thirty-seven years later to redeem his pledge fully; cometh the hour, cometh the man.

Such hugely successful marches to Lahore and Peshawar sent shivers down the General's anatomy and those of his crony chief ministers. The President General, with the full support of the coalition Government of Sindh decided that a stand would be taken in Karachi to stub out the kindling fire. This was like General Custer's last stand. The deposed Chief Justice was not to be allowed to address the Karachi Bar Association in the Sindh High Court. The tragic date of 12 May 2007 had arrived; by the time the day ended, General Musharraf and associates would have much to regret. For four days prior to the scheduled arrival of the Chief Justice, long, tense, and worrisome meetings were held in the Governor's House on the subject attended by a frightened Governor and a casual Chief Minister, as they more than others, would be responsible for the consequences. Also in attendance were a few rather irresponsible federal and provincial ministers and of course the Karachi Chiefs of the Inter-Services Intelligence, Military Intelligence, Intelligence Bureau, provincial Police Chief and his deputy, and the Director General Sindh Rangers. The Civil Administration was represented by me, as Chief Secretary, while the Home Secretary was the respected Brigadier Mohammad Mohtaram.

For an official like me, who had spent his entire career in the Frontier—now the Khyber Pakhtunkhwa Province—Azad Kashmir, and Gilgit-Baltistan (Northern Areas), it was strange to note that in the meetings in Sindh, the views of the civil administration were neither sought nor heeded. Civil servants were there to support and implement the directives, no matter how asinine, and in no case could they question or oppose these directives. Theirs was to 'do or die' so that the politicians, including the Army Chief, achieved their purposes in life. It quickly transpired that on orders from above, the Chief Justice's convoy was not to be allowed to leave the airport building if he did arrive in Karachi and restraining notices were to be served on him and his associates. In the meetings, the general tone of the Chief Minister was unhelpful, though Governor remained amiable and appeared to look for a face-saving solution. What was most painful was the attitude and approach of the Sector Chief of the Inter-Services Intelligence. Perhaps on the prompting from his patron, and in compliance with whatever directives he had received from his seniors, he was even more adamant than the others that the Chief Justice's convoy was not allowed to travel to the High Court. The officer was known for his power and authority in the Sindh Government and his recommendations on policy matters and posting was invariably agreed to. The Chief Minister would always escort him to his car after the meetings.

During the four meetings at the Governor's House, it emerged that not only would the Chief Justice be stopped from leaving the airport but a counter rally, sponsored by the government, was to move towards the Shahra-e-Faisal on 12 May. This further complicated a complex situation and set the stage for a volatile confrontation. The rulers were bent upon displaying the 'people's power' on the streets of Karachi as they had threatened to do a day earlier with a clenched fist. The clenched fist, the emblem of the Army's 1 Armoured Division, should have been unleashed at the country's enemies not its own people. All attempts made by me and supported by the Home Secretary to refrain from the suggested course of action were ignored. The facts were also reported to the Director General of the Inter-Services Intelligence and the Corps Commander Karachi, who appeared concerned but were quite helpless. If the Army Chief orders a line of action, it becomes impossible to recommend any alternate course.

How does one ensure peace in a metropolis like Karachi when both the federal and the provincial governments are intent on taking a series of dangerous steps that will lead to a conflagration? The Inspector General, Sindh Police, and the Karachi Police chief both appeared wanting in courage and a sense of duty. They supported the President, Governor, and the Chief Minister fully while ignoring the law. The wise Additional Inspector General of the Special Branch, Bachal Sangrio tried to put events in the correct perspective but was quickly rebuked and silenced. On the one side were the President, the federal government in Islamabad, the provincial government in Karachi, the Muslim League, and the Muttahida Qaumi Movement, the Police, the Intelligence agencies, and the Rangers. On the other were the Chief Secretary, the Home Secretary, and a clear conscience.

A day before 12 May, a ray of hope was provided by the Chief Justice of Sindh High Court, Justice Sabihuddin Ahmad, a gentleman par excellence. In a communication to the Governor Sindh, he suggested that all demonstrations and protests be prohibited through an ordinance for one month. The choice of the instrument of ordinance instead of preventive action, under the Criminal Procedure Code was to pre-empt any judicial restraint against it. The Governor was quite relieved at the possibility of preventing any untoward happening and sought my immediate advice. As the Chief Secretary, I was relieved and recommended that the recommendation be made effective. Within an hour unfortunately, all hopes were dashed and the peace pigeon lay dead, reportedly shot down by the President. When the Governor was asked about it, he ruefully replied that they did not approve and who else was party to the plural 'they' was left unsaid. The Government and the President did not want to be challenged on the Karachi turf and did not want a repeat of the rousing reception the Chief Justice got in Lahore. The situation was back to square one and looked very ominous.

Meanwhile, I made one final attempt to avert the looming tragedy by speaking to Prime Minister Shaukat Aziz on telephone and in the presence of all concerned senior officials. I called the Home Secretary, the Inspector General Police, Chief Capital Police Officer, District Coordination Officer, Karachi, the Additional Inspector General Police, Special Branch, and the representatives of the three intelligence agencies to my office to hear me speak to the Prime Minister. Despite waiting for a couple of hours the Prime Minister was not available. So I spoke to Khalid Saeed, the Principal Secretary to the Prime Minister. In very straight and candid words, the Principal Secretary was told that the situation in Karachi was very 'ominous' and 'would' result in much bloodshed. It was suggested that the Chief Justice of Pakistan should not be stopped from travelling to the Sindh High Court in order to avoid any chance of confrontation. Winding up, I stated not to ever think that I was panicking in the face of a serious situation and reminded him that during my long career in the Tribal Areas I had experienced many such events. Khalid Saeed promised to convey these forebodings, word for word, to the Prime Minister. In the event, nothing was ever heard from him or the Prime Minister.

In the evening, the Governor informed me that the Prime Minister did discuss the matter with the 'others' and that he did recommend that the march option be reviewed but was overruled. Perhaps my telephone call may have prompted him towards the saner option but to no avail. It appears that the Prime Minister and the Governor wished to avoid a gory confrontation but fate had ordained bloodshed for Karachi. However, the previous orders stood and the Chief Justice was not to be allowed out of the airport and the Government's rally would move unhindered to Shahra-e-Faisal. The police, by the evening, had blocked and barricaded many roads with shipping containers to stop the movement of vehicles and the people. D-Day was only hours away!

Back home that evening, and thoroughly distraught, I wrote a note on the impending crisis for the Governor, the Chief Minister, and the Prime Minister. During the next twenty-four hours regretfully, all predictions were confirmed and the death toll was considerably higher. The President and the Prime Minister studied the letter 'carefully' and later spoke to me about it but the deed was done and the time for action had passed.

The sun rose on 12 May 2007, a bright lit day, to show what the leaders because of their intransigence proposed to do to the people. Early in the morning, all roads leading to the Secretariat and the High Court were blocked. The few vehicles on the roads were being pelted with stones. The Chief Justice of Sindh High Court called me on the telephone to register his concern and I told him that, unfortunately, the matter was out of my hands and I was helpless, as both the Police and the Rangers were taking orders from others. The Chief Justice replied that he knew what this was all about. A short time later, reports started appearing on the television and the District Coordination Officer, Javed Hanif, also informed me about the violence engulfing the city. As is always the case, it was the poor who suffer; daily wage earners like labourers, street vendors, *chowkidars* (watchmen), and drivers were killed by the dozens. By nightfall, forty-eight people eking out a livelihood in Karachi lay dead and many more were wounded. These were people who worked on the roads or in shops and were most vulnerable. In death, ironically, they were claimed as supporters by the two main political parties even though they may have been killed by them. Some Pakhtun dead were claimed as members by the Muttahida Qaumi Movement, the Urdu-speaking party. Nearly four-fifths of the dead and the wounded were poor Pakhtuns.

The scale of the violence and the high death toll surprised and shocked both the rulers in Karachi and Islamabad. General Musharraf's symbol of a clenched fist had lost all meaning and his threatened 'people's power' had an ominous response that he did not want. Whether it was the people's power or state power, it certainly was his Waterloo. He was not the same again and 12 May 2007 soon became a powerful metaphor for the contempt of law. In subsequent meetings and discussions with the rulers, I did tell them confidently that violence could have been forestalled and a peaceful way out could have been chosen, had they wanted it. This was deliberately avoided and to the lasting shame of the Karachi Police and the Sindh Rangers it must be recalled that on that fateful day, they were mainly responsible for allowing the mischief. The Director General Rangers, the Inspector General of Sindh Police, and the Chief of Karachi Police will have to provide explanations to their conscience, if to no one else, on why they permitted wanton killings on their watch. They did not even position themselves in the troubled areas, let alone strive to prevent the violence. Actually they had hidden themselves well and surrendered to the will of one man.

It remains a moot point whether without the administrative changes brought about by the Devolution Plan and the Police Order 2002, the Chief Secretary along with the Home Secretary, the Commissioner, the Deputy Commissioner, and the police hierarchy could have prevented the wanton killings. Perhaps violence could have been pre-empted or the tumult contained, if the option of negotiations was adopted. Administrative norms demand that the officials involve and engage with the protagonists and arrive at a convenient middle ground. Understandably, the mob or the demonstrators cannot be allowed to wield rifles and take the law in their own hands. Peaceful resolution of disputes, has always been accomplished by the District Magistrates and their Executive Magistrates for at least a century in Karachi and elsewhere. There is no reason to believe that May 2007 would have been any different. Karachi in 2007 showed what happens when the physical force of the Police and Rangers is merged with their executive authority to decide the options in dealing with serious law and order situations. This merger was made possible by the Devolution Plan and the reorganized set-up of the Police, at the behest of then rulers. Impartiality was conspicuously absent that day, allowing the situation to aggravate.

In the post-Devolution Plan structure along with the new Police Order of 2002, the Police was made responsible for pre-empting crime and protest without ever being held accountable. The events of 12 May 2007 in Karachi confirmed this. The supposed accountability tiers, cleverly incorporated by police officers working in the National Reconstruction Bureau, in fact ensured that no police officer would be held accountable, let alone be punished for acts of omission and commissions. The ostensible accountability mechanism, incorporated within the District, Regional, and Provincial National Public Safety Committees or the Police Complaint Authority, was never enacted nor was there any plan to enact it. For example, the police officers responsible for the neglect leading to a murderous attack on the Sri Lankan cricket team in Lahore also went scot-free. Public Safety Commissions were mere Trojan horses, established for the police to pre-empt accountability. It was not surprising that the first meeting of the Sindh Public Safety Commission, for example, was held in mid-2007, almost five years after the new policy was introduced. The members were only keen on their perks, offices, vehicles, and protocol than in ensuring police compliance of the law. For a short time, the District Police was made responsible to district *Nazims*, but such was the latter's vicious interference in the posting of officials and police investigation that these orders were soon withdrawn.

In Karachi, on that fateful day, even the Chief Secretary was not being kept fully informed about the violence engulfing the city. The Home Secretary and the District Coordination Officer did send some 'Sitreps' of the situation at intervals but these reports were first vetted by the police. Television coverage was deemed more authentic all along. The police in compliance with government policy was intent in downplaying the violence. However, when the ground situation assumed alarming dimensions on the streets of Karachi, only then did the police start to look for the support of the Sindh administration. The Inspector General Police and City Police Chief were confused and confounded and sought the intervention of the Chief Secretary when it was already too late. The Director General Rangers pretended that the situation was normal and his troops were vigilant. The Inspector General Police was very scared and reluctant even to move towards the airport without the presence of the Chief Secretary. The Home Secretary, Brigadier Mohtaram and the District Coordination Officer (DCO) Karachi, Javed Hanif, were then sent to prop up the IGP at the airport, even though under the new Police Order 2002, the DCO had no law and order, or security responsibilities. These powers lay with the District Police Officer and the *Nazim* of Karachi, who in a sense was the successor to the Deputy Commissioner. The *Nazim*, being a political figure, did not command the trust and confidence of the people as government functionaries like the Deputy Commissioner did. With the situation on the ground desperate, it was suggested, only half in jest, that General Tanvir Naqvi, Daniyal Aziz, Zulfiqar Qureshi, and the other architects of the 'Devolution Plan' and the new district security structure be airlifted to Karachi to take charge and resolve the situation.

As the firing died down, the authors of the blood bath watching from Karachi and Islamabad, became deeply worried. They had not envisioned such extensive death and destruction. Damage control became their foremost priority. It now befell the Chief Secretary, Home Secretary, and the DCO to cool tempers, contain the fires, and restore normalcy. This was a tall order even though in the best of times, Karachi remains unstable where murders and target killings are the norm. For the Chief Secretary to deal with the inferno by himself, at a time like this, was very difficult. The first task now was to provide relief to those who had sustained injuries and lay in the Abbasi Shaheed and Jinnah Hospitals which had coped well inspite of their limitations. Along with District Coordination Officer, I decided to visit the wounded in the hospitals to afford some basic comfort and show the government's concern. Being late in the day, cash was not readily available. Small loans were collected from friends like Ajmal Farooqi, drivers, guards, and the staff of the Chief Secretary's House, enough to provide Rs. 2,000 each to the wounded. It was heart wrenching to see the plight and poverty of the wounded. One young boy in torn clothes, severely dehydrated, was desperately squeezing an empty packet of fruit juice to his mouth. Soiled clothes and blood-stained bed sheets, full of flies caught one's attention immediately. The hospitals had poor maintenance and operation although the doctors and nurses did their best to provide relief. The wounded patients, all extremely poor, must have been at a loss to understand why they were being shot. As representatives of the state, the visiting officers were embarrassed but the answer could only be provided by the rulers in Islamabad. Where was the defiant clenched fist now?

The visit to the Hospital was not without its drama. The Chief Minister, ensconced safely in his official mansion, called to enquire why he was not asked to visit the hospital. He was informed that the Chief Secretary and DCO, being non-partisan, travelled by themselves. The Chief Minister was asked to visit the injured separately but he was too scared to do so. The Governor shortly afterwards tried to visit a Hospital but left quickly due to a hostile reception by the angry citizens, pelting stones. The consequences of the day's killing now started unfolding. The Pakhtun-Punjabi-Balochi Ittehad group called a three-day strike, pledging to withdraw all transport from roads and closing the shops. Such strikes in Karachi lead to serious violence and no wonder the provincial and federal governments wished its cancellation. The obviously worried Governor called endlessly, urging me to try and abort the strike.

It was then that the President telephoned me and beseeched me to do my best to get the strike withdrawn. Knowing well that the Pakhtuns had suffered the most, he entreated me to use my 'ethnic connections' with the Pakhtuns to save the situation. My reply was straight from the official manual; as the head of the civil administration I had no bias or prejudice, that I would do whatever it takes to bring about normalcy, and that he could take my word for it. He was told that as the Chief Secretary, I was completely impartial and it did not matter to me whether the people spoke Urdu, Pashto, Sindhi, Balochi, or Punjabi. I told him that I was duty-bound to avoid the strike and would make all efforts to bring about reconciliation amongst all people. The President appeared worried and spoke about the 'unbalanced' people responsible for the unfortunate events. Which unbalanced person was he referring to? There was more than one around!

The President was however requested that in order to bring about reconciliation quickly, the Inter-Services Intelligence, the ISI, be told categorically to keep away from peace parleys I had initiated, and not to interfere with civil administration. There was a widespread belief that some of those who had instigated the violence would try and sabotage the efforts of the local administration in restoring peace. They were also told not to contact any political figure. The President agreed to the suggestion. Shortly afterward, the Principal Secretary to the President and a senior officer from Inter-Services Intelligence agency called me on the telephone to confirm the content of my request to the President. Both were told that for even a modicum of success on the ground, the Chief Secretary alone must take all decisions. They both agreed and there was no problem on this score.

My reconciliation efforts having been initiated, there was every possibility that someone could sabotage these to prove a trite point or two. The Governor agreed to my advice to visit the hujra, the guest house, of Shahi Sayed where the Pakhtuns had gathered to offer condolences for those killed. This effort, in the interest of peace, led to the emergence of a bit of 'frontier tribal protocol' in Karachi. Anyhow, before the Governor's visit to the hujra, the chief of the intelligence setup in Karachi enquired on phone about the purpose of the visit and the names of those officials accompanying the Governor. He was told that there would be four people in all and that his name was not included. No security detail of the Governor was present and only his Military Secretary and the District Coordination Officer were to accompany him. The Military Secretary raised his concern for the security of the Governor, but he was cautioned that his fears were not well-founded. The Governor's presence was well-received as was expected and the process of generating goodwill was started successfully.

One constant demand of the Karachi transporters, most of whom were Pakhtuns, was financial compensation for the hundreds of their vehicles that were damaged or burned since the 1990s by mob violence. Fortunately, some days earlier, in a meeting with me, their issues were identified and a compensation figure of just under Rs. 100 million was agreed on. The governor was requested to announce this relief but only after the visit to the *hujra*. It was a poor reflection on the successive Governments of Sindh that perfectly legitimate matter like the grant of compensation, could not be resolved in fifteen years and yet when pressure was felt, the amount was sanctioned within hours. It was also sheer callousness on part of the senior officials that such grievances were not sorted out in time. Such dereliction of duties leads to mounting frustrations which tend to blow up at intervals. The Governor's condolence visit went off very well and as expected no recriminations or complaints were even mentioned. The first step taken was positive. For the next three days, the Chief Secretary of the province, functioned as the Deputy Commissioner in Karachi trying to control the situation and to bring about reconciliation. A meeting was arranged with Asfandyar Wali Khan, the President of Awami National Party, with a request to call off the strike. He was most accommodating but did point out that as the call had been given by the provincial chief of ANP, only he could call off the strike. This was the second positive development. Meanwhile, the calls from Islamabad and the Governor House continued unabated, seeking early confirmation of cancellation of the strike. Their desperation knew no bounds, as in the past, strike calls by the Pakhtuns had led to even greater violence in Karachi. The Chief Secretary's House had by then become the de facto Deputy Commissioner's office, as a stream of invited and uninvited visitors thronged in. People from different ethnic and linguistic groups attended, secure in the knowledge that this place, at least, was totally impartial and non-partisan. An overwhelming majority of the people from Chitral to Karachi are law abiding, hardworking, decent folks who do not wish violence or aggression. They want to lead normal lives, despite all the deprivation inherent in our society. Their hard work and thrift have caused deserts to bloom and industry to flourish in Pakistan. The Middle East would not be what it is today without the sweat and labour of Pakistani workers whose remunerations compared to other foreigners, was a pittance. The culprits responsible for the mayhem in our society were the rulers, mostly politicians but with generous representation from the military, business, judiciary, and the pulpit including the bureaucrats.

The Governor's condolence visit, the award of monetary compensation to the transporters, and the efforts of ANP and Pakhtun-Punjabi Ittehad paved the way for the strike to be called off. A great relief was immediately felt. A new problem soon developed when the District Coordination Officer went to distribute the financial relief to the families of those killed or injured. The local Pakhtun elders refused to accept the money and this was considered serious as they wanted to retain the option of avenging themselves. The administration did not want this, of course. Fortunately, I prevailed upon the elders to cooperate with the government and my ethnic connection helped. After the situation stabilized, Prime Minister Shaukat Aziz arrived in Karachi for a briefing on the bloody events in the Governor House. Once again, my views differed from those of the majority present, on the cause and sequence of events leading to the tragedy. The Prime Minister understood it all, even though he said little and actually had some sympathetic words for my stand. He was also appreciative of the note earlier sent by me on the subject. Next, the President arrived with a stern countenance but embarrassment was written all over him. Not a word was uttered on the failure of the provincial government nor was there any mention about the inaction of the Police and the Rangers. The President, however, vehemently disagreed with the Home Secretary about the inadequacies pointed out in the Devolution Plan and the Police Order and emphasized that these reforms would remain intact. He appeared to be in a hurry for the meeting to end. A few relatives of those who had died and leaders of the main linguistic groups met the President which was to be followed by lunch. Two of the Pakhtun speakers however, spoke their mind candidly about the injustices suffered by them over a period of time to such an extent that the President was visibly annoyed, believing he was being held responsible. This was followed by some straight talking by Irfanullah Marwat, a Pakhtun and a minister in the province, who cautioned the President that the outward calm should not be taken as normal, as molten lava was flowing just under the surface. By now the President, who was not accustomed to sustained criticism, decided to end the meeting. The President cut short his visit and did not stay for lunch.

The responsibility for the blood-stained events in Karachi, on 12 May 2012 undoubtedly lay with rulers in Islamabad and their political allies. The poor labourers of Karachi paid a heavy price for the General's misplaced ambitions and his personal vendetta against Chief Justice Chaudhry Iftikhar Ahmad. The Chief Justice, his political supporters, and the lawyers had to be stopped through the 'peoples' power' which in fact was the Government's coercive power. The General had to be re-elected for another five year-term at all costs and he was, although he was also destined to be ousted from power, within a year. Excessive personal interests came first and this too from a person who claimed 'sab se pehlay Pakistan', or 'Pakistan first'. There has been no shortage of pretenders in the country.

The Chief Minister, however, remained very worried because of the note I had written to him on the events of 12 May, which he called a 'charge sheet' against him. He actually wrote a detailed explanatory letter to me, trying to clear his name. This must have been the first time a Chief Minister had done so.

After the restoration of the Chief Justice by the Supreme Judicial Council, an enquiry was initiated by the Sindh High Court on the events of 12 May. But shortly after, Justice Iftikhar's second removal and replacement by Justice Dogar, this enquiry was called off. Poetic justice was nevertheless dealt and the President and the Chief Minister, Sindh were removed from the political scene. Except for them, no one was punished for the 12 May tragedy in Karachi, as is the norm in the country. When no one is ever punished, mischief continues to recur. With Chief Justice Iftikhar restored, there was no difference felt by the silent majority of the people of the country, even in the working of the judiciary. Corruption and delays continued to pillory this pillar of the state. The district courts remained a crying shame while the so-called superior courts continue to be stigmatized as well, by the litigants. Soon after the restoration of the Chief Justice, a litigant swore that he paid Rs. 45,000 to a Supreme Court official to re-adjust the hearing date of his case. In a lower civil court, a lady judge announced one version of an order only to completely change the written text the next day; the lawyer assured this was a routine matter in the Islamic

Republic. Justice Iftikhar was soon bogged down in different controversies with allegations of financial improprieties involving his son and more seriously, charges dealing with the alleged biased conduct of the General Elections of 2013. He and Khalilur Rehman Ramday, a former Supreme Court judge, were accused of influencing the elections by positioning choice judicial officers as Returning Officers in the Punjab elections to favour candidates of one party. However, the Supreme Court absolved them of any wrong doing as no damning evidence was produced. Yet, Chief Justice Iftikhar Chaudhry, more than anyone else from the judiciary, did win the hearts of the people of Pakistan by taking *suo moto* notice of numerous illegal and corrupt actions of some politicians, bureaucrats, and other powerful people. Was this the judiciary's finest hour? Were it not for him, doling out commercial contracts costing tens of billions of rupees without competitive bidding, would have become the norm in the land. The fact that the poor of Manchar Lake now have clean potable water and the Margalla Hills are not littered with hundreds of ugly chalets, is more due to him than anyone else.

Two of the main political actors of the 12 May tragedy, the General and the Chief Minister, Sindh, were discredited and left Pakistan soon after. The other politicians who should have been held responsible, continued to thrive and the police and the intelligence officers who ought to have been penalised, actually rose in ranks. Both the Capital City Police Officer and the Director General Rangers were promoted; the death of forty-eight Pakistanis murdered, was in vain. After nine years charges were laid against some of the alleged perpetrators. Time would tell whether those who planned and executed the deed are penalized. *Kissay wakeel karayn; kissay munsafi chahayn*, or who does one expect justice from!

In the days and months following the tragedy, the newspapers quite openly and some journalists in off-the-record conversations, spoke of official money being used to influence the events one way or the other. The journalists mentioned brief-cases full of cash being provided by Islamabad to ministers in Karachi and also to the leaders of an ethnic party. It was not known to the Chief Secretary or the administration whether this was true because they were not, and could not, be taken into confidence on the alleged payments. What was known, was, that about 100 million or ten crore rupees were paid by the provincial government at the Chief

Secretary's insistence to the transporters for their losses, in mob actions over the previous sixteen years.

The events of 12 May, with a heavy loss of life, were initially thought to be a watershed in the history of Pakistani politics and the justice system. This was to be a defining movement and the patient people were expected to triumph over ephemeral political gains of the tyrants. Unfortunately, nothing much changed. The politicians, the police, and the judiciary remained essentially the same. The welfare of the people takes a back seat when it comes to the interests of power-brokers. Perhaps the silver-lining to the events was the selflessness and resolve shown by the people of the country in resisting injustice.

The gory events did lead to the partial re-alignment of the failed administrative structure, introduced by the Generals. The new Devolution Plan, transferring powers of the provincial government to the District Nazims, the Police Order of 2002 effectively exempting the police from accountability, failed to deal with serious issues. Providing unrestricted powers to the police, without holding them accountable to any judicial or quasi-judicial authority, was a recipe for mischief. The toothless Public Safety Commissions, at various tiers, were soon scrapped. The absence of the Magistrate and the Deputy Commissioner, whose primary function lay in safeguarding the rights of the people against the abuse both, by the Government and private contractors and thugs, was acutely felt. There undoubtedly, were shortcomings in the conventional system, that needed to be remedied, but the bottom line remained that uniformed forces cannot be let loose on a defenseless people. There must be an intermediary tier of quasi-judicial officials in the administration to restrain them.

14

In Retrospect

For Pakistan, 12 May 2007 proved again that the rulers were free to use any means, fair or foul, to achieve their personal objectives. Such tragic happenings have continued to take place at regular intervals because the rulers employed state resources to perpetuate their oligarchic interests at the cost of democratic norms. There are few, if any, effective checks on their arbitrary exercise of power in Pakistan. The founders of the country could never have imagined that their high ideals would be trampled upon, to serve the selfish interests of those in power. Pakistan supposedly means 'the land of the pure people'. This description in hindsight, appears rather presumptuous. A more accurate and factually correct rendition would judge the land pure, while the people inhabiting it falling in a lower category. Other keen observers are convinced that the ordinary people were above reproach and the 'impure' ones mostly those, who have controlled the country since its birth.

Few countries have experienced the turmoil and tumult which Pakistan has suffered in seventy years of existence. There have been numerous insurgencies, rebellions, and civil strife. Crime has been rampant and governance, extremely poor. Ethnic, sectarian, linguistic animosities abound leading to the spilling of blood every now and then. Violence, civil disturbance, and uncertainty appear to be increasing, by the day. A bitter civil war resulted in the secession of half the country and a debate on whether the geographical separation was caused by leadership deficiencies alone or was it the result of the historical experiences of the people during the preceding thousand years. Maybe there was an element of both.

Pakistan, is nevertheless, home to a wonderous landscape and people. A quick glance at the physical and geographical features of the country, reveals an amazingly beautiful land of varied contours and great potential. There are not many countries where the gradient rises to 28,000 feet above sea level of Mount Godwin Austen (K-2) in the Karakoram Range. The area experiences four distinct seasons annually, with a diverse range of climatic zones from the near tropical to the temperate highlands and from the arid wastelands to the lush green plains. The country absorbs heavy monsoon rains in the summers and considerable snows in the winters. The land boasts over 5,000 glaciers with some among them counted as the largest in the world, outside the poles. The country's plains form the largest irrigated expanse in the world watered by the mighty Indus, or Abasin, the father river, supported by the five lesser ones. The diversity of its wildlife is equally spellbinding. From the turtle on the Arabian coastline, one ascends to 15,000 feet to marvel at the majestic *markhor* and the elusive snow leopard. Between the tropical seagulls to the habitat of the Himalayan snow cock or the *Ram Chikor*, at 12,000 feet, there are thousands of species of birds and mammals that display the bounty of nature to the country.

Sadly, though truthfully, the territories that now form Pakistan, inherited much of their present violent streak. The soil, sand, and the mountains of the country have been witness to more invasions and bloodshed than any other tract in the world. The area may also have experienced more than its share of natural calamities like earthquakes, snow storms, pestilence, floods, and cyclones. It was similarly not unfamiliar with genocide, massacre, and the cruelty of man. When these were coupled with the jolts administered by nature, the inhabitants probably developed their peculiar behaviour, character, and instincts. Nearly all major adventurers known to history have ventured hither. They were, without exception, responsible for untold atrocity, sorrow, and misery. These fearsome names included Alexander the Great, Genghis Khan, Tamerlane, Mahmud Ghaznavi, Babur the Mughal, Ahmad Shah Durrani, Nadir Shah Afshar, and many hundreds of lesser known conquerors. They did not bring art or learning with them but left, leaving behind as much killing as their weapons were capable of and as much plunder as their coffers could hold. Theirs was a package tour of blood, flesh, and treasure. Life here was always 'nasty, brutish, and short'.

For sheer survival: deceit, intrigue, lies, and expediency were as useful traits to master as was force and stealth. Death and deprivation had to be avoided at almost any cost; that cost is being borne by all today. Tolerance, magnanimity, and respect towards the weak and the vanquished were not much in evidence. As the historians say, no quarters were expected or given. These tendencies have apparently permeated the genes of the people over the millennia and expecting tolerance and democratic restraint from the people may not be immediately possible. Having inherited such a gory legacy, it is not surprising that the edifice of Pakistan fully reflects its violent past.

The unbroken association with a violent past was accentuated by the birth pangs of the country in 1947. As often happens in history, just when the need for wise and visionary leadership was most in demand, the pompous Viceroy, Earl Mountbatten and the desk-bound jurist, Sir Cyril Radcliffe appeared on the scene and consigned both, India and Pakistan to a benighted era of disputes, killings, and recurrent poverty. Mountbatten was a novice in statecraft, while Radcliffe, the Demarcation Commissioner, was a confused weakling who yielded to the Viceroy's wishes in drawing geographical lines that suited Nehru's India by providing it a corridor to Kashmir. No wonder, the people of Pakistan saw in Pundit Nehru a clever schemer masquerading as a liberal. If hundreds of millions of Indians, and Pakistanis, today, are denied toilets and clean drinking water and if poverty and unemployment remains rife the Indian people can only point a finger towards Nehru. If only Nehru had greater vision and prescience, he would have acted wisely and not conquered Kashmir because this act has caused colossal damage to the people of the subcontinent. The events of the past twenty-five years have shown that India is feeling the pinch of the hot potato stuck in its throat; the voice of the young Kashmiris for independence, will ultimately be heard because such sacrifices cannot go in vain. Over the years, India might have lost a percentage point or two annually in stalled economic growth because of Nehru's egregious adventure. The number of people killed violently in the subcontinent since Pundit Nehru's occupation of Kashmir and those who have died because of the related neglect and deprivation, would place him in the same league of adventurers as Tamerlane and Nadir Shah.

Similarly, the Congress party during its decades-long rule failed to integrate the Muslims and Sikh minorities into a secular India which later paved the way for the extremists like Narendra Modi and company, to wreak havoc on them. Earl Mountbatten and Nehru, as such, bear the greatest responsibility for the million people killed during the Partition massacres, those who have perished since and those who would suffer in future wars and violence. Perhaps the people of India and Pakistan, would have seen greater peace and prosperity if only the more knowledgeable and down to earth Field Marshal Claude Auchinleck, had been selected in place of Mountbatten as the Viceroy. He could have provided a home-grown solution. Sadly, he was not a royal!

Even in the environment of hate and vengeance, with millions of migrants crossing a border marked in blood, there was hope for the future of the new country. This hope was short-lived. The brief interlude of promise of a new dawn in the country soon waned as grim reality took hold. The precipitous fall in the country's fortunes continued. Within a quarter of a century, the most populous province of the country, East Pakistan, seceded after bitter and protracted violence, part of it orchestrated from India, to emerge as the independent state of Bangladesh. The secession of Bangladesh in hindsight, appears to be the result of inherent structural faults in the political makeup of the country. Greater political and economic autonomy, with separate foreign trade, de-centralized national accounts, and representation on population basis, may have been the preferred option for a geographically separated territory. The refusal of Zulfikar Ali Bhutto, who won a preponderance of seats in West Pakistan, to accept the overall majority of Sheikh Mujib ur Rahman in the National Assembly after the general elections in 1970, culminated in military operations leading to the creation of Bangladesh. General Yahya Khan appeared to have abetted Bhutto in his designs. Despite this tragedy, wisdom continued to elude the country's leadership with the result that today the country is seen as a 'patchwork of ethnic groups, increasingly in violent conflict with one another'. Doubts are regularly being expressed about Pakistan's economic sustainability, its political viability, and its capacity of exercising effective sovereignty over its territory. When the rulers who were responsible for serving the best interests of the state failed to do so, the welfare of the people was easily sacrificed.

Following the early death of the Quaid-i-Azam, political stability was noticeably absent during the first decade. Weak political leadership could not address the major provincial and constitutional issues. During the second decade, General Ayub Khan started off well and an economic 'take-off' was imminent but the September war with India in 1965, ensured it was aborted. To begin with, the East Pakistanis were neglected for too long, both in terms of political representation and economic development. General Ayub Khan got one great chance, extending over ten years, but he did not have the vision or the intent to integrate the Bengalis of East Pakistan into the mainstream. By ignoring and then persecuting Huseyn Shaheed Suhrawardy, and popular leaders like him, he aggravated the discontent. There followed, considerable agitation for representative government in West Pakistan and for autonomy bordering on independence in East Pakistan. During the third decade, following the division of the country, the new Prime Minister was Zulfikar Ali Bhutto. He became a victim of his megalomaniacal impulses. He said he wanted to build a new Pakistan but his deeds often belied his words and it seemed he was no different from earlier discredited politicians. Zulfikar Ali Bhutto, despite his distrust of the Sardars, Marri, Mengal, and Bizenjo in Balochistan, did try to develop the province economically. He was unable to make much headway, owing to the nationalistic resistance against his arbitrary style of governing. He was more successful in the Pakhtun Tribal Areas, which he passionately wanted developed economically and socially. The fourth decade belonged to General Ziaul Haq, whose extremist views severely polarized the body-politic from which the country has still not recovered. The fifth decade saw the fragile democratic dispensations of Prime Ministers Benazir Bhutto and Nawaz Sharif which, by and large, were an unhappy period. The last two named, were the first generation of leaders, born in independent Pakistan and much more was expected from them. General Musharraf, the central character of the sixth decade and the principal accused of the failed Kargil misadventure in 1999, had quite amazingly convinced himself that he alone had the capacity to steer the country to progress and stability. The results of his experiments are, before us.

President Musharraf's tenure mercifully ended in 2008 and the elections that year were won by the Pakistan Peoples Party (PPP) with Asif Ali Zardari becoming the President of Pakistan and Yousaf Raza Gillani, the Prime Minister. PPP government remained in power for five unrewarding years when rank incompetence and corruption thrived. However, this was the period when determined and successful operations were launched against the militants in Swat and the Tribal Areas. There was another positive outcome the country witnessed; the peaceful transfer of power, following the elections in 2013 to the Pakistan Muslim League (Nawaz) under whose management the economy was much improved while forceful action was initiated against militancy in Karachi and other areas. Almost immediately after the new government of Nawaz Sharif assumed power, there was widespread agitation against the alleged rigging of the general elections started by Imran Khan of the Tehreek-e-Insaf party. The protest movement initially, drew considerable support and led to a four-month protest *dharna* in Islamabad, seeking to shut down the Government completely. The agitation was called off in December 2014, after the massacre of 150 persons of which 134 were school students, by the militants in the Army Public School, Peshawar. A commission of the Supreme Court, thereafter, did not find much substance to the allegation of widespread rigging. The next five years were marked by severe political polarization in the country when abusive language and intemperate conduct became the norm. This coincided with the revelations from the Panama Papers that hundreds of influential persons from Pakistan, including the Prime Minister Nawaz Sharif and his family, maintained undeclared offshore properties and bank accounts abroad. The Prime Minister was also charged with not truthfully reporting his financial business interests abroad and was disqualified as a result. A new Prime Minister, Shahid Khaqan Abbasi, also of the Muslim League (N), was thereafter elected, who functioned quite competently during the short period he remained in power. The next elections were held in 2018 which finally brought Imran Khan to power twenty two years after he started his political career. Again there were allegations of manipulations in the conduct of elections but these were more muted. How effective the new Government would be in resolving long pending matters, time alone will tell.

Opinions may differ but to be fair, amongst the scores of presidents and prime ministers the country has experienced, arguably the most suitable was Mueen Qureishi. He remained an interim Prime Minister for three months only, pending general elections in 1993. Coming from the international corporate sector, he had spent his life abroad and as such was not expected to be fully aware of the country's issues. Yet he impressed by his correct identification of Pakistan's priorities and a dedication to serve. He had his detractors though. Were he provided a regular term of office perhaps Pakistan would have been a better place today.

Where did the country go wrong and why did it split into two? Why was it not possible to provide decent governance to the people? Was there a design defect, a cardinal failure of idea, or was it the poor leadership that failed the state? Would Pakistan now succeed in dealing with its challenges or fail once more? Some still feel 'it could go either way' yet again.

Over the years, I have raised this question before a number of wise men. They were asked for the reasons behind the apparent failure of the state to develop and serve its people. The replies of sages like Justice Baghwan Das, Professor Khwaja Masud, former President Ghulam Ishaq Khan, Generals Sahibzada Yaqub Ali and Sher Ali, and civil servant, Roedad Khan were in essence, similar. The political leadership in the country, with the honourable exception of the Founding Father, the Quaid-i-Azam, was either devoid of ethical standards or they deviated from the core values required of men in authority. A unity of purpose therefore eluded the people. As pointed out by one of these sages, we listened to more than one *azaan*, the Muslim's call to prayers.

The leadership appeared unequal to the task entrusted to them. Perhaps the wily old fox, the arch-imperialist Winston Churchill, was more prophetic when he predicted years before Partition that after Independence,

> ...power will go to the hands of rascals, rogues, and freebooters. All Indian leaders will be of low calibre and men of straw. They will have sweet tongues and silly hearts. They will fight amongst themselves for power and India would be lost in political squabbles. A day would come when even air and water would be taxed.

These words could have been written specifically for Pakistan of today. The canny and combative debater in Churchill, having lost the imperial battle, may or may not have made this prediction, but if he did his neat description was apt.

In hindsight, it might be argued that the scholarship and intellect of Maulana Abul Kalam Azad, perhaps, led him to a more objective appreciation of the situation. He felt that 'religious affinity cannot unite areas which are geographically, economically, linguistically and culturally different,' and doubted whether East and West Pakistan could bridge their differences. Could the first failure be the result of insufficient understanding of the political realities on ground? Not that Maulana Azad was always right in his assessments; his encouragement of the Khilafat Movement in 1919 was clearly misplaced and led to unnecessary pain and misery.

The founders of Pakistan were visionaries and as men of character imagined that all their differences would be resolved over time, given the common bond of religion. Honourable men with honourable intentions would indeed have resolved most problems but what if less than honourable leaders were placed in authority? Many decades later, a visiting dignitary, after meeting the most reviled of the recent Presidents ruefully remarked that Pakistan deserved someone better than him. He was speaking for all Pakistanis!

The need today is to look to the promise of the future rather than lament the past. In such circumstances, there will be difficulties and challenges but there is much hope and great opportunities as well. In order to succeed, the dangerous trend in the country needs to be checked. A national consensus is long overdue on basic political and economic issues i.e. the limits of provincial autonomy, the role and responsibilities of the military, the content of syllabi and curricula in the education structure, ensuring universal literacy, health care and family planning, the scope of taxes (including agricultural income tax), conservation and pricing of water resources, local self-government, land-use planning, building of water storages, prioritizing development projects, environment conservation, dispensing prompt and cheap justice, the rights of the minorities, and accountability of government officials.

Matters of Concern

There are a number of issues that need to be addressed decisively, and quickly, for Pakistan to establish strong bonds of unity and solidarity.

Firstly, the worrying trend towards ethnic-based and provincial-oriented politics in the country does not augur well. Most of the bigger political parties derive their strength from particular provinces and regions and therefore pay disproportionate attention towards their vote bank especially in allocation of resources. It is extremely dangerous for the Muslim League, as the founding party, to dominate and win only in Punjab and having little or no presence in other provinces. Similarly, for Pakistan Peoples Party, more recently, to remain confined to Sindh, is a matter of concern. The future prospect of the relatively new party, the Tehreek-e-Insaf, depends upon establishing an institutional base in all provinces. Other political parties are more regional in scope and emerge victorious in ethnic pockets which then compel them to focus on regional agendas. If this trend is not reversed quickly by dedicated national leadership, the provinces will continue to elect leaders whose interests remain confined to those who speak their language. For a country as diverse as Pakistan, it has always been the responsibility of the rulers to display benevolence and fairness towards the smaller provinces. This did not happen always. If one were to examine the travel logs of the presidents and prime ministers of the country, with the odd exception, leaders mostly travelled to Lahore, Karachi, and to their hometowns. That was their priority and they made no bones about it. This was an accurate indicator of their limited commitment to the people.

The major political parties would need to establish their presence in all provinces and one way of doing so, is by introducing a variant of proportional representation system. There is a need to reconsider a system where one party gets disproportionate number of seats in Parliament and Provincial Assemblies, on the basis of mere plurality of votes received. The losing parties collectively win much more. There is also a need to create a Saraiki province separate from Punjab so that some balance is restored in terms of size and population. Splitting other provinces, however, would invite trouble. Within the provinces, the chief ministership should also be rotated between geographical regions to make the equation more balanced. In Khyber Pakhtunkhwa for example, if the chief minister in one term is from Peshawar valley, the next term should be reserved for Hazara and the southern districts. Pakistan would be in serious trouble if it dithers toward parochialism and provincialism. The Baloch and Pakhtuns have generally felt that they have been denied patronage despite their acute suffering over the past seventy years, and more so during the present spate of terrorism and insurgency. Increasingly, people feel that not holding power in the centre has led to disadvantages. The two less-developed provinces, for example, must see that they receive more than their share of development resources to make up for the deficiencies of the past. This applies to the erstwhile Tribal Areas, which have now been merged with the Khyber Pakhtunkhwa province. Similarly, all provinces must get a proper share in high-level constitutional, administrative, and military positions in the federation. An informal quota needs to be kept in mind if not in law, while such appointments are made. There is a wider definition of 'merit' than is presently practiced and bearing in mind the needs of a federation this aspect should not be ignored! The Soviet Union suffered because the Russian republic was seen to be in control of all top positions to the chagrin of the others.

It is important to forge a National Development Consensus amongst the provinces, and the regions within these, for all major development and administrative matters. A beginning should be made to focus greater attention on the less developed regions through the China Pakistan Economic Corridor (CPEC) costing over US$50 billion. It would be appropriate to develop the major water storages such as the Diamer Basha, Munda-Mohmand, Akhori, Kalabagh, and Shyok along with smaller ones in Balochistan and the Tribal Areas. A fair distribution of the water resources of the country, having been agreed to through the Water Apportionment Award of 1991, it is important that it be incorporated in the constitution and the releases of water in the inter-provincial canals be monitored by the Water and Power Development Authority (WAPDA). There is similarly a great necessity for a railway line on the right bank of the Indus River from Havelian to Peshawar, Bannu, Dera Ghazi Khan, Kashmore, Khuzdar, and Gwadar. The existing railway line on the eastern bank of the Indus was laid 150 years ago and has been responsible for great economic development in the two provinces. As stated earlier, the consensus amongst the people's representatives must emphasize the provision of full literacy, health and family planning facilities, technical and vocational training, and the conservation of the environment.

Secondly, it has become quite apparent that for a large majority of the people the various organs and agencies of the state barely respond to the needs of the common man. The articles of the constitution may list basic rights guarantees, but in the field the poor, the weak, and those not well connected lead a very wretched existence. The police, the courts, the revenue functionaries, the health and education set-ups neither deliver adequate services nor are they accountable to any. There is little superintendence by district or local government officials. One is either compelled to bribe one's way through or else curse one's fate for being born in the Islamic

Republic of Pakistan. This happens because the main institutions of the
state have failed in effectively undertaking their constitutional and moral
responsibilities. Governance remains poor and the life of the common man
is pathetic. People have little faith in these institutions. The president, the
prime minister, the cabinet, the parliament, the judiciary, and the taxation
authorities have largely become irrelevant to the lives of the common
people. The higher bureaucracy in the headquarters and in the districts has
generally ceased to deliver effectively because of their excessive pliability
to the political bosses and the absence of tenure safeguards. Among senior
officials, a higher premium must be placed on character and courage than
on competence and honesty. They need the support of the state, in the form
of security of tenure and position; integrity and impartiality must replace
the 'master-servant' relationship that the rulers have created.

The superior judiciary bears the greatest responsibility for ensuring the
personal rights of the people and the collective well-being of society. Sadly,
it failed the country very early in the Maulvi Tamizuddin case where it
shielded the rulers and then did no service to the nation by continuously
legitimizing Generals Ayub Khan, Ziaul Haq, and Musharraf whose
performances were unsatisfactory. In the past, the judiciary chose to ignore
the infringement of the law by those who wielded power, both civil and
military. This can no longer be countenanced because now the future is at
stake. Perhaps there is a flaw in the selection process of the judges who sit
in judgment over the citizen. Could a larger body recommend the proposed
judges' names? Could this larger recommendatory body include the major
office holders (and the runners-up) of Bar Councils, the provincial Bar
Associations, some retired judges and officials, prominent journalists, a
couple of Federal Secretaries, and selected parliamentarians and members
from the civil society? The judges need to be persons of integrity without
any ethnic or sectarian bias and prejudice. Fortunately, many of the judges
present in the superior courts offer hope because of their intellect and
integrity; sadly, there may be some who do not have the reputation or the
drive expected of those who dispense justice.

The mind-set of those who are in charge of the country needs to change
for the better, in the years ahead. There must be a lobby for the poor
and the marginalized sections of society. Today, there is little evidence of
tolerance, understanding, and consideration towards others or those who

are not part of the oligarchy, allied with the powerful elite. It would be difficult for democracy to function in this environment. The country may have had better luck if the people were more homogeneous ethnically, linguistically, and culturally, or if the leadership was more devoted, but often that was not the case. It is the leadership which determines whether or not Pakistan advances from corruption and terrorism towards greater homogeneity and progress.

Thirdly, the state must maintain full writ and effective control of all its territories. The last few decades have been difficult. Presently, it appears that the law-enforcing agencies of the state are slowly but successfully turning the tide against militancy all over the country. Their emphasis on intelligence-based tactical operations has been effective although the price paid is at a much higher cost of sacrifice and blood. They, however, have a long way to go before total success is achieved. In many ways, the operations against the insurgents in the former Tribal Areas, Balochistan and elsewhere have been most challenging for the army and paramilitary forces. Time will tell, if there were any operational, strategic, or tactical deficiencies in the conduct of these operations. Fortunately for the country, those involved in violent extremism and terror are few in numbers, testifying to the strong solidarity of the tribes and the common people with Pakistan. Much greater attention would need to be paid to these areas, particularly in the field of development and employment creation in the days ahead. An effective grand strategy for the development of Khyber Pakhtunkhwa and Balochistan would be required.

In the years ahead, the Pakistan Army is likely to play a dominant role in the country. This would continue till greater political and economic stability is achieved. That, in turn, would require greater maturity from the political leadership. The politicians would need to graduate to a higher level of competence and integrity to gain political legitimacy. Faced as the country is, with serious threats from within and outside the borders, the role of the army would remain paramount but increasingly there would be the question of who provides the direction. The army fortunately remains a unifying force to resist the centrifugal elements across the country. For this purpose, there would be the requirement of maintaining a large, strong and effective army for a long time ahead. The security and protection of our 'nuclear deterrence' is a new factor, requiring a vigilant presence of the army across the country. The defence services would require a sizable portion of the resources and this price would have to be paid. With a sound economy, a strong economic rate of growth and effective governance, the budgetary requirements of the forces could be easily met.

It is axiomatic to state, that on account of the limited writ of the state, the violence and uncertainties experienced over the past few decades, foreign powers inimical to Pakistan have taken advantage of our difficulties. It is no secret that India has never lost an opportunity to clandestinely meddle and finance hostile elements in our country. They feel that Pakistan's vulnerabilities should be exploited to the hilt and at negligible financial cost to itself. For a few million dollars, it can tie down substantial Pakistani forces in particular theatres. In 1971, India tasted blood in East Pakistan and would never shrink from adopting a similar course in the future to damage Pakistan. This has to be watched and resisted. Similarly, Pakistan would need to zealously preserve its water rights over the rivers under the Indus Water Treaty of 1960. In the distant past, the fate of the subcontinent was often determined on the battlefield of Panipat. Today, any mischief involving water manipulation or 'Pani-pat' by India, could prove just as catastrophic (*'pat'* in Pushto with a different pronunciation means theft). Any action by India to block waters to Pakistan, should evoke the proper response. There is no other option. The Indians made a blunder in Kashmir in 1947 from which the subcontinent has not recovered and then confounded the blunder by abrogating Article 370 of the Indian Constitution granting Special status to Indian Occupied Kashmir. Both Pakistan and China are unhappy with this precipitate action which has dangerously charged the environment.

Fourthly, it is important that a robust and effective democracy takes root in the country. For democracy to remain meaningful, it must resolve the problems of the people. Moreover, in accordance with our traditions, the heredity factor would remain embedded in our national politics in the immediate future; all assets continue to be transferred to heirs. Many of those who ruled the country, have disappointed us but there is a glimmer of hope among some from the Sharif and Bhutto families, all born with proverbial silver spoon. They could well earn the gratitude of the people of Pakistan but for that to happen they cannot tread the forbidden beaten path. They should be more inclusive and remain focused on 'all people' not just their 'own people'. There is hope also in Fatima Bhutto, the granddaughter of Zulfikar Ali Bhutto, but apparently her interests are more intellectual and artistic. The future prospects of Ameer Haider Hoti, the former Chief Minister of Khyber Pakhtunkhwa, remain bright, as he brings dynamism and hope to the position. Finding dedication in Balochistan would be a tall order but even so, hope exists. Then there is Imran Khan, the cricketer and an acknowledged philanthropist and now the Prime Minister who has the potential for bringing about a meaningful change, *tabdili*, in governance. He would however, need to substitute effective governance in place of rhetoric and keep a safe distance from self-seekers. He has already lost more than a dozen highly reputable persons, including bureaucrats, judges, and generals, who initially gravitated towards him, because in the words of one of them, he was 'very partial towards mercenaries and sycophants'. Is he? Would inertia hold the odds against the new leadership?

Dr Tariq Siddiqui of the Civil Service would say that the country would steer forward rapidly were the elite to enter politics. The elite, though, must be those who are intellectually inclined and public-spirited. It would appear, in hindsight, that the better ones, once in power, seldom distinguished themselves from the rest. There is need for some space for truth, humanity, and tolerance in the country. What Bacha Khan inscribed in his own hand on a copy gifted to me of the book *A Man to Match His Mountains* remains perpetually elusive in the new country: *'Mazab, sachai, muhabbat, aur khudai makhluk ki khidmat ain ibadat hai fakat,'* or 'Service to humanity is the ultimate truth'. This truth remained hidden in the country for long. I remain convinced there is hope for the future. There would always be hope, if leaders like Suhrawardy and Asghar Khan were available who could be trusted in times of adversity. There has never been any shortage of ordinary men and women like Aitzaz Hasan, the teenaged student from Ibrahimzai in Hangu, and Perween Rehman, the social activist and director of the Orangi Pilot Project Research and Training Institute, Karachi, with the courage to embrace danger and death if the moment demanded sacrifice. There would never be a dearth of courage, dedication, and generosity amongst the people of Pakistan. Every now and then, there emerges a bold and devoted individual with the mission to set an example for a polarized and despondent people. In the immediate future, the country would be looking for such a leader with integrity and vision.

The country will survive and prosper through shared values and the force of character of the leadership and not through any other means. This applies even more to the provinces today. There was a time, when higher values and character were absent and the country split apart, after a quarter of a century. Unfortunately, not many tears were shed then and not many lessons learnt. Ahmad Faraz, the highly acclaimed poet, was quite perceptive recalling the tragedy. He once told me that the Pakistanis shed more tears at their defeat in a Cricket World Cup match than at the loss of East Pakistan. The observation was astute!

In the years ahead, only dynamic and dedicated leadership can ensure that the country moves ahead in all spheres of life. A German Army sergeant after retirement, having trained as a leather goods specialist, was deputed under a World Bank project to a small public sector factory outside Bannu. Working conditions in the project were harsh as there was no running water or electricity. The Project Manager, a genial retired Pakistan Army officer, was not seen taking much interest in the project. The German was perplexed. One day he asked the Major how, as an army officer working in his own country, he took scant interest in his work, while he, as a retired Sergeant and a foreigner, worked overtime at no extra cost in the very hot weather. The officer being the leader, was supposed to lead by example. The German sergeant was right; it takes dedicated leadership to run a factory. The same is also true of a country.

Acknowledgements

I owe a great debt of gratitude to my friends and associates for their affection and understanding towards me over the years.

The finest among these were Ahmad Nawaz of Pakistan Railways from Khushab and Nasser Ali Shah of Jehanian Shah in Sargodha, their friendships remain revered long after they passed away. Coming from completely different backgrounds, they were remarkable individuals for their integrity and intellect. May they rest in peace.

Brigadier Zakaullah Bhangoo, a daring pilot and wise in counsel; Liaquat Ali Khan of Income Tax Service with unmatched integrity, Mazhar Sher, an honest police officer and Syed Adil Shah, the gifted hotelier and philanthropist; all departed this life far too early. Much later, the death of my incomparable class-fellow and service colleague, Gulzar Khan was a devastating blow. As a student, bureaucrat, and parliamentarian, he was always witty with the right turn of phrase.

My first school friend was in Presentation Convent School, Rawalpindi in 1952, was perhaps named Muhammad Mazhar, because it could not be 'Manman Mizhar', which, because of my stammer, I thought was his name.

In Lawrence College, there was Shafiullah Babar, serious and honest to a fault; Babar Masood, the high jumper, straight forward as he was genuine; Qamar Aziz, a gentleman who excelled in sports; Mian Shahid, always first in academic studies; Brigadier Jamshed Ali, bright and witty; Major Saeed Akhtar Malik, brilliant and very original; Javed Sadiq Malik, aka 'what's use', competent and correct; Abdul Ghani, who at sixty looked thirty *Mashallah*; Athar Tahir, a Rhodes scholar, an imaginative poet, and an administrator; Major Nisar Ahmad, the marathon man from Samasata; Ahmad Raza, the one who got a rough deal in life; Shaukat Ali, with a Pashto accent of '*choop choop kharay ho zaroor koi baat hai*'; Qaiyum Niazi, a man of many hues and talents; Javed Jalal, the hockey player turned social worker; General Mahmud Ahmad, a genial student and a strict military man; Sherjan Tajik, brave and resourceful; the lively Raza Arshad and the quieter Waheed Ali.

In Edwardes College, Harun Khan, a modest and caring gentleman; Ismail Niazi, who loved a joke at his expense; Salim Jan, Senior Prefect; Azmat Hayat, Vice Chancellor who had in-depth knowledge about the NWFP; Colonel Aftab 'Chacha' and Amanullah, the engineer.

With the passage of time our paths crossed: Javed Khan and his proverbial partiality to food; Brigadier Javed Hasan, always ready for light barbs; Ejaz Saddozai, a direct descendent of Ahmad Shah Baba, with a heart of gold;

421

Colonel Iftikhar Baig of 'fender bender' motor bike fame; Salman Reza Shah, immaculate in his yellow convertible; Major Iftikhar Kiyani, always steadfast; Asif Jamshed Shah, the amiable banker who popularized the shalwar-kameez in New York. There was the inimitable and generous Khalid Shah of Peshawar and Leeds and his talented sons Javed and Daud, one of whom had a small role in the film *Casino Royale*.

In 1971, after my selection in the Civil Service of Pakistan, I got to know many officers that it is not possible to name all of them but there are a few I must mention. There was Rustam Shah Mohmand, the conscientious administrator and diplomat, an expert on Afghanistan; Mian Azhar, always supportive and hospitable; Naveed Cheema, among the best in administration and thorough in his endeavours; Khalid Khattak, the well-read diplomat from Kohat; Khwaja Zaheer Ahmad, with a memory to recall all the articles of the Constitution and most sections of laws; batch mates Masood Rizvi, Chaudhry Ayub, Ziaul Islam, and Hussain Hamid; Hasan Sarmad, Sher Afghan, Tauheed Ahmad, Musa Chouhan, and Iqbal Ahmed from the Foreign Service and from Bangladesh there were Tareque Feroze, Aleemul Haq, Nazim Chaudhry, and Riazul Karim. Police officers Mazhar Sher, Kalim Dil Khan, Asad Jehangir, Zahid Murad, and Zulfiqar Gilani joined after the Sharda Police Academy was lost in East Pakistan. And, of course, there was Anwar Mehmood, the caring information man.

There were few who matched the integrity of Jehangir Bashar, the competent Aitchisonian and the last 'true Englishman'; Rauf Chaudhry, a decent and conscientious civil servant; Khawaja Shamail, one of the finest Deputy Commissioners; Abdullah, an unmatched debater and inspiration; Tasneem Noorani, pleasant company and adept in diverse fields; Ashraf Hayat, the competent bureaucrat and Qamarzaman Chaudhry. Much memorable time was spent with Sangi Marjan Masud and Karim Kasuri from the provincial civil service and with Ahsan Baseer and Mushtaq Marwat from the Ghulam Ishaq Khan Institute of Science and Technology. There were many junior officers who served with me, competently and respectfully but who cannot be named because of space constraints.

There were some amazing friends from the military. The most notable was Brigadier Farooq of 5 Punjab Infantry who epitomized friendship and there is nothing to surpass military friendship. The late Major General Naseerullah Babar, Sitara-e-Jurat and Bar, a fearless and courageous man. General Ehsan ul Haq from Mardan, the cool strategic thinker; Air Chief Marshal Hakimullah, an ace pilot and fellow angler; Lieutenant General Tariq Khan, our own Patton and winner of the sword of honour. There were the three-star Generals Salahuddin Tirmizi, very considerate and dependable, Imranullah Khan, always courteous, and Asad Durrani, with a keen sense of history and strategic matters.

Major General Khurshid Ali Khan, the friendly Governor. Two Lieutenant Generals from the Tribal Areas, Alam Jan Masud and Ali Jan Orakzai, were both sharp and interesting. The late Lieutenant General Afzaal, was bright and affectionate; the courageous Major General Ghaziuddin Rana, formerly of 73 (Thal) Brigade; Brigadier Mukhtar of WAPDA, my former Principal Staff Officer and his brother Dr Nisar Ahmad. Lieutenant General Sayed Amjad along with Air Vice Marshal Rahim Yusafzai were thorough professionals. Major Tariq Mahmood of 10 Baloch Infantry, an amazing staff officer and Major General Ejaz Amjad was most friendly. The former Chief of Army Staff, General Ashfaq Parvez Kayani, a brilliant commander and a visionary. On reflection, most of my military friends were 'Frontiersmen!'

There were friends from the 'services' and there were others, who were 'non-S' so to speak, but all were friends. Fazle Gafoor Khan of Prang, was the ultimate in hospitality; Asmatullah, for whom loyalty was an article of faith and his shikar arrangements were awesome; Jalal ud Din 'Katu Khan' complete with 300 pounds of hospitality perched high in his bar; Nisar Shah, cool and correct 'never more never less than six'; Javed Awan *Chacha* of Haripur and London, consistent and sincere with practical advice 'ishq or love is important but so is a thousand rupee note'; Salim Patel, solid in word and deed; Iftikhar ud Din of Rhode Island. Majeed Khan a compulsive walker; Dr Zahid, steadfast in friendship with the busiest cell phone in the world; Barrister Sultan Mehmood, serious in matters official but with much time for fun and frolic; Shams ul Mulk, former Chairman, WAPDA; Amir Muhammad, the soft-spoken judge; Ghazal Usmani, the one with a grand library whose forte was building bridges. There was also the sincere Kohat *shikar* quartet of Fazlullah Khattak, Sajid, Tasleem Badshah and Rahim, all remarkable men. Dr Masuma Hasan, the academic and diplomat who remained devoted to learning and scholarship. Perhaps the most interesting and dynamic among my friends was Ajmal Farooqi, as popular in London as in Karachi who introduced himself endearingly 'they call me Farooqi', most endearing, supremely confident, and sphinx-like.

It was a pleasure to have known Dr 'Customs' Manzoor, honourable to the core, not always punctilious, having invited the chief guest one day too late for a dinner in Switzerland; Khalid Rehman, perpetually naughty but his wit matched his hospitality; Saeed Khan 'umbaraksha', the jovial and professional Inspector General of Police; Tariq Farook, a top class debater, academically brilliant and he predicted that I would top the competitive examinations; Saud Mirza the quiet and professional police officer; Wilayat Ali Khan, the architect of many buildings and friendships; Momin Khan, flying occasionally but driving perpetually; Shahid Sattar, the consummate power sector expert; Naveed Zaidi, the connoisseur of good food sprinkled with political commentaries; Naeem Khan, Riaz Noor, Javed Iqbal, and Ataullah Toru all extremely witty and friendly Chief Secretaries; Qaim Shah, quiet and solid. There were those like Arbab Arif, Dr Jehanzeb Khan, Khalid Sherdil and Musharaf Rasul who were among the best the bureaucracy had seen. Dr Fida Wazir and Arbab Shehzad were mature and efficient.

Not to be forgotten were the disarmingly amiable and affectionate foursome: Reza Mehdi, Nasir Jibran, Mazhar Sherazi, and Shafiq Abbasi, all from Lahore. The cartoonist, Javed Iqbal was a bonus. To these I would add the name of Khalid Saranjam, an unrecognized genius with amazing wit and talent, who sadly left us early in life.

Then there were Aslam Khaliq, the corporate executive, suave and much concerned with declining wildlife; Shamim Sadullah, 'Sham Lala' of roses and Aitchison College fame; Kamran Aslam, who would pine for America when in Pakistan and vice versa; Asif Shah, the competent son of the very accomplished Judge Safdar Shah; Arbab Zahir, among the best of friends; Wajid Jawad equally at home in corporate management and poetry; Shakeel Mabroor, modest in golf, tall in tales with a great sense of humour; David Eleesha, perpetually calm and composed whose 'sweet dishes' were a delight; Dr Haji Gul, a caring physician; Ashraf from Karachi, the safari driver and businessman; Muhammad Yar Bhuttar, wise and dependable; Khwaja Ghaffar from Srinagar, the author of the unforgettable line 'harking and barking leads to skylarking'; Tariq Rana, the devoted Rajput for whom friendship was the ultimate value. Brigadier Asad Munir, the authority on the Frontier's administration; Khalid Masood of the Civil Service and Harvard Business School; Imtiaz Tajwar, sharp and confident; Hameed Poti, with a golf record of five holes in one and an albatross; Dr Fuad Malik, a dentist in a foreign land, fond of military history; Tariq Pirzada, with an amazing capacity of recalling Persian and Urdu poetry; the young Zaland Khan, well-mannered and talented; Khawaja Shahab, a gentleman and very hospitable; Chaudhry Majeed, one-time Prime Minister of Azad Kashmir but for whom the Mangla Dam Raising project may never have been commissioned; Salim Siddiqui from Campbellpur (Attock), who could argue for hours; Murtaza Durrani, the smart journalist from Azad Kashmir; Amer Mughal, the water sector expert; Waqar Ayub, among the brightest; Tauqir Awan, the one with the fabulous collection of cars and motorbikes; Asad Nawaz, of caviar, champagne, and cigar fame; Salim Khan Masud, the gentleman affectionately called 'Bush Commissioner' because rumour had it that his brother once asked the American President to get him posted as Commissioner.

Ali Baksh Mahar from Sukkur, whose hospitality was unlimited; Bakht Sial, also from Sindh, a generous *shikar* enthusiast; Haji Arbab Riaz, one with an anecdote for every occasion; Malik Sher Afzal Afridi, the person to call on when in dire straits in England; Raja Kamal from Dudial, generous and one who could be serious and joyful at the same time; Tahir Mehmood, always correct, who found answers to all his problems quickly; Iqbal Ratyal, a gentleman and devoted energy professional; Ikram Ellahi, the innovative leather goods entrepreneur from Karachi; Naseeb Jan, the busy *shikari*; Malee Zaman, fondly irreverent who with Ayesha focused on the crystal ball; Dr Aslam and Shaheen, plenty of humour and laughter; Tariq and Saira, genuine and considerate; Nurullah Afridi, who would offer tea and hospitality before greeting one; Ashtar Ausaf, the suave lawyer and urbane conversationalist who was also a food aficionado; Zahir Shah Khan of Och, who knew a thousand anecdotes and two thousand tales; Colonel Murad Nayyar, a record ten years as Commandant of Chitral Scouts; Shamsud Din Chitrali, a rock pigeon was the only bird he could name in English; Siraj of Mirkhani, 'time ho gaya hai', who ploughed his fields having shaved, scented, and in Oxford brogues; Colonel Wahid Jan, meticulous and a consummate big game hunter; Asif Ashraf, the inveterate *shikari* and story teller; Pervez Akhtar, the fighter pilot turned writer; Rashid Bangash, the engineer, for whom honesty was an article of faith; Muhabbat Ali Zafar, amazing man and the last of the generous Nawabs of Kohat; Professor Iqbal Awan, the Kohati, of 'saucy, surly, morose, peevish, irritable' fame; General Farrukh Sair, the blue-eyed doctor, always witty but with a straight face; Asad Alam, an urbane player in more than one field; Javed Akhtar, the media man, always the gentleman; Hafeez Sheikh of Azad Kashmir, a man of unmatched integrity; Shahid Khan of Peshawar, the petroleum man; Aslam and Saleh Bhootani from Lasbela, whose company was a delight and who took trophy hunting to new heights; Hameed Haroon and Hameed Akhund, both devoted to Sindhi culture; Tahir Ahmed, the power sector expert; Fayaz ur Rahman, the high-flyer who I owe one for flying me *gratis* from Zhob; Shuja Alam the diplomat, and his brother-in-law Mahmud Mehsud, the police officer, both very agreeable; Waheed Qazi, responsible for big structures and bigger parties; Mehmood, the Chashma Barrage engineer, whose commitment to duty never waned; Ali Zulqernain, for whom *shikar* and hospitality were one and same and Fawad, fom Shangla.

None could forget the 'Sajjads'; the first a gentleman par excellence and the owner of Royal Hotel in Peshawar, the second Sardar Sajjad, son of Agha Ghulam Hussain also from Peshawar, who was a golden link to the city's history. All who knew the generous Akhtar Ranja from Sargodha, for his merry ways and constant laughter, will miss him.

In England, there was the delightful and well-meaning trio of Ajaib Awan of Blackburn originally from Jhelum, Manzur Chaudhry from Gujrat, and Yusaf Laher of 'brotherly love' from East Africa, who were all such great company. Dr Ashfaq Ahmad, among the most eminent scientists in the country. I cannot forget Muhammad Jamil, 'Emjay' now living in Canada and Mustafa Bajauri, to whom I owe a jacket.

It was my good fortune to have known Syed Babar Ali, the industrialist and philanthropist. Bulleh Shah (1680–1758), the great Punjabi Sufi-poet had something to say about friendship,

'O Bullya dosti sirf uthy karin jithy dosti nibhawan da dastoor howy.'

There are a few politicians who left a lasting mark. One was the gifted former Prime Minister Zulfikar Ali Bhutto, who in 1973 gave the country its first Constitution. In 1991, former Prime Minister, Nawaz Sharif resolved the contentious Water Apportionment issues to his lasting credit. Arbab Jehangir from Peshawar, a former Chief Minister, an honourable and successful politician, who was part of every government in power and when asked whether he was ever jailed, as politicians often are, retorted: *'walay zha darta showda kharum'* or 'do you think I am stupid'.

Former Prime Minister, Shaukat Aziz, a brilliant man, presided over a period of impressive domestic economic growth from 2004–07; Sardar Mehtab Ahmad, the Chief Minister of NWFP, who was a disciplinarian and innovative man; Mian Shahbaz Sharif, Chief Minister of Punjab, a dynamic and indefatigable man who had many achievements to his name; the Chief Minister of Sindh, Murad Ali Shah, whose considerable promise was matched by his talent. The humility of two provincial governors, Iqbal Jhagra of Khyber Pakhtunkhwa province and Rafiq Rajwana of the Punjab province was impressive. Humility was also personified in Malik Meraj Khalid, who rose to become Interim Prime Minister in 1996–97 and who came from a very humble beginning. Then there was a new entrant in Pakistani politics, Chaudhry Sarwar, formerly an MP in the British House of Commons, who, along with Shah Mahmood Qureshi and Jehangir Tareen are known for their commitment.

There were some remarkable politico-administrative functionaries I came to know. Salman Farooqi, Farhatullah Babar, Sartaj Aziz, Aslam Bhootani, and Yusaf Ayub, brought skill and dignity to their office. Salman Farooqi would be long remembered for the dynamism he brought to the telecommunications sector and later in revitalizing disposal of complaints in the Ombudsman office. One of the few inspiring politicians from Punjab was the well-read Sardar Bahadur Siar from Liah district and from Sindh, Zulfiqar Jamote.

The finest ministers I served with were Sheikh Rashid, the cigar smoking Minister of Railways and the competent Salim Saifullah Khan. They never interfered unnecessarily with the working of the departments whether it be the posting of officials, award of contracts, or the recruitment of personnel.

I would like to mention two persons from the Frontier province who became lifelong friends. The modest Khanzada of Peshmal in Swat and Sayed Islam Badshah from Buner.

Much to my delight I also got to know some of my father's friends. They included Brigadier Taskeen ud Din, whose greatest care was his personal car 'da zha na khapa kum' or 'I do not wish to annoy my car by driving over broken roads'; Colonel Qazi Rashid 'Sheedo', a gentleman and one who planted brotherly kisses on both cheeks! Justice Burhanudin, the grand master of repartee and innuendoes; General Sherin Dil Niazi, an amiable gentleman; Major Farooq Shah of Abbottabad, Colonel Rashid Hayat of Multan, Dost Muhammad Khan of Sherpao and Brigadier S. M. Ilyas; Malik Habib, the footballer; Abdur Rahman Khan of Kafoor Dheri, who had a library second to none; Abdul Latif Khan Orakzai, the venerable lawyer and his sons, the gentlemen, Wahab and Yusaf. Aurangzeb Khan, the technocrat from the food department was even better known as the president of the old Edwardes College Association for decades; Finally, there were Dr Majeed and Dr Kabir and the lawyer, Abdul Sattar. So many amazing people in one town!

There were a host of government officers who I met in service who impressed me. Many of the officers serving during Pakistan's early years had enviable reputations for duty and integrity. Perhaps they served in times that were fair. There are memorable names in this galaxy and it may suffice to remember a few. There were the bold and competent frontiersmen like Nasruminallah, Kanwar Idrees, Ijlal Haider Zaidi, Rashid Khan of Matta, Syed Faridullah Shah, Roedad Khan, Wajiuddin, Dr Humayun, Jamil Ahmed, Omar Afridi, Munir Hussain, Karim Lodhi, F. K. Bandial, Usman Ali Isani, Sahibzada Imtiaz, Salim Abbas Jilani, Azam Khan, and Jamshed Burki. They all served with honour.

There were other officers who excelled in the finance, planning, and development departments in the secretariat. They included Masood Rauf, Fazalur Rehman, Bashir Ahmad, Shoaib Sultan Khan, Dr Ishrat Husain, Muhammad Azhar, Zaheer Sajjad, Muzaffar Qureshi, and Mian Tayyab among others. Farid Rehman, the civil servant turned Minister, would be remembered for the increase in the share of the net hydel profits for Khyber Pakhtunkhwa province. Shaukat Tarin,

Advisor, Finance Ministry, made this enhancement possible with the support of the heads of all political parties in Khyber Pakhtunkhwa province.

I also came across many top-class officers from the provincial service like Jehanzeb Khan, Mohibur Rehman Kiyani, Khalid Mansoor, Shaukat Ali Khan, Haider Gul, and Shaukat Zaman Babar, among many others.

There were competent police officers and gentlemen like Yusaf Orakzai, Wajahat Latif, Abbas Khan, Dil Jan Khan, Khawar Zaman, Aziz Khan, Israr Shinwari, Saeed Khan, Malik Asif Hayat, Jehangir Mirza, and the instinctive investigator, Sikander Khan. There were the brave officers like Siffat Ghayur and Malik Saad and many younger officers like Masood Bangash, who left their mark. There were two colourful provincial police officers, the witty Mian Sakinudin and the inspiring poet, Shamsuz Zaman Shams. Engineers like Said Khan, Hisamuddin Bangash, Karim Khan, Sultan Daud, and Nawab Khan Bangash added colour to competence in the much-reviled engineering departments. Engineer Shah Nawaz Khan from WAPDA was a towering figure and a class unto himself.

Dedication was not restricted to the senior officers only. There were some outstanding personal staff officers and juniors like Sohail Khan of Kohat, Iqbaluddin who served in Khyber, Deedan Gul of Hangu, Shafi, the revenue officer from Abbottabad and his brother Saeed, the public prosecutor, Shah Rume (Sultan-i-Rome) in Swat, Najab Khan from Batkhela, Sher Khaibri in Chitral, and Omar Khitab in the Secretariat.

There were competent Magistrates like Sarfaraz of Peshawar, Chiragh of Malakand, Shahjehan Shinwari, Laiq Hussain of Kurram and Pirzada Wazir, the wizard of Wana. There were the more serious ones, including the sagacious Ghulam Farooq Khan of Mansehra, the articulate Waqar Ayub and the courageous Riaz Masud.

The friendship and loyalty of the tribesmen that I came across in the seven tribal agencies, now the merged areas, was amazing. There was Hasan Halimzai, son of Bacha Mohmand, a tribesman who once told me very seriously and most solemnly, that he could be counted as a friend whenever he was needed. As I thanked him, he stated that his words had perhaps not been properly registered. What he meant to say was that anyone could make 'mutton tikka and kebab' for me but if ever I needed him to deal with anything more important, he would be there, waiting for the call. His intent was clear and left me speechless. There were Saida Jan Shinwari, Mir Alam Zargunkhel Adamkhel Afridi, Subedar Major Anwar Shilmani, Said Akbar Kukikhel, Dost Muhammad and Yunas both Zakkakhel Afridis, Mohammad Jan 'Majan' Kukihel, Ghazi Marjan Qambarkhel Afridi, Hameed Shalobar Qambarkhel, Haji Saleh Khan Alisherzai, Bismillah Jan and Akhtar Mangal, Haji Ata Muhammad Mohmand, Bacha Kamali Halimzai Mohmand,

Gulab Sher Halimzai, Ismail and Sardar Khan of Jamrud, Sawab Gul Orakzai, Gul Badshah of 3 SP Artillery and Pindialla, Muhammad Khan Bilandkhel and of course, the unforgettable Lal Badshah from Mardan. Gran, the Afghan Mohmand was very dependable unlike his sons. Subedar Meena Gul Shalobar Qambarkhel, a tall imposing man, who was shot and killed by the Scouts mistaking him for a suicide bomber when he drove his vehicle too close to them. Arsala Khan Alikhel Orakzai at a ripe old age offered to check partridge poaching in Shinwari near Hangu but was soon divested of the responsibility when he became involved in serious brawls with those on the other side of the law. Then there was Shadar Afridi, orderly to Donald, the Political Agent in South Waziristan, kidnapped by Mehsud tribesmen mistaking him for the Agency engineer. On his release, Donald committed suicide in Tank, apparently in disgust he felt over the kidnapping.

Finally, I wish to thank David Page, my teacher in Edwardes College, Peshawar, for his professional advice while writing this book. I would also like to thank Irfan Ahmad of SOPREST for his assistance.

Annexure 1
Of Books and Dedication

During my civil service career, I was fortunate in often being involved with some sensitive issues which often escaped the attention of most government officials and generally of all politicians. Few spoke up for the minorities, animal rights, the family planning, and wild life. Foremost amongst these matters was preventing the extinction of the few remaining Kalash minority community and their heritage in Chitral. Such matters did not get much importance in the power circles. As Deputy Commissioner Chitral, I requested the President, General Ziaul Haq and the Governor, General Fazle Haq, for providing funds for return of the mortgaged walnut trees to the original ownership of the Kalash people. This step helped the Kalash people economically as it was an institutional measure for which Mohammad Alaudin, a civil servant, dedicated his book titled *Kalash: The Paradise Lost* to me, without ever having met me. I would always remain respectful to his name and commitment. Two decades later, I had this book reprinted and added an additional chapter through the efforts of the devoted Maureen Lines and the photographs were provided by the sisters Nadia, Nagin, and Sidra.

Earlier, as Political Agent, Mohmand Agency, I persuaded the distinguished gentleman, Abdur Rashid Khan of Matta of the Frontier Civil Service to pen a short monograph on the civil administration, during the early years of Pakistan. I was greatly flattered to see that the book had been dedicated to me for which I am very grateful.

Later, while serving in the Population Welfare Division in the Federal Government, Feryal Ali Gauhar, the gifted author, environmentalist, and social activist who was then the United Nations Goodwill Ambassador for population activities, dedicated her novel *No Space for Further Burials* to the hundreds of innovative 'Newtonian' awareness and demonstration activities that were initiated. With our population growing at current rate there may actually be little space left for the burials!

A couple of years later, Athar Tahir, the brilliant civil servant, a well-known English language poet and author of several books dedicated his collection of poetry *Body Looms* to me. I am very grateful to him.

Many decades ago, when I was posted as Political Agent, Khyber Agency, a publisher, Mohamed Amin from Kenya, who had authored a series of We Live In *books of different people in the world, wrote one on Pakistan. The article on Khyber Agency is reproduced here in first person for the record.*

430

Annexure 2
We Live in Pakistan
Mohamed Amin (1983)

The Pathans are bound by their code of honour. I'm the chief executive officer of the Khyber Agency—responsible for law and order in a tribal area of 2600 square kilometres (1,000 square miles) where Pakistan's laws are not enforced. To help me, I have two paramilitary forces each larger than a battalion, both headed by a Lieutenant Colonel of the Pakistan Army. I also have my own police force—about 2,000 armed Khassadars (law officers) I try to resolve the disputes between the tribes. The Pathan people—I'm a Pathan myself—are very tough and proud. But if a crime involves the tribesmen themselves, they take care of it. They hold a *jirga*—which is a meeting of the elders – and decide what the punishment should be. The ordinary laws of Pakistan don't apply in the Tribal Areas. Recently, tribesmen shot two Afghan refugees. The killers could give no reason for the shootings so the elders handed them over to the Afghans saying: 'Do what you want with them.' The Afghans shot them there and then in front of their people. This system has been in force for centuries. It's quick and just and also very effective. That may be why there's little crime here. The most common crime is murder. Almost all murders are revenge for a previous killing, perhaps committed many years before. No Pathan ever forgets a murder—or an insult. They are bound by their code of honour: revenge, hospitality and refuge. If anybody asks for refuge—even a total stranger—it has to be given, no matter what the offence of the refugee. When we go after an offender, it's not easy to get him. The whole village, which is probably in an inaccessible area, gives him refuge. We will go after him with a very large force and when we come under fire, we fight back with mortars, rifles and machine guns. Our troops are very tough, but so are the Pathan villagers.

I've been a Political Agent since 1974. I did a degree course in England, and came straight into government service when I returned. Pakistan has seven tribal agencies, with a combined population of about 2.5 million. I've served in four agencies and the Khyber is by far the toughest. I like this Agency. It's very demanding, but I belong to the area and I know it well. I have very wide powers. If I put them to good use—to maintain peace and encouraging development—I get great satisfaction. It's good to bring tribes or families together to end a dispute

431

that's existed for years, and also to see development in the area. In 1947, when Pakistan was created, there were two schools. Now there are 150 schools in the area and many villages are getting water, electricity and health centers. The Pathans have lived around the Khyber Pass for centuries. I'm the fifty-ninth Political Agent since the post was established before the turn of the century. I have three assistants and about a hundred people work in the agency office. I usually work ten hours a day and my phone rings constantly. I love Pakistan and get complete satisfaction from my job. The tribes here have always been independent but they still feel part of Pakistan'.

Shakil Durrani, 36, is married with three small sons, now three grown up men, Masahallah! *He is the Political Agent, civil administrator of four groups of Pathan warriors, who live in the wild and forbidding mountains around the Khyber Pass.*

Annexure 3
Amir Hamza Shinwari

I was most fortunate that a Sufi poet of the stature of Amir Hamza Shinwari, perhaps the most important Pashto poet since the creation of Pakistan, wrote a few lines about me, much to my amazement and appreciation. These verses, although very flattering, may well have been among the last that he wrote, are reproduced below.

> *Khud shakil ye ph maana aw ph soorat kay Chay ye tal khudaiy ph fazal aw rahmat kay*
> *Pakistan ta afsaran sta ghunday boya Mahshahoor chay ye ph adal-o-diyanat kay*
> *Pukhtanh zalmi bh kha taraqi owkaree Rashamel chay shee so sta ph kiyadat kay*
> *Malahat day krray khkula kay deeway baalay Wershamil chay shwaloo sta ph sabahat kay*
> *Ahmed Shah Baba ph shaanay durrania Beryalay ye da zhwandoon ph pani pat kay*
> *Da bemar pursee sunat da payghamber day Chay hesab ye her qadam we ib adat kay*
> *Da dair umer samar okhuray khushal osay Chay mukhlais ye da hamza ph ieyadat kay*

You indeed are 'Shakil' in looks and in spirits
> This surely is due to Allah's grace and blessings

Pakistan needs model officers like you
> Those with a reputation for integrity and justice

The Pakhtun youth is determined to progress
> They need to follow the example you have set

The light of your kindness spreads all around
> It benefits those who associate with you

Durranai, in the great tradition of Ahmed Shah Baba
> May you experience Panipat-like successes all your life

Offering solace to the sick is a *sunnat* of the Prophet (PBUH)
> Such an act is deemed worthy of 'ibadaat'

May you have a long and prosperous life for the concern you showed for the
> ailing Hamza